More praise for *Diet for a Small Planet*

"Frances Moore Lappé's book [*Diet for a Small Planet*] about high-protein meatless cooking really contains recipes for revolution."　　　　　　　　　　　　　　　*—The Boston Globe*

"When Lappé wrote *Diet for a Small Planet,* she changed the lives of an entire generation. Long before anyone was talking about sustainability or climate change, Lappé was doing the math and showing us that the American way of eating was unsustainable. . . . *Diet* has influenced my food choices ever since then."　　　　　　　　　　　　　　—Ruth Reichl

"Some of the 20th century's most vibrant activist-thinkers have been American women—Margaret Mead, Jeanette Rankin, Barbara Ward, Dorothy Day—who took it upon themselves to pump life into basic truths. Frances Moore Lappé is among them."　　　　　　　*—The Washington Post*

"A foundational book for modern vegetarianism, finally providing a thoroughly argued rationale that did not rely on the cruelty-to-animals argument."　　　　　*—Publishers Weekly*

"When Frances Moore Lappé wrote the best-selling *Diet for a Small Planet* back in 1971, she helped start a conversation about the social and environmental impacts of the foods we choose. And, back then, what she had to say was revolutionary. Her idea that a plant-centered diet could be better for the planet—and our health—than a meat-centered diet was considered radical."　　　　　　　—NPR's *Morning Edition*

"Nearly 50 years ago, Frances Moore Lappé's *Diet for a Small Planet* laid out how we could feed the world by using fewer resources, transporting food more efficiently and streamlining our access to protein and calories by consuming them directly from plants. These ideas have only become more relevant and urgent [today]."　　　　　　　　*—Daily News*

Diet *for a* Small Planet

Diet
for a
Small
Planet

50th ANNIVERSARY EDITION

Frances Moore Lappé

Illustrations by Aimée Mazara

BALLANTINE BOOKS | NEW YORK

2021 Ballantine Books Trade Paperback Edition

Published in the United States by Ballantine Books, an imprint of Random House, a division of Penguin Random House LLC, New York.

BALLANTINE and the HOUSE colophon are registered trademarks of Penguin Random House LLC.

Originally published in trade paperback in the United States by Ballantine Books, an imprint of Random House, a division of Penguin Random House LLC, in 1971.

Permissions acknowledgments can be found cn page 389.

Library of Congress Cataloging-in-Publication Data
Names: Lappé, Frances Moore, author.
Title: Diet for a small planet / Frances Moore Lappé ;
illustrations by Aimée Mazara.
Description: Revised and updated edition. | New York: Ballantine Group,
2021. | Includes bibliographical references and index.
Identifiers: LCCN 2021000321 (print) | LCCN 2021000322 (ebook) |
ISBN 9780593357774 (trade paperback) | ISBN 9780593357781 (ebook)
Subjects: LCSH: Vegetarianism. | Proteins in human nutrition. |
Vegetarian cooking.
Classification: LCC TX392 .L27 2021 (print) | LCC TX392 (ebook) |
DDC 613.2/62—dc23
LC record available at https://lccn.loc.gov/2021000321
LC ebook record available at https://lccn.loc.gov/2021000322

Printed in the United States of America on acid-free paper

randomhousebooks.com

4th Printing

Book design by Susan Turner

For Betty Ballantine,
whose foresight, thank God, was better than mine!

Contents

Welcome to the 50th anniversary of *Diet for a Small Planet*. Here, in a new opening chapter—"Our Choice, Our Power"—I share what most keeps me alive in the face of humanity's unprecedented threats. Book One offers a glimpse of history, largely untouched from the original. Book Two, thoroughly revised to today's palate, invites you into the kitchen to experience today's delicious revolution aligning with life. May you delight in learning and eating!

—Frances

List of Figures

Our Choice, Our Power:
Introduction to the 50th Anniversary Edition

To see what is in front of one's nose needs a constant struggle.

—George Orwell, 1946

I began this journey with the realization that growing and eating plant-centered diets was a great choice. Today it is a no-contest necessity: Either we now make a big turn, or life on Earth as we know it is gone forever.

Whoa . . . this blunt declaration rocks me.

I'll admit it's taken me decades to get here, and I am delighted now for this opportunity to share my learning journey with you, dear reader. You'll forgive me, though, if my first thoughts are of my own delight as, over the years, strangers have told me, "Your book changed my life."

One story I'll surely never forget is from friend and long-time head of the Berklee College of Music, Roger Brown: "I was teaching in a small village in Kenya in 1979 when I came across a tattered version of your book," he told me. "I read it on a mountain by moonlight, and it changed the course of my life."

I'm still smiling.

When anyone tells me of the book's effect on them, I always want to blurt out, "Yeah! Me, too." *Diet for a Small Planet* started as a one-page handout when I was 26, and it has profoundly shaped my life's quest. Now, on its 50th anniversary, I strive to capture key lessons that help me to this day and that I hope will help you in these challenging times.

Hmm. "Challenging" doesn't quite do it. Over the past few years, we have been battling the fiercest storm of my lifetime: years of attacks on the integrity of our democracy leading to the first-ever citizens' assault on the Capitol, a pandemic deemed the worst in a century, and murders by police that have fueled the Black Lives Matter movement—furthering, we can hope, our nation's long-delayed reckoning with systemic racism.[1]

At the same time, our climate crisis nears a tipping point that will drastically hasten destruction. And what first shocked me into action—hunger amid plenty—has gotten worse in recent years, even though the world's food supply offers one-fifth more calories for each of us than it did 50 years ago.[2] Here at home, hunger is also rising.[3]

But in a mighty storm, sometimes the biggest tree comes crashing down, and for the first time we can see its roots. Now is such a storm.

So how do we grasp the roots and use what we discover to pull ourselves back from catastrophe and guide us toward life itself?

The great news is that millions here in the United States and many more around the world are grasping the root causes of our intertwined crises and remaking their lives in ways aligned with what humans and nature need to thrive. Fifty years ago, my youthful "ah ha" was that food has special power, as every day our very personal food choices connect us to each other and to all of nature. Shock in discovering the needlessness of hunger triggered in me new ways of seeing what's profoundly amiss in our world and our own power to fix it.

But back then, I had no idea how urgent my message would soon become.

Driven by tightening corporate power over our democracy, harms from meat-centered agriculture and diets have continued to mount—damaging human health, the natural world, and the climate. And now the ultimate harm: We have destroyed so many species, largely in feeding ourselves, that we face the sixth great extinction of life on Earth.[4] To avoid planetary disaster, warns natural historian David Attenborough, we must allow the re-flourishing of life by greatly reducing the land area we farm, and the "quickest and most effective way . . . is to change our diet." Moving beyond the vast inefficiency of meat-centered eating and choosing plant-centered diets, he projects, would cut in half the land used and still produce plenty of food for all.[5]

Now, with vastly more at stake than when my own eyes first opened, it's critical to grasp how we got here. So, let's go for those roots.

Believing Is Seeing

Over the 50 years since I sat in the U.C. Berkeley library pondering the root cause of hunger, I have tried to keep digging to the question beneath the question to help me grasp why we humans have messed up so badly. And here's the deepest question my digging has turned up so far:

Why are we together creating a world that as individuals none of us would choose?

After all, I've never met anyone who gets up in the morning vowing to make another child starve or to turn up the planet's temperature.

In the 20th anniversary edition of this book, I introduced the "power of ideas" to explain what seems inexplicable. (I invite you to read my introduction to that edition directly following this one.) Today, I express the root challenge this way: While "seeing is believing" is a common expression, for our species the reverse is more often true: *Believing is seeing.* Or, as Albert Einstein put it more directly, it is "theory which decides what we can observe."[6]

In other words, our internalized filters can blind us to solutions right in front of our noses—requiring precisely the "constant struggle" George Orwell calls us to in the opening quote.

One filter above all blocks us from solutions: a belief that life is made up of parts, when in truth all life is connected. I can still see in my mind's eye the twinkly grin of the late German physicist Hans-Peter Dürr, who a decade ago laid it out to me so simply: "Frankie, in life there are no parts, only participants."

Got it, Hans-Peter! And I've never forgotten. It is the core truth of our being.

While in the last half century much has changed, the danger in the false lens of separateness shows up in at least three big cases of "believing is seeing" that still blind us. Each has been used by the most powerful, wittingly or not, to keep us on a destructive path, averting our eyes from positive system solutions to our food and farming crises.

WHO WE ARE

Most critical in determining what we can see is our belief about our very nature, as I explain in the following chapter. Much in our culture today teaches us that we can count on humans only to be selfish and competitive. It encourages some of our worst traits—especially blaming "the other." In truth, our species' long evolution has proven our capacities for *both* goodness and unspeakable evil.

Thus, a viable future depends on our together creating rules and norms that elicit our strong, pro-social capacities—cooperation, empathy, and fairness—while restraining the negatives. For me, that's what democracy alone can achieve.

"MAGIC" MARKET MYTH

Another powerful case of "believing is seeing" is the enduring cheery notion of a "free market"—infused throughout our culture by anti-government "true believers," from talk radio to hundreds of Koch-funded university programs.[7] Ronald Reagan famously touted the market as "magic."[8] And with magic, the fun is *not* knowing the magician's secrets, so we become blind to the obvious: No market is "free."

Every market has rules.

And over these 50 years, the economically powerful have increasingly reduced our market economy to *one* rule: Do what brings the most profit to existing wealth. With that driver, it's no surprise that wealth accrues to wealth accrues to wealth.

And the consequences of this magical thinking?

Today, five U.S. companies control almost a fifth of Wall Street wealth.[9] And three Americans now hold as much wealth as the bottom half of our entire population.[10] Within farming is a parallel tightening of power. Now, just 4 percent of farms control almost 70 percent of sales.[11]

Yet half of Americans still cling to the belief that in America "everyone has an equal opportunity to succeed."[12] We are made blind to the depth of our economic inequality. Ours is so extreme that globally we sit between Haiti and Argentina, with income inequality deeper than in more than one hundred countries.[13]

This tragedy is not a given. It has rapidly worsened. Between 1980 and 2019, CEO pay leapt 940 percent, while the typical worker's pay crept up just 12 percent.[14]

The concentration of power throughout our food system feeds inequality. When I wrote *Diet for a Small Planet,* more than 50 seed companies were competing for farmers' business.[15] Now, from seeds to sales, a handful of firms dominate our food system: Just four companies control over 80 percent of beef packing, 85 percent of soybean processing, almost two-thirds of pork packing, and half of chicken processing.[16] Four grocery chains control nearly half of sales.[17]

So it's no surprise that our farmers—made dependent on monopoly suppliers, distributors, and processors—continue to receive a shrinking share of our food dollar, now down to 15 cents.[18] Farm families must turn to off-farm jobs, which now make up more than 80 percent of their household income—up from half in 1960.[19]

Nothing "free" about this market!

This pattern of consolidation has been true since the beginning of my journey, but in the mid-1990s, tightening control over farming and food got a big boost. With virtually no independent testing, our government allowed a new technology—genetically modified seed—to dominate. So today, one company, Bayer (the German pharmaceutical company that bought Monsanto), controls the genetically modified seeds now planted on 85 to 90 percent of acres of our three primary crops—corn, soybeans, and cotton.[20]

Believing in the "magic of the market" has led to another deadly blind spot. Because we think the market efficiently allocates resources, of course, we assume U.S. agriculture has led the world and fed the world because it is so *efficient*.

But when I pulled back the veil 50 years ago, I discovered the opposite: stunning inefficiency.

With so much of our farmland going to feed livestock and to make agrofuel, U.S. agriculture feeds fewer people per acre than does Indian or Chinese agriculture.[21] Only 27 percent of the crop calories we produce end up feeding people directly.[22]

And worldwide? More than 80 percent of agricultural land, including that for grazing, is devoted to livestock and aquaculture, yet they provide less than a fifth of our calories.[23]

Such inefficiency is a form of waste, and to it we must add literal waste. In the United States, up to 40 percent of our food is wasted.[24] And it's gotten worse: Compared to half a century ago, on average, Americans now throw away 50 percent more food.[25] What doesn't end up in our stomachs lands in landfills—emitting greenhouse gases—and drains about $1,800 from the annual budget of a family of four.[26]

Globally, almost a quarter of all calories produced are tossed out, spoiled, or otherwise lost.[27]

DEMOCRACY DELUSIONS

The human trait I've called "believing is seeing" even shapes how we view our nation. From TV to textbooks, the lens through which we're encouraged to see ourselves convinces many of us that our nation is either the greatest or among the greatest anywhere.[28] In this self-image, democracy has been a key element.

In truth, however, for years we have ranked behind 55 countries in the integrity of our elections.[29]

Elections plus a market do not democracy make. We have both. But our economy ensures tightly held economic power that translates into political power and ends up warping public decision-making—that is, democracy itself.[30]

When I first wrote this book, few companies had Washington lobbyists. But today? Corporations pour billions annually into lobbying, and agribusiness is a bigger spender than the defense industry.[31] For every member of Congress we elect to represent us, over twenty lobbyists—mostly corporate—now work to put their own interests first.[32]

This sway of Big Money generates policy choices that don't line up with Americans' values and interests.[33] And Americans get it: Across political divides, three-quarters of us unite in our still-unfulfilled desire to remove the corrupting influence of wealth in politics.[34] And sadly, our failure to end this corruption contributes to Americans' weakening confidence in democracy itself.[35]

Heartbreaking, for sure, but I try to remind myself to pull my head out from under my pillow. Feeling helpless in the face of loss is not fun! In fact, it's awful. What *is* fun is feeling that I'm part of something big—and I mean game-changing—no matter what the odds.

It is this awareness that gave birth to this book and has fueled my passion for democracy ever since.

WHAT IS DEMOCRACY ANYWAY?

For me, at the heart of democracy are the rules and norms for living together that meet our deepest needs—bringing forth the best in our species while keeping our destructive capacities in check.

And what are our "deepest needs"? Here's what now rings true for me.

Beyond food and other physical essentials, we humans need three intangibles: First is power. We need to know that our voices count. Second, meaning. We need to feel that our lives matter beyond our own survival. Third, connection. We need to experience our power and meaning in community with others.

So what rules and norms in our connected world have been shown to enable us to experience these essentials?

Again, I see three: First, those that keep power dispersed—widely. Second, transparency, to keep power accountable. Finally, an ethic of mutual accountability, the opposite of the shaming and blaming so dominant today. Rabbi Abraham Joshua Heschel captures this ethic so simply: "Some are guilty, but all are responsible."[36] No one is off the hook!

All this I pack into one beautiful concept: democracy.

Later in this chapter, I celebrate solutions to our food-and-farming crises as part of such a practice of democracy arising here and around the world beyond anything I imagined 50 years ago. In earlier editions, I called it "citizen democracy," but in the 1990s, "living democracy" began to better capture what, for me, had become obvious: To succeed in ending hunger and saving our planet home, democracy's principles must be alive not only in political life but in all dimensions of our common life—including, of course, the economic.

I hope these three "believing is seeing" traps—a distorted view of our very nature, the market as magic, and the notion that our democracy is "exceptional" and the best we can do—reveal how this human tendency can do us in.

So, the "constant struggle" to which Orwell calls us is worth the effort!

Hope of a Certain Kind

And in that struggle, more and more and more of us are breaking through these deadly delusions to realize we can make new choices. Fortunately for me, the life-changing potential of release from a false way of seeing came early in life. Cracking the then-dominant frame that hunger was caused by "too many people" overrunning our food supply liberated me to envision real solutions.

And that thought brings me to a central theme of my life—hope. Many of us think of hope as "soft." Isn't it for wimps who can't face the truth?

For me, hope is the opposite.

Neuroscientists tell us that hope actually helps to organize our brains toward solutions.[37] So hope is power, and it's just the power we need now.

But it is hope of a certain kind—what I have long called "honest hope." It is not blind optimism. Hardly. It requires that we take in the horrific losses incurred by "believing is seeing" delusions *while* embracing and joining in the most hopeful pathways. It sees possibility even in the dark.

Tears in the Tapestry of Life

One "ah ha" helping me stay in this place is that after 50 years we've been given a huge gift—if we can receive it: the gift of clarity.

It's now clear that to feed ourselves we are killing ourselves and our planet. But equally true is that food and farming solutions are arising, some in surprising places, and proving transformative beyond all expectation.

Let's first take a deep breath as we register the staggering extent to which our supposedly bright species has brought on frightening losses and deadly threats that rip apart the very "tapestry of life," a lovely metaphor I borrow from primatologist Jane Goodall. Only then can we appreciate our species' courage and creativity now bursting forth.

Here are ten food-related assaults on life that have either arisen or greatly worsened during the last half century.

One. Vast hunger continues amid plenty. As the global food supply per person continues to grow, more than enough calories are produced to meet everyone's needs, yet almost

700 million of us go hungry, and one in every five young children worldwide is stunted by malnutrition and unsafe water, bringing lifelong harms.[38]

Two. How we feed ourselves worsens climate chaos. Largely because of the shift to corporate-chemical practices and heavy reliance on meat, our food systems globally generate as much as 37 percent of greenhouse gas emissions. Of that, land use alone—farming, grazing, felling forests, and more—amounts to a quarter.[39] So, get this: Even if the world immediately cut all fossil fuel emissions for energy, food-system emissions alone would make it impossible to meet the targets for limiting global-warming set in the 2015 Paris Agreement.[40] Cows pack such a punch that, if they were a nation, "cow country" would rank as the world's sixth worst greenhouse gas emitter.[41] And if food waste were a country, it would rank still higher—as the third worst.[42]

Three. Food becomes our biggest health threat. Nearly 60 percent of all calories Americans eat now comes from ultra-processed food, providing little nutrition but loads of sugar and salt while exposing us to up to 5,000—mostly untested—food additives.[43] Wow. It's no wonder that nearly our entire population fails to meet national dietary guidelines.[44]

In 2017, 11 million deaths worldwide—one in five—were from diseases in which poor diet is a risk factor, notes *The Lancet*.[45] Included are deaths from cardiovascular disease, cancer, and type 2 diabetes. Since about 1970, the U.S. diabetes rate has jumped almost fourfold, with one in ten of us now afflicted.[46]

And then there's salt. Recently, I was shocked to learn it could be our single biggest dietary peril—linked to as many as 100,000 premature U.S. deaths each year, as it increases our risk of stroke, stomach cancer, kidney disease, and more.[47] We get most of our salt from processed food. Just one cup of Campbell's Chicken Noodle Soup, for example, hits us with almost 80 percent of our daily recommended limit.[48]

And, yes, our diet's health hazards are also hugely expensive. Three-quarters of our health-care spending—about $5,300 every year for each of us—goes toward treating chronic diseases, most of them diet-related.[49]

Four. Hazardous chemicals contaminate our food and the people who work the land. Unfortunately, 90 percent of the top two U.S. crops—soy and corn—are bioengineered to be resistant to Bayer's herbicide Roundup, whose active ingredient, glyphosate, was deemed a "probable carcinogen" in 2015 by the World Health Organization.[50]

Glyphosate use is restricted in over 40 countries and banned in several.[51] So why not here? Recently disclosed internal documents confirm that Monsanto used deceptive marketing strategies, misrepresented the safety of its products to regulatory agencies, and helped secure positions of power in Washington for close associates.[52] So we shouldn't be surprised that the United States, with just 4 percent of the world's population, uses one-fifth of the world's glyphosate—helping it to become the world's most widely used herbicide.[53]

And glyphosate is hardly our only problem. Many other pesticides are still sprayed here, including 72 that are banned or about to be eliminated in the European Union.[54]

Worldwide, almost half of farmers are poisoned by pesticides each year; and here at home as many as 20,000 farmworkers suffer such poisoning, as they still lack essential labor protections.[55] Stricken with cancer, almost 100,000 U.S. farmers and some homeowners filed lawsuits against Bayer, charging that glyphosate had made them sick. To settle, in 2020 the company agreed to pay out almost $12 billion—and, yes, that's a *b*.[56]

Now, as weeds have developed resistance to glyphosate, Bayer and two other companies are spreading the even more deadly herbicide dicamba—vowing to challenge a federal court decision making it effectively illegal for farmers to continue using dicamba.[57]

Five. With no prior health or independent environmental testing, genetically modified organisms (GMOs) are now present in at least 75 percent of U.S. processed foods.[58] In the late 1990s, my family got an early taste of the power behind GMOs: My late husband, pathologist and ethicist Marc Lappé, sounded an alarm in his 1998 book *Against the Grain*, co-authored with Britt Bailey. No surprise, Monsanto threatened to sue, and Marc's publisher pulled out. Fortunately, the (appropriately named) Common Courage Press stepped up to release it.[59] But concerns he raised remain unanswered: "GMO crops still run far ahead of our understanding of their risks [as] scientific controls are often missing," writes scientist Jonathan Latham, a founder of the Bioscience Resource Project. "Results are often ambiguous or uninterpretable," and due to industry influence, "I do not believe that this ambiguity and apparent incompetence is accidental."[60]

Six. We've turned much of modern livestock production into a destructive, cruel, and dangerous nightmare. We have destroyed more than eight in ten wild mammals on Earth. Sixty percent of remaining mammals are livestock we've bred, including a staggering 1.5 billion cattle.[61] And 70 percent of all the world's birds are now farmed poultry.[62] I'm stunned. Just imagine how many life-forms we've deprived of a place in the tapestry of life. Plus, so many creatures who depend on us have miserable lives: For cattle, imagine a thousand or more crammed together, most fed antibiotics primarily to quicken weight gain, emitting a potent greenhouse gas and producing massive waste that pollutes water and air. The pollution triggers breathing and neurological problems for those living nearby, who are disproportionately low-income.[63]

Seven. Soil loss and degradation continue at rates far beyond what nature can rebuild in time. As monocultures spread and crop rotation declines, topsoil across our earth is washing or blowing away at a rate 10 to 40 times faster than nature can build it.[64] At the current pace, topsoil could be gone worldwide in 60 years.[65]

Eight. Underground water for irrigation is disappearing fast, quickened by a meat-centered food system. Producing a pound of beef takes 1,800 gallons of water—nearly 50 times more than for a pound of veggies and about 9 times more than for grain.[66]

As we are effectively "mining" water, at current pumping rates over the next 30 years more than a third of our southern High Plains may no longer support irrigation.[67] Some of our aquifers hold what is essentially "fossil water," meaning that in some areas what we've lost in 30 years would require over 1,000 years to restore.[68]

Nine. A piece of the food and farming crisis unregistered by most of us—nitrogen overload—is wreaking havoc. "We've disrupted the nitrogen cycle even more than the carbon cycle," University of Virginia environmental sciences professor James Galloway, a leading authority, explained to me. Thanks to synthetic fertilizers, we humans have added at least three times more reactive nitrogen to our environment than is produced naturally.[69] Globally, only 4 to 14 percent of fertilizer's nitrogen ends up in what we eat—as a building block of protein.[70]

Nitrogen runoff from fields seeps into streams and rivers and from there into the mighty Mississippi and then the Gulf of Mexico, where it's created a coastal "dead zone" the size of Massachusetts, killing marine life.[71] Worldwide—and doubling each decade since the 1960s—there are 415 such oceanic zones of lifelessness.[72] Nitrogen runoff, explains Professor Galloway, also worsens smog, haze, acid rain, loss of marine species, forest loss, well-water pollution, climate heating, and the stratospheric "ozone hole." Whoa.

And, again, meat production is key in all this harm: Because nitrogen is in the fertilizer used for feed crops as well as in manure runoff, producing meat in the United States is the single biggest avenue by which nitrogen escapes into the environment via food production.[73]

Ten. The overuse of land to produce meat and other destructive farming practices are moving us toward Earth's sixth mass extinction.[74] Primarily due to pesticides and mega-monocultures, we could see the extinction of 40 percent of the world's insect population in the next few decades.[75] Since the early 1990s, U.S. agriculture has become 48 times more toxic for insects.[76] Before you imagine that fewer bug bites might be nice, consider that insects are the largest food source in the animal kingdom.[77] And we have pollinators to thank for one in three food bites we take.[78] Insects are essential in creating healthy soil and decomposing waste. Think about all that!

Worldwide, agribusiness' meat production and marketing is a primary force causing forests and wildlife populations to shrink by two-thirds over the last half century.[79] And, in large measure because so much of our land grows food for livestock, 90 percent of crop varieties have already disappeared.[80] All this contributes to an alarming estimate: One million species are threatened with extinction, and the pace of loss is quickening.[81]

Now, there's a list that breaks my heart. To make honest hope possible, I've got to do something useful with that awful feeling. So together let's dig deeper.

From Choice to Necessity

From all of the above comes this certainty: While 50 years ago *Diet for a Small Planet* was heresy, today plant-centered, chemical-free, whole-foods eating is not only a positive choice. It is essential. Either we make a big turn, or life on Earth as we know it is gone forever.

That turn depends *both* on our everyday choices and on our

courage as empowered citizens to revolt against concentrated power and together achieve democratically set rules putting our health and Earth first.

EATING WITH THE EARTH

In 1970, I never imagined the impact of our diet on the looming life-and-death climate crisis. Nor that 40 years later (proud mom alert), my own daughter, Anna, would tackle this threat in *Diet for a Hot Planet,* enabling me to learn so much about the climate-food connection.[82]

If we achieve a societal shift toward plant-based diets, we can reduce greenhouse gas emissions from farming by as much as 70 percent by 2050—and by even more if we cut food loss and waste, predict University of Oxford's Marco Springmann and colleagues.[83]

Another encouraging way of expressing our gain?

Worldwide, if those eating meat-centered diets simply moved to popular low-meat or no-meat fare—such as traditional Mediterranean or vegetarian cuisine—emissions could be "reduced by an amount equal to the current greenhouse gas emissions of all cars, trucks, planes, trains, and ships," calculate University of Minnesota's David Tilman and Michael Clark.[84] That's huge.

And note, this nutrient balance is hardly novel, as it's what nourished humans throughout our evolution and still characterizes most Indigenous diets today.[85]

Reducing the pressure to fell carbon-absorbing forests to graze livestock and grow feed, our dietary shift away from meat could "prevent the destruction of an area of tropical forests and savannas as large as half of the United States," Tilman and Clark also estimate.[86] (Less deforestation also means less risk of new pandemics, as felling forests for farms and grazing brings humans into greater contact with wildlife that can transmit a virus.)[87]

Some propose shifting to grass-fed beef as part of the climate cure. Certainly, we'd avoid the cruelty of feedlots. But U.S. pastureland could only support just over a quarter of our current demand for beef.[88] Experts differ on whether grass-fed generates more or fewer emissions than feedlot beef, with some even suggesting that with careful ecological practices, grass-fed could even become carbon-neutral.[89]

But regenerating soils with cover crops, compost, and trees does offer climate pluses. It uses half the energy and generates only a third of the greenhouse gases per acre that are released in corporate, chemical-dependent farming.[90] Plus, all plants take in atmospheric carbon and sequester it in the soil, and soils farmed ecologically hold more carbon.[91] If all the land used to produce cattle, goats, and sheep were replaced with natural vegetation, the estimated carbon sequestered could be from one-third to almost five times the greenhouse gas emissions now linked to food production.[92]

In addition to these positives, ecological farming restores the richness of species and thus helps avert the sixth great extinction we've been warned is upon us.

Plus, ecological farming is key in meeting our nitrogen-overload crisis. It uses the nitrogen that soil microorganisms generate, effectively recycling it. Plant-based diets can help, too: In the United States, producing plant protein involves only a third as much nitrogen as producing animal protein.[93]

And here's a not-so-radical nitrogen solution. How about we all consume only the protein we need to be healthy? For many countries, including ours, that's about half our average intake.[94] A study of the European Union found this choice alone could cut the nitrogen involved in producing its food by 40 percent.[95]

AND SO MUCH HEALTHIER, TOO

More heartening news is that changes to farming and eating that benefit our Earth also enhance our health.

Choosing organic is one great example, as a recent study found "higher frequency of organic food consumption was associated with a reduced risk of cancer."[96]

Less meat also brings us big health benefits. Worldwide,

noncommunicable diseases now cause more than 70 percent of all deaths, and red meat is a risk factor for heart disease, cancer, and diabetes, among the biggest of the killers.[97] For our heart health, the largest threat is processed red meat—bacon, cold cuts, and hot dogs—which now makes up a fifth of the meat we Americans eat.[98]

The remarkably positive and diverse health benefits of plant-centered eating are more evident with each passing year. Studying tens of thousands of meat and non-meat eaters, scholars writing in the *Journal of the American Medical Association* found that non-meat diets were "associated with lower all-cause mortality." A study in *Nature* found that centering our eating in the plant world could cut the incidence of type 2 diabetes by up to 41 percent.[99]

Not long ago, then–Brooklyn borough president and, as of fall 2021, NYC Democratic mayoral candidate, Eric Adams, the author of *Healthy at Last*, reached out to thank me for my work. He told me that he had been diabetic and losing sight in one eye. "Then I switched to a whole-food, plant-based diet," he said, "and my sight soon returned to normal, and my diabetes was gone in three months."

I choke up as I think of this one life transformed and its implications for so many of us. I also understand that it might sound too good to be true, but research confirms the possibility of such recovery.[100]

Fortunately, the vast benefits of centering our diets in the plant world are registering broadly. In a 2019 poll, roughly a quarter of U.S. adults across generations reported eating less meat in the last year than previously.[101]

To speed us along, some might celebrate the arrival of fake meat. But it offers nothing to free us from monopoly control or the hazards of ultra-processing and pesticides. The Impossible Burger also uses a genetically modified soy protein—heme.[102] *Consumer Reports* notes that the iron in heme may increase some of the risks associated with meat, such as colon cancer.[103]

What tickles me personally is the fast spread of real and

yummy veggie options. When I first set up the Small Planet Institute in Cambridge in 2001, no nearby lunch options tempted me. Now, within one block of our office, four great new eateries tout plant-rich offerings.

To capture this leap in plant- and planet-centered cuisine over the past 50 years, original recipes in Book Two have been given a 21st-century makeover, curated by my daughter, Anna, and tapping the talents of recipe developer Wendy Lopez, with contributions from some of our favorite culinary heroes.

System Reset . . . Get Ready

I knew even in 1970 that what I discovered called for a system reset—a foundational remaking of the political and economic rules creating outcomes that none of us would want. So I cheered in 1975 when *The Boston Globe* titled Steve Curwood's review of *Diet for a Small Planet* "Lappe's Cookbook for the Revolution."[104]

Yes!

For me, this revolution puts human dignity first. I trust that when humans feel our dignity is protected, we can make new choices that put life itself first.

In our political lives, dignity requires democracy answering not to Big Money but to citizens with equal voice in choosing who represents us in making public choices. In economic life, dignity means equity in opportunity, a voice in our workplace, and assurance of the essentials for life—food, health care, housing, and education. The resurgence of plant and animal life—in all its immense diversity—requires diversity of control in our economy, the opposite of today's monopoly power.

And this revolution is already under way. Imagining such a system reset, though, requires harnessing the power of hope I've long loved to celebrate: Hope arises as we come to appreciate the "tapestry of life" in which all is connected and in continuous change. As we let go of any notion of fixed "parts," we can see signs of empowered, engaged citizens fulfilling the three core needs I believe we all share—our need for power, meaning, and connection.

So, let's start with eight such signs that are igniting our sense of the possible.

EIGHT HEALING STEPS

Here are eight steps citizens are taking to heal themselves, our communities, and our earth:

• *Ecological farming is gaining ground—and fast!* Over just one decade in the United States (2005 to 2015), organically farmed acres almost doubled.[105] And the acreage of certified organic farms grew by 15 percent from 2011 to 2016 to total five million.[106] If you think the word *organic* suggests "elite" and "coastal," think again. Over these five years, six southern states—Arkansas, Alabama, Mississippi, North and South Carolina, and Tennessee—more than doubled their organic farm numbers.[107]

• *More Americans are choosing organic.* Almost 40 percent of us report eating organic at least some of the time.[108] Rising at more than twice the rate of food sales in general, organic-food sales hit $50 billion in 2019.[109]

• *Schools and public agencies are stepping up to offer healthier food using more equitable supply chains.* Farm-to-school programs have grown in the last two decades from just 6 to more than 40,000.[110] So far, more than 60 college and university food services have joined the Menus of Change University Research Collaborative, bringing students more plant-based, sustainably sourced, minimally processed choices.[111] Real Food Generation unites students and food-chain workers to end what it calls "Big Food oppression" and encourages schools to use their purchasing power to support regional economies.[112] And more and more public institutions are tapping the Good Food Purchasing Program to inspire shifts in the billions of taxpayer dollars spent on food toward supply chains valuing sustainability, worker rights, animal welfare, nutrition, economic development, and racial equity.[113]

• *Local farmers' markets are lessening food's travel time.* There are almost 9,000 farmers' markets spread across the nation—more than a fourfold increase since the mid-1990s.[114]

• *Community-supported agriculture (CSA)—families partnering with farmers—is on the rise.* Since their birth in the 1980s, CSAs have grown to include 13,000 farms.[115] Families buy "shares" at the beginning of the season and then collect their fresh produce weekly as it's harvested. (My family loves it!)

• *Food policy councils empowering diverse voices are shaping public action to conquer hunger with healthy food.* Over 400 operate in communities nationwide, some with a statewide mandate.[116]

• *Upward of 29,000 community gardens enrich lives across the country.*[117] They further healthy eating, fight food apartheid, offer community-owned assets, and strengthen neighborly trust.

• *Food hubs—now around 360—bring good food from local and regional farmers to consumers and sellers.* Dotting the country from Harrisburg, Pennsylvania, to Missoula, Montana, to Oakland, California, many food hubs are in low-income neighborhoods where healthy food is hard to come by.[118]

I celebrate these creative steps by everyday Americans exercising their power for democratic innovation.

Food, Land, and Dignity Advances at Home

Now to dig deeper, I want to share two initiatives among the thousands across our country showing us the way. The first is a story of Americans advancing dignity by working to overcome food and farming apartheid.

In 1920, 14 percent of U.S. farmers were Black, but endemic racism has reduced that share to just over 1 percent today.[119] To reverse the injustice, in 2010 Leah Penniman took action, co-founding Soul Fire Farm in Grafton, New York, just north of Albany.[120]

"To free ourselves we must feed ourselves" is one of Soul Fire's great slogans. Its goal? To help end "racism in the food system and reclaim our ancestral connection to land" and to "raise and distribute life-giving food."

So far, Soul Fire has involved almost 8,000 learners from at least 40 states in hands-on exploration of all aspects of farming.

Penniman, who's been farming since the age of 16, stresses that she is honoring her ancestral roots and taking inspiration from her (very great) grandmother who grew up in West Africa. Once her ancestor became aware of the threat of being "thrown into the bowels of a slave ship," she wove her family's seeds into her hair to protect them. "Such foresight," says Penniman.[121]

Soul Fire focuses on crops indigenous to Africa and largely ignored here. In a truly holistic approach, participants learn about saving seeds and storytelling as well as the medicinal and nutritional aspects of their crops.

What thrills Penniman is that a quarter of those coming out of Soul Fire's "immersion program" now farm for a living, and over 60 percent grow food. So many people are responding to Soul Fire's message that the program now has a multiyear waiting list.[122]

Soul Fire links to what Penniman calls its "sister" groups, including the Southeastern African American Farmers' Organic Network operating out of Atlanta and Durham. For 15 years, it's worked to spread Afro-ecological practices among Black farmers in ten states and the U.S. Virgin Islands.[123]

My second story is of those who work tirelessly to make farming safe for workers—which is foundational to human dignity and a heathy food system. Here in the United States, farmworkers are at great risk of harm from pesticides and pollution, and less than 1 percent are protected by a union.[124]

So those in the Farm Labor Organizing Committee (FLOC) are heroes to me.

Since the mid-1960s, they've stood up to corporations as big as Campbell's and Heinz and won protections.[125] Now representing over 23,000 farmworkers, mainly in the Midwest, for more than 50 years, the organization has faced harassment and even the murder of one of its leaders.[126]

When my daughter, Anna, was only 11, we visited a FLOC farmworker camp in Ohio. We got to sit with a farmworker around her kitchen table while her children played outside. She knew she was dying of cancer, likely from pesticide exposure, but her voice carried no bitterness. What we heard was bewilderment.

"Why don't people respect us?" she asked. "We bring you your food." She seemed shocked that anyone could fail to see her job as among *the* most essential. Today, both Anna and her husband work for justice for those laboring along the food chain, and Anna feels part of her motivation flows from this childhood encounter.

Years later, I went to Florida to visit the Coalition of Immokalee Workers, who harvest tomatoes. I'll never forget wobbling as I struggled to pick up even one bucket of tomatoes—what my hosts lift many times an hour. The workers were getting about half in buying power of what they'd earned 30 years earlier and were denied the most basic protections.

But a decade ago their tireless efforts built a broad coalition—from students to religious activists—and a novel strategy called the Fair Food Program. In it, even some of the biggest tomato buyers, such as McDonald's, Subway, Whole Foods, and Walmart, were pushed to agree to a small premium that was passed on to farmworkers, and to sign agreements protecting the workers' basic rights. Three large food-service providers signed, too. Now farmworkers in six other states are likewise engaged.[127]

Clearly, a healthy labor movement is key to the health of farmworkers and to a democracy protecting everyone's voice.

FROM PART TO PARTICIPANT: DEMOCRACY'S JOURNEY

As you now know, ever since I penned my first book—this very one!—I've been trying to weave together the story of food and democracy.

So, in today's democracy crisis, I've been greatly heartened to see citizens across our country stepping up in what feels like a historic first. Across diverse passions—from the environment to racial justice to labor to you name it, more and more of us are catching on. No matter how urgent our particular "issue," we can't succeed without democracy. It's the "mother of all issues."

So, Americans are coming together to create a dynamite Democracy Movement.

A few years ago, though, I admit I doubted whether I could juggle my commitment to the food movement *and* the democracy movement, but soon I came to see my fear as locked in a false sense of competing parts of me.

Fortunately, that fear dissolved in a big inner shift. It happened in April 2016.

Not knowing whether I could walk even 10 miles, I signed up for Democracy Spring, a march that would cover 130 miles from Philadelphia's Liberty Bell to sit in and be arrested on the steps of our Capitol—all to focus Americans on fixing our rigged democracy. Our demands? Limits on money in politics and the end of both direct voter suppression and the unfair drawing of district lines—gerrymandering—that denies citizens an equal voice.

I loved the endless flow of conversation as we put one foot in front of the other, and even sleeping on church-basement floors night after night. We sang, and we chanted: "Whose democracy? Our democracy!" My favorite chant, though, was in the middle of a hailstorm when we spontaneously belted out, "Hail, no! Democracy, yes!"

Finally, as we were approaching the Capitol, something

unexpected happened inside me. As its dome suddenly came into view, a thought popped: "Oh, yeah, of course, *they* work for *me*—those people in the imposing buildings ahead. They work for *all of us*." Tears streamed down my cheeks. *"We citizens are in charge."*

My sense of powerlessness melted away that day, never to return.

Soon our Small Planet Institute got busy co-creating with Democracy Initiative—representing 45 million Americans across a broad range of key issues—a new online hub: www .DemocracyMovement.us.

Our goal?

That millions of Americans will experience the "thrill of democracy" we have, that engaging in this historic moment— restoring and advancing our damaged democracy—will meet our essential human need for power, meaning, and connection.

I realized that my commitment to advancing the Food Movement for healthy farming and eating didn't compete with my devotion to the root: democracy enabling us to make life-serving choices in all dimensions of life.

My decision to join the march also reminded me that every choice we make can open unexpected doorways. On the march I made new friends—including one Adam Eichen, then 23 years old and already a democracy diehard. And by early the next year, in record time, he and I had written a book together, *Daring Democracy*, to capture the exciting heart of this move-ment: regular Americans already winning real system reforms in their states and cities, enabling each voice to be heard and making national reforms more possible.

Despite generations separating us, Adam and I had a blast and agreed on every word!

PROMOTING THE "GENERAL WELFARE"

We marched in 2016 because we believe democratically set public rules are essential for a livable future. Yet much of our nation has been taught to view government as inherently oppressive and to trust "market magic" instead.

Now, with the clarity that such market fundamentalism is threatening life itself, more of us are motivated to liberate the market from monopoly control by embracing democracy in all its dimensions. In pursuing this goal, we can celebrate our alignment with a core purpose of our nation laid out in the Constitution's preamble: to "promote the general welfare."

Appreciating past eras of greater loyalty to this purpose helps me believe it's possible today. So, let's remember these turning points:

During the Great Depression, when grain prices hit all-time lows, Franklin Roosevelt stepped up to help struggling farmers—enacting a principle known as "parity." It supported crop prices to ensure that farmers' purchasing power stayed on par with non-farmers', helping to protect family farms especially during the 1930s and '40s.[128]

In 1944, Roosevelt went much further, calling for an "economic bill of rights" covering health, employment, housing, and more. He argued that political rights alone don't ensure equality for Americans in their "pursuit of happiness."[129] Roosevelt died without passing the bill. Though he did pass Social Security, an economic bill of rights remains urgent.

Later advances from the 1940s into the 1970s brought us Medicare and Medicaid, new labor protections, fairer taxation than we have today, advances in civil rights, and more. In 1965 President Johnson declared a War on Poverty. Its provisions ranged from help for farmers to a Job Corps for the unemployed to a Federal Work-Study Program enabling more students to afford college. It launched Head Start and much more.[130]

Note the stunning impact: Between the late '40s and early '70s, real family income of *all* classes doubled, with the poorest gaining the most.[131] In just one decade after the launch of the War on Poverty, America cut the poverty rate almost in half.[132] In social progress, that's lightning speed.

But two decades after Johnson, Ronald Reagan derided it all, claiming, "We waged a war on poverty, and poverty won."[133]

Oh, so wrong.

My first job—funded by that "war"—gave me a taste of its empowering approach. Knocking on doors in a poor Philadelphia neighborhood, my assignment was to encourage women receiving welfare to join together for united power in standing up to slumlords and gaining home ownership, with the city's help.

But, in the early 1980s, the big reversal I decried earlier began, as "market magic" dogma took hold.

In farming, the policy of parity collapsed, and farmland began moving into even fewer hands. Today, public dollars for agriculture no longer serve the "general welfare"; they concentrate on the largest operators growing what we need less of— including corn and soy for feed and ultra-processed foods.[134] Virtually none goes toward producing the fruits and vegetables that remain out of reach for too many.[135]

But "we aren't doomed to repeat history," says Roger Johnson, president of the National Farmers' Union.[136] We don't have to accept today's stunning inequity, as we step up to remake the public rules that now ensure income and wealth gush upward. One 2020 headline in *Time* magazine captures the power of that upward force during the previous four decades: "the top 1% of Americans have taken $50 trillion from the bottom 90%—and that's made the U.S. less secure."[137]

There is nothing inevitable about this outrage. That we know. Building on the best of our history, and with the clarity that democracy includes not just our political but also our economic lives, *what do we do?*

In food and farming, we work to ensure all voices are heard. We reinstate the principle of parity. We enforce anti-monopoly laws to crack the stranglehold of a few companies at every point in the food chain.

As the essence of democracy is "voice"—having a real say in decisions determining our well-being—we make sure all workers, including farmworkers, are protected by labor laws and encouraged to organize. We create pathways to overcome the huge barriers that Black, Indigenous, and low-income people face in becoming farmers. Specifically, we can reverse the land theft suffered by Black and Native people.[138]

We also encourage power-sharing farming models, especially cooperatives with a voice for all. Here, the Federation of Southern Cooperatives offers inspiration. Growing out of the civil rights movement, it's kept land valued at $125 million under Black ownership.[139]

Plus, we join in the eight "healing steps" celebrated above so they quicken and multiply to help democratize the wider economy.

System reset also means ending the animal-feedlot nightmare. In 2020, more than 300 organizations petitioned Congress to pass the Farm System Reform Act to ban new concentrated animal feeding operations (CAFOs) and eliminate them by 2040. It would also toughen anti-monopoly rules to break up the highly consolidated meatpacking industry.[140] Plus, farmers currently running CAFOs would get help in moving to sustainable uses of the land.[141]

We can also shift significant public support to helping farmers to transition to ecological practices and eaters to access healthy food. We start by moving a sizable piece of the $22 billion in annual farm subsidies to these positive ends, and much larger sums are available once we step up to make sure corporations and the wealthiest among us pay their fair share.

Today corporations provide one-tenth of federal tax revenue. But imagine the resources available if we reinstated the share they paid during the 1950s—a third of tax revenue.[142] Plus, $89 billion a year could be used for healing food and farming if we simply ended offshore corporate tax havens.[143] And how about this? We simply make sure all corporations pay taxes, for in 2018 almost 100 Fortune 500 corporations, including Amazon, paid *zero* federal taxes.[144] Fortifying us for these steps, we can learn from public choices other nations are making, too.

Mexico is helping almost 250,000 low-income farmers adopt agroforestry—mixing trees and crops and restoring the soil.[145] India's state of Andhra Pradesh is assisting all of its farmers in shifting to ecological farming.[146]

The Netherlands is a tiny country but the world's second largest agricultural exporter by value.[147] Since 2000, the Dutch have virtually eliminated chemical pesticides and reduced water used for key crops by 90 percent.[148] Others—from Thailand to Austria to Denmark—are also devoting real resources to making this essential shift to healthy farming.[149] And to tackle food waste, a related problem, in 2016 France became the first country to ban supermarkets from throwing out or destroying unsold food, requiring that stores instead give it to food banks.[150]

Let's learn from the worst and best of our history and also from others as we free our democracy from private power and our economy from the "magical market" mind trap.

Across the Planet, Living Democracy from the Ground Up

In that spirit, and seizing this historic moment, we can also be emboldened by the courage of rural people across our small planet taking their—and thus our—survival and thriving into their own hands. Emerging people's movements are making decisions together to produce healthy food as they diffuse power and sustain the tapestry of life—in the soil, water, and atmosphere.

In other words, they are creating democracy as a way of life—what my 26-year-old self had intuited was the pathway to ending hunger, yet I couldn't imagine way back then.

EIGHT MILLION

For years I've been stoked by the research of Professor Jules Pretty at the University of Essex in the United Kingdom. And just in time for this book's 50th anniversary, he came through again with astonishing new findings.

Pretty and his team published a 50-year perspective on developments in farming, especially in low-income countries. They first confirmed that decades of top-down development approaches, pushed by governments in the Global North, had worsened inequality. But then, a big surprise: Starting around 2000, a radically different approach began to arise—this time from the ground up.[151]

Sprouting with remarkable speed across 55 countries, "intentionally formed collaborative groups" began achieving sustainable farming and forestry. Their life-serving practices harken back to ways we humans cared for ourselves and the earth over eons—through "common rules and sanctions" derived from "shared values," observes the Pretty team. They noted "relations of trust, reciprocity and mutual obligation" as key to their success.

For me, this is living democracy.

The Pretty team's astounding overall finding? While in the year 2000 there were about half a million such groups, in the following two decades eight million more emerged.

Eight million in twenty years—whoa!

So, in all, 8.5 million self-organizing community bodies aligning their farming and forestry with nature have emerged— almost all in low-income countries. Together they're reviving land nearly the size of India.[152]

The brilliance of Pretty and his team, I believe, is that they scoured the world for what others believed to be impossible, and they've turned up lessons of self-empowerment, cooperation, and dogged persistence we all can use.

"WHAT WE FORGOT TO TELL YOU"

Even I might have been skeptical if I had not had my own unforgettable tastes of this global emergence.

One was about ten years ago. I was in Hyderabad, India, for a meeting, and it dawned on me that I wasn't far from one of the 75 villages of the Deccan Development Society (DDS), a women's biodiverse farming initiative I'd admired from afar for years.

So I hired a car, and before I knew it, I was sitting encircled by smiling women wearing gorgeous saris, each with a small mound of seeds decorating the straw mat on which we all sat. The women—of the lowest caste and thus expected never to lead—eagerly shared their stories with me.

Two decades earlier, hunger was their daily reality, and many described feeling powerless in their own households.

But a few women began meeting—and dreaming. More joined, and once a week they began gathering at night after their children were asleep. Their *sangham* (women's group) arrived at common plans for transforming nearby abandoned, barren land into organic, diverse food crops. A savings circle, with each member contributing tiny amounts, made it possible for the sangham to offer members—working in groups— revolving loans to purchase or lease small plots of this land. (Many call the approach Saving for Change, and it's arising in many parts of the world.)[153] Their group savings then qualified the sangham for a bigger loan from the DDS network to be repaid over two to three years.

Today, there is "no hunger in our village," they declared, beaming as they guided me into their fields, each no more than an acre or so, to see for myself at least 20 crops—millet, legumes, greens, and other vegetables—all thriving together.

I also got to visit the women's own radio station, Sangham Radio, where they share farming tips. Plus, every February, a colorful, musical caravan of DDS women travels from village to village sharing and learning about seed saving and more. Today DDS members—who once felt isolated even within their own villages—participate in farmer gatherings as far away as South America.

Deeply moved by all I'd learned, I expressed my thanks and began walking out of the village when suddenly I heard voices. Turning, I saw women rushing toward me calling out, "We forgot to tell you the most important thing!" I stopped, and here's what I heard:

"Most of all, what we get from our sangham is courage."

Their beautiful message goes right to the heart of all I have learned over this half century. The courage we need for system reset comes as we create connections of deep trust.

These women's achievements also reflect the wider rebirth Professor Pretty and his team have documented: Almost 30 percent of farms worldwide "have crossed a redesign threshold" empowering them to better sustain healthy soil, water, and species diversity along with the families depending on them.[154]

You can see why I follow Pretty's work!

What he terms "redesign"—including what many call *agro-ecology*, or regenerative or organic agriculture—is happening across the earth, but I celebrate most the lessons from Africa. There, soil nutrients and crop yields have been dropping, while the continent's share of hungry people is the world's worst.[155] To reverse these deadly trends, farmers are enlisting the power of crops like the pigeon pea and fast-growing trees with nutrient-rich leaves—all called "cover crops" or "green manure" because they fertilize the soil, not deplete it. To learn more, I turned to Roland Bunch, who in the 1970s had driven me and my little kids in his pickup into Guatemala's hill country to see his work with farmers stopping soil erosion. Now, after decades of similar work in Africa, Roland leads the organization Better Soils, Better Lives and shares the story of Malawian farmers who've used these low-cost strategies to double their food-crop yields.[156]

In such breakthroughs, one key is enabling crops and trees to complement each other's growth. In this reimagining of agriculture, Africa offers inspiring lessons.

TREES AND CROPS FEED EACH OTHER, TRANSFORMING LIVES

The African Sahel is a strip of countries south of the Sahara that for decades was linked in my heart to great suffering. From the late 1960s to the early '80s, drought combined with poverty and depleted soils to cause famine that killed many, and Niger—one of the world's poorest countries—was hit particularly hard.

But then another way of being with the earth emerged.

Farmers began growing trees and crops in the same fields. In the right mix, they don't compete. Instead, trees and crops help each other thrive. In Niger, through farmer-to-farmer learning, more and more families came to embrace both "green manure" and cover crops and began nurturing tree stumps and bushes—along with tree roots and seeds in the soil—to sprout and become trees.

By 2009, the approach had regenerated 200 million trees that sequester carbon, improve soil fertility, and significantly increase crop yields.[157] Plus, they offer fruit, fodder, firewood, and even fertilizer—as their leaves enrich the soil—and their shade reduces soil temperature, helping retain soil moisture.

To underscore that farmers are the leaders, these practices are called "farmer-managed natural regeneration."

So effective were these agroforestry practices that in Niger, even by 2009, they'd generated food security for 2.5 million people—a tenth of the population.[158] No one knows for sure how widespread agroforestry is in sub-Saharan Africa today, but Gray Tappan of the U.S. Geological Survey offers an extrapolation from what is known: On-farm trees may have spread to over half a million square miles.[159]

That's more than twice the size of Texas! Amazing. And what does this big shift to agroforestry feel like? To allow me to imagine, agronomist Tony Rinaudo, who helped spark the change, shared a comment from a child in Ghana: "We eat fruits anytime we want to, and if our parents have not prepared food, we can just go to the bush."[160]

Africa's breakthrough in integrating crops and trees has echoes here at home.

One is in the spread of alley cropping—a twist on agroforestry. Since 2013, the Savanna Institute has been working with farmers to spread this practice to Illinois, Iowa, Minnesota, and Wisconsin. In alley cropping, widely spaced "alleys" of trees thrive among companion crops that also help store carbon. The practice increases each acre's total yield by at least 40 percent. Sometimes, it even triples yields.

Plus, alley cropping helps farmers by sequestering carbon, diversifying their income sources, preventing soil erosion, and providing wildlife habitat, Jacob Grace of the Savanna Institute explains. Almost a quarter of "all Midwestern farmland would be more profitable with rows of trees in it, compared to corn and soybean monocultures," Grace writes.[161]

Agroforestry is one face of earth-healing farming. From Africa to our Midwest and beyond, it holds the technical potential to sequester as much as one-sixth of today's total annual global emissions.[162] More broadly, according to Dr. Rattan Lal, soil scientist and World Food Prize winner, "restorative land use" could sequester as much as "one-fifth of today's total annual greenhouse gas emissions." He stresses "the co-benefits to our health, clean water, and so much more."[163]

Restorative, climate-positive farming practices are spreading across our country. The lentil farmers of Montana help bring to soils—and eaters—this healthy crop that fixes nitrogen naturally. The Practical Farmers of Iowa have long pushed forward our ecological transition. And so many more are showing us the way.

Returning to the Roots

I began with the metaphor of a storm so fierce it topples the biggest tree to expose its long-hidden roots. But the metaphor carries another possibility if we ask this question: What is special about trees that the storm *cannot* topple?

Could it be that their roots are more extensive and interconnected? Note that most tree roots are quite near the surface, yet they reach an area two to four times the breadth of the crown.[164] That's huge.

We also now know that trees communicate intensely in mutual aid. Trees use a "network of soil fungi" not just to express their own needs but to "aid neighboring plants," says professor of forest ecology Suzanne Simard.[165]

No wonder healthy trees often weather the fiercest storm.

So, this metaphor now carries a richer meaning for me, as I think back over these stories and the dramatic evidence of transformative change. They are spread widely, for sure. They are connected, and they are firmly rooted in large measure because of those connections.

Yet, they are mostly invisible. And *that* we can and must change if humanity is to make this do-or-die pivot. And to help you connect to these roots, I include Tools for Learning and Action at the end of the book.

Here I've shared my journey to identify the roots of our multiple challenges in the crisis of democracy itself. Democracy is what we decide to do together when all voices are heard, and the events of 2020 have taught us never to take even the basics of democracy for granted. Because of the courageous Black Lives Matter movement and America's rising Democracy Movement, awareness is growing that democracy is the pathway forward. It is the only way of being in community aligned with our own nature—our essential need for power, meaning, and connection throughout our lives.

For the late congressman John Lewis, democracy therefore carried a sacred quality, as the embodiment of human dignity. I agree, Mr. Lewis.

Now, as I close, let me remind us of the truths with which I began. They keep me going.

The nature of nature is never static, and in it there are no parts—only participants. So, in this world of continuous change in which all is connected, there are at least two certainties.

One is that if we ourselves fail to become the change we seek, the unchangeable law of inertia means that today's destructive, even lethal, trends will accelerate.

And the second certainty motivating me: In our connected world of continuous change, *it is not possible to know what's possible.*

And therein lies our freedom . . . and, ultimately, our joy. What a big relief it was years ago when I realized I don't have to be an optimist. That's tough. So I declared myself a diehard "possibilist." And it works. I've learned, thank goodness, that human beings do not need certainty of outcome to achieve great feats. We need only a sense of possibility.

I don't have to be a solid predictor of the future, and that's good—since I would have given virtually none of the stories of innovation and transformation I've just shared much of a chance 50 years ago, as I dug in for answers in the U.C. Berkeley library.

Plus, in our connected reality, the only choice we don't have is whether to change the world. We can't help it. Even our inaction has power, as someone is always watching and affected. Whether we know it or not, we all make ripples.

In this do-or-die moment, it's clear: "Goodness" is no longer good enough. Courage is our call. And, because we are profoundly social creatures, one way to become more courageous is to hang out with courage. So let us bring into our lives those more willing to risk than we are. Let us try what we thought we could not. Who knows, one discovery may be that we are more courageous than we believed.

I admit, I've not always stayed true to my own advice. Yet I am certain that each and every time I have mustered the might to throw myself into the unknown, I've experienced a pivotal moment on my journey.

Like me, you might be surprised, even delighted, by what you discover. So, may we all take in the wisdom that Amanda Gorman, National Youth Poet Laureate, offered us at the 2021 presidential inauguration:

The new dawn blooms as we free it.
For there is always light,
if only we're brave enough to see it,
if only we're brave enough to be it.

—from "The Hill We Climb"

An Extraordinary Time to Be Alive: Introduction to the 20th Anniversary Edition

I begin this introduction to the 20th anniversary edition of *Diet for a Small Planet* with a sense of awe, awe at the rapidity of change. In 1971, I—an intense 26-year-old in search of herself—sat long hours in the U.C. Berkeley library uncovering facts about the global food supply that turned my world upside down. At home in my dining room, working at my manual typewriter, I made seemingly endless protein calculations with a slide rule. And here I am twenty years later, tapping away on my Toshiba "lap top" preparing to FAX this chapter to my editor!

Yes, the pace of technological change has been breathtaking, but our change of consciousness has been yet more dramatic. We who were born in this century are the first generations to experience a perceptible quickening of historical time. The change you or I witness in a lifetime now exceeds what in previous centuries transpired over many, many generations. And we who were born after World War II are the first to know that our choices count: They count on a global scale. They matter in evolutionary time. In our species' fantastic rush toward "modernization" we obliterate millions of other species, transfigure the earth's surface, and create climate-changing disruption of the upper atmosphere, all powerfully altering the path of evolution.

More personally, I feel the quickening of time in realizing that what was heresy, what was "fringe," when I wrote *Diet for a Small Planet* just twenty years ago is now common knowledge.

Then, the notion that human beings could do well without meat was heretical. Today, the medical establishment acknowledges the numerous benefits of eating low on the food chain.

Then, anyone who questioned the American diet's reliance on beef—since cattle are the most wasteful converters of grain to meat—was perceived as challenging the American way of life (especially when that someone came from Fort Worth, Texas—"Cowtown, USA"). Today, the expanding herds of cattle worldwide not only are recognized as poor plant-to-meat converters but are documented contributors to global climate change. They're responsible for releasing enormous quantities of methane into the atmosphere, contributing to global warming. Moreover, commercial invasion of the South and Central American rainforests now implicates cattle ranching in the one-and-one-half acre *per second* destruction of the remaining rainforests worldwide.

Then, anyone who questioned industrial agriculture—fossil fuel and chemically dependent—was seen as a naïve "back to the lander." To challenge industrial agriculture was to question efficiency itself and to wish us all back into the fields at hard labor. Today, the National Academy of Sciences acknowledges the threat of agricultural chemicals,[1] and even the U.S. Department of Agriculture reports that the small family farm is at least as efficient as the superfarms undermining America's rural communities.[2]

Peeling the Proverbial Onion

What an extraordinary time to be alive! More pointedly, in my case, what an extraordinary time to be middle-aged—to perceive, because I have lived most of half a century, the quickening of time.

And with this awareness of humanity's power to remake, to

unmake, our living environment, has come a radical awakening across many disciplines. We thus live in an era of conscious searching, of profound rethinking. It is, I'm convinced, a time of opportunity that may come only once in many centuries. And so, while fear may grip me often, I also feel incredibly privileged to be alive *now:* a time of exploring fundamental questions about who we are and what the role of our species is to be on this lovely planet.

In Part I, you will read "my journey," the path that took me from being the struggling 26-year-old in the U.C. library to being the co-founder of the Institute for Food and Development Policy. In 1981, when I wrote that chapter, my mission was clear. I knew what I had to do. But as the 1980s progressed, I became less sure, and that uncertainty pushed me forward.

Not surprisingly perhaps, I've been thinking in food metaphors all my life—the most persistent being that of the humble onion. I feel I've spent twenty years peeling away at it! Let me now explain by taking you with me through its several layers.

In one sense, what motivated me to write *Diet for a Small Planet* was simple outrage. We feed almost half the world's grain to livestock, returning only a fraction in meat—while millions starve. It confounds all logic. Yet the pattern has intensified. Vast resources move at an accelerating rate toward the production of exports from lands on which people go hungry. Since the 1970s, the rates of growth in food production have been lower in the basic grains and tubers eaten by poor, hungry people than in fruits, vegetables, oil seeds, and feed grains for meat, eaten largely by the planet's already well-fed minority.

My mission was to awaken people to this simple fact: Hunger is human made. I sought to liberate people from the myth that nature's to blame for the massive deprivation hundreds of millions of people now experience. In writing *Food First* and establishing the Institute for Food and Development Policy in the mid-seventies, however, my mission became more ambitious.

I sought, with my colleagues, to explain *how* human-made

institutions create needless suffering. In books like *Aid as Obstacle,
World Hunger: Twelve Myths, Betraying the National Interest,* and *Taking Population Seriously,* we described the growing concentration
of decision making—from the village level, to the national level,
to the level of international commerce and finance. Fewer and
fewer people make decisions that have life-and-death consequences for the rest of us. The problem is not scarcity of land
or food, I became fond of saying: It is a *scarcity of democracy.*

But, for this phrase to make any sense, I had to probe to the
heart and soul of democracy. Surely to have any meaning at all,
democracy must be more than a set of formal rules and procedures. After all, many countries—the Philippines, India, and
many of the Central American countries—have all the trap-
pings of democracy. Yet their people live in misery. Democracy
had to be more—is it less a set of rules, I wondered, than a very
human process? A process grounded in several principles that
can only be realized by people themselves? First is, perhaps, the
accountability of leadership to those who have to live with the consequences of their decisions. Second, the related principle of
shared power, perhaps never equally shared but at least shared to
the degree that no one is left powerless, unable to protect themselves and those they love.

In so defining democracy, it became clear to me that wherever there is hunger, democracy has not been fulfilled.

But the better I got at describing the problem, the more
intense my frustration. What were the solutions? I could describe
the need for greater democracy, making possible, for example,
the reforms necessary for the rural poor in the Global South to
achieve food security and reduce the size of their families. I
could describe policy shifts that could do away with homelessness here. But without a practical path for getting there, all my
descriptions and prescriptions left me profoundly unsatisfied. I
had always enjoyed giving public talks but my enjoyment began
to wane. I realized my audiences wanted more from me. And I
did not feel able to give it.

I had to go deeper. In the early 1980s, I started reading

widely again in political theory and social change. I traveled to countries I thought might have something important to teach. I visited Europe to study the movement for worker participation there. I went to Sweden to examine the much-debated proposal to democratize and decentralize ownership of large industry. In Yugoslavia I studied the troubled path toward worker self-management. I ventured to China to look at its dramatic restructuring of agriculture.

By the mid-eighties my sense of possibilities had been greatly expanded, but I had also come more firmly than ever to believe that no program—no matter how "correct"—could address the problems of our communities and our planet unless many, many more people believed themselves capable of participating in the changes it suggested.

So I was forced to peel away another layer, to go still deeper, again asking why? What blocks us from believing in the possibility of such change—change in the direction of more genuine democracy—and engaging ourselves in the process of bringing it about?

What could possibly be powerful enough to allow us to tolerate and condone as a society what as individuals we abhor? Few of us would allow a child to suffer deprivation in our midst. Yet as a society we do just that. In the United States, we allow one-quarter of our children to be born into poverty, which results in twice the chance of their being physically stunted compared to middle-class children. And what could be powerful enough to allow us to destroy majestic redwoods, to dredge breathtaking coastlines, to drain rich wetlands—to obliterate that which has inspired feelings of security, thanksgiving, and awe in human beings over eons of time?

Perhaps, I thought, it's that as individuals we have come to believe we have neither the capacity nor the responsibility to do otherwise, to do other than acquiesce to forces beyond our control.

We are in large measure who we believe ourselves to be. I had always believed in the power of ideas to shape our reality, but this concept took on new meaning for me as the 1980s progressed. I came to see that what we believe ourselves to be reflects assumptions so taken for granted that they've become like an invisible ether. We live unconscious of their power. I became convinced that as we approach the 21st century, we remain captured in a set of ideas about ourselves which is a legacy of at least three centuries. This may sound strange, especially from someone arguing the quickening of change. But striking also is continuity, continuity in our ideas of ourselves that we now must consciously examine.

The Power of Ideas

To make myself clearer, let me take you the next step in my own quest, peeling away another layer in my "onion" of discovery.

I wanted to bring to the surface the "big ideas"—the assumptions about who we are and the nature of our ties to one another—that lie behind our acceptance of the social structures in which we live. I had become convinced that there was only one thing strong enough to explain our behavior—behavior that was needlessly destroying millions of lives each year from hunger and disease, and undermining the integrity of our fragile planet as well. It is the power of ideas. *But how do we get at those ideas?*

My answer in part became: "through talk." We must talk in order to surface underlying assumptions, to nudge ourselves and each other to reflect upon the reasons *why* we think and act as we do. We must talk in order to discover whether our ideas have simply become unexamined habits of mind, habits which thwart instead of aid effective living.

So I decided to stop writing tracts about just what I believe. I wanted to engage those who had never and would never pick up one of my existing books—books they might dismiss because they challenge the status quo.

I wanted to write a dialogue in order to provoke dialogue—to get people talking. So I set out to write in two voices.

One voice would speak from the inherited assumptions that make up the dominant modern worldview; the assumptions that limit the very questions we're allowed to ask. The other voice would be my own, struggling to articulate an emerging alternative. These voices in print became *Rediscovering America's Values,* published in 1989.

In the years of research required to write *Rediscovering,* I became ever surer that indeed we all do carry unexamined mental baggage, now centuries in the making. This metaphorical baggage we now need to put through the "security check." We must open up this baggage, examining it in light of its consequences and for its security threat to our future.

In considering my case, please excuse my audacity in capturing a few centuries in a few sentences.

In the 17th century, René Descartes located the human soul in its mechanical vehicle, the human body. And Isaac Newton offered an exciting metaphor for understanding the interaction of those mechanical vehicles. He discovered laws of motion governing the physical universe. Having just given up on the ever-so-comforting notion of an interventionist God—one able to put the human house aright—we were left with a frightening void. "Ah ha!" we thought, "there must be parallel laws governing the social world, governing our interaction with one another."

And what became known as the "mechanistic worldview" began to take shape, developed by Western thinkers from the 17th century onward. Dazzling, uninterrupted breakthroughs in technological innovation—from the spinning ginny to steel mills, from bull dozers to dishwashers—permeated ever more aspects of our lives: the ubiquitous presence of machines confirming our sense that indeed the world can best be understood in mechanical terms.

Once absorbing this mechanistic worldview, it was easy to assume that parallel laws governed economic life. Our challenge was to identify them, let them freely function, and, *voilà,* an economic order would fall neatly into place! Human beings are handily off the hook. No moral reasoning required; the job would be done for us.

Critically important, in the mechanistic worldview, everything can best *be* understood by examining its parts. Human beings become distinct "atoms"—insular beings trapped inside our separate egos. Our radical individualism thus does not result from any moral failing; it derives from *our atomistic nature*. We're constitutionally unable to put ourselves in each other's shoes. We can identify only our own distinct interests. But that's not really so bad after all—for private interests serve, conveniently, to drive the giant social machine. No one put it better than Helvetius in the 18th century:

> As the physical world is ruled by the laws of movement, so is the moral universe ruled by the laws of interest.[3]

This view of ourselves has defined the meaning of our most basic social values. Freedom, for example. Freedom is "elbow room": our capacity for self-defense, our success in fending off the intrusion of others. And what better defense than material accumulation? After all, the more we have, the freer we are from dependence upon others. To challenge the unlimited accumulation of material wealth is therefore to challenge the individual's free development. And fairness, what is it? Whatever distribution of rewards follows from each "social atom's" pursuit of its private interests, operating within the "neutral laws" of economic life.

This view of ourselves, driven by narrow self-interest, began to take shape in the 17th century and was picked up in the 18th by many of our nation's founders, including John Adams. He wrote:

> . . . whoever would found a state, and make proper laws for the government of it, must presume that all men are bad by nature.[4]

This combination of notions—social atomism, materialism, and the rule of human affairs by discoverable laws—has had profound implications for the social order we have created. For if indeed we are isolated social atoms, any conscious process of group decision making based on identifying *common* needs—usually called politics—is suspect. We must let absolute laws determine our fate, for self-seeking egos may well twist any other method to their private gain. Any genuine deliberative process is therefore impossible.

Instead of trusting our capacities for common problem solving, we sought desperately, and believed we had found, laws governing the social world—governing life-and-death matters of economics—laws that determine who eats and who doesn't. The more choices we can leave to these laws, the better off we are.

And what are these absolute laws? In much of the West we have established at least two such laws as almost sacrosanct, and adhered to them in varying degrees of faithfulness. They are:

• the market distribution of goods and services;

• not private property *per se* but a particular variant of this institution: the *unlimited* private accumulation of *productive* property.

And here's where the problem arises. It is not the institutions of the market or private property. The problem is converting these handy tools into fixed laws. What happens then? Human responsibility for consequences goes out the window.

If, for example, an inflating market pushes the price of housing out of reach of families on low incomes, leaving them on the street, hey, that's not the community's fault. That's the market at work! *We're* not responsible for that!

Or take income distribution itself. If it is the result of millions of individual free choices in the market, then as a society we're not responsible for the outcome, no matter how wide the resulting chasm between rich and poor. Never mind that during the 1980s perhaps the greatest transfer of wealth occurred in our nation's history—in this case from the nonrich to the rich—largely as a result of deliberate government and corporate policies. But we're absolved of responsibility, as long as we cling to the myth that individual choices in the market "automatically" determine outcomes.[5]

As the market defines more and more of our lives, even the most sacred of human experiences is up for sale: I was saddened but not surprised that the Reagan era brought "surrogate motherhood." In the 1988 debate over Baby "M," parties wrangled over a contract. Few asked what the renting of a woman's womb portended—a world in which any value could be reduced to a market value.

What if, I asked myself, instead of our masters, the market and private productive property could become mere devices in the service of our values, in the service of community-defined ends? The catch-22 is, of course, that those community ends can be defined only through deliberation—public talk—about our values and common needs—a process precluded by the very assumptions of social "atomism" with its self-seeking limits which we've come unquestionably to accept.

In Search of a New Myth of Being

If social atomism and the universe as machine became the dominant "myths" of the modern era, is there an alternative? What might replace these ubiquitous claims on our collective imaginations?

To suggest an answer, let me return to my lifelong focus on food. When I began this quest, I was often dumbfounded when people asked me why I chose *food*. What a funny question, I thought. Everyone knows that all living creatures must eat. If they're not eating, what else matters?

Yet in the 1960s, I only barely understood the implications of my choice to focus on our most direct link to the nurturing earth. Yes, I was aware of being influenced by the birth of environmentalism. In the late 1960s, I attended standing-room lectures on ecology at the "free university" at Berkeley. Most of us were just learning the word for the first time. Something was in the air.

I certainly didn't understand until much later, however, that ecology offered us a new way of thinking about what it means to be a human being.

It's difficult to perceive this possibility in part because the message we hear from environmentalists is too often a scold. "Okay," the environmental preachers tell us, "the party's over. You have all overdone it. Your indulgence must stop! Accept the grim fact that on our little planet we live on limited means, on a fixed income."

Feeling guilty as accused, it's hard to see that while these reprimands may well be deserved there is also a richly positive message for us human beings in the discovery of "nature." Let our guilty feelings not block our capacity to listen. For there is a beautiful irony to appreciate. While the environmental catastrophe sounds the alarm, nature also offers us insights that are essential to addressing not only the environmental crisis but other aspects of social decline as well.

As we begin to see the world through the lens of ecology, subtly, we also begin to reshape our view of ourselves.

To explain, let me again pick up my personal journey.

In 1983, when I began research for what became *Rediscovering America's Values*, I was reacting to the 1980s celebration of narrow self-interest and a materialistic understanding of ourselves. I perceived Reaganism as the last gasp of a tired dogma. In my research and writing, I was struggling to articulate an alternative social understanding of self—self-interest not as narrow selfishness, but as deeply embedded in relationships.

I was struggling to articulate a vision of social change that took us beyond social atomism and beyond "received" Marxism as well. I was influenced by environmental philosophy, Catholic social teaching, feminist philosophy, and historiography. But most fun, I'll admit, was discovering that even within the dominant, Western philosophic tradition were rich insights supporting my own intuitions and life experience. Even from Adam Smith. Yes, the *same* Adam Smith who many view as the Godfather of greed—the supposed celebrator of self-seeking as the engine of the economy. (Officials in the White House during the Reagan years even sported Adam Smith neckties.) But buried has been Smith's profoundly social vision of human nature.

Whereas in the classic Western philosophic tradition, the individual is poised defensively against society, Adam Smith perceived the individual's sense of self and worth embedded entirely within society. Because we not only need the approval of others, but need to feel that approval is deserved, our individual well-being exists more in relationships *with* others than in protection *against* others. In his *Theory of Moral Sentiments*, Smith pointedly reconstructed the Christian precept to love our neighbors as ourselves, writing that:

> . . . it is the great precept of nature to love ourselves only as we love our neighbour; or, what comes to the same thing, as our neighbour is capable of loving us.[6]

This intensely social view of our nature is increasingly confirmed by comparative sociology and anthropology. Indeed, the dominant paradigm's notion of the autonomous individual now appears as philosophical flight of fancy! Its claim to Charles Darwin's imprimatur is suspect when we learn that Darwin clearly believed that evolving human beings could only have expanded their societies because of a "moral sense . . . aboriginally derived from the social instincts."[7] Among primeval people, Darwin observed, actions were no doubt judged good or bad "solely as they obviously affect the welfare of the tribe." Recent studies find the roots of empathy in infancy, noting that infants react to the pain of others as though it were happening to themselves.[8] And psychologists document how human expressions of fellow-feeling respond to a social context which encourages them.[9] In fact, my own intuitions and experience suggest that we ignore our profoundly social nature—our need for approval and to express our feelings for each other's well-being—only at great psychic cost.

But the environmental perspective offers a uniquely moving metaphor for such understanding of self. In 1985, I co-authored an article with environmental philosopher J. Baird Callicott.[10] He, more than anyone I know, views—and eloquently expresses—the social nature of human existence through the lens of ecology. His insights shaped this excerpt from our article:

> Nature is not only human culture's life support system, but its enduring paradigm as well. Human society is not simply embedded in nature. It also imitates nature in crucial ways—as the myths and ceremonies of primal peoples frankly acknowledge.
>
> Ecological science focuses attention on *relationships*. It reveals that organisms are not only mutually related; they are also mutually defining. A species *is what it is because of where and how it lives.* From an ecological point of view, a species is the intersection of a multiplicity of strands in the web of life. It is not only located in its context, *it is literally constituted by its context.*
>
> Once seen through the prism of the biotic community, then, a person's individuality is constituted differently—not by defense against each other but in the peculiar mix of relationships we each bear to family, friends, neighbors, colleagues, and co-workers.[11]

If true, the great environmental awakening we are now experiencing is also reshaping our sense of self. For even the most popular images of ecology involve us in perceiving relationships—the link between acid rain and the forests' health, between the destruction of rainforests in South America and thinning bird populations in North America, between pesticides on crops and the ill health of farmworkers and consumers. They're all about the ties among us and the rest of the natural world. That awareness of *relationship,* I believe, is permeating our consciousness, and ever-so-subtly eroding the notion that we can stake out our own safety and happiness apart from the well-being of the communities in which we live.

Inescapably, awareness of our environment is also awareness of a "commons"—a reality on which we share dependency and therefore mutual responsibility, a commons which defies division into individual goods. I was struck recently by reports of a survey of American youths' knowledge of geography. A shockingly large share could not name the country that borders the U.S. on the south, but almost all had heard of the ozone hole! Its consequences touch us all.

The environmental crisis teaches perhaps more graphically what is true of all our social problems: The health of the whole is literally essential to the individual's well-being. If we are ultimately interdependent, it becomes silly to think in terms of trade-offs between social integrity and the individual's unfettered pursuit of happiness.

I have come to think of this shift in understanding as moving us from a mechanistic to what might be called a *relational worldview.*

Rethinking Farming and Food

These thoughts provide a framework for what you will find in the chapters that follow. *Diet for a Small Planet* identifies the roots of a wasteful, destructive, and hunger-generating food system in underlying economic "rules." In the pages that follow, you will read about how these unquestioned "rules" drive farmers to overproduce, eroding topsoil, polluting groundwater, and decimating farm communities.

But all that I lay out here can also be understood through the inherited "ether" I've just hinted at—the dominant mechanistic worldview. Why have we accepted these "rules" of economic life? They conform to the notion that there are laws governing the social order, just as laws of motion govern the material world. They "fit" neatly with the view of nature as giant machine. And once nature is so perceived, our job is to tinker, even redesigning nature where necessary.

Nonhuman animals become mere cogs in that machine. First Jim Mason and Peter Singer in their book *Animal Factories*[12] and then John Robbins in *Diet for a New America*[13] have told us in horrifying detail how first poultry and now other farm animals were denied expression of their own nature, constrained to the point of pain and ill-health—and, ultimately, reduced to nothing but "food processors" for human convenience and taste. Farm animals, as I discovered early in my research for *Diet*, are to the U.S. Department of Agriculture mere "units of production."

By the 1980s, the view of nature as machine for our tinkering set the stage for genetic manipulation of a new order. Scientists at the U.S. Department of Agriculture spliced a human growth hormone gene into swine. They were delighted with their success: hogs that gain weight faster and are leaner. Never mind that the animals are arthritic and cross-eyed. These problems, as the Land Institute's Wes Jackson puts it, are just aspects of "fine-tuning" the hog.[14]

If, on the one hand, we condemn modern agriculture because it involves the killing of life to sustain life, do we run the risk of furthering the fundamental fallacy: that we human beings are not really *part of* nature; we stand outside and redesign nature by human-made rules? On the other hand, outrage at the cruel treatment of farm animals by "agribusiness" can lead us to question the whole notion of human beings as outside nature. When we reconnect with our place *in* nature, we may well rediscover respectful patterns of interacting with, and even consuming, animals that have long been sources of human sustenance. For many people, the relationship of indigenous North American peoples to the animals they hunted suggests the possibility that human beings can develop humility, awe, and awareness of ourselves within the ever-renewing chain of life and death. Others, discovering as I have that human beings need eat no flesh to be healthy, understandably arrive at a different point. Why inflict any death that is unnecessary to sustaining life?

My own hope is that as we center the critique of modern agriculture in a critique of the machine model of nature, we will move away from the notion of the rights of animals *versus* the rights of humans. We can begin instead to reconceive an organic whole in which a mutuality of interests can be found. Animals re-integrated into mixed farmsteads, with a rich variety of both animal and plant species, can begin to re-attune human beings to our place in nature alongside other animals, rather than over them, outside nature.

This shift allows activists to move away from a morally self-righteous, self-sacrificial tone and to call others toward a positive vision. A "correct diet," one centered in the plant world, one based in less processed and nonchemically treated foods, is not a "should" as much as a freeing step. It helps us find our place in nature. In so doing, we are reminded of the primary fact of our being—that we are defined by relationships.

Toward a Politics of Hope

But, as we all know, it's one thing to have a vision; it's quite another to know how to manifest it. What could be a process for replacing the mechanistic and atomistic worldview with a relational, ecological vision? By the late 1980s, that was the question that pressed itself on me. What did this new worldview mean for our *real-life, everyday existence* in our complex world?

We human beings can come into harmony with the rest of the natural world, and free ourselves from life-stunting hunger and poverty, only as we together make different public choices—not only in agriculture but also across the full range of concerns. For me, however, suggesting what those different choices *should* be was inadequate—almost suspect—if I couldn't also suggest how we might go about arriving at a broad consensus on those choices and actually putting them into practice in our lives.

Surely we need a process for choosing our future that is consistent with our social nature and reflective of the high stakes we now acknowledge. So, to me a most urgent question was no longer "What is the correct policy?" or "What is my vision of the future?" but rather: "What social processes for arriving at public choices best build on our little-tapped but innate capacities for relatedness inherent in the relational worldview?"

To begin to answer that question means to probe, in order to transform, the very *meaning of democracy itself.* For democracy in this culture is the term we use to describe the process of coming together to make public choices.

In other words, I had to stop describing the problem and start developing a philosophy of change. If we are in the midst of a historic shift in understanding, the death of the old worldview and the birth of the new, I believe we can each become conscious midwives to the birth. But not unless we are actively envisioning practical alternatives to our modern, alienating notion of politics.

The word "politics" itself has become debased. In polls of today's young people, public officials are typically characterized as unprincipled. Words like "dishonest," "corrupt," "liars," and "puppets" are common descriptions. Clearly we need a richer, stronger, more active vision of democracy to replace the dominant one, which is increasingly alienating, even insulting, to many Americans.

By mid-1990 I was ready to take the next big leap. I was determined to take on this challenge more directly. Food First, the organization I had founded in 1975 with Joseph Collins, was in good hands. It has thrived and had a major impact in part because of support from members who were readers of *Diet for a Small Planet.* It continues to have a powerful role to play. But I needed a vehicle that would allow me to devote all of my energies to these "how" questions.

But I knew I couldn't do it alone. Were there others ready to take the leap with me? Then, in mid-1990 I received a letter of support for my new direction that also offered a brilliant critique. It came from Paul Du Bois, a person about my age with a remarkable career in community organizing and academic and nonprofit leadership posts. Within minutes, I had Paul on the phone. And in less than two months of intense brainstorming and planning, we made the decision: We would throw in our lots together. We would devote ourselves to creating a vehicle for the thousands of people we sensed were—like us—ready to move from complaint or mere protest to positive work for what Paul and I came to call "citizen democracy." Our goal is nothing less than helping citizens transform the very meaning of democracy.

The year 1990 was a heady time for us. In the fall, we incorporated as the Institute for the Arts of Democracy and began a journey worthy of the rest of our lives. By the end of the year we had volunteers on board and several thousand people who'd expressed interest in our work.

In this work, we are, of course, hardly starting from scratch! Worldwide, people are searching for democracy—democracy that *works*. And here at home, in communities all across the nation, people are experimenting with new, more sustainable, effective ways of engaging citizens in public life. The role of our new center is naming, catalyzing, and further developing a search already underway. By "naming" we mean that we see our role in part as articulating an emergent philosophy—giving conceptual shape to what many are already experiencing. This process is itself empowering.

First we acknowledge that anyone searching for real democracy must start with an admission: There exists no functioning model. No current concept of the social order legitimates the central role of *citizens*—their responsibility, their capacities for common problem solving. All inherited models share the mechanistic assumptions. In the now discredited state-socialist model, the *producer* is central—and who makes decisions? The Party. In the capitalist system, the *consumer* is all important—and who makes decisions? Owners of capital. In welfare capitalism a new role is added: the *client*—and who makes decisions? The professional, the "expert" service provider.

In other words, there is no vision of public life that puts citizen responsibility at its center. Thus, none of our inherited models takes seriously the task of creating capable citizens. In fact, "activists" are oddballs. (I recall judging a debate last year for my daughter's high school. All one debater had to do to discredit an opponent was to label her source an "activist"!)

Here in the United States, democracy's become a thin, weak notion, buttressing social atomism. Democracy and government are conflated. Democratic government is viewed as a necessary evil to sort out collisions of competing "social atoms." Government is traffic cop—or, at best, protector of individual rights. Democracy's only economic job is to keep the market functioning smoothly.

Government and politics are something done *for* us—or, more frequently, *to* us. We feel disconnected, far removed, from the decision makers. On *The Phil Donahue Show* last year, an irate member of the audience challenged funding of the Savings and Loan bailout. Leaping to his feet, he exclaimed: "I don't understand why taxpayers have to pay for the bailout, why can't the *government* pay for it!"

Government is *them*. Not us.

This notion reflects our view of democracy itself. Sitting on a long flight last week I chatted with my seatmates. One was a Marine major; the other an engineer with General Electric. Because they were curious about my work, we started talking about the meaning of democracy. The engineer began quite certain about his views on the subject: "Democracy is the laws we have. It's like they're written in stone. They're fixed. So democracy is protected." In other words, democracy is what we inherited. We were lucky enough to be born into a democracy—there is little left for us to do.

With this perspective, citizenship becomes simply the

defensive posture a prudent person assumes to protect her or his solitary self-interest. A recent poll conducted for People for the American Way found that young people hold a markedly passive notion of citizenship. It means not causing trouble. Eighty-eight percent of the teenagers polled thought that getting involved in politics has nothing to do with being good citizens.[15]

While these views dominate, I sense a profoundly different understanding emerging. I think more and more Americans are realizing that the problems we face are simply too great—too deeply rooted, too widespread, and too complex—to be met without our active engagement. Solutions require the ingenuity of those most affected, the creativity that emerges from diverse perspectives, and the commitment that comes only when people know they have a real stake in the outcome. It takes an active citizenry to create public decision making that works—decision making that is accountable and creative enough to address the root causes of today's crises.

In the emerging alternative, democracy becomes no longer a set of static institutions, but a *way of life*. Democracy as a way of life means we each share responsibility for making the whole work. Democracy is not as much structures or laws as *relationships*.

Democracy as a way of life is what the term "citizen democracy" suggests to us. We see its potential emerging in several distinct themes:

Citizen democracy re-dignifies the public realm. It challenges today's privatization of meaning. The 1980s celebrated only private reward—money, career, family. Such was the good life. Neglected was the deep human need for purpose larger than one's self.

Public life is the larger stage—all our relationships in the workplace, school, religious group, social concern organization, or formal political process. It is on this stage that we express our values—including our commitments to our family's future—and develop distinct human capacities that can only be cultivated in public life. It is on this stage that we express our need to "make a difference."

Thus, the most successful community-based citizen organizing today sees itself as preparing people for effective, sustainable public life—not just achieving victory on a given issue. Ernesto Cortés, a founding force in creating the successful Communities Organized for Public Service in San Antonio, calls citizen groups "universities where people learn the arts of public discourse and public action."[16]

For we're not born citizens, as Cortés' words frankly acknowledge. We *learn* the arts of citizenship. That's why the Institute for the Arts of Democracy is an appropriate name for an organization promoting citizen democracy. These arts include active listening, storytelling, dialogue, critical thinking, mediation, creative controversy, the disciplined expression of anger, and reflection.

In a recent speech, Ralph Nader asked: While one can go to an Arthur Murray dance studio to learn how to dance, where do we go to learn the practice of citizenship? Our answer is that every public encounter—in school, at work, in the community or social group—can become an opportunity for learning.

I'll return to this key theme. Now let me suggest other aspects of citizen democracy coming to life throughout American society.

Citizen democracy is about empowerment through action. Most of us have learned to submerge our common sense, even our own values and tastes, and turn to the "experts"—whether in child rearing, making workplace decisions, or even in decorating our homes. (I recall a few years ago sitting in a café and overhearing a conversation that summed up our sad predicament. One woman confessed to her friend that she felt so intimidated by her interior decorator that she had had to hire a psychotherapist to help her cope!)

We learn at every turn to defer to others "better qualified." But that's changing. Bertha Gilkey, a woman living in the housing projects in St. Louis, got fed up. She wanted to get rid of rampant drugs and crime but was told, she recalls, that "we couldn't do nothing because we were poor folks and not experts." She thought that over for a moment and then responded: "Experts got us into trouble in the first place." Her confidence sparked changes within the project that have transformed it into a desirable place to live and raise a family.[17]

Bertha Gilkey's liberating moment is occurring for more and more of us. With the S&L debacle costing taxpayers the equivalent in real dollars of the entire cost of World War II, with the toxic waste crisis causing vast and needless harm, and with "experts" producing radioactive waste that remains dangerous for millennia while they have no plan for safe storage—more and more citizens are shedding a sense of deference to the authorities "up there."

Understanding citizen democracy as empowering individuals to shoulder responsibility involves us in a radical rethinking of power itself. In the dominant political tradition, power is a one-way force. The cue ball sinks the eight ball in the corner pocket—that's power! As a one-way force, it is also a zero-sum notion: The more I have, the less for you. You must yield to my power, or I to yours. In striking contrast, empowerment as the core of public life returns us to the original meaning of power, from "poder"—to be able. Power is that which enables us to express our interests and values. It is no longer a one-way force, nor zero-sum. Indeed, we can acknowledge the oh-so-frequent instances where my willingness to shoulder responsibility—to assume more power—benefits you. Certainly Bertha Gilkey's story is a case in point: Her power catalyzed community power, benefitting the entire housing project and larger community as well.

Citizen politics is values based and values driven. Most of us have also come to think of public life as a series of "issues" driven by narrow interests. But in the most successful citizen initiatives, issues "are dessert, not the main course," as one effective organizer put it.

The main course is our values. What motivates people to

act, to get involved? To stay involved? What we care about most—our children's future, peace, security, protecting the integrity and beauty of the natural world, fairness for everybody. These are widely shared values. They manifest in issues. But power in public life derives from consciously naming the values that motivate action.

Such an understanding of motivation belies the dominant understanding of self-interest—simply a synonym for selfishness. Realizing the many dimensions of one's own interests makes it possible to see that they cannot be furthered except in relationships—public and private. In fact, self-interest derives from the Latin *interesse*—"to be among." As political philosopher Bernard Crick puts it:

> . . . the more realistically one construes self-interest, the more one is involved in relationships with others.[18]

Thus, citizen democracy is not about learning to give up one's interests for the sake of others. It is about learning to see one's self-interests embedded in others' interests. From concerns about environmental health and neighborhood safety to effective schools and job security—none can be achieved by oneself. Each depends upon the needs of others being met as well.

In this light, we see that selfishness—narrow preoccupation with self—can actually be an enemy of self-interest. In citizen democracy, self-interest is not to be squelched or simply indulged, but to be consciously developed in relationships with others. It is the basis of constructive political engagement.

Citizen politics is about solving problems. In today's political world, moral grandstanding and vicious mud-slinging are the order of the day. Poised against this dominant politics is the politics of protest—we've all learned how to decry what we *don't* like.

Citizen politics takes the next step. It is task oriented. It is less concerned about proving our own righteousness or the others' failings than about taking responsibility for solutions.

Whether it is citizens developing land trusts to keep down the cost of housing or the Kentuckians for the Commonwealth moving from protest over toxic waste to joining a state taskforce to work out solutions.[19]

But *where* do we learn to be problem solvers, rather than merely good complainers?

At home, at school, at work . . . just about anywhere people come together. Among the most effective classrooms in the country are those in which teachers are encouraging students to learn by tackling real problems in their communities. One of my favorite examples is in a grammar school in Amesville, Ohio, where Bill Elasky proves that his sixth graders can plan and carry out long-term problem-solving projects, given encouragement and back-up.

After a chemical spill in a nearby creek, Elasky's students decided they "didn't trust the EPA." Constituting themselves as the Amesville Sixth Grade Water Chemists, they set out to test the water themselves—and succeeded. In the process they had to divide into teams, assign tasks, plan sampling and testing times, and so on. Soon the Sixth Grade Water Chemists became the town's water quality experts, and their neighbors were buying their water testing services. These kids are learning democracy not by memorizing distant structures of government but by "doing democracy."[20]

Citizen democracy assumes that citizen participation is just as necessary in governing economic life as it is in political life. At the time of our nation's founding, the primary unit of economic life was the family. We were family farmers, shopkeepers, and traders. It made a certain amount of sense to think of economic life as private, and therefore not governed by the same democratic principles that we deemed appropriate to political life.

But in the intervening years, what has happened? The determining unit of the economy is no longer the family. Dominating the economic landscape are giant bureaucracies—non-elected, but nevertheless with more power over the quality of our lives than most governments have. We call them corporations. They determine the location and the quality of many jobs, the health of the environment, and—through their political influence—even broader questions.

Today, the world's four largest corporations enjoy a total revenue greater than the combined gross national products of 80 countries comprising half the world's population. Yet we perceive them as *private* entities, beyond democratic accountability!

Citizen democracy—the concept of ordinary people assuming greater responsibility for public decision making—challenges us to ask whether such categories of public and private still make sense.

More and more citizens are taking responsibility for making democratically accountable such "private" economic structures. A consortium of citizen organizations developed the Valdez Principles, guidelines to ensure that oil companies take measures to avoid oil spills, the consequences of which are broadly public in every sense. The Financial Democracy Campaign is providing a vehicle for citizens to take part in devising a fairer burden-sharing of the federal Savings and Loan bailout.

Evidence of the last 20 years seems definitive on one point: Without democratizing *economic* decision making, reversing environmental decline seems beyond our reach. In his 1990 *Making Peace with the Planet*, Barry Commoner updates his earlier classic, *The Closing Circle*. In the earlier work he predicted that only in the few cases where citizen movements were using government to require economic bureaucracies to change their technologies of production could environmental deterioration be substantially turned around. Commoner's predictions proved correct. Real success in protecting the environment has been achieved in just a few instances: taking lead out of gasoline, removing DDT from pesticides, and eliminating PCB from the electrical industry.

In other words, once U.S. corporations have been permitted—through citizen *non*involvement in the process—to emit into the environment each year what now amounts to almost four pounds of toxic substances for every person on earth, *it's simply too late.* To dispose safely of this enormous quantity would require several times the profits of the chemical industry. Commoner argues that the record of the last two decades demonstrates that without citizens taking greater responsibility to ensure the halt of production of toxic substances in the first place, there is no solution.[21]

But, taking a position on *anything,* even speaking out in the classroom or workplace, is a scary proposition for most of us. How do we gain the confidence and the capacity to participate in earth-shaping decisions?

Citizen democracy is a learned art. Earlier I noted that we're not born citizens. True, anyone can respond to a few TV ads and pull a lever in a polling booth. But real citizenship is an art. Like the art of dance, music, or sport, we persevere only as we learn to do it well. If we feel awkward or foolish for too long, we'll just stop! On the other hand, if we are learning the particular *challenges* and *rewards* of an art, we continue even if our "performance" is far from perfect. So, too, with active citizenship.

How do we as a society, and as individuals, come to take seriously building our capacities for expressing our values and interests in common problem solving?

The process can begin in family life. In 1985, my children— Anthony and Anna—and I wrote a book together. It's called *What to Do After You Turn Off the TV.*[22] Our idea was to entice families away from letting TV dominate home life, so they might discover the joys of each other's company. We told of our own experience of eight years without TV and interviewed hundreds of other families to capture their experiences. We were struck by how many close families had developed some version of a "family meeting"—a special time when everyone comes together to make plans and talk over problems that might have gone unresolved. Children in such families gain an early start in acquiring the capacities—for dialogue, compromise, mediation, and reflection—that can make them effective citizens.

Above I suggested a critical role for schools in learning the democratic arts. But equally important are the voluntary associations in which the majority of Americans are engaged—through religious affiliations, or in groups like the PTA, the League of Women Voters, Kiwanis, or Greenpeace. Can we come to see such involvements not just as means to solve a particular problem, or to address a given issue, but as occasions for learning the democratic arts, as opportunities for learning that can sustain our involvement throughout our lives?

So many people who become involved in addressing social problems experience early "burnout." If we do not attend to the arts of reflection and evaluation of our progress, if we do not work to perceive how our particular effort is tied to long-term society-wide change, we soon feel like retreating into our private worlds. We deny our need to make a difference in the larger world. We deny ourselves.

As we begin to value the process of democratic renewal itself, seeing our efforts not as stop-gap measures but as engaging in long-term cultural change, we can attend to making that process *rewarding*—consciously measuring our success in incremental steps, deliberately creating celebration and cultural expressions to sustain our energies.

Growing up, most of us learn that "politics" is about staking out a position and defending it. The "art," if there is any, is winning—not listening in order to understand the interests and values of others. If we are locked into pre-set positions, interaction at best hones our arguments but cannot awaken us to new possibilities. Creativity is lost. Thus, in the emerging citizen politics, listening may be the first art. Many are taking its cultivation seriously; one example is the Listening Project.

The Listening Project, a national program based in North Carolina, is a community organizing and outreach tool that uses in-depth, one-on-one interviews with people in their homes. Instead of the usual quick, check-off survey, organizers ask open-ended questions about people's values and concerns. In one home, a middle-aged European-American man complained that the biggest problem he saw was the noisy black teenagers who hung out on the streets and caused trouble. On a simple survey, that one comment might have gotten him labeled as a racist. But the organizers listened. They didn't argue. Their questions encouraged the man to look deeper. As he talked, he began to reflect as well. By the end of the interview, he himself had restated (and re-understood) the problem in his neighborhood as the lack of recreational facilities and opportunities for young people.[23]

These are some of the themes of citizen democracy. What they add up to is a profoundly different approach to social change than most of us are accustomed to. It means, for both Right and Left, breaking the habit of what I call the "manifesto approach" to social change: We decide on the program, and then "sell" it to others, or preferably, "convert" others to our truths. But if, in drawing up our alternative designs, we appear merely as more "experts" with our own brand of specialized knowledge, we do nothing to diminish the sense of powerlessness that people feel. If our process mimics the dominant instrumental view of politics—or if it fuels the polarized, highly moralized brand—we do nothing to encourage people to take on the joys and frustrations of public engagement. In so doing we fail to address the real crisis. For the real crisis is not that justice, freedom, and biological sustainability have not yet been achieved. It is that people feel increasingly disenfranchised from the public processes essential to their realization.

If this is true, then the real challenge is neither to proclaim beautiful values nor to design elegant answers ourselves; it is to create a politics of practical problem solving—one that is engaging and rewarding, that respects people and allows them to develop their own values in interaction with one another. This means learning, modeling, and mentoring the "democratic arts."

Fully understanding democracy as a process rather than a structure of government means accepting that it can never be fully realized. In his 1990 address to the U.S. Congress, Czechoslovakia's President Václav Havel reminded Americans:

> One may approach [democracy] as one would the
> horizon, but it can never be fully attained. . . . You
> [Americans] have thousands of problems, as other
> countries do, but you have one great advantage. You
> have been approaching democracy uninterrupted for
> 200 years.

Can we come to believe in democracy as an ever-unfolding
dynamic to which there can be no final resting point? Such a
vision suggests a fragile *ecology of democracy*—democracy as ever-
evolving relationships through which people solve common
problems and meet deep human needs.

Midwives to the New

The view I have attempted here would allow us finally to leave
behind the worthless debate about whether we should address
environmental problems by convincing people to alter individual life choices. Or, instead, should we work for changes in our
economic rules and structures?

I've held—and believe my intuition confirmed by people's
experience during the last 20 years—that so-called structural
changes can come only as we reshape our very understanding
of ourselves, gain confidence in our intuitive sense of con-
nectedness, and therefore gain courage. That confidence and
courage, as I argue throughout *Diet for a Small Planet*, come
through making new choices in every aspect of our lives.
Gaining confidence in our capacities and values, we're able to
challenge messages telling us that market exchange is a virtual
divine law whose consequences we must live with; and to
question economic dogma making giant corporations "private" and therefore outside democratic accountability.

As we begin to let go of the notion that there are economic
laws that take us off the hook, the environmental awakening
reminds us that there are indeed laws—*ecological* laws—that we
cannot escape.

There is no "away." (Radioactive wastes cannot be stored away because that place doesn't exist.)

And if that is true, then so is the corollary—everything is connected. We can't do just one thing.

And, finally, since in a wink of historical time we have spent our "fossil fuel" savings, we have no choice but to live on our solar budget.

Now these are pretty obvious truths. And the environmental scolds will tell us that these truths determine our limited means, to which we must now resign ourselves. But is this bad news, really? What such a negative casting ignores is the deep human need precisely *for* limits—for what are limits but guidelines, a coherent context for human conduct, helping us make choices?

Looked at thusly, a feeling of relief might come over us instead of panic. For it is unboundedness, endless choices that make people crazy. If little kids need rules to know they're loved and to be happy, perhaps all human beings have that need. Limitlessness means meaninglessness. Nature's very real, non-arbitrary, and universal laws can offer a sense of boundedness, imbuing our individual acts with meaning and giving us direction in making choices.

As we gain the courage to let go of the human-made laws of economic dogma, in which we have sought relief from choice, perhaps we can discover instead the real laws of the biotic community. In this discovery we can take joy in becoming contributing members, not masters, of that community.

Yes, it *is* an extraordinary time to be alive. Can the 21st century be the era in which human beings finally come home, meeting our deep need for security and meaning not in ignoring or conquering, but in living within the community of nature? Now that the stakes are indisputably ultimate, we can break through the limits of the inherited mechanistic worldview and discover the real meaning of the era of ecology—that our very being is dependent upon healthy relationships. We can find in the focus on relationships—the key insight of ecology—the beginning of what we need to meet the multiple crises affecting us, from homelessness to the environmental crisis itself. We can create an *ecology of democracy*—democracy not as fixed structure but as a rich practice of citizen problem solving, grounded in the democratic arts and equal to the challenges of our time.

Amidst such obvious social decline and environmental devastation—yet with the possibility of rebirth—more than anything we each need to find sources of hope. Hope that we can be part of such a historical awakening. Such honest hope, as opposed to wishful thinking, demands hard work. Cynicism is easy. Honest hope comes only as we experience ourselves changing, and are thus able to believe that "the world" can change. For 20 years, responses to *Diet for a Small Planet* have been for me a primary and continuing source of hope—always reminding me of the words of Chinese writer Lu Hsun I have framed on my bedroom wall:

> *Hope cannot be said to exist, nor can it be said not to exist.*
> *It is just like the roads across the earth.*
> *For actually there were no roads to begin with,*
> *but when many people pass one way a road is made.*

BOOK ONE

Diet *for a* Small Planet

Preface to the 10th Anniversary Edition

I gave my first speech as the author of *Diet for a Small Planet* at the University of Michigan in early 1972. I recall how hard I worked on that speech—locking myself in the basement of my mother-in-law's house while upstairs she cared for my baby son. I remember standing at the podium, shaking like crazy but delivering what I thought was a rousing political speech. Then, the question-and-answer period. A young man far back in the auditorium raised his hand. "Ms. Lappé," he asked, "what is the difference between long grain and short grain brown rice?" In the 1975 edition of this book, I described my reaction:

> I wilted. I had wanted to convey the felt-sense of how our diet relates each of us to the broadest questions of food supply for all of humanity. I had wanted to convey the way in which economic factors rather than natural agricultural ones have determined land and food use. Was I doing just the opposite? Was I helping people to close in on themselves, on their own bodies' needs, instead of using the information to help them relate to global needs?

Five years later, in 1980, before I was to give a lecture at the University of Minnesota, a man approached me. "I have an apology to make to you," he said. "I've been waiting for eight years to make it in person. *I* was that student at the University of Michigan who asked you the difference between long grain and short grain brown rice. I just wanted you to know that, although I am still eating well, *Diet for a Small Planet* also launched me into a broader social commitment. I didn't get stuck—as you thought I did."

You can imagine my surprise. We both laughed hard. And then it dawned on me that, yes, the circle was complete. It was time to do the tenth anniversary edition. It was time to chronicle the change that took me from a narrow, personal concern to the courage to face the bigger questions—questions not so easy to define as the differences among rice varieties.

Part I

Recipe
for a
Personal
Revolution

1

An Entry Point

No one has been more astonished than I at the impact of *Diet for a Small Planet*. It was born as a one-page handout in the late 1960s, and became a book in 1971. Since then it has sold close to two million copies in a half dozen languages. What I've discovered is that many more people than I could ever have imagined are looking for the same thing I was—a first step.

Mammoth social problems, especially global ones like world hunger and ecological destruction, paralyze us. Their roots seem so deep, their ramifications endless. So we feel powerless. How can *we* do anything? Don't we just have to leave these problems to the "experts"? We try to block out the bad news and hope against hope that somewhere someone who knows more than we do has some answers.

The tragedy is that this totally understandable feeling—that we must leave the big problems to the "experts"—lies at the very root of our predicament, because the experts are those with the greatest stake in the status quo. Schooled in the institutions of power, they take as given many patterns that must change if we are to find answers. Thus, the solutions can come only from people who are less "locked-in"—ordinary people like you and me. Only when we discover that we have both the capacity and the right to participate in making society's important decisions will solutions emerge. Of this I am certain.

But how do we make this discovery?

The world's problems appear so closely interwoven that there is no point of entry. Where do we begin when everything seems to touch everything else? Food, I discovered, was just the tool I needed to crack the seemingly impenetrable facade. With food as my grounding point I could begin to see meaning in what before was a jumble of frightening facts—and over the last ten years I've learned that my experience has been shared by thousands of others. Learning about the politics of food "not only changed my view of the world, but spurred me on to act upon my new vision," Sally Bachman wrote me from New York.

To ask the biggest questions, we can start with the most personal—what do we eat? What we eat is within our control, yet the act ties us to the economic, political, and ecological order of our whole planet. Even an apparently small change—consciously choosing a diet that is good both for our bodies and for the earth—can lead to a series of choices that transform our whole lives. "Food has been a major teacher in my life," Tina Kimmel of Alamosa, Colorado, wrote me.

The process of change is more profound, I'm convinced, than just letting one thing lead to the next. In the first edition of this book I wrote,

> Previously when I went to a supermarket, I felt at the mercy of our advertising culture. My tastes were manipulated. And food, instead of being my most direct link with the nurturing earth, had become mere merchandise by which I fulfilled my role as a "good" consumer.

Feeling victimized, I felt powerless. But gradually I learned that every choice I made that aligned my daily life with an understanding of how I wanted things to be made me feel more powerful. As I became more convincing to myself, I was more convincing to other people. I *was* more powerful.

So while many books about food and hunger appeal to guilt and fear, this book does not. Instead, I want to offer you power. Power, you know, is not a dirty word!

Here's how it began for me . . .

In 1969 I discovered that half of our harvested acreage went to feed livestock. At the same time, I learned that for every 7 pounds of grain and soybeans fed to livestock we get on the average only 1 pound back in meat on our plates. Of all the animals we eat, cattle are the poorest converters of grain to meat: *It takes 16 pounds of grain and soybeans to produce just 1 pound of beef in the United States today.*

The final blow was discovering that much of what I had grown up believing about a healthy diet was false. Lots of protein is essential to a good diet, I thought, and the only way to get enough is to eat meat at virtually every meal. But I learned that, on the average, Americans eat twice the protein their bodies can even use. Since our bodies don't store protein, what's not used is wasted. Moreover, I learned that the "quality" of meat protein, better termed its "usability," could be matched simply by combining certain plant foods. Thus, the final myth was exploded for me.

I was shocked. While the world's experts talked only of scarcity, I had just discovered the incredible waste built into the American meat-centered diet. And nutritionally it was all unnecessary! My worldview flipped upside down. Along with many others in the late 1960s, I had started out asking: "How close are we to the limit of the earth's capacity to provide food for everyone?" Then it began to dawn on me that I was part of a system actively *reducing* that capacity.

Hidden Resources Plowed into Our Steaks

What I failed to appreciate fully ten years ago was that the production system that generates our grain-fed-meat diet not only wastes our resources but helps destroy them, too. Most people think of our food-producing resources, soil and water, as renewable, so how can they be destroyed? The answer is that because our production system encourages farmers to continually increase their output, the natural cycle of renewal is undermined. The evidence for this is presented in Part II, but here are a few facts to give you some sense of the threats to our long-term food security:

• *Water costs.* Producing just one pound of steak uses 2,500 gallons of water—as much water as my family uses in a month! Livestock production, including water for U.S. crops fed to livestock abroad, accounts for about half of all water consumed in the United States, and increasingly that water is drawn from underground lakes, some of which are not significantly renewed by rainfall. Already irrigation sources in north Texas are running dry, and within decades the underground sources will be drawn down so far that scientists estimate a third of our current irrigation will be economically unfeasible.

• *Soil erosion.* Corn and soybeans, the country's major animal feed crops, are linked to greater topsoil erosion than any other crops. In some areas topsoil losses are greater now than during the Dust Bowl era. At current rates, the loss of topsoil threatens the productivity of vital farmland within our lifetime.

• *Energy costs.* To produce a pound of steak, which provides us with 500 calories of food energy, takes 20,000 calories of fossil fuel, expended mainly in producing the crops fed to livestock.

• *Import dependency.* Corn alone uses about 40 percent of our major fertilizers. U.S. agriculture has become increasingly dependent on imported fertilizer, which now accounts for 20 percent of our ammonia fertilizer and 65 percent of our potash fertilizer. And even though the United States is the world's leading producer of phosphates for fertilizer, at current rates of use we will be importing phosphates, too, in just 20 years.

A Symbol and a Symptom

The more I learned, the more I realized that a grain-fed-meat diet is not the cause of this resource waste, destruction, and dependency. The "Great American Steak Religion" is both a symbol and a symptom of the underlying logic of our production system—a logic that makes it self-destructive.

Our farm economy is fueled by a blind production imperative. Because farmers are squeezed between rising production costs and falling prices for their crops, their profits per acre fall steadily—by 1979 hitting one-half of what they had been in 1945 (figures adjusted for inflation). So *just to maintain the same income* farmers must constantly increase production—planting more acres and reaping higher yields, regardless of the ecological consequences. And they must constantly seek new markets to absorb their increasing production. But since hungry people in both the United States and the Global South have no money to buy this grain, what can be done with it?

One answer has been to feed about 200 million tons of grain, soybean products, and other feeds to domestic livestock every year. Another, especially in the last ten years, has been to sell it abroad. While most Americans believe our grain exports "feed a hungry world," *two-thirds* of our agricultural exports actually go to livestock—and the hungry abroad cannot afford meat. The trouble is that, given the system we take for granted, this all appears logical. So perhaps to begin we must stop taking so much for granted and ask, who really benefits from our production system? Who is hurt, now and in the future?

In this book I seek to begin to answer such questions.

Diet for an Abundant Planet

The worst and best thing about my book is its title. It is catchy and easy to remember. (Although one irate customer stomped into my parents' bookstore to complain that she'd thought she was buying a gardening book, *Diet for a Small Plant.**) But the title is also misleading. To some it connotes scarcity: Because the planet is so "small," we must cut back our consumption. So when my next book, *Food First,*** came out, with the subtitle *Beyond the Myth of Scarcity,* many people thought I had done an about-face. Yes, my thinking evolved, but for me the message of *Diet for a Small Planet* is abundance, not scarcity. The issue is how we use that abundance. Do we expand the kind of production which degrades the soil and water resources on which all our future food security rests? Do we then dispose of this production by feeding more and more to livestock? The answers lie in the political and economic order we create. The "small planet" image should simply remind us that what we eat helps determine whether our planet *is* too small or whether its abundance can be sustained and enjoyed by everyone. My book might better be called *Diet for an Abundant Planet*—now and in the future.

The Body-Wise Diet

Another part of the good news in this book is that what's good for the earth turns out to be good for us, too. Increasingly, health scientists throughout the world recommend a plant-centered diet. They report that six of the ten leading causes of death in America are linked to the high fat/high sugar/low fiber diet embodied in the Great American Steak Religion. (See Part III, Chapter 1.)

For me, living a diet for a small planet has meant increased physical vitality. And the hundreds of letters I have received testify that my experience is not unique.

---

* Others in search of my book have told me that bookstore clerks pointed them toward the science-fiction department!

** Co-author Joseph Collins, with Cary Fowler (Ballantine Books, 1979).

The Traditional Diet

Over the years many people have been surprised when meeting the author of *Diet for a Small Planet*. I am not the gray-haired matron they expect. Nor am I a back-to-nature purist. (Sometimes I even wear lipstick!) But mouths really drop open when I explain that I am not a vegetarian. Over the last ten years I've hardly ever served or eaten meat, but I try hard to distinguish what I advocate from what people think of as "vegetarianism."

Most people think of vegetarianism as an ethical stance against the killing of animals, unconventional, and certainly untraditional. But what I advocate is the return to the traditional diet on which our bodies evolved. Traditionally the human diet has centered on plant foods, with animal foods playing a supplementary role. Our digestive and metabolic systems evolved over millions of years on such a diet. Only very recently have Americans, and people in some other industrial countries, begun to center their diets on meat. So it is the meat-centered diet—and certainly the grain-fed-meat-centered diet—that is the fad.

I hope that my book will be of value to the growing numbers of people who refuse to eat meat in order to discourage the needless suffering of animals. But I believe that its themes can make sense to just about anyone, whether or not they are prepared to take an ethical stance against the killing of animals for human food.

Many counter the vegetarian's position against killing animals for human food by pointing out that in many parts of the world livestock play a critical role in sustaining human life: Only livestock can convert grasses and waste products into meat. Where good cropland is scarce, this unique ability of grazing animals may be crucial to human survival. Intellectually, I agree. But I say "intellectually" because, although using livestock to convert inedible substances to protein for human beings makes sense to me, I found that once I stopped cooking meat, it no longer appealed to me. If all our lives we handle flesh and blood, maybe we become inured to it. Once I stopped, I never wanted to start again. But this view is a strictly personal one, and it is not the subject of this book.

An Escape or a Challenge?

For many who have come to appreciate the profound political and economic roots of our problems, a change in diet seems like a pretty absurd way to start to change things. Such personal decisions are seen simply as a handy way to diminish guilt feelings, while leaving untouched the structural roots of our problems. Yes, I agree—such steps *could* be exactly this and nothing more.

But taking ever greater responsibility for our individual life choices could be one way to change us—heightening our power and deepening our insight, which is exactly what we need most if we are ever to get to the roots of our society's problems. Changing the way we eat will not change the world, but it may begin to change us, and then we can be part of changing the world.

Examining any of our consumption habits has value only to the degree that the effort is both liberating and motivating. Learning why our grain-fed-meat diet developed and learning what does constitute a healthy and satisfying diet have been both for me. In one area of my life I began to feel that I could make real choices—choices based on knowledge of their consequences. Second, the more I learned about why the American diet developed to include not only more grain-fed meat but also more processed food, the more I began to grasp the basic flaws in the economic ground rules on which our entire production system is based. I learned, for example, that the prices guiding our resource use are make-believe—they in no way tell us the real resource costs of production. Moreover, I came to see how our production system inevitably treats even an essential ingredient of life itself—food—as just another commodity, totally divorcing it from human need. Slowly it became clear that until the production of our basic survival goods is consciously tied to the fulfillment of human need there can be no solution to the tragedy of needless hunger that characterizes our time—even here in the United States.

We Are the Realists

Some call such views unrealistic, visionary, or idealistic. I respond that it is we who are awakening to the crisis of our planet—and to our own power to make critical changes—who are the realists. Those who believe that our system of waste and destruction should continue are the dreamers. Yes, *we* are the realists. We want to face up to the terrible problems confronting the human race and learn what each of us can do right now. At the same time, we are also visionaries, because we have a vision of the direction in which we want our society to move.

My understanding has changed enormously since the 1975 edition of this book. Some say I realized my book's thesis was "naïve." Some claim that since the first edition of *Diet for a Small Planet* I have become more "political." Others say I have shifted my emphasis away from what the individual should do toward a call for group action. All of these judgments contain some truth, but they are not the way *I* see it.

To explain how I do see it, I've written the next chapter— about my personal journey from desperate social worker to co- founder of an international food action center investigating the causes of hunger in a world of plenty. If I believe so much must change, I must be willing to change myself.

2

My Journey

"How did you get interested in food? How did you come to write *Diet for a Small Planet*?" Countless times I have been asked these questions. Invariably I am frustrated with my answers. I never really get to explain. So, here it is. This is my chance.

I am a classic child of the 1960s. I graduated from a small Quaker college in 1966, a year of extreme anguish for many, and certainly for me: the war in Vietnam, the civil rights movement, the War on Poverty. That year was the turning point.

While I had supported the U.S. position on the Vietnam war for years, finally I became too uncomfortable merely accepting the government's word. I set out to discover the facts for myself. Why were we fighting? I read everything I could find on U.S. government policy in Vietnam. Within a few weeks, my world began to turn upside down. I was in shock. I functioned, but in a daze. I had grown up believing my government represented me—my basic ideals. Now I was learning that "my" government was not mine at all.

From that state of shock grew feelings of extreme desperation. Our country seemed in such a terrible state that something had to be done, *now*, today, or all hope seemed lost. I wanted to work with those who were suffering the most, so I did what people like Tom Hayden suggested. For two years, 1967 and 1968, I worked as a community organizer in Philadelphia with a national nonprofit organization of welfare recipients—the Welfare Rights Organization. Our goal was to ensure that welfare recipients got what they were entitled to by law.

Most evenings I came home in tears. Perhaps I had helped someone get her full welfare payment, or forced a landlord to make a critical repair. But I realized that even if I succeeded each day in my immediate goal, I was in no way addressing the root causes of the suffering that was so evident to me. The woman I worked most closely with died of a heart attack at the age of forty-five. I was convinced she died of the stress of poverty.

During these years I became *more* desperate, not less. But I just kept on doing what I was doing, because I did not know what else to do.

In 1968 I ended up in graduate school, studying community organizing at the School of Social Work at the University of California at Berkeley. As part of my training, I worked on fair housing policies in Oakland. But this work did nothing to resolve my questions. I was becoming more miserable, more confused.

The Most Important Decision

Then, in the spring of 1969, I made the most important decision of my life (next to the decision to have children, that is): I vowed not to do *anything* to try to "change the world" until I understood why I had chosen one path instead of another, until I understood *how* my actions could attack the roots of needless suffering.

My first step was to drop out of graduate school. This decision was so agonizing it made me physically ill. I was petrified that people would ask me, "What do you do?" and I would have no answer. My identity had been "social worker." Now I would have no identity.

Friends now tease me when I tell this story. They say, "People in the late 1960s in Berkeley would never have asked you what you 'did.' At most, people might have asked, 'What are you into?'" But the truth was, I didn't have an answer to that either.

So there I was, twenty-five years old and adrift. What would I do? In sixteen years of "learning" I had never known whether I had real interests of my own. Yes, I had pleased my teachers and professors. Yes, I had shed my Southern accent in my first six months of college, to prove that I wasn't an empty-headed Southern female. But all that had been to prove something to others. If I wasn't trying to please a teacher anymore, was there anything left? Any motivation? Any direction? I was skeptical—and afraid.

What gave me the courage to discover my own path? Two things. I knew I couldn't go on as I was; I was just too miserable. At the same time, I was married to a person who gave me absolute emotional support. I was sure Marc would love me even if I never saved the world.

I started studying modern dance and reading political economy—books that attempted to explain the causes of poverty and underdevelopment. Very soon, after only a few months, I began to home in on food.

Why food? In part I was influenced by the emerging ecology movement and the "limits to growth" consciousness. The first Earth Day was in 1970. Paul Ehrlich's book *The Population Bomb* exploded during this same period, and books like *Famine 1975* appeared. Newspaper headlines were telling us (as they still are) that we had reached the limits of the earth's ability to feed us all.

But part of the reason I chose to focus on food was more personal. I became aware of people around me in Berkeley eating differently from the way I did. Some of the foods I had never heard of—bulgur, soy grits, mung beans, tofu, buckwheat groats. What were all these strange things? I was attracted by the incredible variety of colors, aromas, textures. I remember devouring my first "natural foods" cookbook as if it were a novel. Barley, mushrooms, and dill together? Cheddar cheese, walnuts, and rice? How odd. What would that taste like?

Beyond the Food Battle

As I started experimenting, I found my entire attitude toward food changing. Food and I had always been in battle and had reached a stalemate at about ten pounds more than I really wanted to weigh. To hold that line I had to count calories and feel guilty about what I shouldn't eat. But when I started to learn about food, appreciating the incredible variety I hadn't known before and eating more unprocessed foods, I stopped battling. My appetite began to change. I stopped counting calories. I stopped feeling guilty. I had just one rule: If I was hungry, I would eat; if I wasn't hungry, I would say no. I no longer made the decision about whether to eat based on something external to me, only on how I felt inside.

Dancing also helped me make this change. If food and I had been battling, so had my body and I. In the culture I grew up in, the messages were so powerful that my girlfriends and I were wearing girdles to school by the time we were in junior high. When I began to dance, the old battle—me versus my body— was transformed. Instead of being just a problem to reshape and control, my body became a source of satisfaction and pleasure.

My diet was changing. My feelings about myself were changing. At the same time, I was learning about "world food problems." Soon I was reading everything I could find on food and hunger. Something told me that because food is so basic to all of us, if we could just grasp the causes of hunger we would clear a path to understanding the complexities of politics and economics that overwhelm and paralyze so many.

Following My Nose

I read, took notes. I audited courses from soil science to tropical agriculture. And I found an ideal little study niche in the agricultural library at Berkeley. In the quiet basement corridors no one bothered me. No one asked me what I was studying for. The librarians were friendly and helpful.

There I learned to "follow my nose"—a research technique that has served me well for the last twelve years. For me, this meant not having a grand scheme, not knowing exactly where I was going. Instead, I responded to the information I was learning, letting it lead me to the next question.

Overall, I wanted to find out for myself just how close we were to the earth's limits. I wanted to find out for myself the causes of hunger. I wanted to find out what were the important questions to ask.

Then, in late 1969, in my library-basement hideaway, I came across certain facts about U.S. agriculture that changed my life. They changed how I was formulating the important questions.

First, as I recounted in Chapter 1, I learned that in the United States over half of the harvested acreage goes to feed livestock and only a tiny fraction of it gets returned to us in meat on our plate. I learned that most Americans consume about twice the protein their bodies can use.

When I put this all together, I felt like the little boy in the fairy tale who cries out, "The emperor has no clothes!" I could barely believe what I was learning, because it flew so totally in the face of the conventional wisdom. Most important, I saw that the questions being asked by the experts to whom I had turned for guidance were the *wrong questions*.

Newspaper headlines and textbooks were all telling me that we had reached the limits of the earth's ability to feed people. Famine is inevitable, we were (and are still) told. Yet my own modest research had shown me that in my own country the food system was well designed to get rid of a tremendous abundance of grain created by a relentless push to increase production. Because hungry people throughout the world could not afford to buy that grain, it was fed to livestock to provide more meat to the already well-fed.

Suddenly I understood that questions about the roots of needless hunger had to focus not on the simple physical limits of the earth, but on the economic and political forces that determine what is planted and who eats. I began to realize that the experts' single-minded focus on greater production as the solution to world hunger was wrongheaded. You could have more food and still more hunger.

This realization, besides being the motive for what became *Diet for a Small Planet,* was my first step in demystifying the experts—those credential-laden officials and academics who have the answers *for* us. I thought that if I could write up the facts about how land and grain are wasted through a fixation on meat production, and could demonstrate that there are delicious alternatives, I could get people to question the economic ground rules that create such irrational patterns of resource use.

From a One-Page Handout

So I wrote a one-page handout. I planned to give it to friends and post it where sympathetic souls might read it. But I hesitated. "Oh no, you really should know more about this first," I said to myself. So my message became a five-page handout. Then a seventy-page booklet, which I decided to publish myself. I had it all typed up and had bought the paper to print it on when, out of the blue, a friend told me he was on his way to New York to meet with some publishers, including Betty Ballantine of Ballantine Books. He wanted to show her my booklet. What? He couldn't be serious! In my opinion, it might appeal to 500 people in the greater Berkeley community. But he insisted, and finally I agreed.

I was certain that no New York publisher would be interested in my modest effort, but the idea did make me think that some Berkeley-based publisher might be. So I nervously approached one on my own. Theirs was certainly no New York publishing house, they assured me. This firm considered itself part of the "movement," working to revolutionize publishing to "serve the people." I was impressed. Certainly I wanted my book to reach and serve the people.

Suddenly I was being courted by both the "counterculture" publisher and by Ballantine. At first the choice seemed clear. How could I compromise my principles with a New York publisher? Wouldn't they operate like any other big business—looking at only the profit margin, not the value of my book?

But when Mrs. Ballantine telephoned, I couldn't refuse to see her, could I? It wouldn't hurt just to talk with her.

At the same time, the Berkeley outfit was wining and dining me. They took me to a fine French restaurant to "share" with me what they were sure I would want to know about Ballantine. First, did I know it was controlled by the Mafia? "No, really?" Second, did I know what Ballantine did with leftover books? Well, *they* would tell me. It shredded them and polluted San Francisco Bay with them! For a dutiful child of the ecology movement, this was just too much. I broke down in tears.

A few days later, Mrs. Ballantine arrived in Berkeley. I picked her up at the Durant Hotel, expecting to meet a tough businesswoman—maybe not gloves and hat, but certainly someone who could adequately represent a fat-cat New York firm. Out the door came a middle-aged woman in flowered cotton pants and tennis shoes. Her face was warm and natural. No makeup. Her hair was soft and gray. No coloring. But wait! This couldn't be Betty Ballantine!

Betty Ballantine and I spent the day together. I served her a *Diet for a Small Planet* meal—Mediterranean Lemon Soup and Middle Eastern Tacos. She loved it. I told her my concerns about who should publish the book and how I wanted it to be published. Never did she try to convince me to publish with Ballantine. As she left that evening she said, "Whoever publishes the book, I'll buy it."

What was I to do? All my stereotypes had been smashed. If I couldn't make a decision based on my stereotypes, I had to make one based on which choice would ensure that my book got read by the most people. I knew that Ballantine Books reached into grocery stores, bus stations, and airports. The choice became clear. I chose Ballantine and have never regretted it, although the Ballantines later sold the company to Random House, owned by the multinational conglomerate RCA, which in 1980 sold it to the Newhouse brothers.

Betty Ballantine kept her word. She did everything I had hoped for. She didn't change a word I had written. She took great care in choosing the graphics.

The Julia Child of the Soybean Circuit

Nineteen seventy-one was a year of tremendous change. My first child, Anthony, was born in June. I moved to Hastings-on-Hudson, New York, in August. *Diet for a Small Planet* was published in September.

Looking back, I realize I still felt like the little boy who says, "The emperor has no clothes." I was terrified when the book first appeared. My message seemed so obvious it couldn't be correct, I thought.

As the author of *Diet for a Small Planet,* I began a new period of my life. But it was not quite what I had bargained for. Overnight I became the Julia Child of the soybean circuit. I was asked to go on TV talk shows—as long as I brought along my own beans and rice! I was asked to stir them on camera, explaining how to combine protein. As my future colleague Joe Collins later said, "They wanted you to tell people how to lose weight and save money in the coming world food crisis." Such was the intellectual and humanitarian depth of most of these shows.

So I found myself in another apparent ethical dilemma. Did I refuse to be put in the woman's slot on the talk shows, as the writer of a "cookbook," or did I seize the opportunity to reach out to people who would never pick up my book if they knew it was about politics and economics? I chose the latter course. From Boston to San Francisco, from Houston to Minneapolis, I appeared on midday and midnight shows, on morning shows, and on the six o'clock news. Standing there stirring my beans and rice, I would try to get in what *I* thought was important.

The low point of this period came in Pittsburgh on a late-night talk show. Talk-show hosts search for some common ground among their guests; unfortunately that evening the only other guest was a UFO expert. I got only one question the whole evening: "Ms. Lappé, what do you think they eat on UFOs?" I launched from that question into the economic and political roots of hunger. (Now you know why I got only one question.)

Although this was a difficult time, I learned one important rule, useful to everyone in public life—never listen to the questioner, just say what you believe needs to be said!

Rubbing Elbows with the "Experts"

Fortunately, this period of my life came to an end in 1974. In November I attended the World Food Conference in Rome, that much-heralded meeting of government and corporate leaders to design a blueprint to overcome the problem of world hunger. Every major newspaper carried a front-page series on this conference, at which Henry Kissinger announced that in ten years no child would go to bed hungry.

I had gone to Rome at the urging of friends and because I wanted to rub elbows with people who I thought knew a lot more about the problems than I. By now I had two very young children, but I had continued to read and write articles as well as speak and appear on TV. Still, I did not think of myself as especially knowledgeable, certainly not in comparison to the experts gathered in Rome.

Rome was a major shock. People were asking *me* for my opinion. Microphones turned my way. I was asked to appear on a panel of experts. That was pretty startling in itself, but listening to the experts was more shocking still: I discovered that the officials to whom I looked for the answers were still locked into the false diagnoses, and therefore false cures, that I had discarded through my independent study, modest as it was.

This was the second stage in the growing realization which has since formed the basis of my work. I slowly realized that those who have been schooled to direct the powerful institutions which control our economic system are forced to accept and to work within the system that creates needless hunger. Beneficiaries of these institutions, they have been made incapable of seeing outside their boundaries. Rather than preparing them to find solutions, their training has inhibited them from asking questions that could lead to solutions. Those supposed authorities who gathered in Rome in 1974 were still promoting the belief that greater production would solve the problem of hunger, but I had come to see that you could have tremendous production—indeed, I lived in the country with the greatest food abundance in history—and yet still have hunger and malnutrition.

I left Rome feeling I had shed critical layers of self-doubt. I saw more clearly than ever that the real problems in our world—the widespread needless deprivation—will never be solved by the government leaders now in power in most nations. So who will solve them? And how can they be solved? I finally realized that the gravest problems facing our planet today can be solved *only* as part of an overall movement toward a more just sharing of economic and political power, not as separate technical problems. Thus, the solutions will come only when ordinary people, like me and like you, decide to take responsibility for changing the economic order.

In other words, the only way that power will come to be more democratically shared is if you and I take more of it ourselves. If this is true, then the challenge to each of us becomes clear: We must make ourselves capable of shouldering that responsibility.

If I really believed this, then what *I* had to do was clear: I had to take my own work much more seriously. I had to refuse to be dismissed simply as a "cookbook" writer. I had to apply myself with greater diligence than ever in my life.

Finally the veil lifted. I remember feeling like "superwoman" when I returned home that November of 1974. Anything seemed possible. I vowed to completely revise the first edition of *Diet for a Small Planet* and make its political message much clearer. I marched in to talk with the president of Ballantine (the new president, since the Ballantines had sold the company) and presented him with a list of demands concerning the book, its publication date, and its promotion. He agreed to everything.

I completed the revisions in three months, while taking care of two children. It was really a new book. I stressed that I did not believe that a change in the American diet would solve the world food problem. I wrote:

> A change in diet is not an *answer*. A change in diet is a way of experiencing more of the *real* world, instead of living in the illusory world created by our current economic system, where our food resources are actively reduced and where food is treated as just another commodity. . . . A change in diet is a way of saying simply: I have a choice. That is the first step. For how can we take responsibility for the future unless we can make choices now that take us, personally, off the destructive path that has been set for us by our forebears?

I had never worked so hard in my life. It was exhilarating. But when the new book was out (in April 1975) and all the publicity tours were over, I collapsed—from exhaustion, I thought. Soon, however, I learned that fatigue was not my real problem. The real problem was that I did not know where to go next. Here I was, in a suburb of New York, with two small children. I also had a wonderful husband, but his life's work—medical ethics—and his friends who revolved around that work were not mine. I had no political allies and few friends.

My isolation overwhelmed me. I sank deeper and deeper into depression. I saw no escape. Only months earlier my confidence had been at its peak, my calling clear. Now I felt more lost than ever. I knew I had power and energy, but I had no idea how to apply it.

Food First: The Challenge

But a seed had been planted even before the new book was out. On Food Day, in March 1975, I lectured at a conference at the University of Michigan. Among the other speakers was Joseph Collins of the Institute for Policy Studies in Washington. He heard part of my lecture (later he told me that the blah vegetarian meals served during the three-day conference left him so hungry he dashed out midway through my speech for some Kentucky Fried Chicken!) and we were introduced afterward. I learned that Joe was beginning work on a book about the political and economic causes of hunger. He, too, had been at the World Food Conference in Rome the autumn before. He had represented the Transnational Institute and had helped write a report for release there which indicted the conference for failing to address the roots of hunger in the political and economic system. Joe was preparing to take off from that document to write a full-length, more popular book.

I thought no more about it until I received Joe's outline in the mail after I got home. He asked if he might visit me to get my perspective on his project. He came, and slowly it dawned on me that Joe wanted me to write the book with him. But how could I? He lived in Washington; I lived in New York. My children were still so tiny. My daughter, Anna, was barely walking. I said no. While my husband encouraged me, I pulled back.

However, I must not have let go of the idea altogether. I remember saying to my husband, "That man is going to write a book I wanted to write. What am I going to do?" But I felt I wasn't ready for a commitment so enormous.

In April I was invited to speak at a church-sponsored retreat in the Midwest. Gathered there were church leaders, the church experts on world hunger. Again I was shocked. I tried to shift the emphasis from a charity approach to one that focused on the political and economic links between Americans and the causes of world hunger. One church leader responded that he wasn't sure that we should criticize our government's policies, because the government can exert its power over the churches and the churches should not take chances. The general level of discussion was so uninformed that again I found myself thinking: As unprepared as I feel to take on this new book project, if not me, who? I knew that people's unwillingness to take chances was a major factor in allowing needless hunger to continue. Was I also unwilling? If I didn't feel prepared, perhaps I could become prepared. All these thoughts went through my mind. But no decision.

After the evening program on the last night of the retreat, a film was shown. On the screen before us were people actually dying of starvation in the Ethiopian famine. I had never seen anything like this before: babies sucking futilely at shriveled breasts; desperate mothers. The narrative told how the corrupt government of Haile Selassie had created this horror.

The decision to write *Food First* came as I watched this film. It was an emotional decision. Intellectually I had decided I wasn't ready and that my responsibility to my family wouldn't allow it, but emotionally I felt there was no choice. I *had* to do what I could do, no matter how impossible it seemed. I called Joe in Washington at midnight and said I would write the book with him if he could move to New York.

Within three weeks Joe had moved to New York. Within six weeks we had a contract with Ballantine.

When Joe and I started to work, I was terrified. Here he was, the most worldly man I had ever known—fluent in six languages and a world traveler since the age of thirteen. He had gone through a demanding Jesuit education; in my twelfth-grade social studies class we had made Popsicle-stick models of historical events. I was sure that I would be so intimidated that even before we agreed on the book's outline I'd be a humiliated heap of tears. How could my skills measure up to his?

Well, I was amazed.

Joe treated me as a total intellectual equal. It turned out that rather than being unequal, our skills were—and are— miraculously complementary. Joe is a maniac for detail. He will leave no stone unturned in his research. He's also got a lot of chutzpah, so whatever information we need, Joe can figure out some way to get it. Me, I'm a maniac about organization and deadlines.

So it worked. Instinctively we knew we didn't have to compete. Each of our contributions was essential and appreciated by the other. (No one believes this, but I swear it is true: In writing all 412 pages of *Food First,* Joe and I never disagreed over a single word. We edited and reedited each other's material, but we both knew when we hit just the right phrasing.)

In the next year and a half everything in my life—except my relationship with my children—changed. Instead of just writing a book, Joe and I soon decided to use our advance payment for *Food First* to establish an organization to fill a critical gap. We named it the Institute for Food and Development Policy.

We were aware of the growing number of people asking, why hunger? What can I do? By 1975, when we met, every major church body had established a commission or task force on world hunger. Campus action groups were springing up. In courses ranging from nutrition to geography to world politics, students and professors were asking, what are the causes of and solutions to world hunger?

In addition, a new wave of food co-ops had emerged. Learning from their predecessors (which had begun in the 1930s), these initiatives were democratically managed with the goal of providing quality "whole" foods at lower cost than the supermarket. These co-ops were aware of the larger, political implications of the diet they were promoting and the service they were providing.

These initiatives were not centrally coordinated but represented an embryonic movement. Many people, working on many different projects related to food and farming, were becoming aware of and taking encouragement from one another.

What was missing was an independent research and education center to provide ongoing analysis of the roots of needless hunger to these varied projects. This was the gap we set out to fill. At the time, information and analysis came overwhelmingly from agencies funded by corporations, governments, or churches. Each of these sources, we felt, had a vested interest in maintaining the "hunger myths"—the first and most pervasive being that hunger is caused by scarcity.

Exploding the Hunger Myths*

For us, learning began with unlearning these powerful myths. As we studied, traveled, and interviewed, we were able to cut through the media-repeated themes of scarcity, guilt, and fear. As we worked on the book, certain themes emerged that have grounded our work ever since.

• *No country in the world is a hopeless "basket case."* The illusion of scarcity is a product of the growing concentration of control over food-producing resources. From Bangladeshi villages to Wall Street commodity brokerages, fewer and fewer people are deciding how food resources are used and for whose benefit, yet the most wasteful and inefficient food systems are those controlled by a few in the interests of a few.

• *The hungry are not our enemies.* Actually, we and they are victims of the same economic forces. The direct cause of hunger in the Global South—the increasing concentration of economic power—is also accelerating here in the United States: 3 percent

---

* *World Hunger: Ten Myths,* by Frances Moore Lappé and Joseph Collins, one of our Institute's most popular publications, further explodes these myths.

of U.S. farms now control almost half of farm sales. But concentration of production is only one aspect. Economists warn that monopoly power in the food-processing industry results in close to $20 billion in overcharges to Americans every year.[1]

• *Our role is not to go into other countries to "set things right."* Our responsibility is to remove the obstacles facing the oppressed in the Global South—obstacles often created with our tax dollars, such as U.S. economic and military aid that goes selectively to some of the world's most repressive regimes, as in Zaire, the Philippines, and El Salvador.

The logical conclusions of what we were learning put us in conflict with positions we had previously supported, but eventually we came to an understanding that provided us with direction and energy instead of paralyzing us with guilt, fear, or despair.

We worked day and night to write *Food First*. For me the hard work and long hours were not new. What was new was working with other people. For the previous six years I had worked primarily at home or alone in the library. Now I was part of a team. With the advance from Ballantine, Joe and I were able to hire allies like Cary Fowler (now completing a book on the threat of seed patenting) and Robert Olorenshaw to help us. In the process of research and writing I communicated with hundreds more across the country and around the world, people who were willing to offer their ideas and expertise because they believed in what we were doing.

From 1975 on, learning to work as part of a team became a challenge equal to the challenge of writing *Food First* or any of the books I have worked on since. The message of this book and of *Food First* can be distilled into one theme—people can take ever greater responsibility to change the economic ground rules that determine how resources are used, once they understand these rules and can see where to begin. That means we believe in the possibility of genuine democracy. As I began to work in a team, I began to experience this democracy—so abstract and enormous in scope—as something I had to learn to live every day of my life. I discovered how little our society teaches us about how to share power.

A year and a half after we signed the contract, *Food First* was virtually completed. In all the turmoil of that intense work period, Marc and I had separated and he had taken a job with the State of California. To keep the children close to both their parents, we moved the new Institute to California.

On My Own

In January 1977, I landed with my two children, Anthony and Anna, in San Francisco. For the first time I was really on my own. Never before had I alone had to take care of finding housing and schooling for my children, buying a car, dealing with insurance and taxes. Now it was all up to me—and I was terrified. I had spent a year writing about empowerment, yet I was not sure I had inside me what it took to establish my own life. Until that point I hadn't realized how much I had incorporated our society's view of the single mother as social leftover.

Precisely because I had absorbed these images myself, I found my new life a surprise. Rather than experiencing my children as a burden, I discovered that I enjoyed them more than ever. While I was married, I always viewed myself as the mundane mom—reliable but dull. But I discovered that when I was alone with my kids, I changed. I became more spontaneous. My relationship with each of them got better, closer.

Part of the change came from my decision not to have a TV anymore.* To my great surprise, the children never complained. Even though I work until 5:00 every evening, I am home with them every night they are not with Marc. (We share custody.) Between 6:00 and 9:30 every school night is "our

---

* I cannot overstress the importance of this decision. I commend to you Jerry Mander's beautiful book *Four Arguments for the Elimination of Television* (Morrow Quill Paperbacks, 1977).

time." We listen to the evening news on listener-supported Pacifica radio station KPFA, and often talk about what we hear. They do their homework at the kitchen table while I read the newspaper. We play games, listen to records, make up dances, do acrobatic tricks in the living room. On longer summer evenings we skate or ride bikes. Every night we have at least twenty minutes of "story time." After story time is "lie-down time"— I lie down by each of them for five minutes or so. This is the one point in the day when we each have the other's total attention. Feelings come out that would never come out otherwise. Sometimes we sing, or I might write messages on their backs for them to guess. Sometimes we just lie there in silence.

While others sometimes see a conflict between my work and my children, I don't. I couldn't accomplish what I do without them. They are my grounding force. They keep me from working so hard that I would run the risk of burning out. They pull me back from feelings of despair. They are positive. They welcome each day. With people like that around, no wonder I have energy.

But I want them to see my tears and my anger. I want them to understand the injustice in our society and others. When my daughter was three and my son was six, we lived with a Guatemalan family for four weeks while I studied Spanish. In the town of Antigua, where we lived, as in so many Latin towns, the estates of the wealthy are all behind walls, so you can't see who owns how much. One evening we climbed the hillside behind our home. From the top we looked down on the entire valley. For the first time my children saw that just two families owned huge estates (coffee fincas) covering a large portion of the valley. My son was shocked: "But, Mommy, that isn't fair! Those people have so much. But the people we saw this morning on the way to school were just living alongside the road. They had no houses at all." He continued, "I wonder what would happen if we were giants and we could reach down and take all of the rich people and put them in the poor people's houses and all of the poor people and put them in the rich people's houses."

I didn't answer. I only thought how glad I was that we had come. (I still had no regrets even after they both got amoebic dysentery. I do think, however, that their most enduring memory of Guatemala is not the social injustice but that awful green-brown medicine!)

Building the "Food First" Institute

But I've jumped ahead of my story.

A few weeks after I landed in San Francisco, the rest of the Institute arrived—Joe Collins and David Kinley (formerly with the North American Congress on Latin America and the Corporate Data Exchange). We three—plus the cartons of books and papers, a few filing cabinets, and some typewriters—were *it*. That was four years ago. Now the Institute for Food and Development Policy has ten full-time and six part-time staff, plus at least twenty-five work-study students, interns, and volunteers. We have published fifteen books and booklets, dozens of articles, a Food First slide show, and a Food First comic book. We have given dozens of TV and radio interviews and hundreds of speeches.

Most satisfying is the range of people who are using our work—peasant organizers in the Philippines and Bangladesh, teachers here at home (from classes in political science, economics, and ethics to classes in nutrition), members of church study groups of all denominations, food co-op people, and journalists. In one recent week our work was used as the basis for a front-page *Wall Street Journal* article critical of food aid in Bangladesh, we were quoted in *Newsweek*, and one of our new books was favorably reviewed in the *New York Times Book Review*. Yet we feel certain we have just scratched the surface.

Over the four years since *Food First* was originally published, we have seen a dramatic change in the analysis of hunger by groups that we have been trying to reach. The simplistic over-population theories of hunger, for instance, are no longer accepted uncritically. The questions and attitudes of the audiences who hear me speak are also very different. We believe that our work is contributing to that change.

While many discard the overpopulation explanation of hunger, often they still fall back on the idea that greater production alone is the solution; they ignore the most critical issue of control—power. So we have tried to make our message ever clearer: Unless we address the issue of power—who is making the decisions—we can never get at the roots of needless hunger.

The official diagnosis is that the poor are poor because they lack certain things—irrigation, credit, improved seeds, good roads, etc. But we ask, *why* are they lacking these things? In studying country after country, it becomes clear that what the poor really lack is power—the power to secure what they need. Government aid agencies focus on the lack of materials; we focus on the lack of power.

Jimmy Carter's Presidential Commission on World Hunger, for example, identified "poverty" instead of overpopulation as the cause of hunger. We disagree. Poverty is a symptom, not a cause. Poverty is a symptom of people's powerlessness.

Nor is this mere semantic nitpicking. From these very different analyses flow very different "solutions"—and very different roles for us as outsiders.

If, as the official diagnosis would have it, the problem is poverty, then the solution is more government foreign aid to provide the goods to increase production. Billions of dollars of foreign aid is justified this way. But the bulk of this aid goes to governments which the United States sees as its military and political allies, including some of the world's most repressive regimes. For fiscal year 1981, just ten countries received over one-third of all U.S. aid.[2] Among them were India, Indonesia, Bangladesh, Pakistan, and the Philippines, with governments internationally notorious for their neglect of the needs of the poor and their repression of those wanting change. In countries where economic control is concentrated in the hands of a few, foreign aid strengthens the local and foreign elites whose stranglehold over land and other productive resources generates poverty and hunger in the first place. Instead of helping, our aid frequently hurts the dispossessed majority.

In a Bangladesh village, tube wells designed to benefit the poorest farmers become the property of the village's richest landlord; in Haiti, food-for-work projects intended to help the landless poor end up as a boon to the village elite; and in Indonesia, rural electrification which was supposed to create jobs in rural industries actually eliminates the jobs of thousands of poor rural women.

We've had to conclude that U.S. foreign assistance fails to help the poor because it is based on two fundamental fallacies: first, that aid can reach the powerless even though channeled through the powerful; second, that U.S. government aid can be separated from the narrow military and economic strategies of U.S. policymakers. In the 1975 edition of *Diet for a Small Planet* I scolded the U.S. government for being so stingy, and called for an increase in U.S. foreign aid. In researching *Food First* and *Aid as Obstacle,** however, I learned that as a tool of U.S. foreign policy, this aid goes overwhelmingly to the world's most repressive governments, helping to shore up the power of those who are blocking the changes necessary to alleviate hunger and poverty.

Banana Hunger

Six months after we moved to California, I decided that I had to begin traveling in the Global South. Since his teenage years Joe had spent a great deal of time in the Global South, especially Latin America. I had been only to Mexico and Guatemala, and then only briefly. I wanted to experience firsthand what I had been studying for so many years.

I chose the Philippines because the United States has particular responsibility for the underdevelopment of that country.

---

* *Aid as Obstacle: Twenty Questions about Our Foreign Aid and the Hungry,* co-authors Joseph Collins and David Kinley, Institute for Food and Development Policy.

The Philippines was once a colony of the United States and has been heavily influenced by U.S. political, military, and corporate ties. During the five years after President Ferdinand Marcos declared martial law in 1972, U.S. military and economic aid to the Philippines leaped fivefold. In the fiscal year 1982 budget, this aid was scheduled to top $110 million—not including rent for military bases, a disguised form of aid.[3]

For years I had read and written about U.S. corporate invasion of Global South economies. I wanted to see, hear, and touch the impact of that economic force. For years I had read about grassroots resistance to brutal domination by landed elites. I wanted to meet people who were part of that resistance. What did they want? Were they full of hate and anger? Could they accept people like me as allies, or did they see all North Americans as enemies?

I traveled to the Philippines with my buddy Eleanor McCallie, a founder of Earthwork/Center for Rural Studies, also based in San Francisco. Together we learned about underdevelopment in a way that no statistics could ever convey.

Multinational corporations such as Del Monte and Castle and Cook (Dole) tell us that their investments create the wealth and foreign exchange which the Philippines needs to import essential goods; they're the "engines of development," according to the multinational corporations. We visited the products of their interventions—giant banana plantations they have developed in the southern Philippines over the last ten years.

We met workers paid less than $1.50 a day for back-breaking work, sometimes 12 to 14 hours a day. We went inside their living quarters and tried to imagine what it would be like to live with 24 other women in a room not much bigger than my living room back home, with a small curtain over each woman's bunk providing her only privacy. The bunks were simply hard wooden platforms.

A pregnant woman showed us a large, raw wound on her leg. This, she said, was where another worker had accidentally sprayed her with the fungicide used on the bananas. For the first time we became aware of the terrible danger of pesticides everywhere. Besides the pesticides sprayed regularly on each banana tree and the fungicide sprayed on each bunch as it is packed, planes spray the entire plantation from the air twice a month. Water supplies are left uncovered. The workers are not protected, or even given any warning. In fact, we were told pesticide planes have been used to break up the meetings of workers attempting to organize an effective union.

To Del Monte and Dole, this is development. But development for whom? Small farmers had worked the land for over a generation, yet, as is common in the Global South, they had no legal title to it. This made it easier for the corporations to move in. They simply made deals with wealthy local owners of the best banana land. Once these big landowners saw they could make money by producing bananas for Del Monte, Dole, or Standard Brands, they pushed the poor, small farmers off the land, using bribes, false promises of great jobs on the plantations, legal maneuvers, and finally brutal force.

Most of the dispossessed could not get any kind of job on the plantations. Many ended up even worse off—rising at four each morning to line up near the docks in hopes of being picked to help load the banana boats. They had no job security and no place to live except the crowded, dirty "carton" village set up near the docks.

We might have come home demoralized by the degradation and suffering we witnessed, but we didn't, because we also witnessed the strength of the people.

One morning we got up at four to meet with the men waiting for a day's work on the docks. They told us of their attempts to organize a real union to represent them—and how everything had to be carried out in total secrecy. Anyone known to be organizing never got another work assignment. Living with little food and no security in the carton village should have sapped these men's energy, yet they told of their goals and the secret meetings they were planning. They were not resigned.

Maria, a woman who had worked on the banana plantations and was then working through the church community in basic village-level education, was part of the widespread resistance to the Marcos dictatorship. Petite, soft-spoken, Maria did not fit our image of a revolutionary. (But neither did anyone else we met.) Her commitment was not just to the ousting of a dictator but, most important, to the building of a democratic society from the village up. That was why village-level education was a priority. She and her many allies used drama and song to make political and social problems come to life for the peasants.

We asked our new friends how we in the United States could help them. Without hesitation they told us that we should work to end U.S. government support for the anti-democratic dictatorship that rules their country. Without U.S. aid, Maria told us, the Marcos dictatorship would fall. (In 1981 the Philippines was the sixth largest recipient of U.S. development assistance aid and the seventh largest recipient of U.S. military aid.) She urged us to return home to explain to Americans that our security does not rest in supporting dictators abroad.

Maria helped me to understand that our role is not to empower other people. In fact, we *cannot*. Just as only we can confront the unjust concentration of economic and political power within our society, only the poor in the Global South can organize to overcome their powerlessness. We must also understand that wherever people are oppressed, there is *already* resistance. That resistance might appear doomed in light of the mighty forces working against the poor—but many observers belittled the chances of success of our own American Revolution, fought by a minority of colonists. The struggle of the African colonies against Portuguese colonialism was dismissed just two years before its success. And even as late as spring of 1979, many doubted that the Nicaraguans would be able to overthrow the Somoza dictatorship, as they did in July of that year.*

* To understand what has happened in Nicaragua since the fall of Somoza, see our Institute's book, *What Difference Could a Revolution Make? Food and Farming in the New Nicaragua*, by Joseph Collins, 1982.

Three years after my eye-opening trip to the Philippines, Joe Collins, David Kinley, and I wrote *Aid as Obstacle: Twenty Questions about Our Foreign Aid and the Hungry,* fully documenting this analysis. In the process, I learned that ending military and economic aid to repressive governments is not a separate "human rights" cause, because where people's human rights are denied, so are their food rights.

Lessons from Africa

In the summer of 1978 I set out again, this time on a different quest. In so much of our work we study and concentrate on what is wrong in the current economic order—the injustice, the waste, the destruction. Yet we know that we will not be successful unless we are also working *for* something. Here we face a tough dilemma: How can we develop a vision without falling into the trap of believing that there is a "model" social order that everyone can simply follow?

In struggling with this dilemma, we came up with the theme of "lessons, not models." While no society has achieved a model social order, there are powerful lessons that we can learn by studying the experiences of people in other countries, people attempting to establish democratic political and social institutions to meet the needs of all. Behind this belief is the assumption that something new *is* possible—that human beings are capable of building social institutions more life-giving than those known anywhere in the world today.

We try to make "lessons, not models" a basic theme of our work. Yet some people attack *Food First* for offering idealized "models" of alternatives. From these reactions we have learned that our readers—especially North Americans—are not accustomed to thinking in terms of lessons from abroad. Thus, when we praise some feature of another society, we are sometimes accused of suggesting wholesale adoption of their entire system. Wherever possible we seek to break out of this bind by speaking from actual experience and pointing out both the positive and the negative lessons to be learned from other societies.

All this explains why I went to Africa in the summer of 1978 with my colleague Adele Negro. I wanted to see what it was like to be in countries where the land is not owned by a small elite and where the government is not merely the brutal defender of the power of this elite minority. We visited two neighboring African countries whose governments claim to be progressive—Tanzania and Mozambique. At the time, Tanzania was in its eighteenth year of independence from British colonial rule, Mozambique its fourth from Portuguese colonial rule.

In neither country did I see the degradation of the majority of people that I had witnessed in northwestern Mexico, the Philippines, or Guatemala. While most Mozambicans and Tanzanians are poor, I did not see decadent wealth flaunted in the face of miserable poverty. I did not see widespread starvation in the midst of abundance.

In Mozambique we visited a cooperative farm. Begun by 33 families in 1976, it included 300 families by the time of our visit. We talked all afternoon to one of its founders. In spite of setbacks of every imaginable kind—flooding, late arrival of seeds, transportation breakdowns, and theft—the cooperative was thriving. The cooperative could not have been organized without the support of the government, which provided the initial loans. Although it was one of a handful of successful cooperatives at that time, it was the kind of organization for development that the government hoped would flourish.

As I talked with the cooperative's founder, I could not help but flash back in my own mind to the banana plantation in the Philippines. In the Mozambican cooperative, every member had one vote. Those who worked the land decided what to grow and what to do with the profits. On the banana plantation the workers not only were powerless but lived in fear of the power of the owner, backed up by the government's military.

It was dusk by the time my host let us leave. Even though I was exhausted and eager to begin the long drive back to the city, he wouldn't let us go until he had taken us out into the well-tended, irrigated fields. For years he had fought against Portuguese colonialism, but he seemed prouder of these budding crops than of the victory over colonialism. For him, the struggle to build a new society was an even greater challenge. And I think he is right: Societies formed and deformed over hundreds of years of colonial rule will not emerge within a few years as just societies. Patience is a necessity.

My African trip also showed me the inadequacy of the labels used to describe the two dominant theories of economic organization—capitalism and socialism. Americans are taught to associate capitalism with democracy and socialism with totalitarianism. Yet in the world today we see extremely antidemocratic economic structures in both "socialist" and "capitalist" systems. And we can see democratic elements in both systems, too. In the Philippines, a "capitalist" country, I saw few signs of democratic participation; in "socialist" Mozambique I saw the beginnings of democratic participation from the village up. Every member of the production cooperative had a vote; moreover, everyone could participate in choosing representatives for the country's decision-making bodies, the governing party and the representative assemblies.

As our stereotypes crumble, we have to get better and better at perceiving the important distinctions. Instead of talking in "isms," we must learn to determine how power is actually distributed in a society. For example, both of these African countries have a one-party system, so some might place them in the "totalitarian" category. I learned that what matters most is not the number of parties in the government, but whom the government really represents—and whether it is accountable to the majority of people.

Unlearning our rigid categories means learning to think of every society as in a *process of change* rather than static. (A friend of mine once observed: "What's wrong with Americans is that we want progress without change.") Americans do sense the dramatic changes taking place all around us, and many feel overwhelmed and paralyzed. To break out of our fears, we at the Institute believe, we must first make sense out of these changes—we must understand their roots and their consequences. This is the first step toward moving our society in constructive change. So the Institute has launched a major new investigation. It is not taking me to Maputo, Mozambique, or Davao City, the Philippines. Rather, I am asking: What is the meaning of the critical changes taking place in our food and agricultural system here in the United States?

The Underdevelopment of U.S. Agriculture

Studying agricultural problems in the Global South for ten years, I began to see a pattern of "underdevelopment" that included these three elements: the *concentration of economic power* as the gap between the rich and the poor widens; *dependency and instability* both of the society as a whole and of more and more people within it; and finally, *the mining of agricultural resources* for the benefit of a minority.

The agriculture of so many countries can be described in these terms. But what about the United States? Doesn't it have the world's most productive agriculture? Don't we have a system of family farms, not plantations run by a landed elite? And don't we have long-established conservation programs to prevent the mining of our soil and water?

Many believe so, but what I am learning is that each of these patterns of underdevelopment—the kind of society I don't want—is taking hold right here in America.

CONCENTRATION OF ECONOMIC POWER

Control over farmland is becoming increasingly concentrated. In just 20 years, it is predicted, a mere 3 percent of all farms will control two-thirds of farm production.[4] The amount of farmland controlled by absentee landlords will increase. (Already

almost half of U.S. farmland is owned by nonfarmers.)[5] Donald
Paarlberg, among the most highly regarded agricultural economists in the country, warns us: "We are developing a wealthy
hereditary landowning class, which is contrary to American
tradition."[6]

U.S. farmland, at present anyway, is actually much less
tightly controlled than the rest of the food industry, which is
now dominated by what economists call "shared monopolies." This means that in almost any given food category, only
four corporations control at least half of the sales. In 33 categories, only four companies control *two-thirds* of the sales. For
some foods, the monopoly power is much greater: Three
corporations—Kellogg's, General Mills, and General Foods—
capture over 90 percent of breakfast cereal sales.[7]

Such market power spells profits: Between 1973 and 1979,
food industry profits rose 46 percent faster than consumer food
expenditures. And this monopoly power spells higher food costs
for all of us. Monopoly power in the food processing industry
results in close to $20 billion in overcharges to American con-
sumers each year, or almost $90 per year for every single Ameri-
can.[8] That's how much more we pay compared to prices in a
more competitive food economy.

In fact, at every stage of the food industry concentration is
tightening. During just the last ten years, 20 "Fortune 500" corporations have acquired at least 60 U.S.-based seed companies.[9]
In just ten years, the top four pesticide manufacturers increased
their control from 33 percent of the market to 59 percent.[10] Just
two corporations now control about half of tractor sales.[11]

The meat industry is no exception to these trends. Just three
decades ago, cattle were fed in thousands of small feedlots
(fenced areas where cattle are fattened for market). During the
1960s, 7,500 feedlots folded each year. By 1977, half of the
25 million cattle fed in the United States passed through only
400 feedlots.[12]

At the next stage of production—beef packing—four corporations control one-third of the market. One of these, Iowa

Beef Processors, was just grabbed up by Occidental Petroleum. Having made a killing through its control of one scarce commodity—fossil fuel—Oxy is hoping to do the same with another. Its board chairman told *Business Week* shortly before the 1981 merger: "Food shortages will be to the 1990's what energy shortages have been to the 1970's and 1980's."[13]

While nationally four beef packers control about a third of the market for cattle, what's worrying cattle feeders is how few corporations are *in their vicinity* to bid for their herd; for, regionally, control is even more tightly concentrated. Just three packers, for example, now purchase 70 percent of the feedlot cattle in a major Southwest beef-producing area.[14] Cattlemen are sure that such concentrated power depresses the prices they can get for their cattle.

Cattle-feeding, meatpacking, and grain-trading operations used to be owned by separate interests. But today 13 of the 25 biggest feedlot operations are owned or controlled by either meatpacking or grain-trading corporations.[15] Their interest is in keeping the price of feedlot cattle down. Conveniently, these "integrated" firms also control a critically large share of the cattle futures market (trading in contracts for delivery of feedlot cattle), which they can use to depress the price of cattle, helping to drive out of business the smaller feedlots not connected to beef packers. Officers of packing, meat-processing, grain-trading, and feedlot companies also use their insider knowledge to reap incredible personal gain. A 1980 Congressional study revealed that over a 16-month period in 1978 and 1979, those who came out on top in cattle futures trading were a handful of officers in these companies who each profited by an average of $2.5 *million*.[16]

Such concentration of economic power is what I had learned to associate with economies of the Global South.

IMAGES OF THE GLOBAL SOUTH

Miles and miles of coffee or banana trees. Endless fields of sugar cane. Dependency on raw-material production—and dependency on only one or two crops for export. The marketing of these exports through corporations with no accountability, no loyalty to the well-being of the people of the country.

Since these are my images of agriculture in the Global South, you can imagine my alarm as I learned about the parallels in U.S. agriculture.

I began to study the U.S. government's big farm-export push, which began in the early 1970s. Some have called the massive increase in agricultural exports the greatest shock to hit American agriculture since the tractor, and they may be right. In just ten years farm export volume doubled, and in the Corn Belt states almost 30 percent more land came under cultivation—much of it marginal land, highly susceptible to erosion.

Directly related to the export push are two other trends—a reduction in the number of crops produced and the increasing dependence of farmers on foreign markets. In fact, that dependence doubled in only ten years, so that by 1980 almost one-third of farmers' sales went overseas.

What is the significance of these trends for farmers? And for all of us?

Dependence on foreign markets immediately resulted in more volatile commodity prices. The variation in prices farmers received after 1972 was five times greater than during the late 1960s. Boom and bust was the result. While farmers' incomes hit record highs in 1973–74, by 1978 an average farm family's real purchasing power was no greater than it was in the early 1960s. These great income swings hit the moderate-sized family farm the hardest, especially those with big mortgages still to pay off. It favored those farm operators with investments outside farming, those with incomes large enough to weather the price dips, and those with large equity in their land.

THE WINNERS: THE GRAIN TRADERS

If we are right, and the farm export boom has helped only a small minority of farmers, who *has* benefited? We have found that a disproportionate share of the benefits flows to the five major grain-trading companies—Cargill, Continental, Louis Dreyfus, Bunge and Borne, and Andre—that account for an incredible 70 to 80 percent of all U.S. grain trade. What is wrong with that? you may ask.

First, grain traders are able to capture wealth which should rightfully accrue to the farmers. In their role as transporters of farm commodities, traders guarantee themselves a profit because they can add on to their selling price the costs they incur at every transport link in the marketing chain. Because they can pass on costs, grain traders end up profiting while the income of farmers stagnates. Compare the fate of the two: The real income of farmers was about the same at the end of the 1970s as it was in the early 1960s. But the income of the largest trader, the Minneapolis-based Cargill Corporation, has gone up a whopping 441 percent since the late '60s.[17] (And that is *after* adjusting for inflation.)

Second, the interests of the grain traders conflict with the interests of the vast majority of the American people. What consumers and farmers want are stable prices; but traders profit from market *instability.* For grain traders, profit lies in the price *spread;* whether the price goes up or down is less important. Thus, knowledge of price differentials, between locations or between markets, is all that the major firms need to make money.

Third, even though the major grain traders are largely dependent on U.S. producers and U.S. resources, they are virtually unaccountable to the interests of our farm producers or the U.S. government. The grain traders operate in great secrecy and have made themselves immune to many U.S. laws.

Again, take Cargill, the largest. Cargill's major trading arm is Tradax, chartered in Panama and based in Geneva. Cargill calls it an "independent subsidiary," but it is actually 70 percent owned by Cargill and 30 percent owned by the Salevia Foundation—a trust whose beneficiaries are all members of the Cargill and MacMillan families, owners of Cargill.[18] The Panamanian charter gives Tradax (Cargill) significant tax advantages. Based in Geneva, Tradax is protected by Swiss secrecy laws. (Cargill refused to provide some significant information in 1976 Senate hearings, on the grounds that it would be illegal under Swiss law.)[19] Transactions run through Tradax need not all be reported, either to the USDA or to the IRS for tax purposes. This secrecy is both a tax advantage and a trading advantage.

Most major grain-trading firms export grain from every major exporting country in the world. Thus, they have no loyalty to the interests of U.S. producers, and even help to pit foreign producers against U.S. producers.

Fourth, the enormous wealth of the major grain-trading firms gives them power to influence U.S. government policy and to gain access to tax support. The incredible influence of the grain trade came home to us when a high government official confided to us that if he were to question the all-out-for-export strategy, the grain companies would have him out of a job immediately.

Influence helps buy government assistance, too, such as the services of the Foreign Agriculture Service of USDA and even more direct help. Cargill Korea, for example, was started with 95 percent of its financing from the U.S. government. Public assistance has also helped Cargill expand domestically. The Indiana Port Commission, for example, raised $18 million through tax-free revenue bonds for a Cargill-controlled elevator.[20]

Fifth, the size of the major grain traders enables them to prevent competitors—such as farm cooperatives—from entering the export sales market. While farm cooperatives handle 40 percent of domestic grain sales, they have so far garnered less than 10 percent of the export market. Greater export sales by farm cooperatives might allow more of the money from sales to go to producers.

Sixth, the size of the major grain traders, and the wealth they are accruing as export sales mount, allows them to expand into virtually every aspect of the food industry.

Cargill has used its export bonanza to acquire even more *ships* and *elevator space* at major ports (Cargill and Continental already control half the space);[21] to expand its *poultry operations*

(Cargill already ranks fourth in the U.S.);[22] to expand its *animal feed operations* (Cargill is already the nation's second largest producer);[23] and to enlarge its *soybean and sunflower processing operations* (Cargill may already be the largest soybean crusher in the world).

Cargill is also the number one *cattle feeder* in the country.[24] Cargill's new export profits allowed it to purchase the giant *meatpacking firm* Missouri Beef Packers (MBPXL) in 1978. (At that time MBPXL itself ranked 213th of the Fortune 500.) With Cargill's huge assets behind it, it took only one year for MBPXL to push past Swift to become the country's second largest meat packer, just behind Iowa Beef Processors—which itself was just bought by one of the country's biggest oil companies, Occidental, as I just noted. These top two producers are now wiping out smaller competitors. Some investigators suspect that concentration in the meat industry is responsible for a significant chunk of the meat-price increases over the last ten years.[25]

Such increasing vertical integration means that profits, picked up at every stage from raw commodity to sales, accrue to fewer and fewer firms. Not only does this process lead to the concentration of wealth, but also it allows for more market manipulation.

Since our nation was founded, Americans have resisted such economic concentration, believing that mammoth, unaccountable economic units operating behind closed doors are antithetical to democracy. Nevertheless, economic concentration has been quickening and, in the 1980s, it is gaining speed in a "merger mania" blessed by the Reagan administration and fueled by the oil companies' burgeoning profits.

The concentration of economic power, the dependence on unstable international markets, the unaccountability of the most powerful economic forces—all these are characteristics I learned to associate with misery in the Global South. But there is a fourth important parallel that we must face—less visible but equally threatening. It is the mining of agricultural resources for short-term gain. In Part II of this book I describe this threat to our food security.

My path has taken me from years of desperation in the 1960s (desperation because I did not understand the root causes of needless suffering) to a study of the roots of hunger in the Global South of the 1970s and, finally, a return home in the 1980s to face the crises in our own food and agriculture system—shockingly similar to systems I have seen in the Global South. In this twelve-year process I began to see patterns in what before had been an overwhelming jumble. A framework for understanding began to emerge. Using this framework, I have struggled to identify paths of action that are both meaningful and satisfying. Knowing we can't take on the whole system, where do we begin?

First let me make very clear that I am not suggesting every-one become a "food activist." Yes, I do feel that food problems have a special ability to open doors of understanding—everyone eats and everyone likes to talk about food! But I also believe that most of the gravest problems facing our society today have common roots. Whether the issues be education, health, the legal system, or energy policy, the underlying cause is the distri-bution of power and wealth which determines how decisions are made and for whose benefit.

In 1980 the Institute published *What Can We Do? Food and Hunger: How You Can Make a Difference.* For this book we inter-viewed many friends actively involved in transforming our food system into a more democratic and sustainable one. We wanted to know how they kept going in the face of such huge and com-plex problems.

Power and Responsibility: Changing Ourselves

The first struggle for me and for so many of my friends has been to reconcile our vision of the future with the compromises we must make every day just to survive in our society. If we attempt to be totally "consistent," eschewing all links between ourselves and the exploitative aspects of our culture, we drive ourselves—and those close to us—nuts! I still remember my annoyance as a friend, sitting with me in a restaurant in the late 1960s, scornfully picked the tiny bits of ham out of her omelet.

Who wants to be around someone so righteous that they make you feel guilty all the time? But while self-righteousness is not very effective in influencing people, this does not mean we should not try to make our personal choices consistent with our political vision. Indeed, this is exactly where we have to begin.

If the solution to needless hunger lies in the redistribution of decision-making power, we must become part of that redistribution. That means exercising to the fullest our power to make choices in our daily life. It means working with other people to force the few who have more power to share it with the majority. It also means preparing ourselves to share responsibility with others in areas that we now leave to unaccountable "experts" and politicians.

All this implies taking ourselves seriously, which for years I found difficult. In part, taking ourselves seriously means taking responsibility for how our individual life choices either sustain or challenge the antidemocratic nature of our society.

What do we eat? What we eat links us to every aspect of the economic order. Do we allow ourselves to be victimized by that structure, or do we choose a diet that the earth can sustain and that can best sustain our own bodies? Answering that question is the basis of Book One, explored in depth in Parts II and III.

Where do we shop? Do we support the handful of supermarket chains that are tightening their grip over food? In more than a quarter of all U.S. cities, four chains control at least 60 percent of all sales. That tight control means monopoly power and monopoly prices. In 1974 Americans were overcharged $660 million due to concentration of control by supermarket chains alone.[26] Or do we support the growth of a more democratic alternative, the mushrooming network of consumer- and worker-managed retail food cooperatives, which already have more than 3 million patrons? Their consumers have much greater influence over what is sold and where the products come from.

In school, how do we study? Are we studying to please the professor, or to hone our knowledge to heighten our own power? Are we studying toward a narrow career path, or to prepare ourselves for a life of change?

How do we try to learn about the world? Only through the mass media, whose interpretations and choice of stories reinforce the status quo? Or do we seek alternative sources of information that discuss the lessons which we might learn from our counterparts here and abroad? The publications and websites listed in Appendix A suggest some possibilities.

Where do we work? One of the greatest tragedies of our economic system is that few people are able to earn a livelihood and still feel that they are making a meaningful contribution to society. So many jobs produce either weapons of destruction or frivolous nonessentials. Therefore, our struggle is first to find a livelihood that reflects our vision of the world. If that is not possible, then we can do what more and more people are doing—find the least destructive job that pays, then devote our creative energies to unpaid work. (Some of the volunteers at our Institute have chosen this path.) But just as important are these questions:

How do we work? Are we challenging the arbitrary hierarchies that we were taught to accept? Are we struggling to create structures in which responsibilities are shared and accountability is broadened—so that we are accountable not just to one boss but to one another and to ourselves?

Do we work alone (as I tried to do for too many years)? Or do we join with others to learn how to share decision-making power and to experience the excitement of collaborative work? (All the projects I have undertaken in the last six years have involved teamwork, and I'm convinced that the whole is greater than the sum of our individual contributions.)

How do we choose our friends? Do we surround ourselves with people who reinforce our habits and assumptions, or do we seek out people who challenge us?

Obviously these are only some of the questions that we must ask ourselves as we become part of the redistribution of power. Every choice we make that consciously aligns our daily life with our vision of a better future makes us more powerful people. We feel less victimized. We gain confidence in ourselves. And the more convincing we are to ourselves, the more convincing we are to other people.

The less victimized we are by forces outside us, the freer we become. For freedom is not the capacity to do whatever we please; freedom is the capacity to make intelligent choices. This implies knowledge of the consequences of our actions. And that is what this book is all about—gaining the knowledge we need to make choices based upon awareness of the consequences of those choices.

Overcoming Hopelessness: Taking Risks

According to a 1980 Gallup Poll, Americans are more "hopeless" than the people of any other country polled except Britain and India. Fully 56 percent of Americans queried believed the coming year would be worse than the past year. These findings come as no surprise. Hopelessness is a growing American malady. Increasingly, Americans feel alienated from "their" government—witness the lowest voter turnout since 1948 in the Reagan-Carter contest. Americans increasingly perceive that their government operates in the interests of a privileged minority.

This hopelessness is born of the feelings of powerlessness I have been talking about. Consciously working to make our lives more consistent is the first step in attacking the powerlessness that generates despair—but only the first step.

Taking more responsibility for ourselves—and for the impact of our choices in the world—we start *changing ourselves*.

This is the key to overcoming hopelessness. Unless we experience ourselves changing, can we really believe that illiterate peasants in the Philippines, El Salvador, or Chile can change? (After all, they face much greater obstacles and much stronger messages telling them of their own incapacity.)

If, then, belief that "the world" can change depends on changing ourselves, how do we start?

I believe there is only one way—we must take risks. There is no change without risk. To change, we must push ourselves to do what we thought we were incapable of doing.

What do we risk?

We risk being controversial. Personally, I hate being controversial! I hate it when people attack my views—or, worse, attack me. I remember burning inside when a well-known university president tried to dismiss my views on U.S. support for the Marcos dictatorship in the Philippines. "What does *she* know?" he said. "She's just a cookbook writer." I was outraged when a speaker sympathetic to agribusiness who shared the platform with me several years ago in Minneapolis tried to dismiss my positions by suggesting that I was getting personally wealthy from *Diet for a Small Planet* royalties and therefore was a hypocrite. (Royalties have allowed me to work full time on food and hunger issues, and have helped pay the bills at the Institute for Food and Development Policy. The money I earn from speeches goes directly to the Institute.) I grew up wanting everyone to like me (preferably, to love me!), but to change myself and to try to change the world, I have to accept that many people will *not* like me.

We risk being lonely. Maybe this is even harder. Changing yourself often means taking independent positions that those closest to you cannot accept. For me, this meant deciding I no longer wanted to be married. At the prospect of being on my own, I experienced the greatest pain and terror I had ever felt. I can't deny that I do feel lonely sometimes, but I came to realize that many of the most important things I wanted to do, I could only do alone. Yes, I do work in a team. I enjoy our meetings, making plans and reacting to each other's work. But when it comes right down to getting the words on the page, it is me and the typewriter. I came to learn also that there is a reward for being alone in order to do what I believe in: I feel connected to others who share my vision, not only to others at the Institute but to a growing network of people throughout the world.

We risk being wrong. Taking controversial positions is hard enough, but how do we deal with our fear of being wrong? Part of the answer for me was discovering that those learned academics and government officials—whom I had believed—are wrong. They may be mostly correct in their statistics, but how useful are statistics if their questions are the wrong questions? Those "experts" intimidate so many of us and use their grasp of trivial detail to avoid asking the important questions. (In Rome in 1974, all the experts were asking, "How can we increase food production?" But I had already learned that many countries were increasing food production faster than their population grew and yet had more hunger than ever.)

In learning not to fear being wrong, I had to accept that to ask the important questions is to ask *big* questions—and this inevitably entails crossing many disciplines. If you have read our book *Food First,* you know what I mean. The material spans dozens of disciplines, from anthropology to climatology to nutrition to economics. When you ask big questions, it is impossible to be an "expert" in everything that you study. But instead of being paralyzed by that realization, I try to keep in mind the advice of a wise friend. "If you ask a big question you may get something wrong," Marty Strange told me. "But if you ask a small question—as most narrow academics do—it doesn't matter if you're wrong. Nobody cares!"

My positions have changed as I have learned. In the process, I have become more convinced that acting out of sheer emotion, even genuine compassion, is not enough. If we are serious about committing our lives to positive social change, we must always be learning and accepting the logical consequences of what we learn as a basis for what we do.

Yes, we must be able to risk—risk being controversial, risk being lonely, risk being wrong. Only through risk-taking do we gain the strength we need to take responsibility—and to be part of the redistribution of political and economic power essential for a solution to needless hunger.

But How Do We Learn to Take Risks?

Few people change alone. As I have already suggested, we must choose friends and colleagues who will push us to what we thought we could not do. But we must select friends who will "catch" us, too, when we push ourselves too far and need to be supported. Wherever we are, we must not be content to work alone. Only if we experience the possibility and the rewards of shared decision-making in our own lives—in our families, our schools, our community groups, our workplaces—will we believe in the possibility of more just sharing of decision-making in our government and economic structures.

Second, we must learn to associate risk with joy as well as pain. Despite my parents' struggle against racism and McCarthyism through the Unitarian church they founded, the cultural messages were so strong that I grew up believing that the "good life" we all are seeking would be a life without risk-taking. This was my "sailboat" image of the good life. First you work to acquire your sailboat (husband, kids, etc.), then you set your sails, and head off into the sunset. Of course, I assumed that you might have to adjust the sails now and then. But, short of hurricanes, I thought of life as a continuous and relatively riskless journey.

Well, at the age of thirty-seven my view of the good life is different. I discovered that a life without risk is missing *the* ingredient—joy. If we never risk being afraid, failing, being lonely, we will never experience that joy that comes only from learning that *we can change ourselves.*

Third, we can gain inspiration from our counterparts around the world whose lives entail risks much greater than ours. But this requires our seeking out alternative news sources, because the mass media rarely show us the courageous struggles of ordinary people. Learning about our counterparts around the world, we'll come to realize that we do not have to start the train moving. It is already moving. In every country where people are suffering, there is resistance. Those who believe in the possibility of genuine democracy are building new forms of human organization. The question for each of us is, how can we board that train, and how can we remove the mighty obstacles in its way?

But none of what I have presented here makes much sense unless we develop a perspective longer than our lifetimes. Glenn, a volunteer at the Institute, joked with us before he moved to the East Coast. "For a while I considered getting into your line of work—you know, trying to change the world—but I decided against it," he told us. "The problem is that you can go for *weeks* and not see any change!"

We laughed. Glenn was right. It took hundreds and hundreds of years to create the web of assumptions and the unchallenged institutions of exploitation and privilege that people take for granted today. It will take a very long time to create new structures based on different values. But rather than belittling our task, this realization—seeing ourselves as part of a historical process longer than our lifetimes—can be a source of courage. Years ago I read an interview with I. F. Stone, the journalist who warned Americans about U.S. involvement in Vietnam long before antiwar sentiment became popular. He was asked, "How can you keep working so hard when no one is listening to you?" His answer: "I think that if you expect to see the final results of your work, you simply have not asked a big enough question." I've used Stone's answer in several books and probably too many speeches! For me it sums up an attitude we all must cultivate. I call it the "long-haul perspective."

A book on how our eating relates us to a system that destroys our food resources and deprives many of their right to food would seem, on the surface, to carry a message of guilt and self-denial. But not this book!

I don't think the solution to the tragedy of needless hunger lies in either guilt or self-denial. It lies rather in our own liberation. If we do not understand the world, we are bound to be its victims. But we do not have to be. We can come to see the tragedy of needless hunger as a tool for understanding.

We can discover that our personal and social liberation lies not in freedom from responsibility but in our growing capacity to take on greater responsibility. So please take advantage of our Tools for Learning and Action in Appendix A. Alone, we can feel powerless, of course, but with energizing companions we can transform ourselves from victims of change to makers of change. We can choose to seize these tools—not just on behalf of the hundreds of millions who are hungry, but for our own liberation as well.

Part II

Digging
to the
Roots on
Our Small
Planet

1

One Less Hamburger?

I remember ridiculing Hubert Humphrey's comment that if we all just ate one less hamburger a week, the hunger crisis would be conquered. Yet even while I scoffed at that notion in 1974, my own writing was often taken to be saying the same thing. In the 1975 edition I asked my readers to pretend they were seated in a restaurant, eating an eight-ounce steak—and to appreciate that the grain used to produce the steak could have filled the empty bowls of 40 people in the room.

The first two editions implied that our grain-fed-meat diet denied grain to the hungry abroad who lacked the resources to feed themselves. But as I did research for *Food First*, my view began to shift. I came to learn that virtually every country has the capacity to grow enough food for its people. No country is a hopeless basket case. Moreover, only a minuscule fraction of our food exports ever reach the hungry.

Much of our research for *Food First* focused on the food-producing potential of some of the world's most densely populated countries, such as Bangladesh, and some of the most agriculturally resource-poor countries, such as the nations south of the Sahara Desert, known as the Sahel.

In Bangladesh, we learned, enough food is already produced

to prevent malnutrition; if it had been fairly distributed, grain alone would have provided over 2,200 calories per person per day in 1979.[1] And the stunning agricultural potential of Bangladesh, where rice yields are only half as large as in China, has hardly been tapped. I was struck by the conclusion of a 1976 report to Congress: "The country is rich enough in fertile land, water, manpower and natural gas for fertilizer, not only to be self-sufficient in food but a food exporter, even with its rapidly increasing population size."[2]

We focused on the Sahel because severe famine threatened the region in the years just before we began *Food First.* We saw so many TV images of hungry people dying on desolate, parched earth that we were certain that if ever there were a case of nature-caused famine, this had to be it.

But to our dismay, we learned that with the possible exception of Mauritania (a country rich in minerals), every country in the Sahel actually produced enough grain to feed its total population even during the worst years of the drought of the early 1970s.[3] Moreover, in a number of the Sahelian countries production of *export* crops such as cotton, peanuts, and vegetables actually increased.[4]

In researching what became *Diet for a Small Planet,* I was struck by the tremendous abundance in the U.S. food system, and I assumed that many other countries would be forever dependent on our grain exports because they did not have the soil and climate suitable for basic food production. But I learned that while the United States is blessed with exceptional agricultural resources, countries in the Global South are not doomed to be perpetually dependent on U.S. exports.

I learned that what so many Americans are made to see as inevitable dependence on grain imports is the result of five forces:

1. A small minority controls more and more of the farmland. In most countries in the Global South, roughly 80 percent of the agricultural land is, on average, controlled by a tiny 3 percent of those who own land.[5] This minority underuses and misuses the land.

2. Agricultural development of basic foods is neglected, while production for export climbs. Elites now in control in most Global South countries prefer urban industrialization to basic rural development that could benefit the majority. Of 71 underdeveloped countries studied in the mid-1970s, three-quarters allocated less than 10 percent of their central government expenditures to agriculture.[6] Moreover, as the majority of people are increasingly impoverished, the domestic market for basic food shrinks. So food production is oriented toward the more lucrative foreign markets and the tastes of the small urban class. The meager investment in agriculture which does take place is primarily private investment in export crops. In Asia, for example, "the new export-oriented luxury food agribusiness is undoubtedly the fastest growing agriculture sector," the prestigious *Far Eastern Economic Review* notes. "Fruit, vegetables, seafood and poultry [from southeastern Asian countries] are filling European, American and, above all, Japanese supermarket shelves."[7]

3. More and more basic grains go to livestock. As the gap between rich and poor widens, basic grains are fed increasingly to livestock in the Global South, even in the face of deepening hunger for the majority there. Not only is more and more grain fed to animals, but much land that could be growing basic food is used to graze livestock, often for export. Two-thirds of the agriculturally productive land in Central America is devoted to livestock production, yet the poor majority cannot afford the meat, which is eaten by the well-to-do or exported.[8]

4. Poverty pushes up population growth rates. The poverty and powerlessness of the poor produces large families. The poor must have many children to compensate for their high infant death rate, to provide laborers to supplement meager family income, and to provide the only old age security the poor have. High birthrates also reflect the social powerlessness of women, exacerbated by poverty.[9]

5. Conscious "market development" strategies of the U.S. government help to make other economies dependent on our grain. (See "The Meat Mystique," Part II, Chapter 3, to learn how market development works.)

These forces that generate needless hunger are hidden from most Americans, so when they hear that the poorest underdeveloped countries are importing twice as much grain as they did ten years ago, Americans inevitably conclude that scarcity of resources is their basic problem. Americans then urge more food exports, including food aid.

In writing *Food First,* however, we learned that two-thirds of U.S. agricultural exports go to the industrial countries, not the Global South, and that most of what does go to the Global South is fed to livestock, not to the hungry people. In writing *Aid as Obstacle: Twenty Questions about Our Foreign Aid and the Hungry,* we learned that chronic food aid to elite-based, repressive governments not only fails to reach the hungry in most cases, it actually hurts them. Food aid, we found, is largely a disguised form of economic assistance, concentrated on a handful of governments that U.S. policymakers view as allies. Because food aid is often sold to the people by recipient governments, it serves as general budgetary support, reinforcing the power of these elite-based governments. In 1980, ten countries received three-quarters of all our food aid.[10] Among them were Egypt, India, Bangladesh, Indonesia, Pakistan, and South Korea. Notorious for their neglect of the poor, such governments block genuine agrarian reform that could unchain their country's productive potential. Indonesia, for example, squanders its spectacular oil wealth—$10 billion in 1980—on luxury imports, militarism, and showy capital-intensive industrial projects which don't even provide many jobs.

What I have just said does not diminish our responsibility to send food to relieve famine, as was needed in Kampuchea in

1980 and Africa in 1981. (Note that disaster and famine relief are only 11 percent of our government's food aid program.) But even in the face of famine, as in Kampuchea or Somalia, we learned, the U.S. government often operates more out of political than humanitarian considerations—to the detriment of the hungry. Famine relief funds channeled through private voluntary agencies often have a better chance of helping.

In writing *Food First* and the books that followed, I had to learn some painful lessons. In the back of my mind I was always asking, what does all of this mean for the message of *Diet for a Small Planet*?

If our food is not getting to the hungry, if our food exports actually prop up some of the world's most repressive governments, then why exhort Americans to feed less grain to livestock? Why not pour even more of our grain into livestock, so that at least it does not block needed change abroad?

At the same time I was asking myself these questions, I was studying the agricultural system in the United States. In the process, *Diet for a Small Planet* took on new and deeper meaning. The first edition of this book explained how our production system takes abundant grain, which hungry people can't afford, and shrinks it into meat, which better-off people will pay for. But I didn't fully appreciate that our production system not only reduces abundance but actually mines the very resources on which our future food security rests.

Like Driving a Cadillac

A few months ago a Brazilian friend, Mauro, passed through town. As he sat down to eat at a friend's house, his friend lifted a sizzling piece of prime beef off the stove. "You're eating that today," Mauro remarked, "but you won't be in ten years. Would you drive a Cadillac? Ten years from now you'll realize that eating that chunk of meat is as crazy as driving a Cadillac."

Mauro is right: A grain-fed-meat-centered diet *is* like driving a Cadillac. Yet many Americans who have reluctantly given up their gas-guzzling cars would never think of questioning the resource costs of their grain-fed-meat diet. So let me try to give you some sense of the enormity of the resources flowing into livestock production in the United States. The consequences of a grain-fed-meat diet may be as severe as those of a nation of Cadillac drivers.

A detailed 1978 study sponsored by the Departments of Interior and Commerce produced startling figures showing that *the value of raw materials consumed to produce food from livestock is greater than the value of all oil, gas, and coal consumed in this country.*[1] Expressed another way, one-third of the value of *all* raw materials consumed for all purposes in the United States is consumed in livestock foods.[2]

How can this be?

The Protein Factory in Reverse

Excluding exports, about one-half of our harvested acreage goes to feed livestock. Over the last forty years the amount of grain, soybeans, and special feeds going to American livestock has doubled. Now approaching 200 million tons, it is equal in volume to all the grain that is now imported throughout the world.[3] Today our livestock consume ten times the grain that we Americans eat directly[4] and they outweigh the human population of our country four to one.[5]

These staggering estimates reflect the revolution that has taken place in meat and poultry production and consumption since about 1950.

First, beef. Because cattle are ruminants, they don't need to consume protein sources like grain or soybeans to produce protein for us. Ruminants have the simplest nutritional requirements of any animal because of a unique fermentation "vat" in front of their true stomach. This vat, the rumen, is a protein factory. With the help of billions of bacteria and protozoa, the rumen produces microbial protein, which then passes on to the true stomach, where it is treated just like any other protein. Not only does the rumen enable the ruminant to thrive without dietary protein, B vitamins, or essential fatty acids, also it enables the animal to digest large quantities of fibrous foodstuffs inedible by humans.[6]

The ruminant can recycle a wide variety of waste products into high-protein foods. Successful animal feeds have come from orange juice squeeze remainders in Florida, cocoa residue in Ghana, coffee processing residue in Britain, and bananas (too ripe to export) in the Caribbean. Ruminants will thrive on single-celled protein, such as bacteria or yeast produced in special factories, and they can utilize some of the cellulose in waste products such as wood pulp, newsprint, and bark. In Marin County, near my home in San Francisco, ranchers are feeding apple pulp and cottonseed to their cattle. Such is the "hidden talent" of livestock.

Because of this "hidden talent," cattle have been prized for millennia as a means of transforming grazing land unsuited for cropping into a source of highly usable protein, meat. But in the last 40 years we in the United States have turned that equation on its head. Instead of just protein factories, we have turned cattle into protein disposal systems, too.

Yes, our cattle still graze. In fact, from one-third to one-half of the continental landmass is used for grazing. But since the 1940s we have developed a system of feeding grain to cattle that is unique in human history. Instead of going from pasture to slaughter, most cattle in the United States now first pass through feedlots where they are each fed over 2,500 pounds of grain and soybean products (about 22 pounds a day) plus hormones and antibiotics.[7]

Before 1950 relatively few cattle were fed grain before slaughter,[8] but by the early 1970s about three-quarters were grain-fed.[9] During this time, the number of cattle more than doubled. And we now feed one-third more grain to produce each pound of beef than we did in the early 1960s.[10] With grain cheap, more animals have been fed to heavier weights, at which it takes increasingly more grain to put on each additional pound.

In addition to cattle, poultry have also become a big consumer of our harvested crops. Poultry can't eat grass. Unlike cows, they need a source of protein. But it doesn't have to be grain. Although prepared feed played an important role in the past, chickens also scratched the barnyard for seeds, worms, and bits of organic matter. They also got scraps from the kitchen. But after 1950, when poultry moved from the barnyard into huge factorylike compounds, production leaped more than threefold, and the volume of grain fed to poultry climbed almost as much.

Hogs, too, are big grain consumers in the United States, taking almost a third of the total fed to livestock. Many countries, however, raise hogs exclusively on waste products and on plants which humans don't eat. When Nobel Prize winner Norman Borlaug heard that China had 250 million pigs, about four times the number here, he could hardly believe it. What could they possibly eat? He went to China and saw "pretty scrawny pigs." Their growth was slow, but by the time they reached maturity they were decent-looking hogs, he admitted in awe. And all on cotton leaves, cornstalks, rice husks, water hyacinths, and peanut shells.[11] In the United States hogs are now fed about as much grain as is fed to cattle.

All told, each grain-consuming animal "unit" (as the Department of Agriculture calls our livestock) eats almost two and a half tons of grain, soy, and other feeds each year.[12]

WHAT DO WE GET BACK?

For every 16 pounds of grain and soy fed to beef cattle in the United States we only get 1 pound back in meat on our plates.[13] The other 15 pounds are inaccessible to us, either used by the animal to produce energy or to make some part of its own body that we do not eat (like hair or bones) or excreted.

To give you some basis for comparison, 16 pounds of grain has twenty-one times more calories and eight times more protein—but only three times more fat—than a pound of hamburger.

Livestock other than cattle are markedly more efficient in converting grain to meat, as you can see in Figure 1; hogs consume 6, turkeys 4, and chickens 3 pounds of grain and soy to produce 1 pound of meat.[14] Milk production is even more efficient, with less than 1 pound of grain fed for every pint of milk produced. (This is partly because we don't have to grow a new cow every time we milk one.)

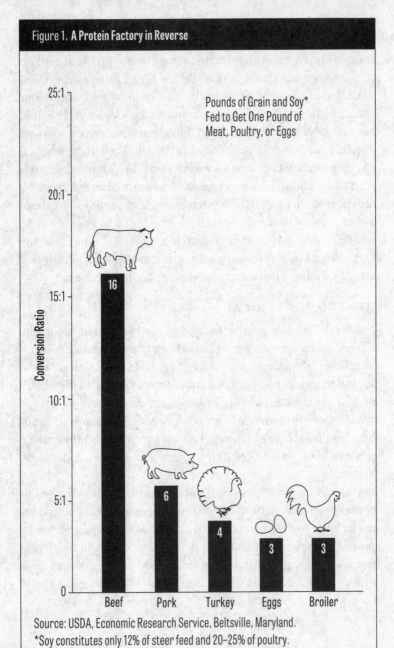

Figure 1. A Protein Factory in Reverse

Pounds of Grain and Soy*
Fed to Get One Pound of
Meat, Poultry, or Eggs

Source: USDA, Economic Research Service, Beltsville, Maryland.
*Soy constitutes only 12% of steer feed and 20–25% of poultry.

Now let us put these two factors together: the large quantities of humanly edible plants fed to animals and their inefficient conversion into meat for us to eat. Some very startling statistics result. If we exclude dairy cows, the average ratio of all U.S. livestock is 7 pounds of grain and soy fed to produce 1 pound of edible food.[15] Thus, of the 145 million tons of grain and soy fed to our beef cattle, poultry, and hogs in 1979, only 21 million tons were returned to us in meat, poultry, and eggs. *The rest, about 124 million tons of grain and soybeans, became inaccessible to human consumption.* (We also feed considerable quantities of wheat germ, milk products, and fishmeal to livestock, but here I am including only grain and soybeans.) To put this enormous quantity in some perspective, consider that 120 million tons is worth over $20 billion. If cooked, it is the equivalent of 1 cup of grain for every single human being on earth every day for a year.[16]

Not surprisingly, *Diet for a Small Planet*'s description of the systemic waste in our nation's meat production put the livestock industry on the defensive. They even set a team of cooks to work to prove the recipes unpalatable! (Actually, they had to admit that they tasted pretty good.)

Some countered by arguing that you get *more* protein out of cattle than the humanly edible protein you put in! Most of these calculations use one simple technique to make cattle appear incredibly efficient: On the "in" side of the equation they included only the grain and soy fed, but on the "out" side they include the meat put on by the grain feeding *plus* all the meat the animal put on during the grazing period. Giving grain feeding credit for all of the meat in the animal is misleading, to say the least, since it accounts for only about 40 percent. In my equation I have included only the meat put on the animal as a result of the grain and soy feeding. Obviously all the other meat, put on by forage, would have been there for us anyway—just as it was before the feedlot system was developed. (My calculations are in note 13 for this chapter, so you can see exactly how I arrived at my estimate.)

The Feedlot Logic: More Grain, Lower Cost

On the surface it would seem that beef produced by feeding grain to livestock would be more expensive than beef produced solely on the range. For, after all, isn't grain more expensive than grass? To us it might be, but not to the cattle producer. As long as the cost of grain is cheap in relation to the price of meat, the lowest production costs per pound are achieved by putting the animal in the feedlot as soon as possible after weaning and feeding it as long as it continues to gain significant weight.[17] This is true in large part because an animal gains weight three times faster in the feedlot on a grain and high-protein feed diet than on the range.

As a by-product, our beef has gotten fattier, since the more grain fed, the more fat on the animal. American consumers have been told that our beef became fattier because *we* demanded it. Says the U.S. Department of Agriculture: "most cattle are fed today because U.S. feed consumers have a preference for [grain-]fed beef."[18] But the evidence is that our beef became fattier *in spite of* consumer preference, not because of it. A 1957 report in the *Journal of Animal Science* noted that the public prefers "good" grade (less fatty) beef and would buy more of it if it were available.[19] And studies at Iowa State University indicate that the fat content of meat is not the key element in its taste anyway.[20] Nevertheless, more and more marbled "choice" meat was produced, and "good" lean meat became increasingly scarce as cattle were fed more grain. In 1957 less than half of marketed beef was graded "choice"; ten years later "choice" accounted for two-thirds of it.[21]

Many have misunderstood the economic logic of cattle feeding. Knowing that grain puts on fat and that our grading system rewards fatty meat with tantalizing names like "choice" and "prime," people target the grading system as the reason so much grain goes to livestock. They assume that if we could just overhaul the grading system, grain going to livestock would drop significantly and our beef would be less fatty. (The grading system was altered in 1976, but it still rewards fattier meat with higher prices and more appealing-sounding labels.)

But what would happen if the grading system stopped rewarding fatty meat entirely? Would less fatty meat be produced? Would less grain be fed? Probably only marginally less. As long as grain is cheap in relation to the price of meat, it would still make economic sense for the producer to put the animal in the feedlot and feed it lots of grain. The irony is that, given our economic imperatives that produce cheap grain, most of the fat is an inevitable consequence of producing the cheapest possible meat. We got fatty meat not because we demanded fatty meat but because fatty meat was the cheapest to produce. If we had demanded the same amount of leaner meat, meat prices would have been higher over the last 30 years.[22]

The Livestock Explosion and the Illusion of Cheap Grain

If we are feeding millions of tons of grain to livestock, it must be because it makes economic sense. Indeed, it does "make sense" under the rules of our economy. But that fact might better be seen as the problem, rather than the explanation that should put our concerns to rest. We got hooked on grain-fed meat just as we got hooked on gas-guzzling automobiles. Big cars "made sense" only when oil was cheap; grain-fed meat "makes sense" only because the true costs of producing it are not counted.

But why is grain in America so cheap? If grain is cheap simply because there is so much of it and it will go to waste unless we feed it to livestock, doesn't grain-fed meat represent a sound use of our resources? Here we need to back up to another, more basic question: Why is there so much grain in the first place?

In our production system each farmer must compete against every other farmer; the only way a farmer can compete is to produce more. Therefore, every farmer is motivated to use any new technology—higher yielding seeds, fertilizers, or machines—which will grow more and require less labor. In the last 30 years crop production has virtually doubled as farmers have adopted hybrid seeds and applied ever more fertilizer and pesticides. Since the 1940s fertilizer use has increased fivefold, and corn yields have tripled.

But this production imperative is ultimately self-defeating. As soon as one farmer adopts the more productive technology, all other farmers must do the same or go out of business. This is because those using the more productive technology can afford to sell their grain at a lower price, making up in volume what they lose in profit per bushel. That means constant downward pressure on the price of grain.

Since World War II real grain prices have sometimes fluctuated wildly, but the indisputable trend has been downward. The price of corn peaked at $6.43 per bushel in 1947 and fell to about $2.00 in 1967. In the early 1970s prices swung wildly up, but then fell to a low of $1.12 in 1977, or about *one-sixth the price 30 years earlier.* (All prices are in 1967 dollars.)[23]

This production imperative doesn't fully explain why production of feed doubled after 1950. In the 1950s the problem of agricultural surplus was seen as too much of certain crops, such as wheat, cotton, and tobacco; so government programs subsidized cutbacks of certain crops, but allowed farmers to expand their acreage in others, such as the feed crops barley, soybeans, and grain sorghum. In Texas, for example, sorghum production leaped sevenfold after cotton acreage was limited by law in the 1950s.[24]

But neglected in this explanation of the low price of grain are the hidden production costs which we and future generations are subsidizing: the fossil fuels and water consumed, the groundwater mined, the topsoil lost, the fertilizer resources depleted, and the water polluted.

Fossil Fuel Costs

Agricultural production uses the equivalent of about 10 percent of all of the fossil fuel imported into the United States.[25]

Besides the cost of the grain used to produce meat, we can also measure the cost of the fossil fuel energy used compared with the food value we receive. Each calorie of protein we get from feedlot-produced beef costs us 78 calories of fossil fuel, as we learn from Figure 2, prepared from the work of Drs. Marcia and David Pimentel at Cornell. Grains and beans are from 22 to almost 40 times less fossil-fuel costly.

Enough Water to Float a Destroyer

"We are in a crisis over our water that is every bit as important and deep as our energy crisis," says Fred Powledge, who has just written the first in-depth book on our national water crisis.*

According to food geographer Georg Borgstrom, to produce a 1-pound steak requires 2,500 gallons of water![26] The average U.S. diet requires 4,200 gallons of water a day for each person, and of this he estimates animal products account for over 80 percent.[27]

"The water that goes into a 1,000-pound steer would float a destroyer," *Newsweek* recently reported.[28] When I sat down with my calculator, I realized that the water used to produce just 10 pounds of steak equals the household consumption of my family for the entire year.

Figure 3, based on the estimates of David Pimentel at Cornell, shows that to produce 1 pound of beef protein can require as much as 15 times the amount of water needed to produce the protein in plant food.

* *Water: The Nature, Uses and Future of Our Most Precious and Abused Resource* (New York: Farrar, Straus & Giroux, 1981).

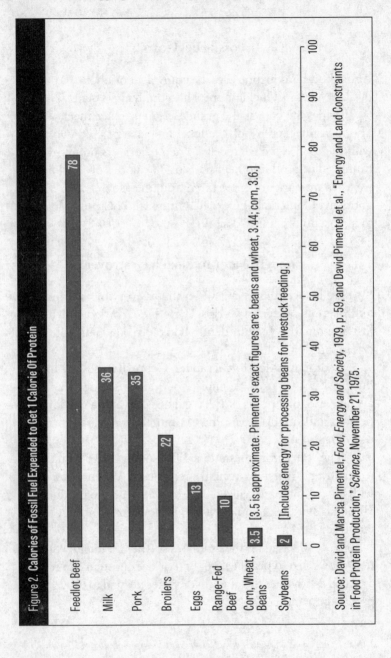

Figure 2. Calories of Fossil Fuel Expended to Get 1 Calorie Of Protein

Feedlot Beef — 78
Milk — 36
Pork — 35
Broilers — 22
Eggs — 13
Range-Fed Beef — 10
Corn, Wheat, Beans — 3.5 [3.5 is approximate. Pimentel's exact figures are: beans and wheat, 3.44; corn, 3.6.]
Soybeans — 2 [Includes energy for processing beans for livestock feeding.]

Source: David and Marcia Pimentel, *Food, Energy and Society*, 1979, p. 59, and David Pimentel et al., "Energy and Land Constraints in Food Protein Production," *Science*, November 21, 1975.

Figure 3. Amount of Water to Produce 1 Pound of Protein from Various Food Sources

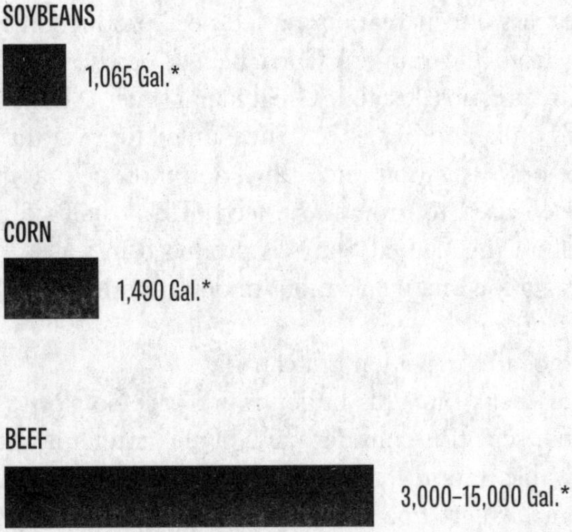

SOYBEANS

 1,065 Gal.*

CORN

 1,490 Gal.*

BEEF

 3,000–15,000 Gal.*

*Includes irrigation water

Source: Dr. David Pimentel, Cornell University, 1981.

MINING OUR WATER

Irrigation to grow food for livestock, including hay, corn, sorghum, and pasture, uses 50 out of every 100 gallons of water "consumed" in the United States.*[29] Other farm uses—mainly irrigation for food crops—add another 35 gallons, so agriculture's total use of water equals 85 out of every 100 gallons consumed. (Water is "consumed" when it doesn't return to our rivers and streams.)

Over the past fifteen years grain-fed-beef production has been shifting from the rain-fed Corn Belt to newly irrigated acres in the Great Plains. Just four Great Plains states, Nebraska, Kansas, Oklahoma, and Texas, have accounted for over three-fourths of the new irrigation since 1964, and most of that irrigation has been used to grow more feed. Today half of the grain-fed beef in the United States is produced in states that depend for irrigation on an enormous underground lake called the Ogallala Aquifer.[30]

But much of this irrigation just can't last.

Rainwater seeps into this underground lake so slowly in some areas that scientists consider parts of the aquifer a virtually nonrenewable resource, much like oil deposits. With all the new irrigation, farmers now withdraw more water each year from the Ogallala Aquifer than the entire annual flow of the Colorado River. Pumping water at this rate is causing water tables to drop six inches a year in some areas, six feet a year in others. And lower water tables mean higher and higher costs to pump the water. The Department of Agriculture predicts that in 40 years the number of irrigated acres in the Great Plains will have shrunk by 30 percent.[31]

In only two decades Texans have used up one-quarter of their groundwater.[32] Already some wells in northern Texas are running dry, and with rising fuel costs, farmers are unable to

---

* Some of this production is exported, but not the major share, since close to half of the irrigated land used for livestock is for pasture and hay.

afford pumping from deeper wells. Why is this water being mined in Texas? Mostly to grow sorghum for the feedlots which have sprung up in the last decade.

When most of us think of California's irrigated acres, we visualize lush fields growing tomatoes, artichokes, strawberries, and grapes. But in California, the biggest user of underground water, more irrigation water is used for feed crops and pasture than for all these specialty crops combined. In fact, 42 percent of California's irrigation goes to produce livestock.[33] Not only are water tables dropping, but in some parts of California the earth itself is sinking as groundwater is drawn out. According to a 1980 government survey, 5,000 square miles of the rich San Joaquin Valley have already sunk, in some areas as much as 29 feet.[34]

The fact that water is free encourages this mammoth waste. Whoever has the $450 an acre needed to level the land and install pumping equipment can take groundwater for nothing. The replacement cost—the cost of an equal amount of water when present wells have run dry—is not taken into consideration. This no-price, no-plan policy leads to the rapid depletion of our resources, bringing the day closer when alternatives must be found—but at the same time postponing any search for alternatives.

Ironically, our tax laws actually entice farmers to mine groundwater. In Texas, Kansas, and New Mexico, landowners get a depletion allowance on the groundwater to compensate for the fact that their pumping costs rise as their groundwater mining lowers the water table. Moreover, the costs of buying the equipment and sinking the well are tax-deductible. Irrigation increases the value of the land enormously, but when the land is sold the profits from the sale are taxed according to the capital gains provisions; that is, only 40 percent of the difference between the original cost of the farm and its sale price is taxed as ordinary income. The rest is not taxed at all.

Few of us—and certainly not those whose wealth depends on the mining of nonrenewable resources—can face the fact that soon we will suffer for this waste of water. Donald Worster, author of *Dust Bowl: The Southern Plains in the 1930s* (New York: Oxford University Press, 1979), interviewed a landowner in Haskell County, Kansas, where $27.4 million in corn for feed is produced on about 100,000 acres of land irrigated with ground-water. He asked one of the groundwater-made millionaires, "What happens when the irrigation water runs out?"

"I don't think that in our time it can," the woman replied. "And if it does, we'll get more from someplace else. The Lord never intended us to do without water."[35]

The Soil in Our Steaks

Most of us think of soil as a renewable resource. After all, in parts of Europe and Asia, haven't crops been grown on the same land for thousands of years? It's true, soil should be a renewable resource; but in the United States, we have not allowed it to be.

We are losing two bushels of topsoil for every bushel of corn harvested on Iowa's sloping soils, warned Iowa state conservation official William Brune in 1976.[36] Few listened. "It can take 100 to 500 years to create an inch of topsoil," but under current farming practices in Iowa, an inch of topsoil "can wash away in a single heavy rainstorm," Brune said after the spring rains in 1980. On many slopes in Iowa we have only six inches of topsoil left.[37]

Few would argue with Brune. Few would dispute that our topsoil loss is a national catastrophe, or that in the last two decades we have backpedaled on protecting our topsoil, or that in some places erosion is as bad as or worse than during the Dust Bowl era. Few dispute that excessive erosion is reducing the soil's productive capacity, making chemical fertilizers ever more necessary while their cost soars. The only dispute is how many billions of dollars topsoil erosion is costing Americans and how soon the impact will be felt in higher food prices and the end of farming on land that could have been abundant for years to come.

Since we began tilling the fields in our prime farming states, we have lost one-third of our topsoil.[38] Each year we lose nearly 4 billion tons of topsoil from cropland, range, pasture, and forest land just because of rain-related water erosion.[39] That 4 billion tons could put two inches of topsoil on all of the cropland in Pennsylvania, New York, and New Jersey.[40] Adding wind erosion, estimated at 3 billion tons, we hit a total erosion figure of nearly 7 billion tons a year.[41]

Robin Hur is a mathematician and Harvard Business School graduate who has spent the last year documenting the resource cost of livestock production for his forthcoming book. "How much of our topsoil erosion is associated with crops destined for livestock and overgrazing of rangeland?" I asked him. "Most of it—about 5.9 billion tons," he calculates, including erosion associated with exported feed grains. This is true not only because feed crops cover half of our harvested acres, but because these crops, especially corn and soybeans, are among the worst offenders when it comes to soil erosion. According to the Department of Agriculture, one-quarter of all soil erosion in the United States can be attributed to corn alone.[42]

MINING THE SOIL

The loss of billions of tons of topsoil threatens our food security only if we are losing topsoil faster than nature is building it. The difficulty is knowing how fast nature works. The most widely accepted rule of thumb is that we can lose up to five tons of topsoil per acre per year without outpacing nature's rebuilding rate—yet one-third of the nation's cropland already exceeds this limit, the Department of Agriculture estimates, and one out of eight acres exceeds the limit almost three times over.[43] This is bad enough, but many soil scientists challenge the standard itself, suggesting it applies only to the top layer of the soil. Soil formation from the underlying bedrock may proceed *ten times* more slowly.[44] If these scientists are correct, we are mining the soil on most of our cropland.

LOST SOIL, LOWER YIELDS

In some areas we are already experiencing lower yields due to erosion and the reduction in fertility it causes. The Department of Agriculture estimates the annual dollar value of the loss just from water erosion at $540 million to $810 million.[45] Adding wind erosion may increase that estimate by 30 percent.

"In our area of Nebraska you see hilltops eroded—completely naked," says Marty Strange of the Center for Rural Affairs. "Yet farmers are still getting 90 to 95 bushels of corn an acre. Farmers don't believe they are losing productivity." They use chemicals to make up for the soil's lost natural fertility, but the cost of fertilizer has risen 200 percent since 1967 and is likely to keep rising. Higher production costs must ultimately mean higher food prices.

We also pay in our taxes, for billions of dollars have gone toward conservation measures (although this spending is shrinking, while the need increases). Moreover, the soil washed from farmlands ends up in rivers, streams, and reservoirs. Dredging sediment from rivers and harbors, the reduction in the useful life of reservoirs, and water purification—these costs amount to $500 million to $1 billion a year.[46]

Thus, the direct and indirect costs of soil erosion already approach *$2 billion a year.*

BUT WHY?

Why is soil erosion accelerating, despite 34 Department of Agriculture programs related to soil and water conservation? There are several reasons:

• The increased tillage of soil so fragile it probably should have remained uncultivated. The government estimates that 43 percent of the land used for row crops in the Corn Belt is composed of highly erodible soils.[47]

• The increased planting of row crops, especially the feed crops corn and soybeans, which make the land particularly susceptible to erosion.

• The growing neglect of conservation practices, including the removal of shelterbelts planted during the Dust Bowl era to protect the soil. By 1975 the total real value of soil conservation improvements had deteriorated over 20 percent from its peak in 1955.[48]

These are the reasons, but what are the causes? Unfortunately, they lie in the economic givens that most Americans take as normal and proper. Squeezed between ever higher costs of production and falling prices, farmers must increase their production. They plant more acres, including marginal land susceptible to erosion, and they plant what brings the highest return, even if this means continuous planting of the most erosion-inducing crops, corn and soybeans. "The most erosive production system—continuous corn—produces the highest net income," according to researchers at the University of Minnesota.[49]

Fertilizers: Becoming Import-Dependent

To determine a price for grain which reflects all its costs would also mean looking at the fertilizers required to mask our lost fertility and continually increase production. Higher yields and continuous cropping deplete soil nutrients, so that ever greater quantities of fertilizer must be used. This vicious circle caused our nation's use of chemical fertilizer to increase fivefold between the 1940s and the 1970s. Just in the last ten years, the use of ammonia (for nitrogen fertilizer) has increased by almost 200 percent and that of potash by almost 300 percent.[50] Corn, the major national feed grain, which occupies about 23 percent of all our cropland, uses more fertilizer than any other crop— about 40 percent of the total.[51]

Because fertilizer has been relatively cheap, farmers have been encouraged to apply ever greater quantities in their desperate struggle to produce. As with topsoil and groundwater, we squander fertilizer resources today without considering the consequences tomorrow. One of the consequences of our heavy consumption of fertilizer is increasing dependence on imports.

Americans might be alarmed at how our dependence on imported strategic metals can be used to justify U.S. political or even military intervention abroad. Americans would probably be even more alarmed about becoming dependent on imported food. But is being dependent on the fertilizer needed to produce food really much different?

Let's look at the three major types of fertilizer:

Nitrogen fertilizer. We won't run out of nitrogen, since it makes up about 78 percent of our air, but the price of natural gas, used to make ammonia, the most common nitrogen fertilizer, has risen so rapidly that we have begun to import ammonia from countries with cheap supplies of natural gas. We now import about 20 percent of our supplies.[52]

Potash. Today we import about 85 percent of our potash (from Canada), and by the year 2000 we are expected to import 90 percent.[53]

Phosphate fertilizer. The U.S. is the world's leading producer, but our high-grade reserves will probably be exhausted over the next 30 to 40 years at the current rate of use, according to a 1979 government report. "We will probably move from assured self-sufficiency and a dominant exporter position to one of increasing dependency on possibly unreliable foreign sources of supply," says the ominous report. "Since phosphates are a fundamental necessity to agriculture . . . *the situation . . . is somewhat analogous to that now being experienced with oil*"[54] (my emphasis).

Livestock Pollution

Some people believe that although we feed enormous quantities of high-grade plant food to livestock with relatively little return to us as food, there is really no loss. After all, we live in a closed system, don't we? Animal waste returns to the soil, providing nutrients for the crops that the animals themselves will eventually eat, thus completing a natural ecological cycle.

Unfortunately, it doesn't work that way anymore. Most manure is not returned to the land. Animal waste in the United

States amounts to 2 billion tons annually, equivalent to the waste of almost half of the world's human population.[55] Much of the nitrogen-containing waste from livestock is converted into ammonia and into nitrates, which leach into the ground-water beneath the soil or run directly into surface water, thus contributing to high nitrate levels in the rural wells which tap the groundwater. In streams and lakes, high levels of waste run-off contribute to oxygen depletion and algae overgrowth.[56] American livestock contribute five times more harmful organic waste to water pollution than do people, and twice that of industry, estimates food geographer Georg Borgstrom.[57]

Cheap Water for Cheap Grain

In a true accounting, the two bushels of topsoil washed away with every bushel of corn grown on Iowa's sloping land would be seen as a subsidy to our cheap grain. In other words, if we were to use all of the conservation measures we know of to prevent this erosion, the cost of producing our grain would go up, as it would if we were to add in all of the costs of dredging the soil from our waterways or charge for feedlot pollution. Failing to account for these costs amounts to hidden subsidies. But in addition, you and I as taxpayers are paying *direct* subsidies right now.

Our tax dollars have paid for more than one-half of the net value of all irrigation facilities in the United States as of 1975.[58] Since the turn of the century the federal government has sponsored 32 irrigation projects in 17 western states where 20 percent of the acreage is now irrigated with the help of government subsidies. A recent General Accounting Office study concluded that even though farmers are legally required to repay irrigation construction costs, in the cases studied the repayments amounted to less than 8 percent of the cost to the federal government.[59]

In some of the projects, the irrigators pay even less. Take the Fryingpan-Arkansas Project near Pueblo, Colorado. This half-billion-dollar project helps farmers grow corn, sorghum, and alfalfa for feed. The GAO calculated the full cost of water delivered to be $54 per acre-foot, but the farmers are being charged only 7 cents per acre-foot.[60] (And the GAO's "full cost" is based on an interest rate of 7.5 percent.) According to *Fortune* magazine, the huge California Central Valley irrigation project is being subsidized at a rate of $79,000 a day.[61]

Cheap water encourages farmers to grow livestock feed. "Because water is so cheap, its use is based on its price and not its supposed scarcity," observes *Fortune*. "Many farmers . . . use inferior land to grow low value crops that require large amounts of water, like alfalfa and sorghum" for feed.[62]

Government subsidies are so large that "the market value of the crops to be grown with federal water is less than the cost of the water and the other farming supplies used to grow those crops," the government study concluded.[63] But Robin Hur has an even dimmer view of the economics of federal irrigation. After studying federal irrigation in the Pacific Northwest, he calculated that in six major projects the value of the crops produced doesn't cover even the cost of the water alone!

Federally subsidized irrigation water helps keep grain cheap. It also helps make people rich. To a farmer with 2,200 irrigated acres in California's Westlands district, the federal water subsidy is worth $3.4 million—that's how much more the land is worth simply because of what the government contributes to irrigation.[64]

A key 1902 federal law stipulated that beneficiaries of the subsidized irrigation were to be small farmers *only*, those owning no more than 160 acres. But the law has never been enforced, despite suits filed by National Land for People and others seeking the irrigated land they are legally entitled to. Today one-quarter of the federally subsidized irrigated land is owned by a mere 2 percent of the landholders, who own far more land than the legal limit. In California, for example, over a million and a half acres of federally subsidized water are controlled illegally—that is, by farms over the legal acreage limit.[65] Southern Pacific alone controls land almost 700 times the legal limit for an individual. (All told, Southern Pacific owns almost 4 million acres in three states.)[66]

Tax Benefits at the Feedlot, Too

Besides directly and indirectly subsidizing the feedlot system by keeping the price of grain low, we taxpayers also subsidize the feedlot operations themselves. Tax laws favoring feedlot owners and investors in feedlot cattle shift the tax burden onto the rest of us. While these tax advantages were cut back in 1976, there are still "income tax management strategies" that can benefit cattle owners who contract with feedlots to fatten their cattle, putting on the last 200 to 600 pounds of each head.[67] According to a Department of Agriculture report, the law that allows farmers to use cash accounting for tax purposes can also profit investors in feedlot cattle, especially those with high non-farm incomes seeking to reduce their taxable income. More than a quarter of "custom feeding" clients in the Southern Plains are such outside investors, including doctors, lawyers, and bankers.[68]

Agricultural economists V. James Rhodes and the late Joseph C. Meisner of the University of Missouri offer this observation of tax favors to feedlot operations:

> Subsidies to large-size feedlot firms, indirect though they be, would tend to lead to survival and growth of those firms on a basis of other than economic efficiency. . . . If the nation seeks to subsidize beef production, direct grants to feedlot firms is an alternative. Then, true economic costs of the subsidies would be more apparent. However, in a world of growing concern for energy supplies, the beef industry would seem to be a most unlikely recipient of national subsidy.[69]

A Fatal Blindness

After reading this account of the resource costs of our current production system, you probably are amazed that more people are not aware and alarmed. I am continually amazed. Again and again I have to learn this lesson: Often those with the most information concerning our society's basic problems are those so schooled in defending the status quo that they are blind to the implications of what they know.

As I was preparing this chapter I came across a book that read as if designed to be the definitive rebuttal to *Diet for a Small Planet*. Three noted livestock economists conclude that "total resource use in this [livestock] production has decreased dramatically."[70] To arrive here, they had, of course, to ignore such hidden costs as I've just outlined—the fossil fuel used, the water consumed (including groundwater that is irreplaceable), the topsoil eroded, and the domestic fertilizer depleted as we attempt to make up for our soil's declining fertility. They also ignore feedlot pollution and hidden tax subsidies. All this I would have expected. What really shocked me was their attempt to prove that we are producing more meat using *less* resources. Their evidence? A decline in labor used and a dramatic drop in acres devoted to feed grains between 1944 and about 1960, while meat production rose. What they fail to tell us is that about one-third of our total cropland was released from feed-grain production between 1930 and 1955 by the rapid replacement of grain-consuming draft animals by fuel-consuming tractors. *Thus, much of the decline in feed-grain acres had nothing to do with increased efficiency of meat production.* Just as appalling, these economists ignore the fact that livestock eat more than feed grains. Since 1960 there has been a spectacular rise in soybean use as animal feed. Tripling since 1960, acres in soybeans now exceed two-thirds of total acres in feed grains.[71] (Almost half of those acres are used to feed domestic livestock,* the rest for export.) Soybeans are not even mentioned by these economists as a resource in livestock production.

While it is useful to keep these gross oversights in mind for the next time we feel cowed by an "authority" questioning *our* facts, they sidetrack us a bit from the basic argument used by such defenders of the status quo. Most economists defend our current meat production system by arguing that feeding grain to livestock is the cheapest way to produce meat. The fatal blindness in this argument is attention only to price. As we have seen, the price of our grain is an illusion. It results from the powerlessness of farmers to pass on their costs of production and the fact that so many of the costs of production—topsoil and groundwater, for example—carry no price at all.

In writing this chapter I came to realize more clearly than ever that our production system is ultimately self-destructive because it is self-deceptive; it can't incorporate the many costs I've outlined here. It can't look to the future. And it blinds those closest to it from even seeing what is happening. Thus, the task of opening our eyes lies more heavily with the rest of us—those less committed to protecting the status quo. As awakening stewards of this small planet, we have a lot to learn—and fast.

But now, let's turn abroad. If the food-producing resources of our country—one blessed with exceptional agricultural wealth—are threatened, what does this production system mean for countries much less well endowed?

---

* The protein concentrate made from soybeans is an excellent livestock ration, and the oil extracted is used to make margarine, salad oil, etc.

3

The Meat Mystique

All that I have said so far might give the impression that the shift toward a meat-centered diet is an American craze. It is not. Throughout the world, more and more grain is being fed to livestock and people are eating more meat—at least, those people who can afford it. When I first wrote *Diet for a Small Planet* ten years ago, about one-third of the world's grain went to feed livestock. Today livestock consume close to one-half the world's grain output; and, by 1985, livestock are expected to eat even more grain than people do.[1] The portion of the world's wheat being fed to livestock has doubled since the late 1960s.[2] And increasingly, even basic staple foods of the poor, such as the tuber cassava, are used as livestock feed.

Grain feeding to livestock outside the United States increased more than twice as fast as population in the 1970s. In Brazil, for example, 44 percent of the staple food crops, mainly grains, are now fed to livestock; in Mexico, 32 percent.[3] In the Soviet Union, not only does a third of the domestically produced grain go to livestock, but the government has made huge foreign purchases of grain to satisfy the Russian people's demand for meat. The 18 million tons of grain which the

Russians bought from us in the infamous 1972 Russian grain deal went largely to feed livestock.

Meat consumption is rising in countries where diets traditionally centered on rice, fish, and soy foods. Thirty years ago, for example, the Japanese people ate almost no meat, but by 1980 meat contributed 20 percent of the calories in the Japanese diet and meat consumption was continuing to rise.[4]

Two questions seem worth exploring. First, why do people want more meat? (Just about everybody seems to want more than they have.) Second, how is it possible that more and more grain is used to produce meat when at least a quarter of the world's people go without even the basic grain they need?

The most obvious answer to the first question is: Meat tastes good. And once any food is considered a favorite, other foods, such as vegetables, are neglected. Mushy string beans accompany the chopped steak plate at Denny's to give it the variety of a classic "home-ec" meal, but don't expect a taste thrill if you eat them!

Meat, especially beef, is also a status symbol. I remember an ad in a progressive newsmagazine for $7-a-pound mail-order steaks. Buy these "when you want to impress your brother-in-law," the ad proclaimed. Like drinking Coca-Cola and wearing Levi's, eating beef is a symbol of the American way of life, imitated from Tegucigalpa to Tokyo. Rising urban middle classes eagerly adopt a meat diet to show how far they have come from the villages where they ate rice, fish, and vegetables.

The Korean diet has historically been based on vegetable protein. But, as Shirley Dorow, a Lutheran missionary who has lived for many years in South Korea, wrote me, "average consumption of beef has risen about 15 pounds a year per person. This means, of course, that some people never eat beef and a few are eating it regularly, for it is a status food."

And to some, I'm convinced, there is an association between meat eating and masculinity. How many women have I heard sigh with pretended exasperation (but real pride) that their husbands are unyielding "steak and potatoes" men. As I was writing this book one of the more amusing letters I received was from a woman in Maine who told me that her efforts to get a good friend to eat more plant foods and less meat got nowhere. He told her that if he didn't eat a lot of meat he would not be able to make love to his wife.

Thus, to challenge a meat-centered diet is to challenge a whole set of feelings and associations. For many, realizing that a meat-centered diet does not bring greater well-being but in fact risks to their health has been one step in rethinking their definition of "progress" or "development." But let's turn to my second question: How can it be that even in the countries in the Global South, more and more grain is used to produce meat while in many of those countries the majority go without the basic food they need?

The answer to this question is much easier than the answer to the first. The sad truth is that those who want and need the grain cannot afford to buy it, so livestock get it. And this is truer every day as the poor are pushed off their lands by the more powerful landowners and as new technology denies the landless poor the jobs they need if they are to buy food.

In researching *Food First* I began to understand that when the "experts" praise underdeveloped countries for "upgrading their diets," the diet of the majority is often being downgraded. This "upgrading" of diets, reflected in statistics showing greater per capita consumption, often means that the well-off minority is eating up hundreds of pounds of grain in the form of meat while the majority is denied even a minimal grain diet.

Brazil is an extreme and tragic example. There, as I've said, almost half of the basic grains go to feed livestock while the majority of the rural poor suffer from malnutrition. Black beans, long the source of cheap protein for the poor, are now expensive and out of the reach of many. The reason? Landowners have shifted from growing black beans to what is more profitable—growing soybeans for livestock feed for domestic and export markets.

The growing power and wealth of the elite in many countries in the Global South means that scarce foreign exchange, often earned by agricultural exports, is used to import feed instead of basic development goods for the benefit of the poor majority. During the 1970s half of the increased livestock feeding abroad relied on imported feed, primarily from the United States.[5]

Exporting the Steak Religion

Most Americans assume that our farm exports go to feed the hungry world. Few appreciate that most of these exports go to other industrial countries, and, overall, *two-thirds of all of our agricultural exports go to feed livestock*.[6] As noted earlier, U.S. farm exports have doubled in just one decade. Much of that spectacular increase is due to feed grain exports, which have leaped fourfold.

The United States has done its part to create a world of hamburger and wheat bread lovers, even in cultures that have thrived for centuries on rice, soy, and fish. From its beginnings in the 1950s, U.S. food aid was officially viewed as a tool for developing commercial markets.[7] American officials understood that food aid could be a foot in the door for converting a nation's taste and food system to dependence on the United States, first on "aid" food, then on commercial exports. The strategy has worked: Among the largest importers of U.S. grain are countries, like South Korea and Taiwan, that not long ago were major recipients of food aid.

But at least most food aid went directly to feed people (mainly the better off); more and more of the current commercial shipments to such countries go into livestock production. This shift to livestock feeding in the Global South was encouraged by a provision in our food aid program during the 1960s. We allowed a percentage of the local currency used to repay food aid loans to be lent at very low interest rates to U.S. corporations. Over 400 U.S. corporations benefited. Some were food firms, such as Ralston Purina, Peavey, and Cargill, which used the cheap loans to establish grain-fed-poultry operations abroad. The development of feed grain markets in the Global South was also encouraged by a law that allowed the federal Commodity Credit Corporation to lend American companies money—over $120 million by 1976—to purchase agricultural commodities. The companies then sell them in the foreign markets, using the proceeds to establish operations there.

At the same time that food aid was introducing Asian taste buds to U.S. wheat and to poultry fed on U.S. grain, the Foreign Agricultural Service (FAS) of the U.S. Department of Agriculture was pushing "aggressive foreign market development" to beat out the "stiff competition" in the race for increased agricultural exports. The Foreign Agricultural Service's cooperation with food export industries includes "market intelligence," "trade servicing," and "product promotion."[8]

If an American corporation wants to know whether it would be profitable to enter a certain market, it turns to one of 100 or so U.S. agricultural attachés in foreign countries. These government employees first make sure the company's product can legally be imported, then call in "professional taste panels" to see if it is acceptable to local tastes. If the company's product makes it past these steps, the FAS helps sponsor a market test.

In addition, the FAS sponsors exhibits around the world for the benefit of U.S. producers. One favorite exhibit is a full-scale reproduction of an American supermarket. Since the United States exports 44 percent of all the wheat in the world trade, the FAS also helps sponsor schools to teach people how to cook with wheat where it is not a traditional food. In Japan the FAS has sponsored a beef campaign, noting that it is "aimed at better-class hotels and restaurants catering to the tourist trade."[9] Its efforts there have also helped to account for the success of fast-food outlets like McDonald's, 90 percent of whose ingredients are imported. Although American-style fast-food outlets began operating in Japan only in 1970, by the end of the decade these chains had taken over a substantial portion of all such sales, displacing many traditional rice, fish, and noodle bars.

Our export strategy thus rests not on shipping our food to a world of hungry people, but on molding the tastes and habits of a relatively small class of people able to afford imported food, making them dependent on products and styles that they never wanted before. American policymakers are encouraging other countries to become more and more food-dependent on the United States, and the United States itself is becoming more and more economically dependent on food exports. Reading the FAS material, one would think that the survival of our nation rested on its success in creating one more hamburger lover in the world.

Meat Imports

We hear almost exclusively about the export side of our agricultural trade. Few Americans are aware that we are also among the world's top agricultural importers. For every dollar our agricultural exports earn we pay out close to 50 cents importing food and other farm products. About one-quarter of those imports are meat and other livestock products, worth almost $4 billion in 1979.[10]

Less than 6 percent of the meat we ate over the last decade was imported. While small in relation to total U.S. consumption, it represents an enormous food resource in relation to the needs of people in some of the countries where it is produced.

As I was finishing this book I received a letter from Sue Pohl of Hillsdale, Michigan. In the early 1970s she lived with her two children in Honduras. "While I was there I experienced the damage our meat-eating habits can do," she wrote. "In 1973 President Nixon increased the quota of imported meat to keep U.S. meat prices down. Instantly many kinds of meat disappeared from our local market, including liver, which I relied on for my iron in our limited diet. (Eggs were in chronically short supply and had to be saved for the children.) So great was the greed of the Honduran meat producers that the government had to issue a decree that a certain percentage of meat must be reserved for the country's own people."

In exporting the Great American Steak Religion, we are exporting a desire for the impossible. The earth could never provide the majority of its people with the grain-fed-meat-centered diet that Americans take for granted. If everyone in the world were to eat the typical American diet, the acreage under cultivation worldwide today would have to double.

4

Democracy at Stake

I have talked of the resources and outright subsidies hidden in our cheap-grain-fed meat and how we are promoting this pattern of eating around the world. But I have left out perhaps the most critical lesson of all: how the production system that mines our resources also undermines social values we cherish. We have been taught that our production system rewards hard work and efficiency while providing abundant food for all, but it actually rewards waste, wealth, and size—and the hungry go without food no matter how much is produced. This is the most painful lesson I have had to learn in the last ten years.

The Blind Production Imperative

In our production system, farmers' profits are in a continually tightening squeeze—between rising costs of production and falling prices for their crops. Their profits are squeezed because farmers are largely price *takers* who must confront price *makers* both when they buy what they need to make the land produce and when they sell their crops.

The first price makers are the manufacturers of farm inputs. Tractor manufacturers, for example, can pass on their rising costs to farmers in the form of higher prices, because farmers must have tractors and there are only a handful of manufacturers. The same holds true for fuel, pesticides, fertilizers, seeds, and other farming inputs. Farmers, however, cannot pass on their higher costs, because in selling their crops farmers meet the second price maker: the marketplace. Farm commodity sales may be the last truly competitive market, with thousands of units competing against one another. Farmers have to take whatever price they can get from relatively few major buyers. Going prices are determined largely by supply and demand, not by the farmers' costs of production.

Because they are at the mercy of price makers both in buying farm inputs and in selling their crops, farmers' profits per acre fall steadily. By 1979 profits per acre in real terms had sunk to one-half the level of 1945.[1] Because of their greater volume of sales, many large farms can survive these lower profits per acre, but smaller farms, *even if more efficient,* may not survive while receiving the very same price per bushel. Thus, ever lower profit margins favor size and force the smaller farms to try to become even larger. Moreover, simply to maintain the *same* income all farmers must try to increase production and lower production costs, regardless of the ecological or human consequences.

So Earl Butz's infamous "Get big or get out" was not a snide crack—it was sound economic advice. But who has the opportunity to "get big"? Only those farmers whose operations are already quite large, particularly those who have considerable equity in their land. They have the advantage when it comes to taxes, government payments, and marketing their crops.

But control of the land is key. Because of this incessant pressure to expand, the most limiting factor in production—land—steadily inflates in value. "Thus, simply owning land comes to be rewarded more highly than producing food on it," Marty Strange, co-director of Nebraska's Center for Rural Affairs, told me. "In other words, unearned wealth is a bigger

factor today in farm expansion than earned income from farming." (For example, a typical farmer with 80 percent of his land
paid for had an annual net income of $18,500 in 1978, but the
value of the land itself increased by $34,600 that year, accord-
ing to a 1979 government study.)[2] As the wealth of those with
considerable equity soars, they have the collateral to buy out
their neighbors down the road. By the mid-1970s almost two-
thirds of all farmland sales involved the expansion of existing
farms, a reversal of the 1950s, when two-thirds of farmland
sales resulted in new farms.[3]

In this process, over four million farms have gone out of
business in the last 40 years. Of those remaining, the top 3 percent now control almost half of all farm sales. By the year 2000,
if trends continue, this 3 percent will control two-thirds of all
farm output.[4]

In place of owner-run farms and widely dispersed control
of our land, we see the possibility of what former Secretary of
Agriculture Bob Bergland called a "landed aristocracy"; that is,
more and more of the actual farming in this country will be
done by tenants, sharecroppers, and day laborers.[5] Already in
the "family farm" heartland of Iowa, more than half of the
farms in some counties are operated by tenants or sharecroppers.[6] And those farms which are still owner-run will operate
increasingly under contract to large export and processing
firms. Newcomers, except the most wealthy, will be barred from
entering farming.

The practice of better established, bigger farms gobbling
up smaller ones is commonly defended on the grounds of more
efficient production, yet already over half the value of all crops
in the United States is produced on farms *larger* than can be
justified on the ground of efficiency.[7] Moreover, costs of production on small to moderate-sized farms are often *lower* than
on the biggest farms, according to the Congressional Research
Service.[8]

Greater production and growing markets have always been
held out to farmers as keys to their prosperity, but the most

straightforward facts of our agricultural history deny this promise:

Our agricultural output has almost doubled in the last 30 years,[9] and agricultural exports have doubled just since 1970, yet the real purchasing power of an average farm family in 1978 was about the same as in the early 1960s.[10] And even this average masks the economic devastation of many (those unable to expand) and the meteoric rise of a minority. Eighty thousand dollars is the *average* net income of the 3 percent at the top, those who now control almost half of U.S. farm sales. The tiny group of 6,000 farms that captures 20 percent of farm sales now enjoys an average annual net income of roughly half a million dollars.[11] At the same time, if two-thirds of American farms tried to live off the sales of their crops alone, their income would fall below the poverty line. Their average income hovers close to the national median only because of increased nonfarm income.[12] And *that* average hides the continuing reality of rural poverty.

Thus, production itself, and efforts to dispose of it through livestock and exports (or, most recently, gasohol), can no longer be accepted as a solution to the plight of the farmer. For we can see where this blind production imperative has taken us—away from values that Americans have always associated with democracy, and toward a "landed aristocracy"; away from dispersed control over the land, and toward a highly concentrated pattern of control; away from a system rewarding hard work and good management, and toward one rewarding size and wealth alone. As I suggested earlier, ours is becoming the kind of farm economy that I have seen at the root of so much injustice and misery in the Global South.

Production Divorced from Human Need

We view our production system as rational, but what makes it go? It is motivated by this year's profits to the individual producer. We proudly cite abundant production as proof of the system's success. But "Does it produce?" cannot be the only question we ask. In judging our system, we must also ask, is it sustainable? Is it fair to its producers? I have already answered "No" to these questions. But the ultimate question which we must answer is, *does it fulfill human needs?* Production divorced from human need is not rational.

Our production is staggering: Over four acres of cropland and pasture are producing food for each person in America. (That's the equivalent of about four football fields just for you!) We produce so much food that although roughly one-fifth is wasted altogether—simply plowed under or thrown out—we are still able to export the output of every third acre harvested. In fact, our production has been so great that one of the biggest government headaches over the last four decades has been the mountains of costly "surpluses."

Yet despite our abundance and the fact that our food prices do not reflect the true costs of production, middle-income families—$15,000 to $25,000 a year—must spend almost 29 percent of their income to eat a "liberal" food plan (as defined by the Department of Agriculture). Poor families must spend from one-half to two-thirds of their income just to buy a "low-cost" food plan.[13]

What's more, there is hunger in America.

"Hunger here?" The Dutch reporter interviewing me looked puzzled. "There can't be. I've never seen anything like your supermarkets. So much food. So many different kinds."

But I have learned that hunger can exist anywhere, within any society that has not accepted the fundamental responsibility of providing for the basic needs of its most vulnerable members—those unable to meet their own needs. And ours, sadly, is such a society. I found myself feeling ashamed when I learned that other societies with which we might compare ourselves—France, Sweden, West Germany—demonstrate by their welfare programs that they do accept this social responsibility. In a recent study of social benefits to needy families with children in eight major industrial countries, the United States ranked among the lowest. In France, a single, unemployed mother caring for two children would receive in benefits 78 percent of the average wage of that country. In Sweden, 94 percent. But in the United States she would receive only 54 percent—and in many parts of our country, much less.[14] (While benefits in other countries are uniform, in our system a person living in the South is likely to get as little as half the benefits of someone living in the Northeast, for example.)

Despite our staggering abundance, millions live in utter deprivation. Who are those denied access to America's abundance?

They are the elderly. Fifteen percent have incomes below the poverty line, and that percentage has begun to climb.[15] Forty percent of all unmarried elderly women in the United States live in poverty.[16]

They are children, and the mothers who must stay home to take care of them. Twelve million American children live below the poverty line, and poverty among inner-city children is climbing at a horrifying rate: Between 1969 and 1975 poverty among related children under five rose, for example, 68 percent in Ohio and 49 percent in New Jersey.[17]

They are the disabled and those unable to find work. By the late 1970s, Americans were being asked to accept as normal an unemployment rate double that of a decade earlier.

In addition to the people who cannot work or cannot find a job, there are many Americans trying to support a family on the money they earn working for the minimum wage. You can work full-time for the minimum wage and still fall below the poverty line.

All told, 29 million Americans—about one in eight of us—live below the poverty line, which the government sets at about $8,400 for a family of four.[18] Poverty-line income amounts to $583 a month, but family incomes of $300 to $400 are more typical. To grasp how there can be hunger and other needless deprivation in our country, all I have to do is try to imagine meeting the needs of myself and my two children on $400 a month.

Many would like to deny that hunger and poverty exist in America. Just after Ronald Reagan's election as President, his chief adviser on domestic affairs declared that poverty had been "virtually wiped out in the United States." Since our system of government aid had been a "brilliant success," he added, it "should now be dismantled."[19] What irresponsible ignorance.

First, our welfare programs do not lift people out of poverty. *Even including food stamp benefits, in few states does welfare bring families even up to the poverty line.*[20] In half the states these programs do not bring families even to 75 percent of the poverty standard.[21] The second fallacy in this statement is that there could ever be a time when government welfare programs are no longer needed. This attitude reflects an unwillingness to accept responsibility for those who—in any society—cannot care for themselves, no matter how bright the economy looks.

But what about hunger? Even though poverty cannot be denied, haven't food stamps eliminated hunger? There is no doubt that food stamps have helped enormously, but they have not eliminated hunger. First, food stamps alone, at about 45 cents per meal, are not enough to supply an adequate diet.[22] The Department of Agriculture concluded that the diets of 91 percent of those families whose food spending is at the level of the food plan on which food stamp allotments are based are nutritionally deprived.[23] If they possibly can, most people supplement their food stamps with cash. But if you are trying to support a family on $400 a month, that means you'll probably have to squeeze some food money out of the rent or heating bill.

Other evidence exists to prove the reality of hunger in America. Poor children have actually been shown to be physically stunted compared to their middle-class counterparts. A Center for Disease Control study in the mid-1970s documented that up to 15 percent of the poor children examined showed symptoms of anemia and 12 percent were stunted in height.[24] Dr. Robert Livingston of the University of California at San Diego told us that "poor children have measurably smaller head circumferences than those in families with adequate income."[25]

Our infant death rate is another powerful indictment of our society. Because the infant mortality rate (deaths of babies less than one year old per 1,000 live births) in part reflects the nutrition of the mother, it is often used to judge the overall nutritional well-being of a people. Even though per-person spending on health care has leapt tenfold in less than 20 years,[26] our infant mortality rate ranks 16th in the world, almost double that of Sweden or Finland.[27] In the United States, 14 babies die for every thousand born alive. This national average is "not enviable," the journal *Pediatrics* sadly notes.[28] But averages do not uncover the real tragedy. Among *nonwhite* babies the infant death rate is 22 per thousand, about the same as that of an extremely poor country like Jamaica.[29] Even assuming much better reporting of infant deaths here, this comparison should alarm us.

Even averages among nonwhites mask the extreme deprivation in some communities. In the Fruitvale area of Oakland, California, just across San Francisco Bay from my home, the infant death rate is 36 per thousand. And in the capital of our nation the rate is 25 per thousand, approximately that of Taiwan.[30]

Perhaps the most convincing evidence of hunger amid abundant production comes from the few people who have the courage to go into our communities to meet and talk with those who are suffering from lack of food. One such person is a woman I met five years ago when we both participated in a Philadelphia "hunger radiothon," 24 hours of commercial-free radio in which all the breaks were used to tell people about hunger and its causes. Investigative reporter Loretta Schwartz-Nobel spoke about people starving in Philadelphia. As I was writing this book, I heard from Loretta again. This time she sent the manuscript that documented the hunger—even starvation—that she had witnessed. Her evidence includes many passages like this one, quoting an elderly former civil service worker in Boston:

> I've had no income and I've paid no rent for many months. My landlord let me stay. He felt sorry for me

because I had no money. The Friday before Christmas he gave me ten dollars. For days I had had nothing but water. I knew I needed food; I tried to go out but I was too weak to walk to the store. I felt as if I was dying. I saw the mailman and told him I thought I was starving. He brought me food and then he made some phone calls and that's when they began delivering these lunches. But I had already lost so much weight that five meals a week are not enough to keep me going.

I just pray to God I can survive. I keep praying I can have the will to save some of my food so I can divide it up and make it last. It's hard to save because I am so hungry that I want to eat it right away. On Friday, I held over two peas from lunch. I ate one pea on Saturday morning. Then I got into bed with the taste of food in my mouth and I waited as long as I could. Later on in the day I ate the other pea.

Today I saved the container that the mashed potatoes were in and tonight, before bed, I'll lick the sides of the container.

When there are bones I keep them. I know this is going to be hard for you to believe and I am almost ashamed to tell you, but these days I boil the bones till they're soft and then I eat them. Today there were no bones.[31]

If your reaction is that Loretta has simply ferreted out a handful of senile old people who refuse government help, read her book *Starving in the Shadow of Plenty* (Putnam, 1981). She is convinced that the people she met are only the tip of the iceberg. "It's happening all over the city," said a social worker in the community where this starving woman lived. "They can't get welfare; they're too old for the job market and too young for Social Security. What can we tell them to do? Tell them to go to the hospital and get treated for malnutrition?" In a Mississippi community, Dr. Caroline Broussard told Loretta, "Whole families come here malnourished. But what's worse is that we know for every hungry child or adult we see here in this clinic there are 20 to 30 others in the area we are not getting to." And in New York City, according to the Community Service Society and a number of public officials, 36,000 people are living on the streets. Again, we think of homeless street people as a Global South tragedy. Yet their numbers are increasing right here in America.

Illusion of Progress

Most Americans believe that since the late 1960s we've made steady progress in eliminating hunger and poverty, due to the introduction of food stamps, school lunch programs, and supplemental feeding programs for pregnant and nursing women. And it's true that these programs have had an impact. In 1967 the Field Foundation sent a team of physicians to investigate hunger in America. Their tour of depressed communities riveted national attention on hunger. Ten years later another Field Foundation team of physicians returned to the same localities. Their 1979 report noted "fewer visible signs of malnutrition and its related illnesses," although "hunger and malnutrition have not vanished." They attributed the improvement *not* to overall economic progress for the poor: ". . . the facts of life for Americans living in poverty remain as dark or darker than they were 10 years ago. But in the area of food there is a difference. The Food Stamp Program, the nutritional component of Head Start, school lunch and breakfast programs, and to a lesser extent the Women-Infant-Children (WIC) feeding programs have made the difference."[32]

Clearly there was progress for those who received the benefits. But these benefits are totally inadequate. (A Texas family of four, for example, is expected to make do on $140 a month in welfare benefits.)[33] Moreover, poverty programs have never reached all those in desperate need of them. The food stamp program reached only half of those eligible for most of its life, reaching two-thirds of those eligible only after rule changes in 1977.[34] Programs for pregnant women and young children have served only one-quarter of those eligible.[35]

Moreover, the value of all our welfare programs has been declining over the 1970s because, except for food stamps, benefits are not tied to inflating prices. And now even food stamp benefits are falling behind. The poor are the worst hit by inflation because they spend a much larger share of their income on necessities, and the prices of necessities (housing, food, fuel, medical care) rose twice as fast as nonnecessities in the 1970s. Inflation has cost welfare recipients 20 percent of their purchasing power over the decade.[36]

In sum, if the lives of the poor have improved at all over the last two decades it has been, for the most part, not because of increases in job-related incomes but because of government programs, such as the grossly inadequate health and food assistance I've just discussed. And even these gains are being reduced by inflation and cut by President Reagan and the Congress elected in 1980.

As to the alleviation of poverty itself? New figures from the Census Bureau show that gains made since the mid-1960s had been virtually wiped out by 1980, even *before* the Reagan administration began to ax social-welfare programs. And in 1981 the nation experienced one of the biggest increases in poverty since the early 1960s, when the Bureau first started collecting poverty statistics. In early 1982, a county administrator in South Carolina told the *New York Times* how he experiences poverty's tightening grip: "The population of the jail has tripled, even though there has been no increase in serious crime," he said. "People get themselves arrested on some minor violation so they can get a meal or two, and I can prove that."[37]

"We're at risk of turning back the clock to a time when hunger and malnutrition were common in this country," Nancy Amidei told me. Nancy is director of the Food Research and Action Center in Washington, D.C. Over the last year she has talked throughout the country with low-income people who are already being affected by the Reagan budget cutbacks. What they told her can be summed up by 82-year-old Luisa Whipple, who told a congressional committee, "I plead with you not to cut back the food stamp program, because as you cut back food stamps you cut back on our health and you cut back on our lives."

Every society must be judged as to how well it meets the basic needs of those unable to meet their own, and on whether it provides a living wage to all those able to work. Our society fails on both counts. How can we act on this judgment? First, we must keep alive in our minds the reality of hunger amid the massive squandering of food resources, for only a sense of moral outrage can keep us probing *how* our society evolved so as to divorce production from human need—and only a sense of moral outrage can force us to question our everyday life choices, asking just how each choice either shores up or challenges the economic assumptions and institutions that generate needless suffering. The "what can we do?" is then answered, not in one act but in the entire unfolding of our lives.

What we eat is only one of those everyday life choices. Making conscious choices about what we eat, based on what the earth can sustain and what our bodies need, can remind us daily that our whole society must do the same—begin to link sustainable production with human need. And choosing this diet can help us to keep in mind the questions that we ourselves must be asking in order to be part of that new society—questions such as, how can we work to ensure the right to food for all those unable to meet their own needs, and a decent livelihood for all those who can work? How do we counter false messages from the government and media blaming the poor and hungry for their own predicament?

Ironically, the notion of relating food production to human needs might strike most Americans as a "radical" idea. We know we're in trouble when common sense seems extreme! But maybe it hasn't gone that far yet. "We've been going at it from the wrong end in the past," Agriculture Secretary in the Carter administration Bob Bergland admitted. "This country must develop a policy around human nutrition, around which we build a food policy, and in that framework we have to fashion a more rational farm policy."[38]

Asking the Right Questions

Once we understand how the ground rules of our economy force greater production yet bypass the hungry, we realize that grain-fed meat is not the cause of our problems. It is a symptom and, for me, a powerful symbol of what is wrong.

If grain-fed-livestock production and consumption were the cause of our problems, then producing and eating less would be the answer. Today Americans *are* eating less beef—16 pounds per person less than in 1976.[*][1] What has been the impact?

Some ranchers, desperate to maintain their livelihood, are planting crops on pastureland. In early 1981, when Eugen Schroeder of Palisade, Nebraska, realized that he stood to lose $200 on each head of cattle, he plowed one-fifth of the 5,000 acres he had previously used for pasture.[2] Along with thousands of other farmers, Schroeder found that it was more profitable in 1981 to grow corn for export than to produce cattle. Thus, given the production imperative basic to our system, a decline in beef eating which helped undercut ranchers' profits led to a

* This drop in beef consumption was made up for by 10 pounds per person more of both pork and poultry.

potentially *more* damaging use of our soil and water, at least in the short term.

Similarly, although the low price of grain is one reason why so much goes to feed livestock, more expensive grain would not be the answer. Would it reduce the mining of our resources? Alone, no. If grain were more expensive, the push to produce it would be even greater, to take advantage of the higher price.

The disturbing discovery is that there is no single change that could alter the self-destructive path we are on. Many things will have to change. But this does not mean that we can wait until they can all happen at once! Eating less grain-fed meat is not the answer in itself, but if this step means that more and more of us will be asking *why* the current American diet developed and *what can we do* to alter the forces behind it, then we are on our way.

The first step is uncovering the right questions.

As long as we focus single-mindedly on increasing production and then on finding ways to dispose of it—through livestock, exports, or gasohol—we can neatly avoid asking the most critical social questions. As our nation was being built, we did not learn how to ask these questions. The continent's vast natural resources, the delusion of "Manifest Destiny" which led Americans to seize most of the United States from its native inhabitants and Mexico, the cheap labor offered by slavery—all these allowed Americans to evade critical questions of justice, resource efficiency, and sustainability in our agriculture. After 200 years we face the consequences: The production system which has provided such abundance for most Americans is now beginning to threaten our food security.

It turned out to be easier to develop new seeds, new machines, and new ways to use grain than to deal with issues of power: how decisions are made and for whose benefit, taking into account not only the immediate return but the long-term impact of these decisions. Our national blindness to the issues of power—how to share it fairly and effectively—has been aided by myths deeply rooted in our national consciousness. So we must begin by looking inside ourselves.

First, a belief that paralyzes many people is the notion that human beings are motivated solely by selfish interests. As a result, democratic economic planning, based on cooperative decision-making instead of a battle of vested interests, is viewed as impossible. And people are bound to doubt any movement or organization claiming to be based on cooperative principles, because if human nature is inherently selfish, people will not cooperate willingly. Claims of cooperation must be masks for coercion.

But look at your own life and the historical record; human beings are much more complex than this. Sure, we all have self-interests. The species would not have survived without them! But most people also want their lives to have meaning beyond themselves. And this is one right denied so many Americans—the "right to feel useful."

So the question is not how to extinguish individual self-interest in the interests of society, but how to begin to build economic and social structures in which the individual can serve her or his own interests and the community's interests at the same time. There need not be an irreconcilable conflict.

The tragedy is that under our current economic ground rules, many feel they must choose: Either ravage our resources today to stay in business or conserve these resources and run the risk of bankruptcy.

Second, we must examine the myth that the essence of democracy is the unbridled freedom of the individual. But wait . . . every responsible society limits people's freedom. In our society freedom is limited by wealth. Those who have wealth have many options; those without wealth have many fewer. Today the "freedom" to own farmland is denied to virtually all those without it, except the few with great wealth. So the question is not *whether* freedom is limited, but *how*. Is our way fair? Is there a more just and democratic way?

Once we accept the myth of unbridled freedom, then placing a ceiling on an individual's "success" is seen as undemocratic. So Americans defend anyone's right to accumulate unlimited wealth. But isn't this a frontier concept? On the frontier it appeared as if there were enough resources for everyone. But the frontier has disappeared; there's only so much farmland in the United States and now it's shrinking, not growing. Yet we give some the right to own 100,000 acres when we know this denies dozens of farm families the right to own any land at all. Is this democratic?

Third, we must probe our deep fear that social planning is always alien and handed down from the top. Hearing the word "planning," we immediately see a grim-faced Politburo officer handing down production quotas. Our stereotypes make us blind to the similarly antidemocratic planning that takes place in our own economy. Industry and government executives here speak English instead of Russian, but their power over our lives may be just as profound as that of economic decision-makers in the Soviet system.

So the question is not *whether* we should have planning. Every society has planning. The issue is *what kind and by whom*. (In Sweden, for example, a committee of local residents decides who can bid on farmland that is for sale, if it is to be sold outside the family. Typically, these committees try to ensure that it does not go to the larger farmers.) But so narrow is our view of planning that it is hard even to imagine developing democratic, accountable planning mechanisms controlled locally and coordinated nationally. In our blind fear we hand over our power—to the unaccountable. What is grown depends only on what will sell to those with money, not on what is needed by those without money. So production is not accountable to need. Neither is production accountable to our children and grandchildren, who will need the resources squandered today. Processing and marketing decisions, moreover, are accountable only to the boards of directors of a handful of corporate giants, as we'll see in Part III.

We have the information to break out of these old fears and misunderstandings. After 200 years we can see where they have taken us. And we can learn from what we see. The destruction of resources, the emergence of a landed aristocracy, and hunger in America are *not necessary*. Shocked into this realization, we can begin to imagine the shape of an economic system truly consistent with democracy. What we need now is courage.

I can't offer you a set of how-to's to get us moving in the direction of greater democracy. But here I would like to offer certain principles that have evolved as the basis of all my work over the last ten years. While there is no blueprint for how we can transform our society, the first step is to develop a sense of the direction in which we want to move—an orientation that more and more people will come to share, so that our distinct tasks become ever more complementary and therefore ever more effective. Here is what I would like to offer to the building of such an orientation.

My Grounding Principles

1. Because scarcity is not the cause of hunger, increasing production alone is not the solution. The solution can be found only by addressing the issue of power. Thus, "development" must be redefined, here and in the Global South, not merely in terms of more production or consumption, but first and foremost in the changing relationships among people. Development must be the process of moving toward genuine democracy, understood as the ever more just sharing of political and economic power.

2. Just as "development" must be redefined to encompass the concept of power, so must "freedom." For what is freedom without power? Freedom to complain about what's wrong in our society without the power to do anything about the problems is virtually meaningless. Thus, *freedom from* interference is only part of what democracy means. We must also have *freedom to* achieve what makes life worth living—the freedom to have safe and satisfying work; the freedom to enjoy security in the

form of food, housing, and health care; the freedom to share in decisions affecting our workplace, community, and nation; and the freedom to share in the responsibility of protecting our resources for coming generations.

3. The concepts of economic and political democracy are inseparable. As the eminent jurist Louis Brandeis said, "We can have democracy in this country or we can have great wealth in a few hands, but we can't have both." Thus, democracy must go beyond the ballot box. It must include the wide dispersion of wealth and control over resources. It must entail the development of accountable, flexible planning structures for resource use from the community to the national level. And the concept of democracy must not stop when we go to work each morning; it must involve the opportunity for self-management in the workplace.

Political and economic democracy are inseparable concepts because where wealth is in the hands of relatively few, laws regulating control over society's basic resources are made in their interest. What's more, this minority's economic might allows it to defy laws not in its interest. (In the United States such monopolies as American Telephone and Telegraph defy antitrust laws; likewise, in California a handful of corporate farming giants have for decades flouted federal law prohibiting their profiting from tax-funded irrigation.)

4. Democracy is not a static model to be achieved once and for all. "Democracy," said William Hastie, "can easily be lost, but is never finally won. Its essence is eternal struggle." Thus, every society is in a process of change and must be judged by the *direction* in which it is moving—toward a more just distribution of power or toward more and more tightly held power. Sadly, I believe my own society is moving away from democracy, toward greater and greater concentration of economic and political power.

5. Within every society, "capitalist" or "socialist," those who have power tend to increase their power. The *only* way to move in the opposite direction is for those who have less power—that means *us*—not only to resist this tendency but to actively take part in the redistribution of power. That means taking on greater and greater responsibility ourselves. In other words, movement toward genuine democracy can happen only when ordinary people realize that they have both the right and the capacity to help make the important political and economic decisions in their society.

With these five grounding principles, the critical question becomes, how can we take part in the redistribution of power?

Part III

Our Dangerous Diet— We Can Do Better!

1

America's Experimental Diet

To eat the typical American diet is to participate in the biggest experiment in human nutrition ever conducted. And the guinea pigs aren't faring so well! With a higher percent of our GNP spent on medical care than in any other industrial country and after remarkable advances in the understanding and cure of disease, the life expectancy of a forty-year-old American male in 1980 was only about six years longer than that of his counterpart of 1900.

Why haven't our wealth and scientific advances done more for our health? Medical authorities now believe that a big part of the answer lies in the new American diet—an untested diet of high fat, high sugar, low fiber, which is now linked to six of the ten leading causes of death. (See Figure 4.)

The first two editions of this book are full of nonmeat recipes, just as this one is. But in my discussion of nutrition I stuck to the protein debate because I wanted to demonstrate that we didn't need a lot of meat (or any, for that matter) to get the protein our bodies need. Now I think I missed the boat, for the *Diet for a Small Planet* message can't be limited to meat. At root its theme is, how can we choose a diet that the earth's resources can sustain *and* that can best sustain our bodies? To answer that, I had to investigate more than meat.

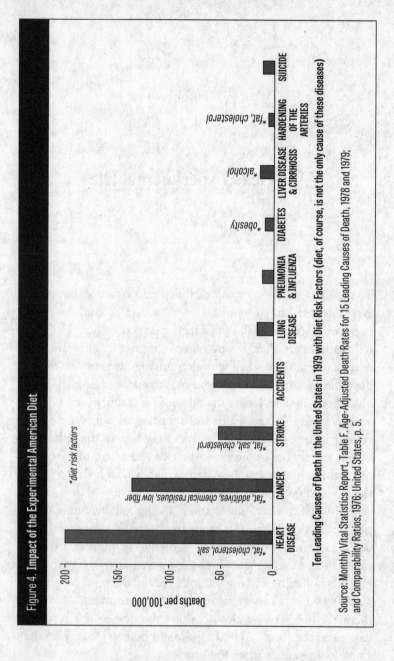

Figure 4. Impact of the Experimental American Diet

Ten Leading Causes of Death in the United States in 1979 with Diet Risk Factors* (diet, of course, is not the only cause of these diseases)

Source: Monthly Vital Statistics Report, Table F. Age-Adjusted Death Rates for 15 Leading Causes of Death, 1978 and 1979; and Comparability Ratios, 1976: United States, p. 5.

As I looked at the radical change in the American diet, I was most struck by our soaring meat consumption. In my lifetime beef consumption has doubled and poultry consumption has tripled. What I didn't adequately appreciate was how much our *entire* diet had been transformed. In the 1977 *Dietary Goals for the United States,* health authorities summing up information gathered by the Senate Select Committee on Health and Nutrition concluded that Americans are eating significantly more fat, more sugar, and more salt, but less fiber and too many calories. No fewer than 16 expert health committees, national and international, now agree that each of these changes is linked to heightened risk of disease.[1] Many other people are concerned that the food additives and pesticide residues we are ingesting may also pose health hazards.

Most striking is that each of these health-threatening dietary changes is actually a by-product of two underlying ones: *more animal food,* and *more processed food.* "Processed" simply means that between the ground and our mouths someone takes out certain things and puts in other things—and not always things that are good for us. The problem is not that Americans are adding more sugar and salt to their recipes or cooking with more fat; the problem is that these are being added *for* us. All we have to do is take the fatty, grain-fed steak from the meat counter, the potato chips from the shelf, or the Big Mac from its styrofoam package.

Eat at Your Own Risk

You'll notice that when scientists speak of diet and disease they are careful to say that such-and-such a way of eating affects the "risk" of getting a particular disease. That's because it is almost impossible to *prove* that diet causes a particular disease. For instance, you can't prove that your father's heart attack was caused by high blood pressure that was caused by his high-salt diet.

Scientists must largely rely on "guilt by association." By comparing populations, they can observe which diets are associated with which types of disease. But comparing different societies with different diets is less than convincing, since there is always the possibility that genetic differences among populations and other environmental factors play a decisive role. So the most telling observations are those of a single population group which changes its diet. Here is a sampling of such evidence:

• The traditional Japanese diet contains little animal fat and almost no dairy products. Japanese who migrate to the United States and shift to a typical American diet have a dramatically increased incidence of breast and colon cancer.[2]

• The citizens of Denmark were forced to reduce their intake of animal foods by 30 percent during World War I, when their country was blockaded. Their death rate simultaneously fell 30 percent, to its lowest level in 20 years.[3] Denmark's experience was not unique: In a number of European countries, where World War II forced people to eat less fat and cholesterol and fewer calories, rates of heart disease fell.

• In some countries in the Global South, a small class of urbanites have adopted the new American diet over the last 20 years. Coronary heart disease now occurs more and more frequently in some of those countries, such as Sri Lanka, South Korea, Malaysia, and the Philippines, the World Health Organization reports.[4]

Other important evidence comes from different diet and disease patterns in populations that are similar in most other ways. For example, a study of 24,000 Seventh-day Adventists living in California showed that the nonvegetarian Adventists had a three times greater risk of heart disease than those eating a plant food diet.[5]

In her fascinating, thoroughly researched book *Jack Sprat's Legacy* (Richard Marek, 1981), Patricia Hausman convinced me that health authorities around the world virtually all agree: The typical American diet is a high-risk diet. The "debate" over the risks associated with the new American diet is perpetuated by the media and vested interests in the meat, dairy, and egg industries, who have spent millions of dollars trying to publicly deny these risks, despite overwhelming evidence to the contrary.

Eight Radical Changes in the U.S. Diet

The food industry was quick to attack the Senate Select Committee on Nutrition and Human Needs for daring in 1977 to suggest a change in the American diet. How ironic. Never has a people's diet changed so much so fast as ours has over the last 80 years. And that change, as we shall see, has been in large part caused by the food industry itself.

I have looked at each of these changes and asked, what are the risks associated with this change? And *why* the change? (By the way, the best detailed source on the "Changing American Diet" is an excellent 1978 book by that name written by Letitia Brewster and Michael Jacobson of the Center for Science in the Public Interest in Washington, D.C.)

I will discuss each change separately, but as nutritionist Dr. Joan Gussow wisely observes, our bodies don't experience these changes separately. "One of the handicaps of most 'scientific' investigations of the impact of dietary change is that each is studied separately, whereas the greater threat may be their cumulative impact," says Dr. Gussow. So we have to look at the whole cluster.

Dangerous Change No. 1:
Protein from Animals Instead of Plants

Contrary to what I thought, the dramatic change is *not* in our protein consumption. It has actually varied little over the last 65 years, fluctuating between 88 grams and 104 grams per person per day (roughly twice what our bodies can use). The change is in how our protein is packaged. Sixty-five years ago we got almost 40 percent of our protein from grain, bread, and other cereal products. Now we only get 17 percent of our protein from these sources. In their place, animal products, which then supplied about half of our protein, now contribute two-thirds.[6]

U.S. consumption of animal products began to climb after World War II, with beef consumption almost doubling and poultry consumption almost tripling by the late 1970s.[7]

THE RISKS

There is no medical consensus about the risks of diets high in protein generally or about diets high in animal protein specifically. (There is general agreement about the risks of what results from this new "packaging" of our protein—more fat and less fiber. But I'll deal with those risks later.) While no consensus exists, there are some intriguing warning signals.

The Senate Select Committee notes: "One series of investigations found that diets that derive their protein from animal sources elevate plasma cholesterol levels to a much greater extent than do diets that derive their protein from vegetable sources. Another line of basic research demonstrated that, in almost all cases, high protein diets are more atherosclerotic than are low protein diets."[8] (Atherosclerosis is a hardening of the arteries caused by fatty deposits accumulating along the artery walls.)

High-protein diets have also been linked to osteoporosis, the thinning of the skeleton, in some studies. Osteoporosis, which now affects four out of five elderly American women, occurs when calcium is drawn from the bones, weakening them. Pain, fractures, and even the collapse of part of the vertebrae can result. Because more calcium is excreted in the urine in a high-protein diet, this kind of diet may promote osteoporosis. (Apparently, eating more calcium doesn't help.) One recent investigation found that animal protein did contribute to increased calcium excretion. But there is still much that's not understood.[9]

Dangerous Change No. 2: More Fat

Americans eat 27 percent more fat than did our grandparents in the early 1900s. And more than one-third of that increase has come just in the last ten years. As a result, fat's contribution to our total calorie intake climbed from 32 to 42 percent, though there are signs that the average may be lowering.

THE RISKS

The risks appear to lie in too much total fat, too much saturated fat, and too much cholesterol. Saturated fats, found in animal foods and in some vegetable foods (especially palm and coconut oil), and cholesterol, found only in animal foods (especially eggs, some seafood, and organ meats), generally increase the blood cholesterol level. Eating saturated fat raises blood cholesterol levels more than does eating cholesterol itself.[10] As Patricia Hausman explains in *Jack Sprat's Legacy*, the higher the blood cholesterol, the greater the rate of fatty deposits that harden the arteries. The more severe the fatty deposits in the arteries, the greater the risk of heart disease, stroke, and other complications of atherosclerosis.

Reducing the cholesterol in the diet does not automatically reduce the cholesterol in the blood for everyone. There may be genetic factors which determine why some people respond to lowered dietary cholesterol and others do not. But to be on the safe side, it would seem prudent to assume that lowering our cholesterol consumption will make a difference.

In a survey of 200 scientists in 23 countries, 92 percent recommended that we eat less fat to reduce our risk of heart disease.[11] In addition to increased risk of heart disease, says Hausman, "studies, spanning up to 40 countries worldwide, confirmed that the total amount of fat in the diet does correlate with some forms of cancer. Studies link six forms of cancer with dietary fat, including cancers of the breast and colon, two of the top cancer killers in the United States."[12]

Dietary Goals for the United States suggests we return to a diet in which 30 percent of our calories come from fat, instead of the 42 percent we're averaging now. (The Japanese, notable for their low incidence of heart disease, traditionally have gotten only 10 percent of their calories from fat. Unfortunately, this is rapidly changing as hamburger joints displace the traditional rice, fish, and noodle bars.)

The good news is that eating polyunsaturated fats— safflower, sunflower, corn, and soybean oils—actually *lowers* the blood cholesterol levels, and may help control hypertension as well.[13] So the recommendation is that at the same time as we reduce our total fat, we shift from animal fats and palm and coconut oils to more of these polyunsaturates.

WHERE IS THE FAT IN OUR DIET?

We are eating more fat, not because we are pouring more oil on our salads or frying more foods at home. Again, we are letting someone else put the fat in for us. In our "choice" and "prime" steaks, grain has been turned into fat. In those French fries at Burger King, a very low-fat food—the potato—has been transformed into one in which most of the calories are from fat, mostly saturated fat.

Where is the fat in our diet?

In animal foods. Over half the fat in the American diet comes from animal foods, with red meat alone contributing almost one-third. Although our consumption of butter and lard has fallen drastically (Americans eat about one-quarter the butter we ate in 1910),[14] we're eating much more fat in meat, poultry, cheese, and margarine. We're eating two or three times as much of these foods as we did in the mid-1940s.

In fattier meat. Not only do we eat more meat and poultry, but those products contain more fat today than in our grandparents' time. As we've seen, one important effect of grain feeding is to put on more fat. During their last 120 to 150 days before slaughter, cattle are fattened up (or "finished," as cattlemen say) so they will receive USDA's "choice" or "prime" grade rating and command a premium price. A choice-grade carcass has about 63 percent more fat than one fed less grain and graded only "standard." (In the last several years the meat industry has begun to respond to the public's concern about fat by offering more lean meat and even a few reduced-fat processed meats, such as hot dogs.)

In snack foods. Just as important in explaining our increase in fat consumption are snack foods—French fries, potato chips, corn chips, crackers, and other snack foods. Eating potato chips, we get 63 percent of calories from fat—fully double the recommended proportion for our total diet. Even in Ritz crackers, we get 46 percent of the calories from fat.[15]

In other processed fat surprises. Ironically, some of the processed foods we purchase in an attempt to avoid fat or cholesterol have more fat than the product we are trying to avoid. Nondairy coffee whitener, for example, has three times the fat of natural half-and-half.[16]

Prepared foods such as TV dinners and fast foods also contribute to the fat surge in the American diet. In a Big Mac or Kentucky Fried Chicken or a TV dinner, Americans are getting about half their calories from fat.[17] At home we *could* eat a meal with just as much fat, but once we pass under the Golden Arches we have no choice.

The vegetable oils most commonly used in processed foods—coconut and palm kernel oils—contain largely saturated fats, the type medical authorities warn us against. Virtually all of the fat in powdered coffee whitener is saturated fat.[18] So is the fat used in processed foods such as "breakfast bars" and some imitation ice creams. Thus, even though we might never use coconut or palm oil in our own kitchens, if we eat a processed diet we get plenty of these saturated vegetable fats. They now account for 16 percent of total vegetable oil consumption.

Dangerous Change No. 3: Too Much Sugar

Since the turn of the century Americans have doubled their daily sugar dose; just since 1960 it's gone up 25 percent.

One-third of a pound of sugar is now consumed each day for every man, woman, and child in America.[19]

THE RISKS

The problem with sugar is both what it does to us and what it displaces. The link between sugar and tooth decay is well established. In virtually all societies studied, the incidence of tooth decay rises as people eat more sugar. Half of all Americans have no teeth at all by the time they reach the age of fifty-five.

Sugar also fills us up with calories while giving us no nutrients or fiber. Filled on sugar calories, we inevitably eat less of other nutrient-rich foods such as breads and cereals, fruits and vegetables. Unfortunately, sugar makes us need the nutrients in these foods even more. Sugar increases the body's need for thiamin and perhaps the trace mineral chromium as well, according to Dr. Jean Mayer.[20]

WHERE IS THE SUGAR IN OUR DIET?

As with fat, Americans are not buying more sugar and confections directly. In fact, Americans are eating significantly less candy today than they did in the early 1940s. Candy has its ups and downs, but per capita intake has been falling steadily since 1970.[21] The household use of sugar has dropped to half of what it was in the early 1900s.[22]

We are eating more sugar because it is being added *for us* by the food-processing corporations and we are eating more of their processed foods.

Since the early 1900s the per capita consumption of sugar in processed fruits and vegetables has tripled. So much sugar is added to processed fruits and vegetables that Americans eat almost as much sugar in these foods as they do in cake and candy. Since the early 1900s, the per capita use of sugar in beverages, mainly soft drinks, has increased almost sevenfold.[23] By 1976 the equivalent of 382 twelve-ounce cans of soft drinks— each with six to nine teaspoons of sugar—was consumed for every person in the country—up about two and one-half times just since 1960.[24] (The next time you reach for a Coke, remember that you're about to drink the sugar equivalent of a piece of chocolate cake, including the icing.) Fully one-quarter of our intake of cane and beet sugar now comes from soft drinks.[25] Among processed foods, cereals and baked goods give us the most sugar; the country's second most popular breakfast cereal, Sugar Frosted Flakes, is *half* sugar.[26]

Dangerous Change No. 4: Too Much Salt

Americans now eat 6 to 18 grams of salt (sodium chloride) a day—10 to 30 times the average human requirement, and as much as three times the recommended level.[27] *Dietary Goals for the United States* recommends that we eat no more than one teaspoon of salt (5 grams) a day (about 2,000 mg of sodium). Since the average human *requirement* for salt is probably one-twentieth the recommended maximum of one teaspoon, there is virtually no danger of insufficient salt even if we never add salt to any food ourselves.[28]

THE RISKS

Health scientists are widely agreed that high salt intake markedly increases the risk of hypertension, or high blood pressure, and they estimate that as many as 40 percent of the older people in the United States are susceptible to hypertension. High blood pressure increases the risk of heart attack and stroke. High-salt diets also cause edema, or water retention, in some people.

WHERE IS THE SALT IN OUR DIET?

Again, as with fat and sugar, the problem is not so much that Americans are reaching for the saltshaker more often. The greater problem is that many Americans eat two to three times the recommended daily intake without ever seeing a grain of salt. In a Kentucky Fried Chicken dinner, for example, you consume a teaspoon of salt—enough for a whole day.[29]

Figure 5. Sodium* in Fresh Versus Processed Foods

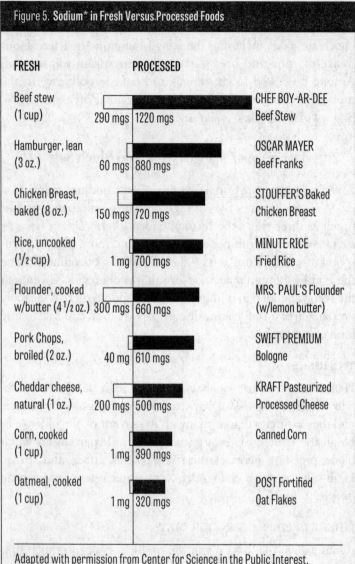

FRESH	PROCESSED
Beef stew (1 cup) — 290 mgs / 1220 mgs	CHEF BOY-AR-DEE Beef Stew
Hamburger, lean (3 oz.) — 60 mgs / 880 mgs	OSCAR MAYER Beef Franks
Chicken Breast, baked (8 oz.) — 150 mgs / 720 mgs	STOUFFER'S Baked Chicken Breast
Rice, uncooked (1/2 cup) — 1 mg / 700 mgs	MINUTE RICE Fried Rice
Flounder, cooked w/butter (4 1/2 oz.) — 300 mgs / 660 mgs	MRS. PAUL'S Flounder (w/lemon butter)
Pork Chops, broiled (2 oz.) — 40 mg / 610 mgs	SWIFT PREMIUM Bologne
Cheddar cheese, natural (1 oz.) — 200 mgs / 500 mgs	KRAFT Pasteurized Processed Cheese
Corn, cooked (1 cup) — 1 mg / 390 mgs	Canned Corn
Oatmeal, cooked (1 cup) — 1 mg / 320 mgs	POST Fortified Oat Flakes

Adapted with permission from Center for Science in the Public Interest, Washington, D.C.

*Roughly 2,000 mg sodium = 1 teaspoon salt (total daily recommended maximum)

Not only does fast food come salt-laden, so do many processed foods. (See Figure 5.) A mere ounce of processed Swiss cheese—less than you might put in a sandwich—has almost one-quarter teaspoon salt. Natural Swiss cheese has one-sixth that much.[30] A frozen beef dinner contains almost a full teaspoon of salt, 20 times as much as an unsalted hamburger.[31] Two hot dogs give you one-half teaspoon, as does a cup of Campbell's soup.

Almost all canned vegetables are salt-heavy. Fresh or frozen corn, for example, has almost no salt; but a cup of canned corn has 20 percent of the salt recommended for a whole day. Even processed foods that we think of as sweet are really salty, too. One piece of cake made from a devil's food cake mix contains as much salt as a 1.5-ounce bag of potato chips.[32]

Other salt-laden foods are cured meats, such as smoked ham, chipped beef, and corned beef, and the pickles Americans love on hamburgers.

In addition to the invisible salt in processed foods, Americans are eating more and more salted snacks. In 1980 Americans spent almost $4 billion on potato chips, nuts, corn chips, pretzels, and prepopped popcorn.

Dangerous Change No. 5: Too Little Fiber

Until very recently, most of us did not know that lack of fiber in the diet was a risk; most of us didn't even know what fiber was. Scientists define dietary fiber as the skeletal remains of plant cells that are not digested by our bodies' enzymes.

As significant as any other change in the human diet over the last 20,000 years is the "fiber revolution." The diets of our early ancestors probably contained ten times the dietary fiber of contemporary diets.[33] Our long digestive tract undoubtedly evolved to handle this higher-fiber diet. The antifiber revolution has taken its most extreme form in the United States, where today 70 percent of our calories come from food containing little or no fiber.[34]

The fiber in fruits, grains, beans, seeds, and vegetables differs, and serves different beneficial functions. Some, for example, shorten the time it takes food to pass through the intestines; others promote the growth of bacteria useful in altering potentially harmful substances. So it is important to eat a variety of fiber.

THE RISKS

Of all the diet-disease connections, the role of dietary fiber may be hardest to pin down, since the fiber content of our diet has no direct biochemical effects but promotes physical and secondary physiological changes. Nevertheless, low-fiber diets have been implicated in heightened risk of bowel cancer and other intestinal diseases. "Dietary fiber appears to aid in reducing the onset and incidences of diabetes, cardiovascular disease, diverticulosis, colon and rectal cancer, and hemorrhoids," states Dr. Sharon Fleming of the Department of Nutritional Sciences at the University of California, Berkeley.[35] More than one scientist believes that fiber in the diet appears to be even more strongly linked to reduction of blood cholesterol levels than does a lowering of fat consumption.[36] Another problem associated with lack of fiber is plain old constipation.

WHY SO LITTLE FIBER IN OUR DIETS?

Whole cereals, fruits, vegetables, and legumes (peas, beans, lentils) are good fiber sources. But we are eating less of many of these fiber foods and more of foods without fiber. For example, we eat less than half the flour and cereals our grandparents ate in 1910,[37] and the refined cereal products we do eat have been stripped of their fiber. A slice of white bread has only one-eighth the fiber of a slice of whole wheat bread. (See Figure 6.) Since 1930 we have cut our fresh fruit consumption by one-third.[38] The amount of dried beans in our diets has dropped by a third since its peak in the 1930s. One of the few fiber foods whose consumption is not declining is fresh vegetables.

As with fat, the real reasons for lack of fiber in the American diet are the increase in animal foods (which have no fiber to begin with) and the increase in processed foods (which have theirs removed).

Figure 6. Fiber in 4 Slices of Bread and Other Foods	
White bread	0.2 gm
Whole wheat bread	1.6 gm
Rye bread	1.1 gm
1 small apple	1.0 gm
½ cup cooked dry beans	1.5 gm
1 cup grated carrots	1.0 gm
¾ cup raw cabbage	0.8 gm

Dangerous Change No. 6: Too Much Alcohol

Ever since Prohibition, Americans have been drinking more alcohol. They drank the equivalent of 2.69 gallons of *pure* alcohol per person in 1975, 24 percent more than during the 1961–65 period. Of course, this figure is misleading, because while many people drink little or no alcohol, others drink far more than their share.[39] The biggest increases have come in wine, with 490 million gallons sold in 1979, and beer, up from 82 million barrels in 1950 to 175 million barrels in 1979.[40] (Some 25 percent of the cereal grains directly consumed in the United States are used to make alcoholic beverages.)[41]

Alcoholic beverages offer us few nutrients but lots of calories—210 calories per day in the average adult diet in 1975. (Again, this is misleading: Since many Americans drink no alcohol, others must get 500 or even 1,000 calories a day from alcoholic drinks.)[42]

THE RISKS

Alcohol leads to cirrhosis of the liver, the sixth leading cause of death in the United States. It can also cause birth defects and mouth cancer. Even more deadly is alcohol's effect in traffic accidents: Half of all traffic deaths involve a drinking driver. Moreover, alcoholism destroys—only more slowly—the lives of millions of Americans every year.

Despite these undisputed dangers, sales of alcoholic beverages amount to more than $45 billion a year. Anheuser Busch, which controls 26 percent of the beer market, spends $120 million a year on advertising, and the alcohol industries have enormous political power.[43]

Dangerous Change No. 7: More Additives, Antibiotic Residues, and Pesticides

FOOD ADDITIVES

"It is impossible to know exactly how many pounds of artificial colors, flavors and preservatives we ingest annually" is the sober assessment of Letitia Brewster and Michael Jacobson. In *The Changing American Diet,* these authors note that the only accurate records made public are the amounts of coal-tar-based colors certified each year by the Food and Drug Administration. But Brewster and Jacobson suggest that the increase in the use of food coloring is probably a pretty good indicator of the increase in other additives. The use of certified food coloring has increased about *elevenfold* since 1940.[44]

THE RISKS

The debate over the risks of food additives continues. The Center for Science in the Public Interest, co-founded by Jacobson, has spent ten years looking into these risks. Jacobson's first book, *Eater's Digest* (Doubleday, 1972), is a valuable encyclopedia of food additives and their risks.

"But there are hundreds of common additives," I said to Michael Jacobson in a recent phone conversation. "What do *you* tell people to do?" He answered with a list of five additives about which he believes there is enough evidence to warrant concern.

Read labels and avoid these additives, Michael suggests. "But it's not so difficult," he says. "Basically, if you avoid junk food, you'll avoid most of them."

	WHERE YOU FIND IT	SUSPECTED TO INCREASE RISKS OF
Caffeine	3 Cokes have as much as 1 cup of coffee	Birth defects and other reproductive problems when consumed by pregnant women, fibrocystic breast disease (breast lumps), irritability, insomnia
Saccharin	"Diet foods" (diet soda accounts for half of all saccharin used)	Bladder cancer
Nitrite	Hot dogs, bologna, bacon, sausage, etc.	Cancer*
BHT†	Many processed foods, such as potato chips, oils, and yeast	Cancer
Colorings	Many processed foods, especially candy, soft drinks, and gelatin desserts	Cancer

*The debate about whether nitrites are cancer-causing continues. But what is often overlooked, according to the Center for Science in the Public Interest, is the fact that even if nitrites themselves are not shown to cause cancer, nitrosamines may be formed from the nitrites either in cooking or in the digestive process, and nitrosamines have been linked to cancer.

†Butylated hydroxytoluene (BHT) prevents oils from oxidizing and becoming rancid. But it increases the shelf life of a product only slightly and is not necessary if one consumes the product within a normal time range.

ANTIBIOTICS

Livestock consume nearly half of the 25 million pounds of antibiotics produced in this country every year, an output that has shot up 400 percent in the last 20 years. Livestock eat most of these antibiotics in their feed, which contains low-level doses to enhance growth and prevent disease. Penicillin and tetracycline are the most common.[45]

Cancer-causing sulfa residues from antibiotics are still occasionally found in pork above the levels now considered safe, according to my former husband, pathologist Marc Lappé, author of *Germs That Won't Die: Medical Consequences of the Misuse of Antibiotics* (Doubleday/Anchor Press, 1981). In addition, the carcinogenic growth hormone DES has been discovered in some cattle, even after its banning several years ago.

Marc and other scientists fear that such widespread use of antibiotics in animals could lead to the evolution of bacteria resistant to common antibiotics. "The drugs are used in livestock production in total disregard of the possibility that they could create resistant bacteria which might directly or indirectly cause disease in humans, or even human epidemics," Marc warns.

The Food and Drug Administration is now considering banning the use of penicillin and certain types of tetracycline in animal feed.

The antibiotic explosion is just one more aspect of the destructive production imperative. Since poultry producers can get as much as 12 percent more weight gain from the same amount of feed when antibiotics are used, they feel they have no economic choice. Antibiotics also reduce disease and death, problems greatly exacerbated by the large-scale, high-density livestock production our economy encourages.

PESTICIDES

Pesticide use doubled from 1966 to 1976, reaching about 600 million pounds of active ingredients. When livestock eat tremendous volumes of treated grass and grain, pesticide residues concentrate in their tissues. Not surprisingly, a Food and Drug Administration study of our diet found the most (22 percent) pesticide detections in meat, fish, and poultry. (Virtually all the detections of DDT were in this group.) Oils and fats were next, with 18 percent of all detections.[46]

Studies of human breast milk offer strong evidence linking animal fat in the diet with heightened concentrations of pesticides. Stephanie Harris, formerly with the Environmental Defense Fund, told me that her study, using matched controls, found a significant correlation between pesticide levels in breast milk and the diet of the mother. "The more animal fats in the diet, the more pesticides we found in the mother's milk," Stephanie told me. "To reduce our intake of pesticides," she suggests, "means not only cutting back on our meat intake but also on full-fat dairy foods—butter, whole milk, and fatty cheeses."[47]

Our national intake of DDT is going down. But you might be surprised that there is any DDT in our food at all, since it was banned for use here in 1972. Unfortunately, the life span of organochlorine pesticides already introduced into the environment ranges from 7 years to over 40 years. And while the amount of DDT in our food may be going down, our intake of other pesticides, like malathion, toxaphene, and captan, is going up.[48]

THE RISKS

No one knows. Our intake of pesticides does not exceed what the government calls safe "tolerance" levels. But these toxicity standards are established on the basis of short-term toxicity tests on small animals. They tell us little about the long-term risks to humans.

Moreover, when officials of the Environmental Protection Agency checked up on Industrial Biotest Laboratories, the mammoth lab which conducted most of the studies establishing the "safe" levels for pesticides consumed by Americans, it found that more than 75 percent of the tests audited were invalid. They involved faulty test procedures or downright falsification of data.[49]

We may not know for 10 to 20 years (or we may never know) the true health risks of pesticides in our food. In the meantime, one way to reduce our exposure is to limit our intake of meat, poultry, fish, and fats. Fruits and vegetables come next in line as carriers of pesticides. Chemists recommend that we wash commercially produced fruits and vegetables with detergent to reduce the amount of pesticides we eat.

In 1981 our Institute published *Circle of Poison: Pesticides and People in a Hungry World,* a book by David Weir and Mark Schapiro. It reveals that American chemical corporations are legally exporting to the Global South pesticides that have been banned or heavily restricted in the U.S. Residues of these banned pesticides have been found in some of the food we import. Therefore, avoiding imported meat, fruits, and vegetables makes sense as another way to lower your pesticide intake.

Dangerous Change No. 8: Too Many Calories

I probably don't have to present evidence to convince you of one of the key consequences of the new American diet. A government study confirms what our scales are telling us: As of the early 1970s the average American man was six pounds heavier and the average woman seven pounds heavier than their counterparts of 15 years earlier.[50] Twenty percent of all Americans are either clinically overweight or obese.[51]

THE RISKS

Extra pounds can aggravate hypertension and heart disease.[52] (Even a 10 percent reduction in weight can lower blood pressure significantly, according to a recent study.)[53] It is less widely known that obesity is also believed to promote diabetes.

But why are Americans getting fatter?

We are not eating more calories, but we are burning up less because our lives are more sedentary. Moreover, with the typical American high-fat, low-fiber, high-sugar diet you can eat a lot of calories without eating very much bulk, so you just don't feel full. A gram of fat has more than twice as many calories as a gram of carbohydrate. This means that for the calorie "cost" of just one pat of butter or two bites of hamburger, you could eat a whole cup of plain popcorn, a slice of bread, most of a small potato, a cup of strawberries, or an entire head of lettuce.

Eating more plant food and less animal food allowed me not only to shed my extra ten pounds (never achieved as a chronic dieter) but to maintain the same weight for the last ten years. And my experience is apparently not exceptional. Says the *Journal of the American Dietetic Association:* "Persons who were previously omnivores and became vegetarians in adulthood report weight loss rather than gain."[54] It suggests that increased physical activity might also play a part, as was true for me. Most important, I was liberated from the stifling preoccupation with weight that plagues so many Americans.

The Good News

The flip side of the message in this chapter—that so many of our most dreaded diseases are related to the food we now eat—is the good news: We can reduce our chances of getting these diseases since *we* control what we eat. And it's easy. We don't have to memorize a book of tables and walk through the grocery store with an electronic calculator, adding up grams of fat, salt, and sugar. Since the eight threats to our health derive mainly from animal foods and processed foods, achieving a healthy diet involves only a few steps: reducing our consumption of animal foods (limiting eggs to three a week and cutting back on full-fat dairy products), enjoying a variety of *whole* foods, and using safflower, sunflower, corn, or soybean oil at home. Remember, what the medical authorities are recommending today is not some newfangled way of eating that requires a Ph.D. to put together. It is a pattern of eating that sustained human life for thousands of years.

The lesson is clear: The more we let the food industry create what we eat, the more we expose ourselves to risk. The more control we take over our diet, the better able we are to reduce those risks. (I am not suggesting a corporate plot to make us sick; it is simply that the logic of corporate expansion is frequently in direct conflict with our body's logic, as we'll see in the next chapter.)

And the word is getting out. Americans *are* starting to modify their diets, at least in part for reasons of nutrition and health. Many people nationwide have cut back on fatty meat, eggs, and oil, while eating more fruits and vegetables.

The single most important first step in rediscovering the traditional, healthy diet is *changing where you shop.* As long as you are wading through 15,000 choices in a supermarket, coming up with something healthy will seem like an incredible challenge. But if you are shopping in a community cooperative store filled with whole foods and foods from local producers, all your senses will be tantalized—but in the right direction for your health.

2

Who Asked for Froot Loops?

At a party not long ago I was talking with a man I hardly knew about the ideas in this edition—how I was struggling to grasp the forces *behind* these eight radical and risky changes in the American diet. "Well, don't blame the corporations," he told me. "If people are stupid enough to eat junk food, they deserve to get sick. Naturally corporations are going to make what sells best."

I think he summed up pretty well how most Americans view these changes in our diet. They are seen as the more or less inevitable consequences of combining the corporate profit motive with human weakness. And since you can't change either, why stew about it?

I'm convinced that this view is popular because while it *appears* to assign responsibility (to the gullible individual), it is really a way to evade responsibility for our economic ground rules. Once accepted, these ground rules justify such practices as feeding 145 million tons of grain to livestock. And they make the expensive, energy-consuming, life-threatening changes in our national diet inevitable.

To understand corporate logic, pretend for a few minutes that you are the chief executive of Conglomerated Foods, Inc.

From the Point of View of Conglomerated Foods, Inc.

Get off the elevator on the top floor. Enter the executive suite. Say hello to your secretary, settle down in your big leather chair, and gaze for a moment out the picture window. Think. How would *you* make Conglomerated Foods prosper? Even if you don't have a degree from Harvard Business School, I think you'll find that certain obvious strategies come to mind.

Ah, yes . . . first *expand sales*. But how?

The "Takeover" Strategy

Your most obvious step in expanding sales is to squeeze out, or buy out, smaller, often regional, producers. (As Procter & Gamble did when they bought a small southwest coffee company called J. A. Folger about ten years ago.)[1] Then you launch an advertising blitz and a deluge of coupons and even reduce the price of your product below your cost. (You can follow International Telephone & Telegraph's example—it sold its Wonder, Fresh Horizons, and Home Pride breads at a loss to drive smaller bakeries out of the market.)[2] Since you're a conglomerate selling many different products, you can make up for any losses simply by raising prices in your other product lines. And why not expand your sales overseas through takeovers? (As Borden did when it bought Brazil's biggest pasta manufacturer.)[3]

THE IMPACT OF YOUR STRATEGY

Walking into the supermarket, customers still see Aunt Nellie's Pickles and Grandma's Molasses. This illusion of diversity hides the reality that your strategy has succeeded in making the food industry one of the most tightly controlled in America. In the scramble to capture national markets, *half* of American food companies have been bought out or closed down during my lifetime. Most of them were not inefficient producers; they simply could not withstand the financial muscle of the cash-laden conglomerates.

Take Beatrice Foods, for example, a company whose name is unknown to most Americans. This one company has bought out more than 400 others.[4] Names like Tropicana, Milk Duds, Rosarita, La Choy, Swiss Miss, Mother's, and Aunt Nellie's, and even Samsonite and Airstream—all these should really be called "Beatrice."

As a result of the surge of takeovers, 50 of the remaining 20,000 companies have emerged at the pinnacle. These 50 corporations now own two-thirds of the industry's assets. Based on present trends, these 50 firms—one-quarter of 1 percent of them all—will control virtually *all* the food industry's assets in another 20 years.[5]

By the 1970s the supergiants had begun to gobble up the giants. In what *Business Week* called the "great takeover binge," Pillsbury plunked down $152 million for Green Giant (frozen vegetables). For $621 million, R. J. Reynolds seized Del Monte's vast fruit and vegetable empire. Nabisco merged with Standard Brands (Chase & Sanborn coffee, Blue Bonnet margarine, Planters peanuts, etc.).

Now, in most food lines—such as breakfast cereals, soups, and frozen foods—four or fewer firms control at least half of the sales. (See Figure 7.) Economists call that a "shared monopoly"—and with it come monopoly prices, an estimated $20 billion in overcharges to consumers each year.[6] Anticompetitive practices cost consumers a 15-cent "monopoly overcharge" on every dollar's worth of cereal, according to a four-year study by the Federal Trade Commission.[7]

And who's to resist? The combined budget of the antitrust divisions of the Justice Department and the Federal Trade Commission is $20 million a year, the sum that a corporate food giant can put into promoting just one "new" processed food. Spending only $20 million to counter the monopoly abuses in a trillion-dollar economy is what Ralph Nader calls a "charade."[8]

Figure 7. **Control of Our Food by Shared Monopolies***

INDUSTRY	PERCENT OF SALES CONTROLLED BY TOP FOUR COMPANIES
Coffee, ground	51
Oil, salad and cooking	51
Peanut butter	51
Baked goods, dry cookies	52
Fish and seafood, canned	58
Cigars	59
Beans, canned and dry	65
Corn, wet milling	65
Grain mill products, mixes, and prepared flours	70
Milk, canned	70
Spice	70
Baked goods, dry crackers	71
Chocolate and cocoa	71
Milk, dried	73
Cereal, to be prepared	80
Cigarettes	80
Coffee, instant	81
Tomato products, catsup	81
Baking powder and yeast	86
Dessert mixes	86
Grain mill products, refrigerated doughs	87
Soft drinks, bottling	89
Soft drinks, syrup	89
Cereal, ready to eat	90
Gum	90
Soup	92
Baby food	95

Source: Food Price Investigation, Senate Hearings, 1973.

*When as few as four firms control in excess of 50 percent of the sales of a given food line, economists usually find "oligopolistic" practices, such as overcharging, in comparison to prices under more competitive conditions.

The "Grab a Bigger Market Share" Strategy

But now where are you? In most major food categories, a few giants now make over half the sales. Procter & Gamble (Folgers) and General Foods (Maxwell House, Sanka) together control nearly 60 percent of the ground-coffee market.[9] Kellogg's, General Foods, and General Mills divvy up 90 percent of the dry-cereal market.[10] Campbell's alone controls nearly 90 percent of the soup market.[11] And on it goes. Industry studies show us that at least half of the shoppers in a supermarket buy mainly the top two brands, even though they usually cost more. So you've got to become number one, or at least number two. You'll have to lure some customers away from the other Big Food companies. But you can't compete in ways that hurt your long-term profits—like offering better quality or lowering prices. Hmmm. Why not up the advertising budget? And you can come up with some eye-catching "new" products in some eye-catching new packages. If you can't compete in price or quality, you must compete in visibility—and the more snazzy the packaging, the more visible. With more products, you can squeeze your competitors off the supermarket shelf.

To create consumer loyalty, you have to have brand names. And that's a lot easier with processed foods. (You did stick labels on bananas, but lettuce and mushrooms were a lot more trouble.) And since you want to sell the products from your giant assembly lines all over the country, you'll need to add such delicacies as BHT and polysorbate for indefinite "freshness."

THE IMPACT OF YOUR STRATEGY

Food advertising costs shot up from about $2 billion a year in 1950 to a record $13 billion in 1978.[12] "On the average, six cents of every dollar we spend on processed foods will go directly to buy ad time on television and other promotion," says food researcher and writer Daniel Zwerdling. "But when we buy one of industry's hot-selling brands, we pay far, far more. In

Figure 8. The Price of a Brand Name			
	PRICE OF HOUSE BRAND	PRICE OF NAME BRAND	PERCENT HIGHER
Flour, all-purpose, 10 lb.	$1.35	$2.75 Gold Medal, Pillsbury	104
Salt, iodized, 26 oz.	0.22	0.33 Morton	50
Sugar, granulated, 5 lb.	1.89	2.49 Domino	32
Corn oil, 1 qt.	1.99	2.25 Mazola	13
Spaghetti, 1 lb.	0.59	0.85 Mueller's	44
Rice, enriched, parboiled, 32 oz.	1.05	1.69 Uncle Ben's	61
Nonfat dry milk, ten 1-qt. envelopes	3.79	4.49 Carnation	18
Cut green beans, 16-oz. can	0.30	0.50 Libby's	67
Raisin bran, 20 oz.	1.19	1.63 Kellogg's	37
Orange juice, frozen concentrate, 16 oz.	1.04	1.49 Minute Maid	43
Graham crackers, 16 oz.	0.79	1.09 Nabisco	38
Peanut butter, smooth, 12 oz.	0.83	1.15 Jif, Peter Pan	39
Coffee, instant, 6 oz.	3.19	3.99 Nescafé, Folgers	25

Source: Center for Science in the Public Interest, 1980.

a recent year, breakfast eaters who bought Kellogg's Country Morning, a so-called 'natural cereal' that better resembled crumbled cookies, paid 35 cents of every dollar merely to finance Kellogg's ads. . . ."[13] But the costs of the ads themselves are only a fraction of what the consumer ends up paying for advertising. Because advertising is power, people are willing to pay more for a highly advertised brand-name item than they would for exactly the same product sold under a less well-known or store brand name. (See Figure 8.)

Since launching just one new item nationwide can cost as much as $20 million, only the corporate giants can afford to play this game.[14]

Because of the huge expense of advertising, Zwerdling concludes, the advertising strategy and the takeover strategy are closely tied: "Food corporations merge in part to amass the financial power they need to launch massive advertising campaigns."[15] Other studies confirm that the more any industry relies on advertising, the faster the concentration of market power.[16]

More eye-catching packaging was also part of your strategy. What has this done for us? Well, by 1980 the cost of the package exceeded the cost of the food ingredients for a fourth of the food and beverage product industry. (Soft drink containers cost two times as much as their contents; beer containers five times as much!) Over the last decade packaging costs have gone up 50 percent faster than the labor costs in our food. Today one out of every 11 dollars we spend on food and drink goes to pay for packaging.[17]

And the impact of your new product strategy? "In the beginning, there was just Campbell's chicken rice soup," quips journalist A. Kent MacDougall. "Today, besides chicken with rice soup, Campbell Soup makes chicken gumbo, chicken noodle, chicken noodle-Os, curly noodles with chicken, cream of chicken, creamy mushroom"[18] plus five others. That's what economists call "product proliferation." ("To grow dramatically you have to introduce new products," says General Foods' Peter Rosow, general manager of the company's dessert division.) It's the battle of the giants for supermarket shelf space. And it works. Today, just five companies use 108 brands of cereal to control over 90 percent of cereal sales.

Such product proliferation requires more and more shelf space. Just since the early 1970s, shelf space devoted to candy and chewing gum has gone up 75 percent; that for dog and cat food, 80 percent.[19] All this means bigger stores, more clerks—costs which must mean rising prices.

And product proliferation, almost by definition, means more processed foods. You can't easily proliferate new fruits. If you want endless varieties of colors, flavors, and shapes, the answer is more and more processing and ever greater use of food colorings and flavorings. Firms like International Flavors and Fragrances are delighted by your product proliferation strategy. They introduce more than 5,000 scents and 2,000 flavors each year, and estimate that three-quarters of what we buy at the supermarket contains either artificial flavors or scents.[20]

The energy cost of all this processing is staggering. We use twice as much energy to process our food as to produce all of our nation's crops, according to the Department of Agriculture.[21] And the energy our food system uses off the farm is rising much faster than that used on the farm. The energy consumed in food processing and transportation doubled between 1960 and 1973.[22]

Food processing generates yet another cost that few of us ever think about—water pollution. Food processing corporations in the United States contribute more waste to water pollution than does our entire human population.[23]

Not only do we pay for this processing, for burgeoning advertising, for bigger stores and the labor to stock them, but we also pay for the "research and development" of these "new" foods. In 1981 just one company—General Foods—budgeted almost $100 million for developing "new" foods. Food corporations tell us that they are responding to our needs, yet rarely do we get a glimpse of how new products really come to be. This description from Foremost-McKesson is a candid exception.

According to a company spokesperson, the first step is a brainstorming session that produces all kinds of crazy ideas. Typically, only 50 out of 200 ideas are chosen for a preliminary technical analysis. These 50 are presented to "focus groups" of sophisticated consumers (formerly called housewives), and their reactions whittle the number down to 10 ideas, leading to perhaps 5 prototype products. Then test marketing brings the selection down to one.

We, the consumers, ultimately foot the bill—even if the product never makes it. Foremost-McKesson, with $3.3 billion in annual sales, spent a whole year and $200,000 developing "Quick 'n Saucy" sloppy joe lunches, then ditched them before they ever hit the supermarket.[24]

While product proliferation has gone wild, with 60,000 brand-name processed food items introduced in ten years, only 100 basic foods still account for three-quarters of the food we eat.[25] Doesn't this suggest that the billions of dollars spent on processing, advertising, and packaging are peripheral to our real diet? Most of us have plenty of variety with a minuscule fraction of what is offered.

The "Don't Just Make It, Serve It" Strategy

More than a third of America's food dollars are spent on food eaten away from home. To profit on this trend, you'll need to buy into the fast food business and spread your stores throughout the nation.

THE IMPACT OF YOUR STRATEGY

Into every city and town enter the fast food outlets, their invasion often fueled by the big money their new conglomerate owners can put behind them. (See Figure 9.) The same food giant that brings us Pillsbury flour brings us Burger King hamburgers. The same conglomerate that feeds our dogs Gaines-Burgers feeds us Burger Chef hamburgers. The same multinational company that brings us Pepsi serves us Pizza Hut pizzas. These giant corporations have driven out of business the roadside diners and Mom and Pop cafés which once served us local specialties and real cooking—soda biscuits, corn bread, and homemade soup. After a tour of over 26 fast food restaurants in a five-mile stretch outside Tucson, MIT nutritionist Judith Wurtman reported: "Despite the number and variety of these places, their menus were relatively similar . . . pancakes, doughnuts, fried or 'char'-broiled meats, hotdogs, fried potatoes, soft drinks and soft ice cream. . . . None served carrots, chopped liver, whole wheat bread, vegetable soup, baked potatoes, yogurt, skim milk, bananas or broccoli."[26] Forced to select foods only from these places, she concluded, "one might begin to feel deprived." Deprived not only in variety but nutritionally, too, because the fast food joints hit us with every nutritional hazard from high fat to high salt to low fiber.

Figure 9. **Who Owns the Fast Food Giants?**	
CHAIN	**OWNER**
Burger King	Pillsbury Co.
Burger Chef	General Foods
Jack-in-the-Box	Ralston Purina
Kentucky Fried Chicken	Heublein Co.
Pizza Hut	PepsiCo., Inc.
Arby's Roast Beef	Royal Crown Cola
A & W Root Beer	United Brands

All but Royal Crown Cola are among the 200 largest industrial corporations in the country.

The "Cut the Calorie" Strategy

Now that you've captured the national market, how can you expand U.S. sales? Our population is growing very slowly. And while some Americans might aspire to owning 20 pairs of shoes, most can eat only three meals a day. Since you can't produce bigger people, you could launch a "fat is beautiful" campaign. No, that might not go over . . . Why not just take the calories out of food? That will appeal to the weight-watchers, and since the food will have no calories, people can eat almost unlimited amounts!

This ingenious sales expansion strategy also increases your profit on each item. For while you can charge the consumer the same price, or even a premium price, manufacturing low-calorie "foods" costs you less. Saccharin is cheaper than sugar. "Light" beer costs less to produce.

THE IMPACT OF YOUR STRATEGY

Diet sodas and low-cal foods are born. By the late 1970s, three diet sodas were among the top ten bestselling soft drinks in America.[27] By using less expensive ingredients but charging the same for diet sodas, soft drink makers are overcharging American consumers $300 million each year, estimates the Center for Science in the Public Interest. No one's added up the overcharges for "light" beer, but buying Michelob Light means paying a higher price for regular Michelob plus water.[28]

The "Salt Plus Soft Drink" Strategy

Now there must be another angle on this. Since people can eat only so much at any given meal, what about *between* meals? Can't you make some progress there? Snack food—that's it! With plenty of salt and sugar. Bet you can't eat just one! (And if more people are eating salty snacks, certainly that must help push up your soft drink and beer sales.)

THE IMPACT OF YOUR STRATEGY

Americans bought almost $4 billion in salty snack foods in 1979. Since 1949, soft drink consumption has increased almost four times.[29]

The Popcorn Institute even arranged for joint popcorn-Coke ads on television in the 1950s.[30] Enormously successful, the campaign led to more and more Americans munching and sipping in front of their TVs. The connection was completed in 1965, when PepsiCo bought Frito-Lay Corp., makers of Fritos corn chips and Lay's potato chips, and the first company to sell $1 billion worth of snack foods in one year.[31]

. . .

So far you've explored five possible strategies to expand sales. The second path to corporate prosperity is to ring up more profit on every item you sell.

The "Up the Price for the Same Ingredients" Strategy

Raw produce and even unprocessed frozen foods aren't so profitable. But if you turn these ingredients into some "new" specialty, you can charge more for them. "The biggest growth and profit potential lies in prepared foods—frozen entrees, vegetables in special sauces and 'ethnic' combinations—products that command higher margins for the producers," *Forbes* advises.[32]

THE IMPACT OF YOUR STRATEGY

Your strategy means higher prices and more and more processing. In fact, that seems to be a recurring theme here! How else can you take macaroni (55 cents a pound), add a bit of "dried cheese" and some chemicals, and convince consumers that Betty Crocker will stretch their food budget with Hamburger Helper? Hamburger Helper costs $2.38 a pound; a few aisles away hamburger itself sells for just $1.50. (By the way, Hamburger Helper is 23 percent sugar, according to *Consumer Reports*.)

The "Reduce Your Costs" Strategy

If you can cut your costs while charging the customer the same price, your profits will rise. To do this, you can use fewer expensive ingredients and more of the cheaper ones, invent cheap flavorings that taste like quality ingredients, and use synthetic flavor enhancers or MSG while reducing the amount of real, expensive ingredients. You can also try to use fewer ingredients which are imported or in unreliable supply. After all, if the prices of basic ingredients are constantly changing, your financial planning becomes a nightmare.

THE IMPACT OF YOUR STRATEGY

Your strategy has led to more salt, more sugar, more artificial flavors. To clam chowder with an almost invisible portion of clam, but the clam flavor enhanced by one whole teaspoon of salt in every cup. To "chocolate" candy bars with little chocolate. (Cocoa prices are unpredictable.) To soft drinks sweetened with saccharin. (Saccharin costs about one-tenth as much as sugar.) And to raspberry and blueberry pies actually made from apples and flavorings. (Berries are too expensive.)

But What's Good for Conglomerated . . .

Your logic as a Conglomerated Foods executive was impeccable. There was only one problem: Virtually *every one* of your sales strategies added one more health risk for everybody who buys your products. More salt, more sugar, more fat, less fiber, more additives (not to mention higher prices and more energy wasted).

Ironically, at least four of our giant food corporations—Borden's, Nestlé, General Foods, and Kellogg's—were started by men whose prime motive was to make people healthier. Dr. Kellogg was a strict vegetarian working in a world-famous sanatorium when the first wheat flakes were developed in 1894.[33] Yet the logic of corporate profit-seeking is so powerful that today Kellogg's boasts two of the most sugared cereals. General Foods, the same company that was launched with Postum by a man who wanted to free us from the evils of caffeine, now sells seven brands of coffee plus Pop Rocks and Dream Whip.[34]

The man I met at the party would respond: "But people *buy* the stuff. And more than ever. So it must be what they want."

While he's right that Americans are buying more and more high-risk foods, this justification for defending the status quo doesn't hold up.

First of all, the same corporations that sell us food also control virtually all of the information bombarding us every day about food. The top 50 food firms control 90 percent of all food advertising on TV. A typical television-watching child is exposed to between 8,500 and 13,000 food and drink commercials each year.[35] Hundreds of times a week Americans hear that nutritionally empty foods will actually make our lives better: Coke "adds life"; Betty Crocker cake mixes help us show our love better; Jell-O helps us "have fun." In other words, health-risky food is continuously promoted as an antidepressant in a society where depression is epidemic. (Valium was the most widely prescribed drug in America in the last decade.)

TV's power of persuasion is well demonstrated by the history of presweetened cereals, disclosed in a Senate hearing on TV advertising aimed at children. When the cereal industry first introduced presweetened cereals, before World War II, consumers vetoed them. Yet now they are among the bestselling cereals. Sidney Margolius testified, "I attribute this [change] largely to the development of television as a very powerful selling medium for children, and I think if we had television before World War II, the housewives would not have been able to reject it [presweetened cereal]."[36]

Almost half of all TV commercials are for cereals, candy, and gum. The sweetest cereals of all—some half sugar—have the highest advertising budgets.[37] TV advertising promotes such low-nutrition foods specifically to children. General Foods' Tang was advertised 24 times on Saturday mornings, but only once each on Sunday and Monday evenings, according to one study. Similarly, Nabisco aired its Cream of Wheat commercial only once—on a Monday evening—but 16 Nabisco commercials for its Chips Ahoy, 12 for its Fig Newtons, and 16 for its Oreo cookies were shown on Saturday mornings during a two-week period.[38] The food corporations know what they are doing. Almost half the time children are successful in influencing what their parents buy, according to surveys by psychologist Joanne Paley Galst. Other studies have shown that the more time children spend watching TV, the stronger their desire for advertised foods—and the more they eat of them.[39]

Needless to say, very few unprocessed foods are advertised.

Does it make sense to say that the risky new American diet is what people *want*, when their choices are so heavily influenced by the corporations which have the most to gain by these choices?

PepsiCo and Nabisco and General Foods also benefit from the fact that although the sugar and salt in high-risk foods are not biologically addictive, as far as we know, they often seem to be psychologically addictive. From my own experience, from the experience of friends, and from dozens and dozens of letters I have received over the years, I'm convinced that "the more you eat, the more you want." (On the other hand, the less you eat, the less you want.)

Whose Convenience?

The explosion of processed foods is frequently explained as a response to the needs of working women. "Working wives haven't the time to cook, and they've got the money to pay a bit more for frozen foods," is how *Forbes* puts it.[40] There is some truth to this, but the presumption is always that cooking with whole foods is more time-consuming than using "convenience" foods. Yet in my own experience this is simply not true, although it takes some extra time and thought to change habits in the beginning. If you know what to have on hand for easy meals, shop in a small whole-foods store (which takes much less time than a supermarket), and lay out your kitchen so that everything, including a few time-saving utensils, is within easy reach, whole-food cooking can be fast and convenient. (I discuss these points in more detail in Book Two.)

Thousands of processed foods and mammoth supermarkets purport to save us time. But do they really? Although the average time spent in preparing food in an urban household fell by half an hour between the 1920s and the late 1960s, we never really gained more free time, according to a *Journal of Home Economics* report.[41] With longer distances to stores, bigger stores, and other complexities of life, an extra 36 minutes each day were used in food marketing and record keeping. We actually lost 6 minutes!

Another reason processed foods have taken over is that they require less imagination. (There are no instructions on a raw potato, says Michael Jacobson, but there are on a box of instant potatoes.) While I believe people are inherently creative, so much in our culture stifles creativity. Uniform images of what is beautiful, acceptable, and of high status bombard us. And the easiest way to be sure that we don't deviate from those images is to buy what is *pre*packaged and *pre*pared. In cooking and eating whole foods, however, we break loose from these standardized images. By taking charge of our food choices, we gain confidence in our judgment and creativity. Feeling less like simple-minded followers of instructions in one area of our lives can help us feel capable of assuming responsibility in unrelated areas.

A Right or a Privilege?

The man I met at the party who claims that Americans are getting what they ask for also was concerned about any attempt to interfere with corporations' "right" to advertise what they want, to whomever they want. "We can't violate their First Amendment rights," he said.

He got me thinking. When they advertise, *are* General Foods and Coca-Cola exercising their First Amendment rights? A lot of Americans would agree that they are. But, I wondered, should we include in the definition of "free speech" the capacity to dominate national advertising? Isn't there something amiss in this definition of rights?

Perhaps the concept of "rights" should be limited to those powers or possibilities which are open to *anyone*. For example, our right to say what we think, to associate with whom we please, and to practice whatever religion we choose. These are rights. But actions such as advertising on TV, open only to those with vast wealth, should be called something else—perhaps "privileges." For how many of us could spend $340 million a year for advertising, as General Foods does? The $20 million spent just to promote one new sugared cereal amounts to more than 40 times the entire budget of the Center for Science in the Public Interest, which has provided vital information for this book.

Ideally, I suppose, there would be no such privileges in a society. If it were impossible for everyone wanting to participate in an action to do so, some would be selected on the basis of merit or some other fair system open equally to everyone. But that is pretty dreamy. So what can we do in the present, when there *are* privileges because some are incomparably more wealthy than others?

We can work to limit the privileges of wealth and to make those with wealth and power accountable to us all.

In campaigns for public office, for example, we have already limited the privileges of wealth by limiting the size of any one contribution. Why not regard access to TV advertising the same way? If we placed a low ceiling on the amount of money that any one company could spend on TV advertising, this would diminish the privileges now held by a handful of giant corporations. As we have seen, it's because the biggest corporations can spend such enormous sums on advertising that they can squeeze out the smaller producers—and then charge us more.

Once we realize that advertising is a privilege, not a right, isn't it reasonable to grant that privilege only on certain conditions? An obvious condition would be that the advertising—with its proven power to influence—not be used to promote products that threaten our well-being. Society has already banned cigarette advertising on TV. There is virtually unanimous opinion in the health community that high-sugar, low-nutrition foods— those which monopolize TV advertising—threaten our health. So why not ban advertising of candy, sugared cereals, soft drinks, and other sweets?

As long as our society rewards wealth by allowing it such

disproportionate ability to influence public opinion, we cannot build a genuine democracy in America. But our vision must extend beyond the need to make advertising responsible to society's well-being. The theme of this book is that we must work toward more democratic decision-making structures governing all aspects of our resource use. Those who process and distribute our food must be accountable, not just to their shareholders but to a broad, representative, elected, and recallable group of Americans whose concerns are wider than expanding sales and increasing profits. Only through such structures can we put into action our choices affecting the health and well-being of our earth and our bodies.

Where Do We Begin?

If this vision of a genuine democracy seems a long way off, we might be tempted to give up. Or we might look around us for signs of change and ask, how can we support them? We might look at ourselves, at our own lives right now. To build a democracy in America, we must redistribute power. We can be part of that redistribution *right now* by taking greater and greater responsibility for our own lives and the problems right in our own communities. I have met and heard from thousands of people across the country who are realizing that the redistribution of power in America begins with them.

Michelle Kamhi is one. She lives in New York City's Upper West Side. In 1978 she decided that if the diet in her son's school lunchroom—Twinkies, white bread, and bologna—was to change, it was up to her. "But how to change things?" she wrote. "Answer: form a committee, however small. Our Nutrition Committee at first consisted of one other concerned parent and myself." From these two parents grew an innovative program on teacher and parent education. Kindergartners tried making their own whole wheat flour and bread. Third-graders, who were studying "desert people," experimented with Middle Eastern delicacies, using beans and whole wheat pita bread. So nutrition entered the classroom not as a negative "don't" but as a positive and tasty "do."

And nutrition entered the lunchroom, too, according to Michelle.

Raw carrot and celery sticks are displacing mushy canned vegetables. Fruits canned in syrup have been banished in favor of fresh fruits on most days; occasionally, unsweetened canned pineapple or applesauce is substituted. No more white bread; only whole wheat is served. And meats containing nitrates/nitrites have been banned, thanks to a school-wide poll of parents.

Nutrition also entered the regular curriculum:

The day my son came home with a vocabulary list of "glucose, maltose, dextrose, fructose, honey, corn syrup, etc.," I could see that my efforts had begun to reap benefits close to home. His second-grade class's assignment was to see how many packaged foods containing hidden sugar he could find at home. This was a perfect example of how teachers were using the information disseminated at the workshops. . . .[42]

Learning about food was obviously a powerful first step for Michelle, and her decision to seize the power she had is changing hundreds, maybe thousands of lives.

I have heard from many other people like Michelle. But first let's tackle the protein debate, because that was where *Diet for a Small Planet*—and the vision it embodies—began over ten years ago.

Protein Myths: A New Look

Note to reader: Protein nutrition research and recommendations shared here were updated in 2021.

Having read of the vast resources we squander to produce meat, you might easily conclude that meat must be indispensable to human well-being. But this just isn't the case. When I first wrote *Diet for a Small Planet* I was fighting two nutritional myths at once. First was the myth that we need scads of protein, the more the better. The second was that meat contains the *best* protein. Combined, these two myths have led millions of people to believe that only by eating lots of meat could they get enough protein.

Protein Mythology

Myth No. 1: Meat contains more protein than any other food.

Fact: Containing 20 to 25 percent protein by weight, meat ranks about in the middle of the protein quantity scale, along with some nuts, cheese, beans, and fish. (See Appendix C for percent of calories from protein in a range of foods.)

Myth No. 2: Eating lots of meat is the only way to get enough protein.

Fact: Americans on average eat roughly twice the protein allowances recommended in *Dietary Guidelines for Americans, 2020–2025*. Thus, most Americans could *completely eliminate* meat, fish, and poultry from their diets and still get the recommended daily allowance of protein from all the other protein-rich foods.

Myth No. 3: Meat is the sole source for certain essential vitamins and minerals.

Fact: Even in the current meat-centered American diet, nonmeat sources provide more than half of our intake of each of the 11 most critical vitamins and minerals, except vitamin B12. And meat is not the sole source of B12; it is also found in dairy products and eggs, and even more abundantly in tempeh, a fermented soy food. Some nutrients, such as iron, tend to be less absorbable by the body when eaten in plant instead of animal foods. Nevertheless, varied plant-centered diets using whole foods, especially if they include dairy products, do not risk deficiencies.

Myth No. 4: Meat has the highest-quality protein of any food.

Fact: The word "quality" is an unscientific term. What is really meant is usability: how much of the protein eaten the body can actually use. The usability of egg and milk protein is greater than that of meat, and the usability of soy protein is about equal to that of meat. All plant foods commonly eaten as sources of protein contain *all* nine essential amino acids. Those eating only plant foods can take care to include nuts, seeds, beans, and lentils—all of which are rich in protein.

Myth No. 5: Plant-centered diets are dull.

Fact: Just compare! There are basically five different kinds of meat and poultry, but 40 to 50 kinds of commonly eaten vegetables; 24 kinds of peas, beans, and lentils; 20 fruits; 12 nuts; and 9 grains. Variety of flavor, of texture, and of color obviously lies in the plant world . . . though your average American restaurant would give you no clue to this fact.

Myth No. 6: Plant foods contain a lot of carbohydrates and therefore are more fattening than meat.

Fact: Plant foods do contain carbohydrates but they generally don't have the fat that meat does. So ounce for ounce, most plant food has either the same calories (bread is an example) or considerably fewer calories than most meats. Many fruits have one-third the calories; cooked beans have one-half; and green vegetables have one-eighth the calories that meat contains. Complex carbohydrates in whole plant foods, grain, vegetables, and fruits can actually aid weight control. Their fiber helps us feel full with fewer calories than do refined or fatty foods.

Myth No. 7: Our meat-centered cuisine is key to a nutritious diet and overall superior to that eaten in lower-income countries.

Fact: For the most part the tragedy of malnutrition in low-income countries is not the poor quality of the diet but the inadequate quantity. Traditional diets in most countries are probably more nutritious and less hazardous than the meat-centered, highly processed diet most Americans eat. The dramatic contrast between our diet and that of the "average" Indian, for example, is not in our higher protein consumption but in the amount of sugar, fat, and refined flour we eat. More and more health professionals are advocating less meat for health reasons, as discussed in the new opening chapter.

As long as we are getting adequate calories by eating a diverse diet and avoiding heavily processed food, we are virtually certain of getting enough protein. This is true because the vast majority of unprocessed foods can supply us with enough protein to meet our daily protein allowance without filling us with too many calories. In Appendix C, I present a simple rule of thumb for judging any food as a protein source. There you'll see that most plant foods excel.

The simplest way to prove the overall point is to propose a diet which most people would consider protein-deprived and ask,

Figure 10. Hypothetical All-Plant-Food Diet (Just to Prove a Point)

BREAKFAST	CALORIES	TOTAL PROTEIN (GRAMS)
1 c. orange juice	110	2
1 c. soy milk	131	8
1 c. cooked oatmeal	158	6
1 oz. sunflower seeds	163	5.5
1½ tbsp. brown sugar	77	0
4 tbsp. raisins, dried seedless	108	1
LUNCH		
3 tbsp. peanut butter	226	9.6
2 slices whole wheat bread	138	7.2
1½ tbsp. honey	128	0.1
½ apple, medium, raw	57	0.3
2 carrots, small, raw	50	1.2
DINNER		
½ c. cooked beans	122	7.6
1 c. cooked brown rice	248	5.5
1 c. chopped kale	33	2.9
4 mushrooms, large, raw	20	2.6
2½ tbsp. oil	300	0
1 c. apple juice	113	0.2
1 banana, medium, raw	105	1.1
SNACK		
2 c. popcorn, cooked in oil	118	1.6
Total:	**~2,400**	**~63**

Totals take us to the male caloric recommendation below from the Department of Health and Human Services (Health.gov). Our point is simply to illustrate the abundance of plant-protein sources.

Female: 1,800 to 2,200 calories and 46 grams of protein

Male: 2,400 to 2,600 calories and 56 grams of protein

does its protein content add up to the allowance recommended? In Figure 10 I have put together such a day's menu. With no meat, no dairy foods, and no protein supplements, it offers plenty of protein without exceeding calorie limits.

Clearly, this day's diet contains more protein, about 63 grams, than the Department of Health and Human Services recommendation of 56 and 46 grams for adult males and females respectively in its *Dietary Guidelines for Americans 2020–2025*.[1] (I am pleased to point out that these guidelines include vegetarian and plant-centered options.) While weight and protein allowances relate to typical moderately active adults, the same pattern would hold true for *any weight* person, since the protein allowance and calorie needs rise proportionately as body weight increases.

Note that my hypothetical diet, while not intentionally protein-packed, is a healthy one. It contains few foods with no or almost-no protein: only sugar, honey, oil, an apple, and apple juice. They comprise only about 25 percent of the calories. The more of these protein-free foods one eats, the more the rest of the diet should be filled with foods with considerable protein.

Most vegetarians eat some dairy products, so in Figure 11 let's look at basically the same day's diet but this time put in two modest portions of dairy foods, one cup of milk and a one-inch cube of cheese. These changes bring the total protein up to about 68 grams—well above the required intake for moderately active adults.

Protein Prudence

First, let's keep in mind that Americans on average eat roughly twice the protein our bodies can use as protein. We use what's "extra" as an energy source or store it as fat.[2]

Next, of course, we are each unique. Scientists point out that even the most prudently arrived-at recommendations—covering 97.5 percent of the population—should not be followed blindly. As we choose foods more consciously for our health and the

Figure 11. Hypothetical Mixed Plant and Dairy Diet (Just to Prove a Point)

BREAKFAST	CALORIES	PROTEIN (GRAMS)
1 c. orange juice	110	2
1 c. cooked oatmeal	158	6
1 oz. sunflower seeds	163	5.5
1½ tbsp. brown sugar	77	0
1 c. milk	149	7.5
4 tbsp. raisins, dried seedless	108	1
LUNCH		
2½ tbsp. peanut butter	226	9.6
2 slices whole wheat bread	138	7.2
1½ tbsp. honey	128	0.1
½ apple, medium, raw	57	0.3
1 carrot, small, raw	25	0.6
DINNER		
1 oz. cheddar cheese (1 inch square)	112	7.0
½ c. cooked beans	122	7.6
1 c. cooked brown rice	248	5.5
1 c. chopped kale	33	2.9
4 mushrooms, large, raw	20	2.6
2 tbsp. oil	240	0
1 c. apple juice	113	0.2
½ banana, medium, raw	52	0.8
SNACK		
1½ c. popcorn, cooked in oil	88	1.2
Total	~2,400	~68

Totals take us to the male caloric recommendation below from the Department of Health and Human Services (Health.gov). Our point is simply to illustrate the abundance of plant-protein sources.

Female: 1,800 to 2,200 calories and 46 grams of protein

Male: 2,400 to 2,600 calories and 56 grams of protein

planet's, we can also become more sensitive to our own well-being. In Part I, "My Journey," I shared how my move to plant-centered eating was liberating—giving me new energy, pleasure, and freedom from preoccupation with my weight.

Note also that protein allowances are calculated for healthy people, and ill health and age, as well as genetic differences, could result in differing needs. Genetic differences may play a role not only in our needs but also in our taste for foods.[3] Physical stress—pain, for example—or psychological stress—even from exam pressure—can push one's protein need up. But, because most of us are eating so much more protein than our bodies can use, we can likely get the "extra" protein needed under stress from what is already in most of our diets.

A World Health Organization report discussed these stress conditions: (1) *heat:* unacclimatized individuals lose nitrogen (a primary component of protein) in heavy sweating; (2) *heavy work:* athletes and others may need additional protein when they are increasing their muscle mass, although the amount needed is not likely to be large (some studies, though not widely substantiated, suggest an additional 25 percent intake over the totals recommended here if you are building muscle mass); (3) *inadequate energy intake:* when overall calorie intake is not adequate, some dietary protein is used for energy and thus is not available to meet protein needs; (4) *infection:* infections, especially acute ones, cause some depletion of body nitrogen due to increased urinary excretion and poor intestinal absorption (as with diarrhea); these losses need to be replaced with additional protein during recovery.

Moreover, pregnant and breast-feeding women need more protein. A pregnant woman is advised to up her protein intake by an additional 14 to 54 grams a day—an increase of 30 to 117 percent.[4] Breast-feeding women are advised to increase protein intake to a comparable level, and in both cases, it is always best to talk with one's physician about what levels are best. With high protein needs, it becomes important to choose protein-rich options, including legumes—beans, peas, and lentils—as well as nuts and seeds.

Only recently did I grasp that too much protein itself can be harmful, taxing the kidneys and increasing one's risk of kidney stones.[5] Plus, if that extra protein is from meat, especially processed meat, health risks increase.[6]

As you cultivate body wisdom—how our diet affects our energy level, general health, and temperament—be aware that some nutritional deficiencies show up as deterioration in the hair, skin, and nails and in the slow healing of wounds. And, because certain nutritional deficiencies negatively affect appetite and choice of foods, just feeling "satisfied" is not enough.

Finally, some are concerned about the protein needs of children. While they do not need more protein in relation to their calorie intake than adults, infants and young children cannot digest certain plant foods as easily as adults. So some care is needed in meeting their needs on a largely plant-food diet. You can turn to the *Dietary Guidelines for Americans, 2020–2025* to find protein recommendations by age.[7] To enrich children's experience of healthy eating, we include children's cookbooks in Appendix A.

Why Do We Need Protein Anyway?

Given protein's importance to the body, perhaps it is not so surprising that a certain mystique grew up around it. We simply cannot live on fats and carbohydrates alone. Protein makes up about one-half of the nonwater components of our bodies. Just as cellulose provides the structural framework of a tree, protein provides the framework for animals. Skin, hair, nails, cartilage, tendons, muscles, and even the organic framework of bones are made up largely of fibrous proteins. Obviously, protein is needed for growth in children. Adults also need it to replace tissues that are continually breaking down and to build tissues, such as hair and nails, which are continually growing.

But talking about the body's need for "protein" is unscientific. What the body needs from food are the building blocks of protein—amino acids, specifically the nine that the body cannot manufacture itself, which are called "essential amino acids." Even more precisely, what the body actually requires are the carbon skeletons of these essential amino acids that the body cannot synthesize, although it can complete them by adding nitrogen, if the nitrogen is available. The body needs many more amino acids than just these nine essential ones. The body can, however, build the others *if* it has sufficient "loose" or extra nitrogen to build with. Thus, what is popularly referred to as the "protein" the body needs to eat are the nine essential amino acids and some extra nitrogen.

The body depends on protein for the myriad of reactions that we call "metabolism." Proteins such as insulin, which regulate metabolic processors, we call "hormones"; other proteins, catalysts of important metabolic reactions, we call "enzymes." In addition, hemoglobin, the critical oxygen-carrying molecule of the blood, is built from protein.

Protein is not only necessary to the basic chemical reactions of life, it is also necessary to maintain the body environment so that these reactions can take place. Protein in the blood helps to prevent excess alkalinity or acidity, maintaining the "body neutrality" essential to normal cellular metabolism. Protein in blood serum participates in regulating the body's water balance, the distribution of fluid on either side of the cell membrane.

Last, and of great importance, new protein synthesis is needed to form antibodies to fight bacterial and viral infections.

BOOK TWO

Plant- and Planet-Centered Cooking *for* Everyone, 50th Anniversary

Preface to the 50th Anniversary Edition

From Anna:

In 1971, the year my mom's *Diet for a Small Planet* was first published, the Pentagon Papers rocked *The New York Times'* front page and the Black Panthers were feeding tens of thousands of children through their free breakfast program. Pleats were popular, and Carole King was belting it out. The Vietnam War raged on. Flash forward fifty years and so much has transpired in politics, fashion, culture—cuisine is no exception.

The 1970s food scene saw the rise of "hippie food," influenced in part by books like the one you have in your hands. It was a cuisine that put its politics on the plate, rejecting food industry spin and ultra-processed products. It focused on whole grains and brown rice, eschewed sugar, and gave birth to relatively new advents in the U.S. culinary scene: the stuff of tempeh and tofu, textured vegetable protein and carob, nutritional yeast and soy grits. And for my mother, among many others, it meant questioning the roots of the corporate-driven, industrialized meat industry and a diet centered around its products—as you've read all about in Book One.

A half century later, the "good food" plate has evolved.

Knitting together social justice with the culinary arts, eater-and-farmer solidarity with the celebration of culturally diverse food traditions, those questioning the processed products lining supermarket shelves have contributed to radical changes in how we eat and what we cook at home. And—no offense to textured vegetable protein—key ingredients have changed, too.

In thinking about the recipes for this 50th anniversary edition, we reflected on all these transformations. We wanted to retain the essence of those early recipes—easy, plant-centered meals—but align them with today's palate (sorry, soy grits!). We also wanted these recipes to reflect how much we've learned about nutrition, particularly the importance of eating foods in their whole state. An astute reader will notice that we've scrapped margarine for butter, egg whites for eggs, low-fat cottage cheese and yogurt for their full-fat forms. For this edition, we also wanted to make the recipes more accessible for readers avoiding all animal products, so we flagged recipes that are either vegan or easily made so with this symbol: ♥

We've also taken a different approach to protein, again reflecting all that we've learned. Fifty years ago, many saw my mother's idea that we could get more than enough protein from a diet without animals as heretical. In fact, it was so threatening to the meat industry that the National Cattlemen's Beef Association hired nutritionists to prove her recipes inedible. Today, as you read in her new introduction, "Our Choice, Our Power," there is now a long history of proven plant-centered health. Because of all we now know about how easy it is to meet our protein needs without meat—no need for complicated complementary protein combinations—recipes were changed to reflect the new understanding, as my mom explains in the next section.

While it's increasingly common knowledge that a plant-centered diet can provide more than enough protein, there's still work to do to mainstream that message. A friend was recounting a recent trip to a make-your-own salad restaurant. After ordering hers—kale, carrots, roasted beets, tomatoes, avocado, quinoa, chickpeas, edamame, black beans—the person taking the order asked, "Would you like any protein with that?" My friend laughed (through her COVID-19 mask) and told her it already had ample! So, yes, there is still plenty of work to do to help people understand that vegetarian diets can provide all the nutrients we need. We hope this book continues to play a part in doing so.

For those of you with dog-eared copies of *Diet*, you may notice recipes that were left on the editing room floor or catch the big changes in the ones we kept. We hope you enjoy all the new flavors you find here—and revisit your yellowed original for your favorite classics!

As we thought about celebrating this anniversary milestone, we also wanted to invite contributions from some of the countless chefs and social justice activists transforming our plates with inspired creations, pulling from culinary traditions around the world. These are among the growing chorus of chefs speaking out for the inherent wellness of Indigenous diets, from Mesoamerican cuisine to Native American dishes. These contributors also reflect the growing efforts to reclaim incredibly nutritious, biodiverse foods that have long been denigrated, foods like amaranth from Mexico, wild greens from North America, teff from Ethiopia and Eritrea, millet from West Africa, and the list goes on. Many of these traditional foods had long been condemned by either colonizers or those with economic interest in pushing commodities for export markets. In the recipes that follow, we tried to reflect the incredible variety and bounty of the plant kingdom—and the political nature of the revival of such diversity.

As we invited these chefs' contributions, re-developed the classic recipes, and introduced new ones, we kept the *Diet for a Small Planet* spirit. The recipe development in the earlier editions of this book was always collaborative: Many headnotes referenced friends and readers who contributed ideas and tweaks. In that spirit, we sought out a recipe developer who shared our food values and were so pleased Wendy Lopez came on board and brought her masterful touch and creative vision. Along with our appreciation for Wendy, we are immensely grateful for the chefs who contributed—and for all those who share our belief that access to good, healthy food, and the means to procure it, should be a basic right for all.

The original *Diet for a Small Planet* was all about putting knowledge in your hands, including, when it came to the recipes, knowledge about how to cook your own food. The original recipes were intentionally approachable, designed with a you-can-do-it attitude, crafted from the belief that recipes should inspire and empower, not intimidate. So are these. To be honest, I always thought it was ironic that my mother wrote a cookbook—with actual recipes!—because she rarely follows them. She is the master of taking what's in the fridge, especially leftovers, and whipping them into delicious meals. As you explore, tap your intuition to play fast and loose with the instructions, particularly as you swap ingredients with what you have on hand.

As Wendy and I worked on these recipes and connected with the chef contributors, I thought about the words of a food company executive I heard at an industry conference many years ago. To a packed audience of fellow business leaders, he shared his vision: a future, he said, where consumers would consider it just as absurd to sew their own jeans as it would be to cook their own food. I consider every one of you home cooks, every chef and food educator, to be doing your part in thwarting the dreams of that food industry executive.

From Frances:

I am thrilled that the 50th anniversary gives us the opportunity to offer recipes with many new delights—all in keeping with the book's original spirit.

When I was growing up, my brother and I used to say that although our mother was no gourmet cook, she was perhaps the best short-order cook in the world. Judging from the reaction to the first edition of this book, I'd say that a lot of people have the same approach to cooking as my mom. They like recipes that they can whip up from memory, vary according to what they have on hand, and get on the table in a hurry, but that have a flair of originality to them. This is certainly the way I cook most of the time, except for those special meals for friends when some extra preparation and care add to the pleasure of the occasion.

If you've read earlier editions, you might recall my emphasis on "complementary protein"—the recommendation that we choose foods in the same meal, or same day, whose amino acid patterns "complement" each other so our bodies get the most usable protein. I loved the idea of being a "chemist in the kitchen" when making these combos. However, over the decades, science has progressed, and now we know that we can eliminate that concern altogether. In 2019, scientists at the University of Paris and Stanford clarified that if we eat a variety of foods, the "amount and proportions of amino acids consumed by vegetarians and vegans are typically more than sufficient."[1] End of story.

More generally, in focusing on how to get protein without meat in earlier editions, I fear I reinforced an unnecessary preoccupation with protein. So, in this 50th anniversary edition, we want to emphasize how easy it is to get the protein we need from plant-centered sources. Freed from that concern, you'll notice simplified recipes without ingredients like instant milk powder, sesame seeds—there were a lot of sesame seeds in the original!—and soy flour: ingredients that were added just for their protein. Keen-eyed readers will also notice we've changed section names, dropping Baked-In Protein and Protein for Dessert for simplified sections, like Appetizers and Sides, Main Dishes, and so on.

As we appreciate that many plant foods contain significant grams of protein and most foods provide some protein—even green vegetables—we gain much more flexibility in meal planning. We no longer feel the need to pack scads of protein into a dish filled with cheese and eggs. We can use more vegetables, grains, and fruit. We achieve greater variety and lighter meals.

Once meat is no longer the center of the menu, anything goes. We're free. In planning menus, we can respond to our own appetites. In my family, what has come to feel most natural is a one-dish meal into which we put our care and imagination, accompanied by a side dish such as salad or roasted vegetables and, often, good, hearty bread.

Letting go of the meat-starch-vegetable formula and experimenting with new foods was, for me, satisfying in yet another way. I became more experimental. I recall the first non-meat dinner party I ever gave, for which I made a Walnut Cheddar Loaf (page 304). Never too confident about my cooking, I was comforted by the thought that at least no one would be comparing my dish with Julia Child's version—because there wasn't one! After you become comfortable with the ingredients, you will become a creator, taking foods that are in season and on hand and creating your own favorites.

For those for whom moving meat out of the center of your plate is new, let me offer one important caveat I also included in the first edition of this book: Don't expect yourself to change overnight. Maybe start with one new meal a week or even one new ingredient; gradually build up a repertoire of dishes you enjoy. Suddenly changing lifelong habits of any kind does not strike me as very realistic or even desirable, however great the revelation. At least, that is not the way it has worked for me.

In Book One, as I explained, I am advocating a return to the plant-centered diets on which our bodies evolved—a diet in which animal foods play a supplemental role, if any at all. This shift is especially critical in countries where levels of meat consumption have run wildly off course. (I'm looking at you, USA.) While I personally don't eat meat for the reasons I lay out in this book, I'm aware that for cultural, spiritual, and geographic reasons, many communities around the world include animal foods in their diets. So my personal preference for a completely meatless diet does not mean I feel everyone must eschew all meat, dairy, and seafood to embrace plant- and planet-centered eating. While the recipes you'll find here are indeed meatless, they're for everyone. They are meant to spark or further stoke what I hope is a lifelong passion for the bounty and pleasure of plant foods, whether you choose to add animal proteins into your diet or not. There is room here for everyone.

In 1971, I had to assure readers that plant protein was also a less expensive option. Today, it is widely appreciated that plant sources of protein—especially peas, beans, lentils, and sunflower seeds, for example—are our best protein bargains. (See Appendix D for price comparisons.)

One of the other pushbacks I addressed in the early editions of this book is that cooking whole foods takes too much time. I thought about this as I reflected on my experience writing the original book and its recipes. For most of my children's early years, I was a single mom, working full-time. Figuring out shortcuts for meals was a key part of keeping my family healthy. But consider that when my kids were young—the late 1970s and early '80s—the country was a different place: I could work one job, with reasonable hours, and still have enough to buy a single-family home and put food on our table. Today it's much harder for most families to get by on one salary—and many have to take on two, sometimes even three jobs to make ends meet, particularly as health care, education, and housing costs have skyrocketed while wages have stagnated.

And it's not just how much more time we spend at work; it's also the time it takes for many of us to access healthy food options. Many don't have nearby grocery stores well stocked with fresh food, let alone farmers' markets to access just-picked produce. So, as I pen these pages, I realize just how much time has become a real barrier: We have less of it to spend cooking. For this reason any conversation about food, cooking, and what we eat must always be tied to the bigger conversation about achieving equity in our society, as found in the opening chapters.

Having acknowledged the time challenge, I also have learned that plant-centered cooking can be quick. And the biggest draw for me was the discovery that within the plant world lies a vast range of color, texture, taste, aroma, combination, and seasoning possibilities. What fun to break free!

Part I

Kitchen Tips for Eating Well on a Small Planet

Keeping in mind the pressures on our time, in this edition we streamlined ingredients and prep for many of the recipes. I've also found these time-saving tips to be incredibly helpful as I navigate my own meals: Keep the basics on hand, invest in time-saving equipment, cook extra for the freezer, and love your leftovers.

What to Have on Hand

There are probably certain foods that you always have, that you shop for automatically because you know that, with these basic ingredients, you can always produce a good meal. As you begin to change your eating habits, your buying and stocking habits will change, too. To help, we share some suggestions of items that we are almost never without. Of course, in each of these categories there are many more possibilities, but with these you could make most of the recipes in this book. (You might have to substitute a little, but that is part of the fun!)

We are not suggesting you go out and buy a lot of new ingredients all at once. To get started, find one recipe that looks good. Buy any ingredient you don't already have, then try discovering all the other possibilities for it. You'll be amazed at the variety that is possible when cooking with plants.

For some of the basics, we suggest stocking up on a few different kinds, ranging from the more expensive (use sparingly!) to the more affordable (use with abandon!). This is one small way to keep your food costs down as you stock up. Another is to take your wasted food seriously: As I mentioned earlier in the book, the typical family of four in the United States wastes about $1,800 worth of food every year.[1] Reducing our food waste isn't just good for the planet—it is a money-saving proposition!

A note on organic foods: The original *Diet for a Small Planet* was published three decades before the U.S. Department of Agriculture (USDA) developed an official definition for organic food, a certification that prohibits the use of genetically modified organisms (GMOs), synthetic fertilizer, and nearly all synthetic pesticides. Even back then, farmers were already rejecting the advent of chemical agriculture out of concerns about human health and harm to ecosystems from a mounting arsenal of pesticides born in World War II. (To be clear, "pesticide" might sound like it's just about "pests," but it's an umbrella term for herbicides, insecticides, fungicides, and more—any substance used for "preventing, destroying, repelling, or mitigating any pest.")[2]

Fifty years ago, the threats from pesticides were already becoming clear; since then we've learned so much more. We have vast evidence of the dramatic impact of chemical farming on our ecosystems, including devastating populations of those all-important pollinators.[3] We now know that many of the pesticides regularly used on nonorganic crops are associated with serious health harms, increasing the risk of certain cancers, and impacting hormonal systems, fertility, and more.[4] Many pesticides have also been tied to neurotoxicity, particularly impacting children's brain development.[5] While most of the research on health impacts has focused on people who are highly exposed to pesticides—like farmers and farmworkers or agricultural communities exposed especially by pesticide drift[6]—a growing body of data is showing that organic diets can also reduce eaters' risk for a range of health problems from cancer to infertility.[7]

All of which is to say, seek out organic products when and where you can. Look for the USDA organic seal or shop at farmers' markets where you can ask farmers directly about whether they use toxic pesticides. Unfortunately, for many of us it's still hard (sometimes impossible!) to find organic options, but don't let that stop you from a diet rich in fruits and vegetables, whether or not they're organic.

You can use this knowledge about the very real, manifold benefits of organic farming—including that no one should be exposed to toxic pesticides to grow food for our plates—to inspire others to join the chorus calling for policies that will support farmers who transition to nonchemical farming and make organic food accessible for all.

PASTA, RICE, AND OTHER CEREAL GRAINS

One of the wonderful changes I've witnessed in 50 years is the flourishing of whole grains in mainstream markets in the United States. Here are some suggestions from the world of grains:

• *Rice (brown, basmati, jasmine).* I like to have a variety of rice on hand, but especially short grain brown rice. *Please see note on next page about rice prep.*

• *Bulgur.* Great as breakfast cereal, dinner grain, soup thickener, and cold salad with vegetables, bulgur's nutty flavor is enhanced by sautéing before cooking.

• *Couscous.* Originating in North Africa, couscous is a type of pasta made from semolina, or coarsely ground durum wheat. It's quick-cooking and makes a good complement to stir-fried vegetables and a wonderful addition to salads.

• *Farro.* Another delicious grain. You'll want to soak the whole-grain variety overnight or choose semi-pearled. It's got great flavor and chewiness.

• *Millet.* A wonderfully nutritious grain, millet is considered one of the first domesticated cereal grains in the world. It's perfect for adding crunch (and nutrition) to muffins, pancakes, and waffles.

• *Quinoa.* Technically a seed, quinoa is often grouped with cereals from a culinary standpoint. It was traditionally cultivated by Indigenous communities across the Andean region of South America. A highly nutritious crop, quinoa holds spiritual and medicinal importance as well. Today, the Andean plant, high in fiber and protein, has had a resurgence.

Preparing your rice. In 2012, *Consumer Reports* released an alarming study about the levels of inorganic arsenic found in rice grown in the United States, noting the crop absorbs both organic and inorganic arsenic more effectively than many other plants. To protect yourself, *Consumer Reports* recommends rinsing your rice thoroughly in a strainer until the water runs clear and limiting the amount of rice milk, rice crackers, and other rice-based products you consume. A 2014 follow-up noted that millet, quinoa, and buckwheat are all low in arsenic and great alternatives. Among the rice varieties analyzed, basmati rice from California and most types of sushi rices, including those from the United States, rated half as high in arsenic residues as most other types.[8] The arsenic findings were particularly worrisome because even small amounts of inorganic arsenic can increase risk of certain cancers and heart disease, among other health concerns. While there are many forms of arsenic, and while organic arsenic is generally considered to be less toxic, it can convert to inorganic arsenic in nature. In some places, high levels in water are a result of naturally occurring inorganic arsenic in rock that leaches into drinking water or groundwater used for irrigation. Poultry waste applied as fertilizer is another possible source—for decades, poultry feed commonly contained organic arsenic as a growth promoter, which converted to inorganic arsenic in poultry manure used as fertilizer. And though inorganic arsenic-based pesticides were banned in the 1980s, arsenic residues from those sources can also still be found in soils today.

FLOURS

• *Whole-wheat flour.* Whole-wheat flour is, like it sounds, made with the whole wheat kernel: the endosperm, bran (the kernel's exterior), and germ (a part of the inner seed). This is why whole-wheat flour provides more protein as well as fiber and nutrients (and flavor, too) than all-purpose—and why the original *Diet* included only whole-wheat flour in its recipes.

• *All-purpose flour.* All-purpose flour is made by removing the bran and germ, making a lighter (and far less nutritious) flour. You can replace some all-purpose flour with whole wheat. But because whole-wheat flour is a little tricky to work with—in general, a one-for-one substitution with whole wheat will make for denser baked goods—we like Mark Bittman's rule of thumb: You can substitute up to half of a recipe's all-purpose flour with whole wheat without radically changing the finished product. (In fact, it's usually better.)

• *Almond, amaranth, and other alternative flours.* Since *Diet* was published, a world of new flours is more commonly available. Try experimenting with them to discover ones you particularly enjoy. We like using almond flour in pancakes, biscuits, and cookies. Amaranth flour is a great gluten-free alternative to whole-wheat flour.

A note on wheat: The industrialization of wheat in the mid-19th century meant wheat flour could last longer on your shelf—and was whiter, much whiter. But the industrial milling process separates wheat's germ and bran, and what's left behind in white flour is devoid of most of the nutrients and the beneficial synergy between micronutrients and fiber naturally found in wheat. The industrialization of wheat also meant the loss of community-based wheat processing. As Community Grains founder Bob Klein has noted, in the middle of the 19th century, 22,000 stone flour mills were producing wheat flour for communities across the country; that number has dropped to just 166 mills. Much of the flour branded today as "whole wheat," Klein says, is "essentially white flour with some germ and bran mixed back in."[9] When choosing your wheat flours, seek out producers committed to real whole grain, and look for organic certified, too. As of this writing, many wheat growers across the United States still use glyphosate—an herbicide classified as a probable human carcinogen by the International Agency for Research on Cancer—just before harvest to speed up the drying process, a practice that started several decades ago. Organic-certified wheat growers don't.[10]

NUTS AND SEEDS

• *Sunflower and sesame seeds.* Wonderful additions in salads, casseroles, stuffing, or granola, or mixed with peanuts for snacking. Toast lightly to bring out the flavor.

• *Peanuts and peanut butter.* Both are great in bean croquettes, casseroles, salads, cookies, candy, vegetable sauce for pasta, and curries.

• *Almonds, cashews, walnuts.* A healthy source of fiber, fat, and protein, nuts are great to have on hand for many dishes. If you're not going to use right away, store in the freezer or fridge.

• *Pine nuts.* Delicious in pesto or sprinkled on top of salads.

• And so many more—have your favorites on hand for a healthy addition to salads.

LEGUMES

• *Green, brown, red, or yellow lentils.* Wonderful for soups, curries, sauces, and—with cooked grain—in patties.

• *Black lentils.* This variety is especially good for salads.

• *Black beans.* My favorite for tacos and soups.

• *Chickpeas/garbanzo beans.* Good for soups and salads.

• And so many more to try—including lima beans, white beans, and black-eyed peas.

FATS

• *Butter.* At the time the original *Diet* was published, nutritionists were warning about the saturated fats found in butter. Today, we understand that while more than two-thirds of us consume about 70 percent more than the recommended limit for saturated fats, we don't have to fear butter![11] In this edition's recipes, we replaced the margarine with either butter or oil. Eating these healthy recipes, we needn't worry about too much saturated fat.

• *Oils.* For a well-stocked kitchen, we recommend having on hand a range of oils, including vegetable oils with a high smoke or burn point such as canola or grapeseed. These are well suited for cooking at high heat. We also recommend refined olive oil for cooking and roasting, and a more flavorful extra-virgin olive oil for dressings. (Note: Where these recipes call for oil, use the vegetable oil of your choice.)

Neutral oils, e.g., grapeseed, avocado, canola, corn
Olive oil and *extra-virgin olive oil*
Oils for flavor, e.g., coconut, peanut, or toasted sesame

FRESH FOODS AND CITRUS

• *Carrots.* In carrot and onion soup, grain dishes, salad, curries.

• *Onions.* Key for soups, casseroles, curries, and so much more.

• *Potatoes.* In soups, salads, casseroles, pancakes.

• *Garlic.* Another key ingredient to always have on hand.

• *Lemons.* A key to many recipes, lemon zest and juice bring out flavor.

CANNED FOODS

• *Kidney beans, black beans, and chickpeas.* Great to have on hand when you're in a rush or have a last-minute meal idea.

• *Crushed whole tomatoes.* For soups and casseroles.

• *Coconut milk.* Add to rice for a flavor boost and use in curries.

FREEZER FOODS

• *Leftover beans.* I like to cook more than the recipe calls for and freeze the rest for quick meals. You can put cooked and cooled beans in a small freezer-safe storage bag and lay them flat in your freezer.

• *Pita, tortillas, whole-grain bread.* Bread keeps well in the freezer and, when toasted, tastes fresh for any meal.

• *Frozen corn, chopped spinach, and peas.* All are lovely ways to add color, taste, and nutrition to soups, stews, salads, and more.

HERBS

You can substitute fresh herbs for dried herbs, or vice versa, by using this rule of thumb: For every teaspoon of dried herbs, use roughly one tablespoon of fresh. Taste as you go; herbs vary greatly in flavor.

DAIRY PRODUCTS AND PLANT-BASED DAIRY ALTERNATIVES

• *Yogurt.* A dressing for fruit salad and ingredient in smoothies, cold summer blender soups, and sauces.

• *Buttermilk.* You can make your own by adding a tablespoon of lemon juice for each cup of whole milk.

• *Cheese.* Less is more when it comes to cheese. Having a good Parmesan is a delectable addition to many meals, and a little goes a long way. Rinds can be used when making stock.

• *Ricotta cheese.* The basis of sauces, salad dressings, casseroles, and pancake filling—or simply a scrumptious spread on bread.

• *Plant-based alternatives.* Since *Diet* was published, the world of plant-based alternatives to milk, butter, and cheeses has flourished—and gotten a lot better tasting! These products are not all created equal: Some are much healthier—and more palate-pleasing—than others, so investigate ingredients lists, and don't let one dud stop you from exploring the vast variety of new options out there.

SOY FOODS

When *Diet* was first published, soy foods like tofu and tempeh were just gaining popularity in the United States, many, many millennia after soybeans were first enjoyed in what is modern-day China, Japan, and Korea. (Some date the origins of the first domestication of soy as far back as 7000 B.C.) Today, soybean products—from soy milk to tofu, tempeh, and miso—can easily be found in most U.S. supermarkets.

• *Tofu.* With the consistency of firm custard, tofu readily absorbs the seasonings and flavors with which it is cooked. Uncooked, silken tofu can be blended for salad dressings and sauces. Firm tofu is good for sautéing with vegetables and seasonings.

• *Tempeh.* Fermented soy curd, tempeh is tasty in stews or sandwiches.

• *Miso.* Made by fermenting a combination of soybeans with rice, wheat, and/or barley. We love keeping miso on hand to add flavor to soups and sauces. You'll find a variety of misos—white is slightly sweet; red has a stronger umami pop and is great for heartier dishes; experiment to suit your taste buds. Stored in a tightly sealed container in the refrigerator, miso is at its best flavor within three months, but can be stored and used even longer.

• *Tamari and soy sauce.* Both tamari and soy sauce are made from fermented soybeans. Tamari is a little thicker, less salty, and contains less wheat than soy sauce. Some tamari brands are even certified gluten-free, so for those with a gluten intolerance, it's a great option.

SUGARS

• *Raw cane sugar, brown sugar, and granulated white sugar.* All are made from sugarcane, the differences a reflection of how refined they are. We like to have some of each in stock, but use them all sparingly!

• *Molasses.* We also like to have molasses (also made from sugarcane) for whenever its strong flavor is just what's needed.

• *Maple syrup.* Adds rich flavor to dishes that call for it—and is an essential topping for breakfast favorites like pancakes, waffles, and French toast.

SALT

We recommend stocking up on several different kinds of salts, from expensive and high-flavor to cheap, everyday options. Have on hand a fine salt to use in water for blanching vegetables or boiling pasta. In addition:

• *Sea salt.* For roasting vegetables and adding to soups and sautés.

• *Flavorful flaky sea salt.* For sprinkling on top of casseroles, salads, or soups as a finishing touch, like Maldon.

A note on salt: Most of us are consuming way too much of it, but the biggest source in our diets is from fast food, fast casual dining, and ultra-processed foods—not from our kitchens. Processed meats (fake or real) are another big source of sodium. Cooking for ourselves is key to reducing our sodium intake.

INTENTIONAL LEFTOVERS

When you are exhausted after a long day, it's nice to just take a delicious dish out of the refrigerator, heat, and serve. That's why I embrace the habit of preparing more than we will eat in one meal and freezing the rest (in containers that can go right into the oven, if appropriate). It gives me the option to have our favorite foods ready for us when we are too tired to cook. You can cook extra beans and store them in the freezer to be added later to soups, casseroles, or salads. Extra cooked grain keeps well for a couple of days in the refrigerator. (If it hardens a bit, add a little water when you reheat it.)

Keeping It All Within Reach

Preparation time is not just how long something takes to cook; it's getting the ingredients to the cooking stage, too. That's why the organization of your kitchen can help. Kitchen counters and open shelves can be beautiful and handy storage areas for your whole foods. Flours, seeds, beans, lentils, and even pasta can be kept within easy reach. Large glass jars with tight-fitting lids are a nice storage option; seeing ingredients can spur the imagination. I often end up tossing in a little of something that I had not planned to, just because I see it. I keep herbs and spices in easy reach on a little shelf above my stove. Measuring utensils can also be in easy reach of your basic ingredients. I've found that even small shifts in my kitchen have helped inspire me to get cooking—and make it easy for me when I do.

Helpful Kitchen Tools

No-hassle cooking with plant foods requires some basic tools; the investment pays off with a greater ease of cooking. Almost every kitchen tool we suggest will last years, some even a lifetime! Note that you don't have to refit your kitchen! While handy, virtually none of these tools is essential—except a good knife, for sure, and for some recipes, a blender.

Mortar and pestle. You may not use yours a lot, but when you need it, nothing else achieves the same texture as does pounding ingredients together in a mortar and pestle.

Garlic press. You'll never again have the frustration of trying to mince a tiny clove of garlic with a knife. Just put the cloves in and squeeze.

Citrus squeezer. This handy device helps get all the juice out of your citrus. They're made in sizes for lemons, limes, and oranges, but you can make the lemon squeezer work for all.

Mandoline. This is a godsend for creating perfectly sliced vegetables, but it can be dangerous. You need to be careful not to trim off the tip of a finger! Used with care, this slicing wonder is great for cutting vegetables into nice, even sizes. It works especially well with carrots, potatoes, and zucchini, and for shredding cabbage for slaws.

Zester. There is no better way to get the flavorful zest off lemons, limes, and oranges. A number of recipes you find here call for lemon zest—a great way to add zing to a dish.

A good knife. A good knife is another great investment. As it dulls, you can get it professionally sharpened at many farmers' markets or kitchen supply stores. What kind you will enjoy most is a personal preference. My culinary life changed when I bought my first Japanese *nakiri* knife. Designed for cutting vegetables, it resembles a thin, light meat cleaver. The other knives we have are nothing to write home about. Investing in at least one good knife will help you enjoy slicing and dicing, which makes a world of difference for everyday plant-centered cooking.

Salad spinner. Essential for all those salads you're going to make!

Parchment paper. We love using parchment paper for baking and roasting vegetables. It prevents all your yummy food from sticking to your roasting and cake pans. (Again, another timesaver: You don't have to break a sweat scrubbing crusted food off your baking sheets.)

Wok. Woks are our go-to for stir-fries. They're nice to have but, depending on your cooking style, not essential; a large sauté pan can work just as well.

Immersion blender. This handheld device easily turns any foods you want to purée into a creamy wonder!

High-speed blender. There wasn't a single smoothie recipe in the original *Diet*. Now you can find entire books of smoothie recipes! (We include three yummy ones submitted by readers in this edition.) For smoothies—and many sauces—a powerful blender is key.

Small blender. For many dressings and sauces, a small blender is much easier to work with (and to clean) than a larger blender or food processor. If you've got the budget and space, this is another nice-to-have appliance.

Electric pressure cooker. Although I still swear by my stovetop pressure cooker, I know they are history. Anna and many of my friends use the handier electric pots for cooking grains, legumes, and soups. I admit, the convenience of plugging them in, turning them on, and walking away has appeal, and to save money they are easy to find secondhand, too.

Rice cooker. If you have a stovetop pressure cooker or an electric one (see above), you don't necessarily need a separate rice cooker, but for big meals that include rice with beans or stews, for instance, having both can be a time-saver—cooking away at the same time. Like with an electric pressure cooker, you can walk away: When finished, it will turn off automatically and keep your rice warm.

Stand mixer and/or hand mixer. A stand mixer is also not cheap, and it takes up room, but depending on how much baking you do, it's really useful. We don't have a lot of recipes in this book that require it, but if you are interested in expanding your home-cooking game to include breads and more baking, it's good to have. If you don't have a stand mixer, a hand mixer for whipping eggs, cream, and butter works, too.

Part II

Recipes—
Discovering the Pleasures
in Planet-Centered Eating

Appetizers AND Sides

Most of these recipes can be served either before a meal or as a side dish. Some are particularly easy to scale up for parties: Louisa's Mirza Ghasemi (eggplant spread, page 200), the Spicy Hummus (page 197), and Cheesy Pinto Bean Dip (page 198) all make great dishes to serve to guests.

Spicy Hummus

4 servings

A hummus recipe is a wonderful, versatile dish. Pair it with pita bread, use it on sandwiches, or add it to salads for a nice protein punch. This is a creamy and flavorful version of the classic with a bit of a kick.

1½ cups cooked chickpeas, or one 15-ounce can, rinsed and drained
2 cloves garlic
2 tablespoons tahini
½ tablespoon chili paste (sambal oelek)

Juice of 1 lemon
½ teaspoon salt
2 ice cubes
Extra-virgin olive oil, toasted sesame seeds, and chopped fresh herbs for topping

Pour the chickpeas into a bowl filled with water and rub them together so the skins come off. This will help create a creamier texture. Drain, discard the skins, add the peeled chickpeas to a food processor or small blender, and pulse for a few seconds. Add the garlic, tahini, chili paste, lemon juice, salt, and ice cubes and continue pulsing for 3 to 4 minutes, until you get a smooth, creamy texture. Enjoy it topped with olive oil, toasted sesame seeds, and fresh herbs. We love it served with pita triangles and carrot sticks.

Cheesy Pinto Bean Dip

4 servings

Easily made 🥬 by omitting the cheese

This makes for a hearty appetizer, but you can also serve it with rice, beans, tortillas, and/or eggs for a more complete meal.

1½ cups cooked pinto beans, or one 15-ounce can, rinsed and drained

½ teaspoon each of chili powder, garlic powder, and cumin

½ teaspoon salt

1 tablespoon oil

¼ cup shredded cheddar or jack cheese

Chopped fresh cilantro and pickled jalapeño pepper for topping

In a food processor, pulse the beans with the spices, salt, and 2 tablespoons water until puréed. In a pan, heat the oil, add the puréed beans, and cook for 1 to 2 minutes, until warmed through. Sprinkle the cheese over the beans, let it melt, then top with chopped cilantro and pickled jalapeños and enjoy with tortilla chips or tostadas.

Garlic and Leek Ricotta Spread

4 servings

New for this edition, this rich and savory spread is delicious atop toasted bread and served alongside a bowl of greens. Great as an appetizer for a small gathering or for a special lunch.

1 small head of garlic
Olive oil
1 medium leek (white and light green parts only), rinsed well and roughly chopped

1½ teaspoons tamari
1 cup ricotta cheese
Salt and freshly ground black pepper

Preheat the oven to 400°F. Cut and discard about ¼ inch from the top of the garlic head, exposing the cloves. Place the garlic on a sheet of aluminum foil and drizzle 1 teaspoon oil over the exposed head. Wrap it with the foil and bake for 25 minutes.

While the garlic is roasting, heat a pan with 1 tablespoon oil and add the leeks. Sauté for 3 to 4 minutes until the leeks are translucent, then add the tamari and cook until browned. Place the ricotta in a serving bowl.

Once the garlic is done roasting, allow it to cool and then squeeze the garlic cloves from their skins into a small bowl and mash them with a fork. Discard the skins. Mix the smashed garlic along with about half of the sautéed leeks into the bowl with the ricotta. Top with the remaining leeks and sprinkle with salt and pepper to taste.

Louisa's Mirza Ghasemi
(Garlicky Eggplant and Tomato Spread)

4 to 6 servings

Ochre-hued mirza ghasemi is a singing combination of flavors derived from charred eggplant, tomatoes, turmeric, whisked eggs, and an abundance of garlic and lemon. Slathered on flatbread or spooned over grains, it makes for a quick, satisfying meal. The spread is stellar when served warm but can also be enjoyed cold or at room temperature.
—Louisa Shafia

3 tablespoons olive oil, plus more as needed

1 large eggplant (1 pound), sliced in half lengthwise

3 medium to large tomatoes (1½ pounds), diced, or one 16-ounce can of crushed tomatoes

6 cloves garlic, minced

2 tablespoons tomato paste

½ teaspoon ground turmeric

2 eggs, whisked

3 tablespoons freshly squeezed lemon juice

Salt and black pepper

Preheat the oven to 350°F. Generously grease a baking sheet with olive oil.

Lay both eggplant halves facedown on the baking sheet, score the skin with a fork, and bake for about 1 hour, until very tender. Set aside to cool, then scoop out the flesh and coarsely chop it.

Heat the oil in a large, deep skillet over medium heat and add the tomatoes, eggplant, garlic, tomato paste, and turmeric. Simmer, stirring occasionally, for 10 minutes, until the tomatoes are softened and the flavors of the garlic and turmeric have mellowed.

Whisk about 1 cup of the warm vegetables into the eggs. Add the mixture back into the skillet and return it to a simmer, stirring occasionally, for about 20 minutes, until the eggs are fully cooked. Remove from the heat and stir in the lemon juice. Season with salt and pepper and transfer to a serving bowl. Serve warm, topped with a glug of olive oil.

—From *The New Persian Kitchen* by Louisa Shafia

Yasmin's Eggplant and Feta Kefte

4 to 6 servings

The Palestinian kitchen is filled with a variety of meat, fish, and vegetable kefte, which are balls of seasonal ingredients that are molded, stuffed, baked, or fried. This is my interpretation of a vegetarian kefte, using eggplants married with fragrant fresh herbs and tangy white cheese. These are perfect for picnics and keep well for a few days in the fridge.
—Yasmin Khan

1⅓ pounds eggplants (about 2 medium ones), chopped into ¼-inch squares

3 tablespoons olive oil or any neutral oil, plus more for greasing

Sea salt and freshly ground black pepper

1⅓ cups bulgur

½ teaspoon cumin seeds

½ teaspoon coriander seeds

1 clove garlic, finely chopped

3 tablespoons finely chopped fresh mint leaves

3½ tablespoons finely chopped fresh parsley leaves

6 ounces feta cheese, crumbled

⅓ cup sunflower and pumpkin seeds

2 eggs, lightly beaten

Zest of 1 lemon

Preheat the oven to 400°F. Place the eggplant pieces on a baking sheet and drizzle with the oil and ½ teaspoon salt. Use your hands to mix everything, then roast for 25 minutes, or until soft. Transfer to a large mixing bowl and let cool. Increase the oven temperature to 425°F.

Bring a saucepan of water to a boil, add the bulgur, reduce heat, and cook for 15 minutes. Drain, rinse with cold water, drain well again, and add the bulgur to the eggplant.

Toast the cumin and coriander seeds by stirring them in a dry pan over medium heat for a few minutes until their aromas are released, then grind them in a mortar and pestle or a spice grinder. Stir this into the eggplant and bulgur along with all the remaining ingredients and season with ½ teaspoon each salt and pepper.

Oil or line a baking sheet with parchment paper. Using your hands, divide and shape the mixture into 12 equal-sized round kefte and place them on the prepared baking sheet.

Roast for about 20 minutes, or until the kefte are golden all over, turning halfway. Serve as part of a mezzo with a selection of salads and rice.

—From *Zaitoun: Recipes from the Palestinian Kitchen* by Yasmin Khan

Vegetable and Tofu Tempura

6 servings

This fun recipe is meant to be enjoyed immediately. Serve on a bed of shredded green cabbage for a beautiful appetizer or as a side dish. Make a simple dipping sauce—mixing mirin and tamari to taste—or try with the Savory Barbecue Sauce (page 260) or the Spicy Peanut Sauce (page 261).

1 small green or red cabbage, halved lengthwise, cored, and shredded
¾ cup all-purpose flour
¼ cup cornstarch
½ teaspoon salt
1 cup seltzer water
1 egg, beaten
Oil for frying

2 to 3 cups diagonally sliced raw vegetables (such as mushrooms, sweet potatoes, carrots, eggplant, onion, zucchini), bite-sized broccoli or cauliflower florets, and/or one 14-ounce package firm tofu, sliced crosswise and then into ½-inch-wide squares

Line a platter with the shredded cabbage. If you're using root vegetables, steam them in a steamer basket for 5 minutes to cut down frying time. Dry well.

In a medium bowl, make a tempura batter by whisking together the flour, cornstarch, salt, seltzer, and egg. Heat the oil in a deep pan. Make sure your cooking oil is deep enough to at least mostly cover your ingredients. Using tongs, pick up each piece of vegetable or tofu one at a time, dip in the batter, and drop it into the hot oil. To determine your oil's readiness for frying, test a drop of batter. When it's frying nicely, carefully add a batch of ingredients. Cook each piece, turning several times, until golden brown on all sides. Cooking time will vary depending on the heat of your oil and your vegetables: Carrots take much longer than mushrooms, for example. Most will take between 2 and 5 minutes. They'll be a nice golden brown when done and tender to cut into. Remove with tongs as the vegetables or tofu are done and place them on the cabbage-lined platter. Enjoy right away!

Claire's Cool Spinach Dip

2 cups

For the original Diet, *Claire Greensfelder developed this recipe in an effort to re-create the great taste she had in an Afghan restaurant. My kids always loved this simple appetizer.*

1 pound fresh spinach,
  stems removed
1 cup plain yogurt
1 tablespoon tahini, or
  more to taste

Juice of 1 lemon
1 clove garlic, crushed

Steam the spinach, drain, and let cool. Once cooled, press out any excess water. In a serving bowl, blend the yogurt, tahini, lemon juice, and garlic. Chop the cooled spinach and mix it thoroughly with the blended yogurt mixture. Great on pita bread or crackers.

Crispy Potato Latkes with Parsley

8 to 10 latkes

This yummy potato pancake recipe pairs well with sour cream and/or applesauce. Easy to scale up for bigger crowds or hungry eaters!

1½ pounds russet potatoes (2 or 3)
½ onion
2 tablespoons all-purpose flour
¼ cup finely chopped fresh parsley, or more to taste

2 eggs, beaten
1 teaspoon salt
Freshly ground black pepper to taste
Oil for frying

Using the shredding disk of a food processor or a cheese grater, shred the potatoes. Wrap them in cheesecloth or paper towels and squeeze as much liquid from the potatoes as possible. Grate the onion and, in a large bowl, combine the potatoes and onion with the flour, parsley, eggs, salt, and pepper. Drop spoonfuls of batter into a skillet of hot oil, flatten them slightly with the back of a spoon, and cook for 3 minutes on each side, or until both sides are browned. Place on a paper-towel-lined plate as you finish frying up the rest of the batch. Enjoy with sour cream and/or applesauce.

José's Ensaladilla Rusa with Vegan Allioli

4 servings

Ensaladilla Rusa is one of my very favorite tapas in the world, one with a complicated history—a Belgian chef created it in Moscow before it made its way to Spain to become its true self. This is my updated version for the 21st century, featuring a delicious way to use aquafaba—the canned chickpea water—to make a garlicky, rich allioli. In today's world we do not want to waste a thing, even the chickpea water! —José Andrés

4 medium russet potatoes, peeled

1 large carrot

One 15½-ounce can chickpeas, drained and liquid reserved for allioli

1 cup frozen petite peas, thawed

1 tablespoon sherry vinegar

About 1 cup Vegan Allioli (recipe follows)

Salt and freshly ground black pepper

¼ cup fresh chopped parsley leaves, for garnish

1 tablespoon extra-virgin olive oil, for drizzling

Flaky sea salt, such as Maldon

Put the potatoes in a large saucepan, cover with water, and bring to a boil. After about 15 minutes, add the carrot and cook until all vegetables are tender, another 15 to 20 minutes. Check the vegetables frequently so that they do not overcook. Remove each one as soon as it's tender and transfer to a plate. Let the vegetables cool to room temperature.

Roll-cut the carrots by slicing them on the diagonal at ¾-inch intervals, rotating the carrot a quarter turn after every cut. Cut the potatoes into ¾-inch dice.

Transfer the carrots and potatoes to a large bowl, along with the chickpeas and peas. Add the sherry vinegar and allioli and mix well to coat the vegetables. Season with salt and pepper.

Transfer to a serving bowl, sprinkle with the parsley, drizzle with olive oil, and sprinkle with a few flakes of Maldon salt.

Vegan Allioli

Liquid reserved from one
    15½-ounce can chickpeas
3 medium cloves garlic
1 tablespoon fresh lemon
    juice

Kosher salt
1½ cups extra-virgin
    olive oil

Pour the chickpea liquid into a small saucepan, bring to a simmer, and cook until reduced to ½ cup, about 15 minutes. Remove from the heat and let cool completely.

Transfer the reduced chickpea liquid to a blender, add the garlic, lemon juice, and a pinch of salt and blend on low speed until the garlic is finely chopped. With the blender running on low speed, gradually drizzle in the olive oil in a very thin stream; don't rush it or the sauce won't emulsify properly. Once all of the oil has been incorporated, season the allioli with salt to taste.

—Contributed by Chef José Andrés

Sean's Roasted Corn with Wild Greens Pesto

4 to 6 servings

Corn, when it's just picked, is full of natural sugars that caramelize to perfection on the grill or in a hot oven. Nothing could be easier or more satisfying than freshly roasted sweet corn. —Sean Sherman

4 to 6 large ears fresh sweet corn
Sunflower or hazelnut oil

2 to 3 tablespoons Wild Greens Pesto (recipe follows)

Prepare a hot charcoal grill or preheat the broiler to high. Shuck the corn and rub it lightly with the oil. Set the corn directly on the grill or under the broiler and roast, rolling the cobs occasionally, until all sides are nicely browned but not burned, 5 to 7 minutes total cooking time. Serve with dollops of the pesto.

—From *The Sioux Chef's Indigenous Kitchen* by Sean Sherman with Beth Dooley

Wild Greens Pesto

About 1 ½ cups

To make a bold, flavorful pesto, try to balance a range of flavors: fragrant mint, potent mustard, citrusy sorrel or purslane, bitter dandelion, neutral lamb's-quarter. Wood sorrel, like its domestic cousin, adds a bright lemony flavor. Making pesto the old-fashioned way by pounding together the greens, nuts, and oil in a mortar and pestle will yield a thick, rough sauce. If you'd like something smoother, blend it all together in a small food processor. —Sean Sherman

2 cups wild greens, some combination of sorrel, dandelion greens, purslane, lamb's-quarter, wild mint, and mustard

1 wild onion or shallot, chopped (roughly ½ cup)

¼ cup toasted sunflower seeds

⅔ to ¾ cup sunflower or hazelnut oil

Pinch of salt

Pinch of maple sugar

Pound together the greens, onion, and sunflower seeds with a mortar and pestle or by whizzing them in a food processor. Slowly drizzle in the oil and season to taste with the salt and maple sugar. This pesto keeps for a week or more in a covered container in the refrigerator.

—From *The Sioux Chef's Indigenous Kitchen* by Sean Sherman with Beth Dooley

Greens with Sesame Seeds and Orange Slices

4 servings

These lightly cooked greens pair nicely with rice and beans. The sesame seeds add a delicious roasted flavor and crunch.

¼ cup olive oil
½ onion, chopped
3 cloves garlic, minced
1 pound trimmed greens
   (such as beet or mustard
   greens or collards)

Salt
Cayenne pepper
¼ cup toasted sesame
   seeds
1 orange, sliced, for
   garnish

In a skillet, heat the oil and briefly sauté the onion and garlic. Add the greens and cook until wilted, 5 to 6 minutes. Add salt and cayenne pepper to taste, top with sesame seeds, and garnish with orange slices.

Bryant's Slow-Braised Mustard Greens

4 to 6 servings

This is one of my favorite recipes in my book Afro-Vegan. *I was so proud of transforming what can be a mundane side dish—mustard greens—into a flavorful standout. Warm, savory, and tangy-sweet, this dish is inspired by smoor tomatoes and onions—a traditional South African dish eaten as a sauce, relish, or side. Caramelized onions and tomato paste give the dish a textured richness; minced jalapeños and hot-pepper vinegar provide a pop. —Bryant Terry*

Greens	Onions
1 tablespoon plus ½ teaspoon coarse sea salt	3 tablespoons extra-virgin olive oil
1 pound mustard greens, stems and leaves chopped separately	3 large yellow onions, sliced into thin rings
1 tablespoon extra-virgin olive oil	2 teaspoons raw cane sugar
1 large clove garlic, minced	6 tablespoons tomato paste
4 cups vegetable stock	1 jalapeño pepper, seeded and minced, for serving
	Hot-pepper vinegar, for serving

To prepare the greens, in a large pot over high heat, bring about 12 cups water to a boil. Add 1 tablespoon salt, then add all the greens (leaves and stems) and cook, uncovered, until soft, about 5 minutes. Drain well.

Warm the oil in a large sauté pan over medium heat. Add the garlic and the remaining ½ teaspoon salt and sauté until the garlic is fragrant, about 3 minutes. Stir in the greens and stock, increase the heat to high, and bring to a boil. Decrease the heat to low, cover, and simmer until the greens are meltingly tender, about 45 minutes.

Meanwhile, prepare the onions. Warm the oil in a separate large sauté pan over medium-low heat. Add the onions and sugar and sauté until they are deep golden brown and quite soft, about 15 minutes. Stir in the tomato paste and 1 tablespoon water and cook, stirring often, until the onions are thoroughly coated and hot, about 3 minutes.

To serve, portion the greens along with some of their liquid into small bowls. Top with the onions, sprinkle with jalapeño, and drizzle some hot-pepper vinegar on top.

—From *Afro-Vegan: Farm-Fresh African, Caribbean & Southern Flavors Remixed* by Bryant Terry

BREAKFAST
AND
BAKED GOODS

When I was researching the original *Diet for a Small Planet*, I was struck by the burgeoning of breakfast junk food all around me. By that, I mean the cereal aisle. Today, the breakfast cereal industry is booming, bringing in more than $20 billion annually in the United States alone and delivering a huge amount of sugar—and often additives and preservatives—in every serving. Store-bought cereal is also really expensive! The following recipes offer ideas for liberating you from the cereal aisle and include some of our family favorites, like the granola recipes you find here. (For a reason I can't remember, my nickname for Anna when she was really little was Crunchy Granola, which—she teases me now—was very "on-brand.")

Crunchy Granola

8 to 10 servings

Personalize this granola recipe easily by adding flaxseeds or your favorite nuts, or toss in chia seeds when you serve it. Pair with yogurt and fresh fruit for a satisfying breakfast or snack.

4 cups rolled oats
½ cup sesame seeds
Pinch of salt
½ cup oil
¼ to ½ cup maple syrup

1 tablespoon vanilla extract
½ to 2 cups shredded unsweetened coconut

Preheat the oven to 350°F. Combine the oats, sesame seeds, and salt in a large bowl. In a separate bowl, mix the oil, maple syrup, and vanilla. Add this to the bowl with the oats and work it in well with a spatula so that all the oats are coated. Bake for 30 minutes, stirring it once halfway through. Stir the coconut into the granola and bake for an additional 5 minutes. Allow to cool and enjoy.

Cinnamon Ginger Granola

8 to 10 servings

The original recipe came to us from Susan Weber of Willits, California, whose family called it "Cookie Crunch Granola"—but she thought that sounded too much like a General Foods concoction. This version swaps out buckwheat groats for more oats and adds in subtle traces of cinnamon and ginger. Choose the nuts and seeds of your liking: Walnuts, almonds, and sunflower and pumpkin seeds are our favorites. Enjoy for breakfast or as a snack with your favorite milk or yogurt.

3 ½ cups rolled oats
2 cups chopped nuts and/
   or whole seeds
Pinch of salt
½ teaspoon ground cin-
   namon

1 teaspoon ground ginger
½ cup maple syrup
½ cup oil

Preheat the oven to 350°F. Combine the oats, nuts/seeds, salt, and spices in a large bowl. In a separate bowl, mix the maple syrup and oil. Add this to the bowl with the oats and work it in with a spatula so that all the oats are coated. Bake for 30 minutes, stirring it once halfway through. Allow to cool and enjoy.

Wendy's Maple Amaranth Porridge

3 servings

Amaranth is a nutritious seed from the amaranth plant that works beauti-fully in this comforting porridge recipe. Feel free to customize your toppings based on what you have on hand. —Wendy Lopez

1 cup amaranth
¾ cup unsweetened
    almond milk or other
    plant-based milk
1½ tablespoons maple
    syrup
¼ teaspoon vanilla extract

½ teaspoon ground cinna-mon
2 teaspoons coconut oil
Figs, blueberries, sliced
    almonds, pumpkin seeds,
    and/or dried cranberries
    for optional toppings

In a medium pot, bring 3 cups water to a boil and add the am-aranth. Cook over low heat, covered, for 20 minutes, or until most of the water has been absorbed. While the amaranth is cooking, stir it occasionally. Once done, remove the pot from the stove and add the almond milk, maple syrup, vanilla, cin-namon, and coconut oil. Stir well.

Ladle the mixture into bowls and top with any of the suggested toppings or your favorite fruits, nuts, and/or seeds! Leftovers can be stored in the fridge for up to a week.

When it's time to reheat, add additional almond milk and mix it in so the porridge isn't so thick. Enjoy!

—Contributed by Wendy Lopez

Spinach and Leek Frittata

4 to 6 servings

You can enjoy this frittata on a slow morning with family and friends or make it in advance and enjoy slices throughout the week. Can be refrigerated for up to one week in an airtight container. Serve with crusty bread.

2 tablespoons oil for sautéing

1 medium leek (white and light green parts only), rinsed well and roughly chopped

2 cloves garlic, minced

½ teaspoon paprika

2 cups chopped spinach

6 eggs, beaten

½ teaspoon salt

3 ounces cheese, preferably Muenster, diced or grated

Freshly ground black pepper

In a medium broiler-safe skillet, heat the oil and add the leeks and garlic. Sauté over medium heat for a few minutes until the leeks are translucent. Add the paprika and spinach, stir, and continue sautéing for another couple minutes, until the spinach has wilted. In a medium bowl, whisk the salt and cheese into the beaten eggs and add to the skillet. Cook over low-medium heat until the eggs have set around the edges, 8 to 9 minutes. Turn on the broiler and broil for an additional 2 to 4 minutes, until the top is browned and completely cooked. Allow to cool, then slice and enjoy with a sprinkling of freshly ground black pepper and fresh bread.

Challah French Toast

4 servings

Enjoy this special twist on basic French toast. The original recipe was shared with us by Irma Timmons of Shawano, Wisconsin.

2 eggs
⅓ cup whole milk
1 tablespoon maple syrup
½ teaspoon vanilla extract
¼ teaspoon ground cin-
  namon
Pinch of salt

Unsalted butter for the pan
4 thick challah slices
Chopped walnuts, maple
  syrup, fresh berries or
  fruit, butter, and/or
  lemon zest for optional
  toppings

In a wide, shallow bowl, whisk together the eggs, milk, syrup, vanilla, cinnamon, and salt. Butter a large skillet or pan and dip each slice of challah into the mixture so that both sides are coated. Cook in the skillet over low-medium heat until both sides are golden, 2 to 4 minutes per side. Enjoy with the toppings of your choice.

Black Bean Breakfast Tostadas

4 servings

This breakfast makes a festive and delicious family meal.

One 15-ounce can black
beans, rinsed and
drained (1½ cups
cooked)
½ teaspoon ground cumin
Juice of ½ lime
Salt
6 eggs, beaten
1 jalapeño pepper, seeded
and chopped
1 medium tomato,
chopped
Oil for sautéing
¼ cup shredded cheddar
cheese
8 tostada shells
Sour cream, sliced avo-
cado, and chopped
fresh cilantro for
optional topping

In a food processor, pulse together the beans, cumin, and lime juice until you get a thick paste. Salt to taste and set aside. Whisk the jalapeño, tomato, and ¼ teaspoon salt into the eggs. Heat oil for sautéing in a pan set over low-medium heat, and scramble the egg mixture. When cooked to your liking, remove from the heat and sprinkle the cheddar cheese over the eggs and let it melt. Layer the tostadas with the bean purée and cheesy scrambled eggs and top with sour cream, sliced avocado, and cilantro.

California Scrambled Tofu

4 servings

Easily made 🍅 by omitting the cheese

Karla Peterson of Point Richmond, California, contributed the original recipe. We love this classic vegetarian breakfast as a flavorful alternative to scrambled eggs.

1 tablespoon oil
1 large onion, chopped
1 cup sliced mushrooms
¼ teaspoon each of curry powder and ground turmeric
12 ounces firm tofu, drained, squeezed in dry towel, and crumbled

Dash of freshly ground black pepper
½ cup grated cheddar cheese, or 2 tablespoons nutritional yeast
½ teaspoon salt
Sliced avocado for topping

In a medium skillet, heat the oil and lightly sauté the onion, mushrooms, and spices. Add the tofu, pepper, cheese or nutritional yeast, and salt, mix together, and cook over low heat until the tofu is thoroughly heated, 5 to 10 minutes. Enjoy topped with sliced avocado and served with toasted wholegrain bread or English muffins.

The Ultimate Zucchini Bread

1 small loaf

This recipe is a fabulous way to put zucchini to good use. Enjoy layered with nut butter and a side of yogurt and fruit for a satisfying breakfast. It's also delicious as a snack on its own or dressed up as dessert with a scoop of vanilla ice cream.

½ cup oil, plus more for the pan
1 cup all-purpose flour
¼ teaspoon salt
½ teaspoon baking soda
½ teaspoon baking powder
½ to ¾ cup packed dark brown sugar, depending on how sweet you like it
1 teaspoon ground cinnamon

¼ teaspoon ground nutmeg (optional)
2 eggs
1 teaspoon vanilla extract
1 cup grated zucchini (1 to 2 medium zucchini)
½ cup chopped walnuts (optional)

Preheat the oven to 350°F. Grease an 8 × 4-inch loaf pan. In a bowl, combine the flour, salt, baking soda, baking powder, sugar, and spices. In another bowl, combine the eggs, oil, and vanilla; add the zucchini and mix well. Mix the wet ingredients into the dry with a rubber spatula until all ingredients are worked in. If using walnuts, fold them into the batter. Spread the batter in the prepared loaf pan and bake for 50 minutes, or until a toothpick inserted in the center comes out dry. Allow to cool on a wire rack. The bread will keep in an airtight container for up to 1 week in the refrigerator.

Mollie's Buttermilk Bran Muffins

12 to 16 muffins

A muffin recipe is always great to have up your sleeve. These muffins—from my breakfast-ideas cookbook Sunlight Café—*are still an all-time favorite. Add raisins or some chopped walnuts if you like. Enjoy these muffins as a breakfast treat or a special midday snack.*
—Mollie Katzen

Oil for greasing
2 cups all-purpose flour, or
1 cup all-purpose flour
and 1 cup whole-wheat
flour
Rounded ½ teaspoon salt
1 tablespoon baking pow-
der
¼ teaspoon baking soda
¼ to ½ cup granulated
sugar
½ cup light brown sugar

2 cups wheat bran, or
replace ¼ cup of the
wheat bran with ¼ cup
millet
2 cups buttermilk
2 eggs
½ cup (1 stick) unsalted
butter, melted
½ cup raisins (optional)
½ cup chopped walnuts
(optional)

Preheat the oven to 375°F. Grease 12 standard muffin tins with oil.

Combine the flour, salt, baking powder, baking soda, and granulated sugar in a medium bowl. Crumble in the brown sugar, rubbing it with your fingers to break up any clumps. Stir in the bran (and millet, if using). Mix thoroughly.

In a bowl or 4-cup liquid measure, whisk together the buttermilk and eggs until smooth. Slowly pour this mixture, along with the melted butter, into the dry ingredients. Mix until the dry ingredients are all moistened. Don't overmix; a few lumps are okay.

Spoon the batter evenly into the prepared muffin cups. For smaller muffins, fill the cups about four-fifths full; for larger muffins, fill them to the top. If you have extra batter, grease additional muffin cups and fill them with the remaining batter.

Bake in the middle of the oven for 20 to 25 minutes, or until the muffins are lightly browned on top and a toothpick inserted into the center comes out clean. Remove the pan from the oven, then remove the muffins from the pan and place them on a rack to cool. Wait at least 30 minutes before serving.

—From *Mollie Katzen's Sunlight Café* by Mollie Katzen

Betty the Peacenik's Gingerbread

1 loaf

A favorite of Claire "Betty the Peacenik" Greensfelder, who earned her nickname back in 1970 when she was simultaneously the Betty Crocker Homemaker of Tomorrow and the co-chair of her high school's Students for Political Action in Oakland, California. We've replaced the soy flour from the original with amaranth or another alternative flour, like almond flour. This recipe produces a rich, dark brown loaf, with bold flavors of molasses and ginger. The optional millet gives the recipe a nice crunch.

½ cup (1 stick) unsalted butter, cut into small pieces, at room temperature, plus more for greasing pan

½ cup packed dark brown sugar

½ cup molasses

½ cup boiling water

1 egg

1¼ cups all-purpose flour

¼ cup amaranth flour or your favorite heirloom flour

¼ cup millet (optional)

½ teaspoon each baking powder and baking soda

½ teaspoon salt

1 teaspoon each ground ginger and cinnamon

Preheat the oven to 350°F. Grease an 8 × 4-inch loaf pan and set aside. In a large bowl or the bowl of a stand mixer, combine the butter, sugar, and molasses and add the boiling water. Stir until well mixed. Add the egg and stir again. In a separate bowl, mix the flours and millet (if using), baking powder, baking soda, salt, and spices. Pour the dry ingredients into the wet and mix until dry ingredients are incorporated, being careful not to overmix. Pour into the prepared pan and bake for 45 minutes, or until a toothpick comes out clean. Serve with applesauce or yogurt.

Mark's No-Knead Bread

1 large loaf

We wanted to include a bread recipe, and this one was the clear winner! This recipe is great for anyone intimidated by bread making. The food industry loves to sell you bread, but you don't have to be a skilled baker to liberate yourself from the store-bought stuff. The recipe first appeared in The New York Times *in 2006 and, over the years, has seen several updates, but the main recipe hasn't changed much. What you find here is the most recent version from Mark Bittman's completely revised 20th-anniversary edition of* How to Cook Everything.

This innovation—the word "recipe" does not do the technique justice—came from Jim Lahey, owner of Sullivan Street Bakery in New York City. Jim created a way for regular home cooks to nearly duplicate an artisan bakery loaf with its crackling crust, open-holed crumb, light texture, and fantastic flavor, all without kneading or special equipment. A wet dough and slow fermentation are the keys to success, as is the baking method— a heated covered pot, which essentially creates an oven within an oven to trap steam as the bread bakes.

Since the method was first published in 2006, many people— including me—have tinkered with the formula. This is the original, simplest version. The only thing required is forethought. Ideally, you will start the dough about 24 hours before you plan to serve it. After all these years, I still say with confidence the results will blow your mind. —Mark Bittman

4 cups all-purpose or bread flour, plus more for dusting (Note: You can substitute up to 1 cup of whole-wheat, rye, spelt, or kamut flour, though you won't get the same doming and open crumb.)

2 teaspoons salt
Scant ½ teaspoon instant yeast, or ½ rounded teaspoon active dry yeast
Cornmeal, semolina, or wheat bran (optional)

Mix the flour, salt, and yeast together in a large bowl. Add 2 cups warm water (it should be about 70°F) and stir until blended. You'll have a shaggy, sticky dough; add a little more water if it seems dry. Cover the bowl with plastic wrap and let sit for about 18 hours at room temperature (a couple of hours less if your kitchen is warm; a couple more if it's cool). The dough is ready when its surface is dotted with bubbles.

Transfer the dough to a lightly floured work surface and fold the dough once or twice; it will be soft but not terribly sticky once dusted with flour. Cover loosely with plastic wrap and let rest for about 15 minutes.

Using just enough flour to keep the dough from sticking, gently and quickly shape the dough into a ball. Generously coat a cotton kitchen towel (not terry cloth) with cornmeal, semolina, or wheat bran, or use a silicone baking mat; put the dough seam side down on the towel (or baking mat) and dust with more flour or cornmeal. Cover with another cotton towel or plastic wrap and let rise for about 2 hours. When it's ready, the dough will be more than doubled in size and won't spring back readily when poked with your finger.

After the dough has been rising for about 1½ hours, put a 3- or 4-quart ovenproof cast-iron, enamel, Pyrex, or ceramic pot and its lid in the oven and heat to 450°F. When the dough is ready, carefully remove the pot from the oven, uncover it, and turn the dough into the pot, seam side up. (Slide your hand under the towel and just turn the dough over into the pot; it's messy, and it probably won't fall artfully, but it will straighten out as it bakes.) Cover with the lid and bake for 30 minutes. (If at any point the bread starts to smell scorched, lower the heat a bit.)

Remove the lid and bake for another 20 to 30 minutes, until the loaf is beautifully browned. The bread's internal temperature should be about 200°F when you insert an instant read thermometer. Remove the bread from the pot with a spatula or tongs and cool on a rack for at least 30 minutes before slicing.

—From *How to Cook Everything: Completely Revised Twentieth Anniversary Edition* by Mark Bittman

Smoothies

The original *Diet* didn't have any smoothie recipes, but we wanted to include some in this edition because they're a great option for a nutritious snack or start to your day. We invited fans of the original to submit their favorites and were flooded with amazing suggestions. We chose these wonderful three. Tweak to your own tastes and to what you have on hand. For any of these recipes, simply throw the ingredients into a blender and let it whirl until the ingredients are mixed well. For a smoother smoothie, blend for longer. Feel free to add more of any of the liquids called for if you'd like a less thick drink.

Suzette's Blueberry Co-op Smoothie

2 servings

This recipe comes to us from the Neighboring Food Co-op Association's Suzette Snow-Cobb and combines blueberries with light hints of vanilla and cinnamon. Suzette encourages all of us to seek out products from cooperative enterprises, helping food producers build stronger, more resilient communities and strengthen local economies. She suggests yogurt from Organic Valley, for instance, and Frontier Natural Products ground cinnamon.

1½ cups frozen blueberries
⅔ cup plain yogurt
½ cup brewed hibiscus tea, cooled

¼ teaspoon vanilla extract
Dash of ground cinnamon or to taste

Reyna's Morning Rocket Smoothie

2 servings

Make this smoothie with the apple variety of your choice. Experiment with a tart Granny Smith or a sweeter Gala or Fuji. Packed with nutrients, this smoothie is designed to start your day with a boost of natural energy and immunity-boosting nutrients, says Reyna Franco, who shared this recipe with us.

- 1 apple, cored
- 1 tablespoon freshly grated ginger
- 1 cup fresh or frozen blueberries
- 1 teaspoon ground turmeric
- 2 tablespoons flaxseeds
- 1 cup fresh spinach
- 1 cup plant-based milk, such as almond milk or oat milk

Note: You can also grind the flaxseeds in a coffee grinder before adding them to the blender.

Mishy's Watermelon Meets Blueberries and Mint Smoothie

2 servings

Contributed by Mishy Lesser, the mint and watermelon make a tasty combination with the sweetness of dates in this refreshing smoothie.

- ¾ cup unsweetened almond milk or oat milk
- ½ cup frozen blueberries
- 2 pitted dates
- 2 cups watermelon chunks
- Fistful of fresh mint leaves

SOUPS

Many of these soups can be prepared with a few basic ingredients we recommend having on hand: carrots, potatoes, canned tomatoes, and onions. For a satisfying meal, put some homemade muffins or bread in the oven or prepare a hearty salad—see our DIY Salad Ideas (page 247).

Golden Gate Minestrone

8 generous servings, plus leftovers

Easily made ♥ by omitting the cheese

The original contribution came from our friend Claire Greensfelder—she once served 15 gallons of it to the Golden Gate Audubon Society Bird Counters! It is indeed a special soup to come home to after a long winter's day of birdwatching. As with any minestrone recipe, use creative license: Cut some of the suggested vegetables, add potatoes if you have them. Include both these beans, just one, or another type of your choice. Feel free to add more stock for a brothier version.

¼ cup plus 1 tablespoon
 olive oil
1 or 2 medium onions,
 diced (roughly 1 cup)
Salt
2 cloves garlic, minced
1 small green bell pepper,
 seeded and chopped
2 medium carrots, sliced
 into rounds
2 or 3 stalks celery,
 chopped
One 28-ounce can peeled
 whole tomatoes
6 cups vegetable stock
1 bay leaf
1 teaspoon each dried
 thyme and parsley

1 medium zucchini,
 sliced into rounds,
 then quartered
1 medium yellow squash,
 sliced into rounds,
 then quartered
1½ cups cooked kidney
 beans, or one 15-ounce
 can, drained and rinsed
1½ cups cooked chickpeas, or
 one 15-ounce can, drained
 and rinsed
1 cup uncooked shells or
 other small pasta
Grated Parmesan cheese
 for topping (optional)

Heat ¼ cup oil in a large pot and sauté the onions and 1 teaspoon salt until translucent. Make a well in the onions and add the remaining 1 tablespoon oil and the garlic. Cook just enough to release the flavor, about 30 seconds, being careful not to burn the garlic or onions. Stir well. Add the green pepper, carrots, and celery, and cook, stirring occasionally, until the vegetables soften, 7 to 10 minutes. Meanwhile, break up and crush the whole tomatoes with your hands. Add the tomatoes, stock, bay leaf, herbs, zucchini, squash, and any other vegetables you're including. Bring to a boil, then lower the heat to medium-low. Cook until the vegetables are softened, another 15 minutes. Add the beans and pasta and continue simmering, uncovered, for 15 to 20 minutes or until the pasta is al dente. Taste for seasoning and add more herbs and/or salt, if needed. Top each serving with grated Parmesan. The soup keeps well in the refrigerator. Add more stock before reheating if you need more broth.

Minestrone con Crema

4 servings

This minestrone is a creamy version of the classic soup. It is also a great way to put your favorite vegetables—or any vegetables you happen to have around—to good use.

¼ cup oil
½ onion, chopped
2 cloves garlic, minced
2 cups milk
2 cups vegetable stock
1½ cups cooked chickpeas, or one 15-ounce can, drained and rinsed
2 cups roughly chopped seasonal vegetables (zucchini, potatoes, turnips, carrots, etc.)

Salt
2 cups chopped beet greens or spinach, without stems
Black pepper
¼ cup chopped fresh parsley
½ cup grated Parmesan cheese

In a large pot, heat the oil and sauté the onion and garlic until translucent. Add the milk, stock, chickpeas, vegetables, and ½ teaspoon salt and simmer for 20 minutes, or until the vegetables are tender. Stir in the greens and cook for another 2 to 3 minutes. Add salt and pepper to taste. Top with fresh parsley, Parmesan cheese, and more black pepper.

Comforting Carrot and Onion Soup

4 to 6 servings

This uncomplicated soup is a family-favorite comfort food. Any home-made bread goes nicely with it.

4 cups vegetable stock
2 bay leaves
4 medium carrots, roughly chopped
1 medium onion, roughly chopped
2 large potatoes, roughly chopped
2 cloves garlic
3 sprigs fresh thyme
1 cup milk
Salt to taste
Homemade croutons for serving (optional)

In a large pot, bring the stock to a boil and add the bay leaves, carrots, onion, potatoes, garlic, and thyme. Turn down the heat to medium-low and cook at a low simmer for 25 minutes, or until the carrots and potatoes are tender. Allow to cool slightly, remove the bay leaves and thyme, and then purée with an immersion blender. Stir in the milk and simmer for 3 to 5 minutes, or until hot. Be sure not to bring to a boil. Adjust for salt, top with homemade croutons, if desired, and enjoy.

Hearty Quinoa Chili

4 servings

Easily made 🌱 by omitting the cheese

The quinoa in this recipe adds another level of flavor and satisfaction. You can feel free to improvise with whatever beans you have in your kitchen, or even mix it up by using a few different types of beans.

2 tablespoons oil
½ onion, finely chopped
2 cloves garlic, minced
1 jalapeño pepper, seeded
    and minced
2 medium tomatoes,
    chopped (roughly 2 cups)
1 teaspoon ground cumin
2 cups pasta sauce or
    Homemade Marinara
    (page 262)

1½ cups cooked beans
    or one 15-ounce can
    pinto beans, rinsed
    and drained
½ cup dry quinoa
¼ cup jack or cheddar
    cheese, or more to taste
    (optional)
Salt to taste
Chopped fresh cilantro
    for topping

In a medium pot, heat the oil and add the onion, garlic, and jalapeño. Sauté for a couple minutes and then add the tomatoes and cumin. Continue sautéing for another couple minutes and then add the pasta sauce, ½ cup water, the beans, and the quinoa. Cook, covered, over low to medium heat for 25 to 35 minutes, stirring occasionally. Add the cheese and continue simmering until the cheese has melted. Adjust for salt, as needed, and top with cilantro.

Classic Lentil Soup

4 to 6 servings

A classic from the original Diet. *We enjoy this lentil soup with corn muffins or cornbread, or pair it with brown rice or quinoa for a comforting meal on cool nights.*

¼ cup olive oil
2 large onions, chopped
1 carrot, chopped
½ teaspoon each of dried
  thyme and oregano
4 cups vegetable stock, plus
  more as needed
1 cup brown lentils, rinsed
  and picked over

¼ cup chopped fresh
  parsley
2 cups canned diced
  tomatoes, a little less
  than one 28-ounce can
Salt to taste

Heat the oil in a large pot, add the onions and carrots, and sauté for 3 to 5 minutes. Add the thyme and oregano and sauté for 1 minute. Add the stock, lentils, parsley, and tomatoes. Cook, covered, until the lentils are tender, about 45 minutes. Stir occasionally, being sure to add water or stock as needed if the soup starts to dry out. Adjust for salt, and enjoy with your favorite cooked grain.

White Bean and Basil Tomato Soup

4 to 6 servings

Earlier variations of this came to us from Myra Levy and Charlie Varon of San Francisco. This savory soup is great when you want something simple and fast. All you need to do is throw everything into a pot, simmer, and enjoy. It pairs well with grilled cheese or crusty bread.

2 tablespoons oil
2 cloves garlic, minced
1 onion, chopped
1 stalk celery, chopped
One 28-ounce can diced
 tomatoes

1 teaspoon salt
1 cup cooked white beans
1 cup vegetable stock
1 cup chopped fresh basil
Black pepper and Parmesan
 for topping (optional)

Heat the oil in a large pot, add the garlic, onion, and celery, and sauté until the onion is translucent. Stir in the tomatoes, salt, beans, and stock and cook, covered, for 10 minutes over low heat. Stir in the fresh basil, and top with freshly ground black pepper and Parmesan, if desired.

Quinoa-Cauliflower Soup

4 to 6 servings

Here's our variation on a favorite of Robin Bryce Lasobeck of Gaines-ville, Florida. The miso adds a nice umami touch, but if you have trouble finding miso, you can omit it.

2 tablespoons oil
1 small onion, chopped
2 cloves garlic, minced
3 stalks celery, finely
  chopped
1 tablespoon tomato paste
1 bay leaf
1 large carrot, chopped
½ cup quinoa
3 sprigs fresh thyme, or
  ¼ teaspoon dried

Salt
1 medium head cauliflower,
  broken into small florets
1 cup vegetable stock
2 tablespoons yellow miso
  (optional)
¾ cup raw cashews
½ cup nutritional yeast

In a large pot, heat the oil, add the onion, garlic, celery, and tomato paste, and sauté for 3 to 5 minutes. Stir in 6 cups water, the bay leaf, carrot, quinoa, thyme, and 1 teaspoon salt. Cook, covered, for 20 minutes. Remove the bay leaf and, if using, thyme sprigs. Add the cauliflower and stock. In a blender, blend the miso (if using), cashews, 1 cup water, and nutritional yeast until smooth, and add that to the soup pot. If you want the soup a bit less thick, add more stock or water until you reach the desired consistency. Salt to taste. Simmer for 10 minutes and enjoy. You can use an immersion blender to make a soup with a smooth consistency.

Chickpea Mulligatawny

4 to 6 servings

Easily made ♥ by using a vegan butter alternative

In the 1970s, the San Francisco Ecology Center was known for its soups. The original version of this delicious and easy-to-make soup was shared by the Center's Ed Lubin, who swore it was the favorite of their lunchtime patrons. This version hews close to the original, with added coconut milk to boost richness and flavor. The longer it cooks, the more the flavors pop. Enjoy with your favorite grain; brown rice or quinoa are great options.

3 to 4 tablespoons unsalted butter

2 onions, coarsely chopped

3 cloves garlic, minced

1 carrot, chopped

2 stalks celery, chopped

1 green bell pepper, seeded and chopped

1 large apple of your choice, peeled, cored, and chopped

1 teaspoon curry powder

⅓ cup tomato paste

2 tablespoons finely chopped fresh parsley, plus more (optional) for garnish

3 cups vegetable stock

One 13-ounce can coconut milk

2 cups cooked chickpeas

Salt to taste

Melt the butter in a large pot, add the onions and garlic, and sauté until the onions are translucent. Stir in the carrot, celery, green pepper, apple, curry powder, tomato paste, parsley, vegetable stock, coconut milk, and chickpeas and cook for 45 minutes over low heat, stirring occasionally. Adjust for salt and enjoy with your favorite grain and topped with more parsley, if you like.

Luz and Catriona's Sopa de Milpa

4 to 6 servings

Easily made 🌱 by omitting the optional queso fresco

This simple soup honors the milpa, the sustainable crop-growing system used throughout Mesoamerica. More than just a system of agriculture, it is a worldview that honors the connection between farmers, crops, land, and the cosmos. Our soup features the life-affirming flavors of the summer garden, from blossom to tender squash to mature corn and chiles. Because this soup celebrates the land used to grow food, feel free to add a vegetable that you have grown yourself or that you purchased from your farmers' market. Fresh green beans, squash tendrils, carrots, chayote, or seasonal mushrooms would be wonderful additions or substitutions. In Mexico, this soup has hundreds of variations. —Luz Calvo and Catriona Esquibel

1 tablespoon olive oil

½ medium white onion, finely chopped

2 cloves garlic, minced

6 cups homemade vegetable stock (see Note)

2 to 6 fresh poblano chiles, roasted, peeled, seeded, and torn into thin strips

2 medium zucchini, sliced into bite-sized quarter-rounds

2 cups fresh corn kernels (from 2 or 3 ears)

2 tablespoons chopped fresh epazote or cilantro

15 squash blossoms (roughly 6 ounces) or a large handful from the summer garden's bounty, torn into bite-size pieces

Salt and freshly ground black pepper to taste

2 avocados, peeled, seeded, and cubed

6 ounces queso fresco, cubed (optional)

In a large saucepan over medium heat, heat the oil, add the onion, and sauté about 10 minutes, until golden brown. Add the garlic and stir until its fragrance is released, about 30 seconds. Stir in the vegetable stock, chiles, zucchini, corn, and epazote or cilantro. Simmer for 20 minutes, or until the zucchini is crisp-tender. Remove from the heat and add the squash blossom pieces. Season the soup with salt and pepper. Ladle the soup into bowls and serve topped with avocado cubes and queso fresco, if using.

Note: We encourage you to make your own vegetable stock while you're making this soup, using discarded corncobs, chile peels, and other vegetable scraps.

—Adapted from *Decolonize Your Diet: Plant-Based Mexican-American Recipes for Health and Healing* by Luz Calvo and Catriona Esquibel

SALADS

When they were young, my kids would tease me about how crazy I was for salad. There's family lore about a potluck we once hosted for the Institute for Food and Development Policy. As guests arrived, seven-year-old Anna pointed to the two big salads bursting with fresh produce atop our dining room table: "That one's for my mom," she said. "That one's for all of you." Everyone cracked up.

DIY Salad Ideas

It's true: I do love salads, and there are countless ways to put them together. Here are a few tips for making salads that are nutritionally balanced and satisfying. Aside from greens, adding proteins, carbohydrates, and/or fats can easily turn a salad into a nourishing meal. Following this section, you'll also find one of our all-time favorite salad dressings from our friend Alice Waters, whose farm-to-table restaurant, Chez Panisse, opened the same year *Diet* was first published. Her dressing goes well with a huge variety of salad combinations.

Leafy Greens

- Baby spinach
- Kale
- Arugula
- Butter lettuce
- Mixed greens

Fruits and Vegetables

- Cucumber
- Tomatoes
- Mushrooms
- Peppers
- Red onions
- Carrots
- Broccoli
- Berries
- Pears
- Apples
- Dried fruit
- Olives
- Corn
- Fresh herbs

Carbohydrates and Proteins

- Cooked quinoa
- Legumes (chickpeas, black beans, lentils, etc.)
- Hummus
- Grilled tofu
- Eggs

Fats

- Avocado
- Nuts/seeds (pumpkin, almonds, walnuts, etc.)
- Cheese (feta, burrata, halloumi, etc.)
- Dressings

Alice's Creamy Meyer Lemon Dressing

About ½ cup

This creamy dressing coats lettuce in a luscious way. The flavor is light and sprightly, filled with lemon juice and zest. It's especially nice on sweet lettuces such as butterhead or romaine or a mix of small chicories and radicchio. —Alice Waters

1 tablespoon Meyer
   lemon juice, plus more as
   needed
1 tablespoon white wine
   vinegar
Grated zest of 1 Meyer
   lemon

Salt and freshly ground
   black pepper to taste
3 tablespoons extra-virgin
   olive oil
3 tablespoons heavy cream

In a large bowl, stir together the lemon juice, vinegar, zest, salt, and pepper. Taste and adjust as needed. Whisk in the olive oil and heavy cream, or any of the variations suggested below. Taste for salt and acid and adjust as needed. Enjoy!

VARIATIONS:

- Add a pinch of cayenne pepper along with the salt for a bit of spice.
- Stir in a tablespoon of chopped tender fresh herbs such as chives, chervil, parsley, dill, tarragon, summer savory, or anise hyssop to the finished dressing.
- Try rangpur lime, bitter orange, lemon, lime, or another sour citrus instead of Meyer lemon.
- Use red wine vinegar instead of white wine vinegar.
- Omit the cream and use 5 tablespoons extra-virgin olive oil instead.
- Substitute 2 tablespoons buttermilk or crème fraîche for 2 table-spoons of the cream.

—From *The Art of Simple Food II* by Alice Waters

Black Bean Rice Salad with Creamy Avocado Dressing

4 servings

A new twist on an old favorite, this tasty black bean and rice salad makes a colorful meal for a summer evening. For this version, we used a dressing with the kick of jalapeño.

1½ cups cooked rice
(¾ cup uncooked), at
room temperature
1 cup cooked black beans
or one 15-ounce can,
drained and rinsed
½ cup diced tomatoes
½ cup coarsely chopped
fresh cilantro

Dressing

½ avocado
½ jalapeño pepper,
seeded
Juice of 1 small lime
¼ teaspoon salt

Toss all the salad ingredients in a bowl.

For the dressing, pulse the ingredients together in a food processor until smooth; add up to 1 cup water, depending on the desired texture and taste preferences. Drizzle the dressing over the rice salad.

Colorful Macaroni Salad

6 servings

Easily made 🟢 by using a mayonnaise alternative

*Great for a summer-evening salad—light and satisfying. An uncompli-
cated side for a variety of main dishes, it can be served on a bed of lettuce
for extra crunch. Toss in any or all of the optional additions for more
complex flavor—and even more color!*

Salt
½ pound macaroni noodles
½ cup mayonnaise or
  vegan alternative
½ teaspoon Dijon mustard
1 large carrot, finely
  chopped
1 green bell pepper, finely
  chopped
½ cup fresh or canned
  sweet corn

½ small red onion, finely
  chopped
Freshly ground black
  pepper to taste
Optional additions:
  ¼ teaspoon paprika,
  ½ teaspoon garlic powder,
  sliced kalamata olives,
  chopped fresh parsley,
  dill, pinch of cayenne pepper for a kick

Boil the macaroni in salted water according to the package
directions until tender; drain. In a small bowl, mix together
the mayonnaise, mustard, and salt to taste (½ to 1 teaspoon).
In a large bowl, combine the macaroni with the mayonnaise
mixture and the remaining ingredients (including any desired
add-ins). Chill before serving.

Lebanese Tabouli Salad

4 servings

This recipe has been updated from the one that appeared in the original Diet, *which was contributed by Susan Kanaan, one of my oldest friends. This traditional Lebanese dish can be scooped up with lettuce, grape, or cabbage leaves instead of spoons. Look for fine (#1) bulgur available in Middle Eastern markets.*

½ cup bulgur (#1 or fine
  bulgur, if possible)
2 cups minced fresh flat-
  leaf parsley
½ cup minced fresh mint
  leaves or additional
  parsley
¾ cup chopped scallions
  (white and firm green
  parts)

3 medium tomatoes,
  finely chopped
½ cup fresh lemon juice,
  or more to taste
¼ cup olive oil
Pinch of ground allspice
Salt and freshly ground black
  pepper to taste

In a large bowl, pour 2 cups hot water over the bulgur, cover, and let stand until light and fluffy, 20 to 30 minutes. (The finer the bulgur, the less time this will take.) Drain or squeeze out any excess water. Add all remaining ingredients to the bulgur, stir, and chill for at least 1 hour. Before serving, adjust for more lemon or salt, if necessary.

Lentil-Bulgur Salad with Tangy Yogurt Dressing

6 to 8 servings

Enjoy this hearty salad for lunch or with soup for supper.

1 cup French (green) lentils, rinsed and picked over
4 cups vegetable stock
Oil for sautéing
1 onion, chopped
1 cup bulgur
1 cup plain yogurt
2 tablespoons mayonnaise
1 or 2 cloves garlic, crushed
1 teaspoon Dijon or other prepared mustard
2 teaspoons lemon juice, or more to taste
4 cups chopped spinach or baby spinach
4 chopped scallions (white and firm green parts)
¼ cup chopped fresh mint (optional)

In a saucepan, cook the lentils in 2 cups of the stock until tender but not mushy, 20 to 30 minutes. Drain any excess liquid. Let cool uncovered.

While the lentils are cooking, cook the bulgur: Heat a bit of oil in a heavy skillet over medium heat and add the onion. Sauté until soft, then add the bulgur and sauté together for 5 to 10 minutes. Heat the remaining 2 cups stock, add it to the bulgur and onion, cover tightly, and cook over low heat until light and fluffy, about 10 minutes. Drain any excess liquid. Let cool.

For the dressing, mix together the yogurt, mayonnaise, garlic, mustard, and lemon juice in a small bowl. In a large bowl, combine the bulgur, lentils, spinach, scallions, and mint (if using) and toss with the dressing. Chill, if desired, or serve at room temperature.

Greek Salad with Arugula and Chickpeas

4 servings

Easily made 🟢 by omitting the cheese

A fabulously nutritious salad. Mix and match with ingredients you have on hand—any greens will do, for instance.

1½ cups cooked chickpeas, or one 15-ounce can, drained and rinsed

2 cups arugula

1 tomato, chopped

1 cucumber, peeled and chopped

¼ medium red onion, chopped

½ cup crumbled Greek feta

¼ cup chopped fresh parsley

Salad dressing of your choice

1 avocado, sliced (optional)

Combine all ingredients except the avocado in a large bowl. Toss with your favorite dressing and lay the sliced avocado across the top. Delicious served with crusty bread or warm pita. If you're not going to eat it all, leave some undressed; it lasts up to 3 days in the refrigerator.

Everyday Egg Salad

4 servings

New for this edition, this protein-packed egg salad works well on toast or with your favorite crackers.

1 stalk celery, finely chopped

¼ small red onion, finely chopped

¼ cup mayonnaise

2 teaspoons Dijon mustard

Juice of ½ lemon

6 hard-boiled eggs, chopped

Salt and freshly ground black pepper to taste

¼ cup finely chopped fresh parsley (optional)

In a bowl, combine the celery, onion, mayonnaise, mustard, and lemon juice. Mix in the eggs and salt and pepper to taste. Top with chopped parsley, if using. Refrigerate before serving.

Sauces

A key to quick, easy vegetarian cooking for me has always come down to sauces. Develop a selection of go-to sauces you love, and you can turn any combination of vegetables, pasta, your favorite grain, or sautéed tofu into a delicious dinner. Most of the sauces we include here keep well in the refrigerator for up to five days. Others can be frozen for up to three months for best flavor, and taken out any morning for a quick evening meal.

Easy Almond Pesto

6 servings

This pesto is a twist on the classic, which is traditionally made with pine nuts. Almonds are an affordable alternative and give a subtle and unique flavor. We like serving this with hot or sweet marinated Italian peppers and garlic bread.

½ cup olive oil
2 cloves garlic
¼ cup roasted, unsalted almonds

2 cups chopped fresh basil
½ cup grated Parmesan cheese
¼ teaspoon salt

In a food processor, process all of the ingredients until coarsely chopped and blended together. Enjoy tossed with pasta, on fresh bread, or drizzled on vegetables, raw, grilled, or roasted.

Mushroom Garlic Cream Sauce

About 2 ½ cups

2 tablespoons unsalted
butter
2 cups thinly sliced button
mushrooms or a variety
of your choice
2 tablespoons all-purpose
flour

1½ cups milk
3 cloves garlic, minced
½ tablespoon soy sauce
or tamari
Salt and freshly ground
black pepper

Melt the butter in a large skillet and sauté the mushrooms until soft. Add 1 tablespoon of the flour to coat the mushrooms, stir, and cook to toast the flour. Add the milk, garlic, soy sauce, and salt and pepper to taste. As the sauce cooks, whisk in the remaining tablespoon flour slowly to avoid clumps forming. Cook for a couple of minutes, whisking often, until the sauce thickens. Enjoy with pappardelle pasta drizzled with olive oil and freshly chopped rosemary.

Sweet and Sour Tahini Sauce

About 1 ½ cups

1 tablespoon oil
½ onion, chopped
2 ½ tablespoons maple
   syrup or honey, or to
   taste
1 tablespoon tamari
1 tablespoon rice vinegar

1 tablespoon tahini
½ teaspoon grated fresh
   ginger
1 scallion (green parts),
   finely chopped
3 teaspoons cornstarch

Heat the oil in a medium skillet and sauté the onion until translucent. Add 1¼ cups water, the maple syrup, tamari, vinegar, tahini, ginger, and scallions and bring to a boil. In a small bowl, dissolve the cornstarch in 2 tablespoons water, then stir it into the sauce. Cook until the sauce thickens, 6 to 8 minutes. Drizzle the sauce over pan-fried tofu and enjoy with brown rice or rice noodles. You can also enjoy this sauce stir-fried with vegetables, tempeh, or your favorite protein.

Savory Barbecue Sauce

About 1 cup

The original recipe came to us via Joan Donaldson-Van Voorhees of Fennville, Michigan.

1 tablespoon toasted
   sesame seeds
3 scallions (green parts),
   chopped
4 cloves garlic, minced
¼ cup tamari

2 tablespoons sesame oil
2 tablespoons maple syrup
2 to 4 tablespoons balsamic
   vinegar
Red pepper flakes to taste

Blend all ingredients in a blender or food processor until thoroughly mixed. This sauce keeps well in the refrigerator. Serve with brown rice and cubed tofu or as a dipping sauce for Vegetable and Tofu Tempura (page 203). You can marinate slices of tofu in the sauce for several hours, grill, and serve with additional sauce, or marinate whole mushrooms for a special appetizer.

Spicy Peanut Sauce

About 2½ cups

One of the classics from the original book, just slightly updated for flavor and texture. This versatile sauce is great for dipping and marinades and was contributed by public-interest lawyer Kathy Severens of Rosalie, Nebraska.

1 tablespoon oil
3 cloves garlic, minced
½ medium onion, finely chopped
One 1-inch knob of fresh grated ginger, or more to taste
½ teaspoon red chili powder, or more to taste

1 tablespoon soy sauce or tamari
2 tablespoons tomato paste
Juice of ¼ lime
1 cup coconut milk
1 cup smooth peanut butter
Salt to taste

In a saucepan, heat the oil and sauté the garlic and onion until the onion is translucent. Add the ginger and cook for 2 minutes, stirring occasionally. Add the remaining ingredients and cook gently for 5 minutes, stirring frequently to prevent the sauce from burning. Adjust for salt. If you want a smooth sauce, use a small blender or food processor to purée, adding warm water to reach your desired consistency.

We love serving this as part of an Indonesian-inspired gado-gado salad, layering brown rice with roasted vegetables and protein (tofu, tempeh, or eggs) and then smothering it all with this spicy sauce. For the best flavor, make the sauce a day ahead. It keeps well for up to 1 week in the refrigerator.

Homemade Marinara

About 4 cups

This sauce can be enjoyed with your favorite pasta or as a base for a savory stew.

2 tablespoons olive oil
2 large cloves garlic, minced
1 onion, minced
1½ cups sliced button mushrooms
2 stalks celery, chopped
1 medium green bell pepper, diced
One 28-ounce can crushed tomatoes

1 teaspoon salt
2 tablespoons maple syrup (optional)
1 bay leaf
½ teaspoon dried oregano
1 sprig fresh thyme
Dash of dried marjoram (optional)

In a large skillet or heavy pot, heat the oil and sauté the garlic and onion for 1 minute. Add the remaining ingredients, bring the sauce to a boil, then turn the heat to low and simmer, covered, for 15 minutes, stirring frequently. For best flavor, refrigerate overnight to let the flavors marry. Remove the bay leaf, reheat, and serve over hot pasta.

Creamy Cashew Gravy

1 ½ cups

Easily made 🌱 with a vegan butter alternative

This great alternative to traditional gravy can be drizzled over mashed potatoes or your favorite vegetables. It's inspired by a recipe from Barbara Cuomo of Freedom, Maine.

½ cup cashews (raw or roasted)
1½ cups vegetable stock
1 tablespoon unsalted butter or vegan alternative
3 cloves garlic, minced

1 cup sliced button mushrooms
1 tablespoon tamari
Salt and freshly ground black pepper to taste

In a blender or food processor, blend the cashews with 1 cup of the stock; set aside. In a medium saucepan, melt the butter, add the garlic and mushrooms, sauté over low heat for a couple minutes, and then add the tamari. Stir in the cashew blend and the remaining ½ cup stock and simmer over low heat for 3 to 4 minutes, until the texture is thick like gravy. Add salt and pepper to taste. Serve over vegetables, mashed potatoes, or cooked grains.

MAIN DISHES

Sandwiches

DIY Sandwich Ideas

For a meal that is simple and new each time, fill sliced bread or pita with a variety of combinations driven by your taste buds and the ingredients in your kitchen. Here are some of the favorite filling ingredients at my house. Pick your favorites, try one of the recipes in this section, or explore something new!

Bottom Layer

- Falafel patties
- Grilled tofu or our Fried Turmeric Tofu (page 291)
- Beans, especially pinto beans or chickpeas, whole or puréed

Top Layer

- Chopped nuts
- Sliced red onion
- Sweet peas
- Shredded lettuce or cabbage
- Chopped spinach
- Sliced cucumbers
- Grated beets
- Cheese (sliced, grated, crumbled)
- Toasted sunflower seeds
- Tomatoes
- Sliced or smashed avocado

Seasonings

- Fresh herbs (basil, parsley, cilantro, dill, etc.)
- Dried spices (curry powder, chili powder, ground cumin, dried oregano, paprika, etc.)

Dressing

- Alice's Creamy Meyer Lemon Dressing (page 248)
- Yogurt or labneh
- Tahini sauce

Brooks's Superiority Burger

8 to 10 patties

This is not fake meat, nor is it vying to be. The un-likeness to the real thing is canny. Think of these as vegetable-and-grain croquettes that are put on buns. These are our namesake, they are absolutely recognizable as food, and they are meant to be a Luddite response to the modern gaggle of vegetable patties that bleed and squirt and ape. —Brooks Headley

Oil for sautéing and roasting

1 medium yellow onion, chopped

Salt and freshly ground black pepper

2 teaspoons ground toasted fennel seeds

1 teaspoon chile powder

1 cup cooked chickpeas, a bit less than one 15-ounce can, drained and rinsed

1 teaspoon white wine vinegar

1 cup red quinoa, rinsed vigorously, cooked, and cooled (see Note)

1 cup small-diced carrots (about 2 medium carrots)

½ cup coarse bread crumbs

¾ cup walnuts, toasted and crushed

Juice of 1 lemon

1 tablespoon chopped fresh flat-leaf parsley

1 tablespoon hot chili sauce

2 tablespoons unmodified potato starch (or cornstarch if you can't find potato starch)

Grapeseed oil for searing the patties

Burger buns

Shredded lettuce, roasted tomatoes, pickle slices, sauerkraut, and/or sliced Muenster cheese (or other cheese of your liking) for topping (optional)

Honey mustard, Dijon mustard, mayonnaise, and/or ketchup for serving (optional)

Preheat the oven to 425°F.

In a pan, heat the oil and sauté the onion until translucent and browned, then season with ½ teaspoon salt, black pepper to taste, the fennel, and chile powder. Add the chickpeas and cook for 5 to 10 minutes, stirring constantly, until nicely browned. Deglaze the hot pan with the vinegar, scraping everything stuck to the bottom of the pan back into the mixture. Using a potato masher, roughly smash the onion-chickpea mixture. Mix the chickpea mash by hand with the cooled quinoa.

Coat the carrots with olive oil and salt and pepper to taste, toss, and roast in the oven until dark around the edges and soft, 20 to 25 minutes. Add to the chickpea-quinoa mixture. Add the bread crumbs, walnuts, lemon juice, parsley, and chili sauce and season again with salt and black pepper until it tastes sharp. Mix the potato starch with 1 tablespoon water to create a cloudy, thick slurry. Fold the slurry into the burger mix as the binding agent. Form the mixture into 8 to 10 patties and sear them in grapeseed oil in a hot sauté pan or cast-iron skillet until fully browned, about 3 minutes per side. To serve, place each patty on a toasted bun and top with shredded iceberg lettuce, roasted tomatoes, pickle slices, sauerkraut, and/or cheese and the condiments of your choice.

—From *Superiority Burger Cookbook* by Brooks Headley

Note: Here are some tips for cooking quinoa. Always start with rinsing quinoa thoroughly in a fine-mesh strainer under a rush of cool water. Using a 1-part quinoa to 2-parts water ratio, add quinoa to salted water. Bring to a boil, then lower heat, cover, and let cook over low for 15 minutes. Turn off the heat and let stand, still covered, for 5 more minutes, then fluff with a fork. As tempting as it might be to peek, keep the lid on to keep the steam inside!

Chickpea-Stuffed Pita Pockets

6 pita sandwiches

Of all the recipes that appeared in the 1971 edition, this is the one we have eaten most often. With precooked beans, the whole dish can be put together in no time. It's wonderfully tasty and satisfying. Increase any of the spices to taste.

3 cups cooked chickpeas,
   or two 15-ounce cans,
   drained and rinsed
¼ cup tahini
2 cloves garlic
Juice of 1 lemon
¾ teaspoon ground coriander
½ teaspoon salt
½ teaspoon ground cumin
¼ to ½ teaspoon
   cayenne pepper
6 pita breads
Garnishes (optional):
   shredded lettuce,
   chopped tomatoes,
   chopped cucumber,
   chopped onion,
   1½ cups yogurt

In a food processor, pulse together the chickpeas, tahini, garlic, lemon juice, coriander, salt, cumin, and cayenne pepper to taste, adding a little water, if necessary, to make blending easier. The mix should be mostly puréed with some chickpea chunks. Let stand at room temperature for at least 30 minutes. Cut each pita in half and fill the pockets with the chickpea mixture. Set out garnishes and let everyone assemble their own.

Terry's Take-Out Tofu Sandwiches

4 pita sandwiches

Easily made ♥ by using a mayonnaise alternative

Writes Terry Gips about his recipe, "Fast food never had it so good. Look out, hamburger!" These sandwiches are easily thrown together, and you can customize with your favorite vegetables.

Oil for sautéing
1 medium onion, sliced
   crosswise into rings
1 cup sliced mushrooms
1 cup vegetables (sprouts,
   leafy greens, thinly sliced
   carrots, zucchini, shredded cabbage, etc.)
4 slices firm tofu, one
   14-ounce package cut
   lengthwise about ½ inch
   thick

2 tablespoons soy sauce
   or tamari
2 teaspoons chili paste
   (sambal oelek)
1 tablespoon rice vinegar
Mayo and sriracha for
   spreading
4 pita breads, sliced in
   half

Heat the oil in a large skillet and sauté the onion rings for 2 minutes. Add the mushrooms and vegetables and sauté another 2 to 3 minutes. Remove the vegetables and coat the skillet with more oil for pan-frying. Fry the tofu slices for 4 to 5 minutes on each side, until golden. You may need to do this in batches if all the slices don't fit in the skillet. While that's happening, whisk together the soy sauce, chili paste, and vinegar. Once the tofu is done, drain the oil from the pan, add the soy sauce mixture, and pan-fry the tofu for a minute on each side. Spread mayonnaise and sriracha into each pita and add the cooked tofu and vegetables.

One-Pot Meals

As you dive into these one-pot meal ideas, consider making more grains, beans, or rice than you need for the recipe. Leftover grains or beans can be turned into lunches and added to salads. Leftover rice is great for fried rice. You can cook more beans than you need for a recipe and freeze what you don't use. Beans keep well in the freezer; grains can be stored for several days in the refrigerator.

One-Pot Spinach, Beans, and Rice

4 servings

Easily made 🌱 by omitting the cheese and sour cream

Make this meal when you want to minimize time spent in the kitchen. Prepare the brown rice in advance, throw everything in a pot, and, in less than 10 minutes, you have a complete meal and just one pot to wash. Make it colorful by serving with a contrasting vegetable, like sautéed carrots or yellow squash.

2 tablespoons oil
½ medium onion, chopped
1 teaspoon ground cumin
¼ teaspoon cayenne pepper
2 cups pasta sauce or Homemade Marinara (page 262)
1½ cups cooked red kidney beans, or one 15-ounce can, drained and rinsed

2 cups cooked brown rice (¾ cup uncooked)
6 cups chopped fresh spinach
¾ cup shredded cheddar cheese
Chopped fresh cilantro and sour cream for topping

In a large pot, heat the oil over low-medium heat and add the onion and spices. Sauté for 1 to 2 minutes, then add the pasta sauce, beans, and rice. Mix well. Add the spinach and cook, covered, for 3 to 4 minutes, until all the spinach has wilted. Stir together thoroughly and top with cheddar cheese. Place the lid back on to melt the cheese. Remove from the heat and enjoy topped with fresh cilantro and sour cream.

Quinoa and Beans Skillet

2 servings

This one-pot dish can be made into a complete meal simply by adding some fresh greens on the side, or try serving it with a crispy cucumber and tomato salad.

2 tablespoons oil
1 clove garlic, minced
½ onion, chopped
½ green bell pepper, diced
1½ cups cooked kidney
   or pinto beans, or one
   15-ounce can, rinsed and
   drained

½ cup diced tomatoes
   (canned or fresh)
1½ cups cooked quinoa (see
   page 269)
1 teaspoon paprika
Dash of cayenne pepper
Salt to taste

In a skillet, heat the oil and sauté the garlic, onion, and green pepper until the onions are translucent. Add the beans, tomatoes, quinoa, and spices and sauté for 5 minutes. Adjust for salt and enjoy.

Mediterranean Eggplant and Zucchini Skillet

4 servings

Easily made 🅥 by omitting the yogurt

For a special dinner, serve with a Greek salad of lettuce, tomatoes, Greek olives, and feta cheese.

2 tablespoons olive oil
1 medium onion, chopped
1 clove garlic, minced
1 small or medium egg-
   plant, peeled and diced
   into 1-inch cubes
1 large zucchini, diced
1 teaspoon chopped
   fresh mint
1 teaspoon chopped
   fresh dill

1 tablespoon chopped
   fresh parsley
Juice of 1 lemon
1 cup canned diced
   tomatoes
One 8-ounce can tomato
   sauce
Salt and red pepper
   flakes for topping
Brown rice and yogurt
   for serving

Heat the olive oil in a skillet and sauté the onion and garlic until the onion is translucent. Add the eggplant and zucchini and sauté for 5 minutes. Stir in the herbs, lemon juice, tomatoes, and tomato sauce, then cover and cook for 15 minutes. Adjust for salt as needed and top with red pepper flakes. Enjoy with rice and a dollop of yogurt on each serving.

Roman Rice and Beans

8 servings

Easily made ✹ by omitting the cheese

This dish has been one of my family's favorites since publication of the 1971 edition. With a green salad and crusty bread, it is a satisfying meal. It's well suited for serving large gatherings, too.

¼ cup oil for sautéing
2 cloves garlic, crushed
1 large onion, chopped
1 or 2 carrots, chopped
1 stalk celery, chopped
⅔ cup chopped fresh parsley
2 teaspoons dried oregano
2 or 3 large tomatoes, coarsely chopped
1¾ cups cooked red kidney beans

Salt and freshly ground black pepper to taste
4 cups warm, cooked brown rice (1 cup uncooked)
½ cup grated Parmesan cheese, plus more for serving
Chopped fresh parsley for topping

Heat the oil in a skillet and sauté the garlic, onion, carrots, celery, parsley, and oregano until the onion is translucent. Add the tomatoes, beans, and salt and pepper. Simmer for 3 to 4 minutes over low heat. While that's happening, combine the rice and Parmesan cheese in a bowl. Once the beans are ready, serve them over the rice mixture, garnished with parsley and more grated cheese.

Frankie's Feijoada

6 servings

This recipe was one of the favorites from the first edition, with updates from a Brazilian friend for the 20th anniversary edition.

¼ cup oil for sautéing
1 large onion, chopped
2 cloves garlic, minced
2 scallions (white and light green parts), chopped
1 green bell pepper, seeded and chopped
1 tomato, chopped
3 cups cooked black beans, or two 15-ounce cans, rinsed and drained

2 cups vegetable stock
1 bay leaf
1 teaspoon white wine vinegar
2 stalks celery, chopped
½ sweet potato, diced (optional)
1½ teaspoons salt
Chopped fresh cilantro and 1 sliced orange, for topping

Heat the oil in a large pot and sauté the onion, garlic, scallions, green pepper, and tomato until the onion is translucent. Add the beans, stock, bay leaf, vinegar, celery, sweet potato, and salt. Bring to a boil, reduce the heat, and simmer, covered, for 20 minutes.

Mash some of the beans in the pot to thicken the mixture and continue cooking for 5 more minutes. Remove the bay leaf and top with chopped cilantro and orange slices. Enjoy with rice and greens.

Rice with Green Chile Sauce

6 servings

Easily made ♥ by omitting the optional queso fresco

The sauce provides a spicy upgrade to the rice and can be prepared in just a few minutes. Add avocado and queso fresco for a Mexican-inspired twist. We like serving this with Frankie's Feijoada (page 277) and Greens with Sesame Seeds and Orange Slices (page 210) for a complete meal.

Rice	*Sauce*
2 tablespoons olive oil	1 tomato, roughly chopped
1 onion, chopped	One 4-ounce can California green chiles
3 cloves garlic, minced	1 teaspoon salt
2 tomatoes, peeled, seeded, and coarsely chopped	2 cloves garlic
About 4 ½ cups cooked brown rice (2 cups uncooked)	Juice of 1 lemon
½ cup crumbled queso fresco (optional)	1 onion, cut in chunks
½ avocado, sliced (optional)	¼ cup white wine vinegar
	¼ cup cilantro or to taste (optional)

For the rice, heat the oil in a pot and sauté the onion and garlic until the onion is translucent. Add the tomatoes and simmer for a few minutes. Stir in the cooked rice and keep warm over low heat.

For the sauce, purée all the sauce ingredients in a blender. Drizzle over the rice to taste. Top with optional avocado slices and queso fresco.

White Bean Kale Fettuccine

4 servings

Throw most of the ingredients into a high-speed blender and then cook them down to make a creamy sauce that will serve as the base for the fettuccine. Toss with the pasta and enjoy with your favorite toppings.

2 cups chopped kale
2 cups whole milk
1 cup cooked white beans
½ cup grated Parmesan cheese
3 cloves garlic
Salt
¼ teaspoon black pepper
½ pound fettuccine or another pasta of your choice

¼ cup (½ stick) unsalted butter, cut into 4 pieces
Olive oil, chopped basil and/or other fresh herbs, grated Parmesan cheese, and/or red pepper flakes for topping (optional)

Start by blending the kale, milk, white beans, Parmesan, garlic, ½ teaspoon salt, and black pepper in a high-speed blender until you get a smooth sauce. (A high-speed blender is helpful to break down the kale.) The end result should be smooth without any chunks.

Add the sauce to a medium pot and bring to a light simmer. Cook for 5 minutes over low heat, stirring frequently until the sauce thickens, being careful not to boil. Set aside. Add the pasta to a pot of salted boiling water. Boil for 9 to 10 minutes without the lid, stirring occasionally. Drain well, then add the pasta to a bowl with the butter. Toss together until all the butter is melted into the pasta. Add the kale sauce to the bowl and continue tossing everything together until the pasta is completely coated with the sauce. Enjoy with your favorite toppings!

Anthony's Leek, Shiitake, and Miso Butter "Casserole" and Soy-Pickled Peppers

4 to 6 servings

This is a comfort food mash-up of Hong Kong noodles and leek chowder that plays to the strength of the angel hair–like pasta, fideo. The final result is a savory umami bomb. The Soy-Pickled Serrano Peppers (recipe follows) provide a good counterpoint. If you're serving it with the peppers, start those pickling before you begin making the pasta dish. —Anthony Myint

1 medium leek
8 tablespoons (1 stick) un-
    salted butter, plus more
    for sautéing
Salt
6 ounces shiitake mush-
    rooms, or more if you
    want it more mushroomy
    (chanterelle and oyster
    are also good options)
2 shallots, peeled, halved
    lengthwise, and thinly
    sliced, for garnish
4 ounces Bloomsdale
    spinach or other sweet,
    tender green

2 tablespoons miso, light
    or dark are both fine;
    red miso is especially
    good here
1 cup half-and-half, plus
    more as needed
12 ounces fideo or angel
    hair pasta, broken into
    1-inch pieces
Chopped fresh cilantro
    for garnish

Clean the leek thoroughly and reserve the tough greens for stock or other use. Cut the tender interior lengthwise into quarters, then slice finely crosswise and place in a microwave-safe bowl. Cut the butter into small pieces, toss it with the leeks and a generous pinch of salt, and microwave for 30 to 60 seconds until the butter is melted and the leeks are completely relaxed. Add more time as needed. Meanwhile, bring a large pot of salted water to a boil.

Remove the shiitake stems. (You can reserve them for stock as well.) Slice the shiitake caps into thin strips. Heat a large pan—

large enough to eventually toss all the pasta—on medium-high heat, spoon 4 or more tablespoons of the butter from the melted leeks into the pan, and salt generously. Sauté the shiitakes until golden brown, about 6 minutes, tossing occasionally.

In a small pan, melt a bit more butter, about a tablespoon, and add the shallots, frying them until golden brown and crispy, 2 to 4 minutes. Set aside.

Wash, drain, and cut the spinach into ½- to ¼-inch-wide strips.

Add the leeks, butter, and miso to the large pan with the shiitakes and break up any miso clumps. Add the half-and-half and chopped spinach and simmer until spinach has just softened, 1 to 2 minutes. Turn off the heat.

Meanwhile, boil the pasta until just cooked, approximately 2 minutes. Drain, reserving about a half a cup of the pasta water, add the pasta to the large pan, and toss and fold to incorporate. The result should be a slippery and savory pasta. Add salt to taste and another generous splash of half-and-half or reserved pasta water right before serving to ensure slipperiness. Garnish with cilantro and the crispy shallots and serve with soy-pickled peppers.

Soy-Pickled Serrano Peppers

6 serrano peppers   ¼ cup soy sauce or tamari

Halve the peppers lengthwise, remove the stem and seeds, and thinly slice them crosswise. In a small bowl, combine them with the soy sauce. These soy-pickled peppers are a great complement to the mild leek pasta. They're also delicious atop tacos and sandwiches.

—Contributed by Anthony Myint

Aileen's Ginataang Gulay
(Coconut-Simmered Vegetables)

4 servings

Each July, Sama Sama Cooperative camp gathers in its outdoor garden in Oakland, California, to cook and share lunch. Woven into a summer rich with Filipino language, eskrima *(a Filipino martial art form), history, and social justice curriculum, collective meals are embedded into the camp's practices. Under the shade of oak trees, children cut kabocha squash, mince garlic, and reflect on food memories and practices past, present, and future. Kawayan, a young alumni, summed up best what the Sama Sama kitchen is really about: "Cooking is ancestral practice, because food is about nourishing each other."*

Ginataan (simply, to cook in coconut) is a flexible recipe, meant to reflect place. Encoded in its comforting flavors are memories of survival and collective care. Adapt the recipe with ingredients accessible in your community— for example, wilt spinach into the dish, use zucchini in the summer or winged beans if you can find them. You can also substitute another winter squash for kabocha, or make a heartier dish by adding crispy tofu. —Aileen Suzara

1 tablespoon olive oil
1 onion, diced
5 cloves garlic, minced
2 tablespoons grated fresh
   ginger
4 cups cubed kabocha
   squash (no need to peel,
   as the skin is edible!)
3 cups coconut milk, about
   two 13.5-ounce cans
1 or more bird's-eye chile
   or jalapeño pepper, sliced
   (optional; keep the seeds
   for more heat)

2 cups snapped or cut
   yardlong beans (green
   beans or haricots verts
   work well, too)
Sea salt and black pepper
   to taste
Lemon or calamansi to
   taste
Scallions, crispy garlic,
   or shallots for topping
   (optional)

Heat the oil in a heavy saucepan over medium heat. Sauté the onion until soft, add the garlic and ginger, and sauté until fragrant, about 3 to 4 minutes. Add the kabocha and coconut milk. Cover and simmer about 10 minutes or until tender. If you're using the chiles for heat, add them now. Add the beans (or other soft vegetables) and simmer until tender-crisp. Season generously with salt, pepper, and a squeeze of citrus. For a creamier texture and brilliant hue, mash some of the cooked kabocha into the sauce. Serve with rice, toppings, and a splash of your favorite sawsawan (dipping sauce), like a mixture of soy sauce, chiles, lemon juice, and raw garlic.

—Contributed by Aileen Suzara

Lentil Curry with Green Peas and Cauliflower

4 servings

Easily made ♥ by omitting the yogurt

This straightforward curry can be whipped together relatively quickly. We encourage you to experiment by adding your favorite vegetables to the dish. The original was contributed by Deborah Wheeler of Mar Vista, California.

1 cup red lentils or waxed
  dal (yellow split peas),
  rinsed and picked over
Salt
3 tablespoons oil
1 medium onion, chopped
2 cloves garlic, minced
2 tablespoons curry powder
1 cup fresh or frozen peas

½ head cauliflower, broken
  into small florets
Cayenne pepper to taste
1 cup yogurt
½ cucumber, peeled and
  chopped
Chutney, raisins, and/or
  chopped nuts for serving
  (optional)

Fill a pot with 2 cups water, add the lentils and ¼ teaspoon salt, and bring the water to a rapid simmer, then reduce heat and simmer until the lentils lose their distinct shape and are tender, 15 to 20 minutes. Add more water as needed so lentils are consistently covered; drain. Heat the oil in a large skillet and sauté the onion, garlic, and curry powder until the onion is translucent. Add the cooked lentils, peas, cauliflower, cayenne pepper, and 1½ to 2 cups water as needed to achieve a thick stew consistency. Simmer, covered, for about 10 minutes, stirring occasionally. In a small bowl, combine the yogurt and cucumber.

Serve the lentils over rice, with a generous dollop of cucumber yogurt for coolness and condiments on the side.

Padma's Yellow Velvet Lentil Soup with Cumin and Dried Plums

6 to 8 servings

I once went to the annual kite festival in Ahmedabad in Gujarat, in western India. It's a day of celebration when most people can be found on their roofs flying so many kites that the sky looks peppered with locusts. My host, the lovely and beautiful Kinnari, usually makes a feast for the 60 or so people who come through her home on that day. Gujarati food is known for its incredible variety of vegetables, lentils, and fruits. I love the lentil soups, or dals, the best. Gujarati dal has a slightly sweet and hot taste to it. This soup is inspired by the many luscious soups I tasted that weekend at Kinnari's house while flying colorful kites on the roof with the rest of the townsfolk. —Padma Lakshmi

3 cups masoor dal (orange lentils), washed well with warm water and drained
1 bay leaf
1 teaspoon salt
2 tablespoons olive oil
1 teaspoon cumin seeds
½ cup chopped shallots
1½ tablespoons minced fresh ginger
2½ tablespoons shredded unsweetened coconut
1 cup halved lengthwise grape or cherry tomatoes
3 plum tomatoes, quartered
2 teaspoons curry powder
Juice of 1 lemon
10 dried plums, pitted, chopped to bits
1 cup chopped fresh cilantro leaves

Fill a deep stew pot with the lentils, bay leaf, salt, and enough water to cover by 1 inch. Simmer on very low heat for 1 hour.

Heat the oil in a skillet and add the cumin seeds. After 2 minutes, add the shallots and ginger and cook until the shallots are glassy. Add the coconut and stir until the coconut is golden brown. Add all the tomatoes and the curry powder and sauté on medium heat for about 5 minutes, until the tomatoes start to wilt and lose their shape. When the mixture forms a cohesive paste, add it to the lentils, stirring over low heat until nicely combined.

Remove the bay leaves. With an immersion blender, pulverize the lentils so that the whole mixture is roughly blended but not totally liquefied. Remove the soup from the heat and stir in the lemon juice, chopped plums, and cilantro. Serve hot.

—From *Tangy Tart Hot & Sweet* by Padma Lakshmi

Stir-Fries

One of our favorite cooking methods, stir-frying is a great way to make quick and satisfying meals. A large nonstick pan or a wok will work well for most of the recipes in this section.

Couscous with Savory Vegetable Bowls

4 servings

Couscous is a light, partially refined wheat product that is a common ingredient in many Middle Eastern dishes. It's ready within minutes, which makes it perfect when you want a quick meal. Couscous pairs well with stewed vegetables and your favorite protein. This is just one riff on a couscous bowl with vegetables. Feel free to experiment with the vegetables of your choice.

¼ cup oil
1 large onion, chopped
1 stalk celery, chopped
2 cloves garlic, minced
2 sprigs fresh thyme
1 teaspoon ground cumin
2 cups canned diced
  tomatoes

2 cups sliced mushrooms
2 cups diced zucchini
2 cups cauliflower florets
Salt
1 cup (6 ounces) uncooked
  couscous

In a large wok or skillet, heat the oil and sauté the onion, celery, garlic, thyme, and cumin for a couple minutes. Add the diced tomatoes and remaining vegetables and simmer, covered, for 15 minutes.

Meanwhile, in a medium saucepan, bring 1¼ cups lightly salted water to a boil and stir in the couscous. Cover, remove from heat, and let stand for 5 minutes. Fluff the couscous lightly with a fork before serving.

Season the vegetables with salt and enjoy over the prepared couscous.

Crunchy Peanut Rice Noodles

4 servings

New for this edition, this dish is delicious with a fried or soft-boiled egg, fresh herbs, toasted sesame seeds, and crushed peanuts for an added crunch.

8 ounces pad Thai rice
noodles
¼ cup toasted sesame oil
½ onion, chopped
1 red bell pepper, seeded
and sliced lengthwise in
thin strips
2 cloves garlic, minced
One 1-inch knob fresh
ginger, finely chopped

1 medium carrot, julienned
2 medium zucchini,
cubed
2 cups sliced mushrooms
Chopped fresh cilantro,
finely chopped
peanuts, toasted
sesame seeds, fried
egg, and sriracha for
optional toppings

Sauce

3 tablespoons soy sauce
or tamari, or (for
pescatarians)
2 tablespoons fish
sauce

2 teaspoons chili paste
(sambal oelek)
2 tablespoons rice vinegar
¼ cup vegetable stock

In a large pot, bring 4 to 5 quarts water to a boil and add the noodles. Cook for 4 minutes, or until tender, stirring occasionally. Drain under cold water and set aside. In a wok or large pan, heat the sesame oil over medium heat and add the onion, bell pepper, garlic, and ginger and sauté for 1 to 2 minutes. Stir in the carrot, zucchini, and mushrooms and sauté for another 4 to 5 minutes. While that's happening, mix all the ingredients for the sauce in a small bowl and set aside. Add the cooked noodles and the sauce to the wok, mix well until all ingredients are worked in, and cook for another minute or until all ingredients are warmed through. Remove from the heat and serve with any, or all, of the optional toppings: cilantro, chopped peanuts, toasted sesame seeds, a fried egg, and sriracha.

Fried Turmeric Tofu

4 servings

The original concept for this recipe came from Eric Dunder of Green-bush, Maine. The flavors blend together and make a fresh twist on fried tofu. You can take the edge off by omitting the jalapeño—it's still just as delicious!

¼ cup oil

One 12-ounce block extra-firm tofu, drained and cut into ½-inch cubes

½ teaspoon each ground turmeric, dried thyme, ground cumin, and curry powder

2 cloves garlic, minced

1 jalapeño pepper, seeded and chopped (optional)

2 tablespoons tamari

2 tablespoons nutritional yeast

Heat the oil in a large pan and sauté the tofu over high heat for 6 to 8 minutes, until the tofu is golden. If you want crispy tofu, make sure you give the pieces enough room and sauté until each side is golden, then flip. Depending on the size of your pan, you may need to cook in multiple batches. Once crispy, add the spices and stir until the tofu is nicely yellowed with the turmeric mixture. Then stir in the garlic, jalapeño (if using), tamari, and nutritional yeast. Sauté a little longer, until uniformly golden brown. Serve warm over fried rice, dribbling the extra sauce over the top.

Napa Cabbage and Mushroom Stir-Fry

4 servings

*The original came to us from Julya Ripsam of Alamosa, Colorado. Use
a wok or your favorite big skillet for this simple, healthy dish.*

2 tablespoons toasted
  sesame oil
1 tablespoon grated fresh
  ginger
½ head napa cabbage, cut
  into bite-sized pieces
1 cup sliced mushrooms
3 tablespoons tamari, or
  more to taste

½ teaspoon cayenne
  pepper
One 12-ounce block firm
  tofu, drained and cut into
  1-inch squares
Toasted sesame seeds
  and chopped scallions
  (white and light green
  parts) for topping

In a wok or large skillet, heat the oil and sauté the ginger
briefly. Add the napa cabbage and mushrooms and cook, covered, for a few minutes, stirring occasionally until the cabbage
starts to wilt. Add the tamari, cayenne, and tofu and cook for
another 5 to 10 minutes, stirring occasionally. If you want the
tofu to be crunchy, fry it in oil in a separate pan before adding
it to the wok. Serve over brown rice or rice noodles and top
with toasted sesame seeds and chopped scallions for a quick
and tasty dinner.

Vegetable Sesame Fried Rice

4 servings

This one-pan dish can be enjoyed as a complete meal on its own or paired with your favorite protein and vegetables. A great way to use whatever vegetables you have on hand.

¼ cup toasted sesame oil
1 onion, chopped
One 1-inch knob fresh
   ginger, minced
3 eggs, beaten
3 cups chopped vegetables
   (cauliflower, broccoli, bell
   peppers, zucchini, leafy
   greens, and/or carrots)
2 cups cooked long grain
   brown rice (1 cup un-
   cooked)

1 tablespoon tamari
½ tablespoon fish sauce
   (optional)
Salt to taste
Chopped scallions (white
   and green parts) and
   toasted sesame seeds
   for topping

In a wok or large pan, heat the oil and add the onion and ginger. Sauté until the onion is translucent. Move the onion and ginger to one side and, on the other side, add the eggs. Scramble until cooked slightly, then add the chopped vegetables, brown rice, tamari, and fish sauce (if using). Stir and cook, covered, over medium heat for 5 minutes. Salt to taste. Remove from the heat, top with chopped scallions and toasted sesame seeds, and serve.

Baked and Roasted

While the cooking time for these dishes may be longer than for stovetop meals, your actual work time is not necessarily greater. And like many of the recipes in this book, you can feel free to adapt ingredients to what you have in your kitchen. Remember, never feel you have to follow the recipe to the letter!

Three-Cheese Spinach Lasagna with Fresh Tomatoes

6 to 8 servings

An undemanding vegetarian lasagna that includes good-for-you spinach and fresh tomatoes instead of the usual marinara sauce.

Salt
½ pound lasagna noodles
  (about 9 noodles)
2 to 3 tablespoons oil
2 cloves garlic, minced
1 medium onion, chopped
2 medium tomatoes,
  chopped
2 cups sliced button mushrooms
½ teaspoon dried oregano
1 teaspoon minced fresh
  rosemary

2 cups washed, drained,
  and chopped spinach
1 cup ricotta cheese
½ cup grated Parmesan
  cheese, plus more
  (optional) for topping
2 cups grated mozzarella
  cheese
Chopped fresh basil for
  topping

Preheat the oven to 350°F. In a pot of boiling salted water, cook the noodles until al dente according to package directions. Drain and set aside.

Heat the oil in a large skillet and cook the garlic, onion, tomatoes, and mushrooms for 4 to 5 minutes over medium heat. When the onion is translucent, add the oregano, rosemary, and spinach. Cook, covered, for a few minutes until the spinach is wilted. Mix together and turn off the heat.

In a large bowl combine the ricotta, Parmesan, and 1½ cups of the mozzarella. Pour the sautéed vegetables into the cheese mixture and mix thoroughly. Layer the noodles alternately with the vegetable-cheese mixture in an 8 × 13-inch baking pan. Top with reserved ½ cup mozzarella and more Parmesan cheese, if desired. Bake for 30 minutes. Let sit 5 to 10 minutes before slicing and serving. Enjoy topped with fresh basil.

Stuffed Ricotta Eggplant

2 servings

A creation of Mary Sinclair of Albany, California, and Julie Rosenbaum of Ann Arbor, Michigan, both of whom helped test many recipes in the original Diet. *For this edition, we simplified the recipe and swapped out cottage cheese for ricotta, among other changes, to bring the flavors to life in this hearty and beautiful dish. Perfect with a green salad and crusty bread.*

1 medium eggplant	½ teaspoon ground cumin
2 tablespoons oil	¼ teaspoon cayenne pepper
½ onion, chopped	½ cup cooked rice
½ green bell pepper, seeded and diced	½ cup ricotta cheese
1 tablespoon tomato paste	¼ cup chopped fresh parsley for topping
½ cup sliced mushrooms	Crumbled feta cheese and red pepper flakes for topping
1 clove garlic, minced	
½ teaspoon ground coriander	

Preheat the oven to 350°F. Cut the eggplant in half lengthwise and scoop out the flesh with a small knife, leaving about ¼-inch-thick flesh in the eggplant. Set the shells aside. Heat the oil in a skillet and sauté the onion, bell pepper, and tomato paste for 1 to 2 minutes. Stir in the eggplant flesh, mushrooms, garlic, and spices and sauté for about 15 minutes, covered, over low-medium heat, stirring occasionally. Turn off the heat, let cool 2 to 3 minutes, and add the cooked eggplant mix to a bowl along with the cooked rice and ricotta cheese. Mix well. Put the eggplant shells in a tight-fitting baking dish and fill evenly with the sautéed mixture. Cover with aluminum foil and bake for 45 minutes. Remove the foil and bake another 10 minutes. Enjoy sprinkled with fresh parsley, feta, and red pepper flakes for additional heat!

Sesame Eggplant Parmesan

4 servings

Even eggplant doubters like this dish. It is easy to make but elegant enough for guests. A meal by itself with a fresh green salad and crusty bread, it can become a heartier dinner if you add your favorite pasta or rice as a bottom layer under the eggplant.

Oil for sautéing
1 medium eggplant, sliced crosswise ½ inch thick
2 cups pasta sauce or Homemade Marinara (page 262)
¼ teaspoon each dried oregano and fresh thyme and rosemary
½ onion, finely chopped

3 cloves garlic, minced
1 tablespoon tamari
¼ cup grated Parmesan cheese
½ cup whole toasted sesame seeds
½ pound mozzarella cheese, sliced
Toasted bread crumbs for topping (optional)

Preheat the oven to 350°F. Heat the oil in a large skillet and sauté the eggplant slices until browned and becoming soft on both sides. You may have to do this in batches if all the eggplant slices don't fit. Remove the eggplant, set aside, and add the pasta sauce, herbs, onion, garlic, tamari, Parmesan, and sesame seeds to the skillet. Simmer for 15 minutes. Arrange the eggplant slices on a large ovenproof platter or in a shallow 2-quart casserole. Cover with the sauce and top with the mozzarella slices. Bake for about 15 minutes, remove from the oven, and then broil for 1 to 2 minutes or until the top layer browns. If you like, top with toasted bread crumbs.

Lentil Pasticcio

4 servings

A favorite recipe of Sue Pohl of Hillsdale, Michigan. We recommend serving it with a Greek Salad with Arugula and Chickpeas (page 253) or your favorite tossed salad. This dish resembles a vegetarian version of the classic Hamburger Helper.

8 ounces macaroni noodles
2 tablespoons oil
1 small onion, chopped
1 cup brown lentils, rinsed
  and picked over
3 cloves garlic, minced
1 cup tomato purée
1 tablespoon tamari
½ teaspoon chopped fresh
  rosemary
2 cups ricotta cheese

¼ cup all-purpose flour
½ cup grated Parmesan
  cheese
1 egg
1 cup milk
1 teaspoon salt
½ teaspoon grated nutmeg
1 teaspoon ground
  cinnamon
Bread crumbs for topping
  (optional)

Cook the macaroni according to the package directions until al dente, drain, and set aside. Preheat the oven to 350°F.

In a pot, heat the oil, add half of the chopped onion, and sauté for a couple minutes. Stir in the lentils, garlic, tomato purée, tamari, rosemary, and 2¼ cups water and simmer at medium-low heat until the water is absorbed and the lentils are tender, about 30 minutes. Meanwhile, in a bowl, whisk together the ricotta, flour, remaining onion, Parmesan, egg, milk, salt, nutmeg, and cinnamon until well blended.

Pour half the macaroni into a 9 × 9-inch baking pan or casserole. Pour a third of the cheese mixture over it, then make a lentil layer (using all the mixture), topped with another third of the cheese mixture. Add the remaining macaroni and top with remaining third of the cheese mixture. Sprinkle with bread crumbs for a crusty top, if desired. Bake for 35 minutes, or until nicely browned.

Spinach and Cheese Bake with Black Olives

6 to 8 servings

Simpler than a quiche, this dish has a distinctive and rich taste. It was improved for the 20th anniversary edition by Myra Levy and Charles Varon of San Francisco and updated again for this edition.

4 eggs
2 cups ricotta cheese
½ cup all-purpose flour
4 ounces Greek feta cheese, crumbled
1 teaspoon salt
½ pound (5 cups) spinach, washed and chopped or torn

Oil for greasing
Black olives, halved, for garnish
Freshly ground black pepper to taste

Preheat the oven to 350°F. In a bowl, beat the eggs, ricotta, and flour together until smooth. Add the feta, salt, and spinach and mix thoroughly. Pack the mixture into a large greased pie plate and bake for 60 minutes. Top with black olives and black pepper and enjoy with fresh bread.

Pesto Portobello Mini Pizzas

4 servings

A delightful and easy way to enjoy a pizza-like meal when you don't want to make a crust. Serve with a salad and crusty bread.

4 portobello mushrooms, stems removed
½ cup fresh basil leaves
¼ cup walnuts
¼ cup grated Parmesan cheese
¼ cup olive oil
Salt to taste
1 cup chopped tomatoes, canned or fresh
1 cup shredded mozzarella cheese
Red pepper flakes for topping

Preheat the oven to 425°F. Line a baking sheet with parchment paper. Place the mushrooms, top side down, on the baking sheet. In a food processor, pulse the basil, walnuts, Parmesan, and olive oil into a pesto, season with salt, and spread it evenly on the mushroom bottoms. Layer the chopped tomatoes and shredded mozzarella on top and bake for 20 minutes. Adjust for salt as needed and enjoy topped with red pepper flakes.

DIY Pizza

Who doesn't love pizza? Part of what makes this such a fun food is that you can customize it with your favorite sauces and toppings. You can use our Everyday Pizza Dough recipe (page 302) as the base or purchase a pre-made dough if you're short on time. Pita rounds or naan also work as an effective base for pizza. Once you have your base, layer on your favorite ingredients and pop it in the oven! Avoid overlayering or using too much sauce, since either can result in a soggy crust.

Crust

- Everyday Pizza Dough (page 302)
- Pre-made dough
- Pita rounds
- Naan

Sauce

- Tomato sauce
- Pesto sauce
- Arrabbiata sauce
- Homemade Marinara (page 262)

Cheeses

- Ricotta
- Mozzarella
- Gorgonzola
- Burrata
- Parmesan
- Gruyère

Toppings

- Kale
- Arugula
- Spinach
- Onions
- Mushrooms
- Broccoli
- Peppers
- Olives
- Fresh herbs (basil, rosemary, thyme, etc.)
- Dried herbs (oregano, red pepper flakes, garlic powder, etc.)

Everyday Pizza Dough

6 servings

Ready to be enjoyed the same day, this simple pizza dough provides an impressive base for your favorite cheeses and toppings. Bake to golden perfection and enjoy alongside a bowl of crispy greens.

3 ½ cups all-purpose flour   1 tablespoon olive oil,
½ teaspoon active dry yeast   plus more as needed
½ tablespoon salt

If using a stand mixer, mix flour, yeast, and salt together for a minute with the paddle attachment. Add oil to 1¼ cups warm water and stir. Pour into mixing bowl and mix for another 1 to 2 minutes on low, until ingredients are well integrated. Switch to the kneading attachment and knead for 5 minutes, until dough becomes smooth. If using a metal spoon, mix the flour, yeast, and salt together in a bowl. Add in 1¼ cups warm water and the oil until all ingredients are worked in together, then use your hands to knead the dough into a ball. The dough should be sticky enough to adhere to the bottom of the bowl but not so sticky that it clings to your fingers. Add a few teaspoons of water as needed to better work the dough. Oil a large bowl, add the dough, cover with plastic wrap, and allow to rise for 2 hours at room temperature.

When you're ready to bake, preheat the oven to 450°F. Stretch and fold the dough into itself a few times until it is smooth and elastic. Remove the dough from the bowl, place it on a flat surface, brush with more olive oil as needed, and roll it out into a 12-inch round. Lift the dough and stretch it out from the middle with your fists. Place on a parchment-paper-lined baking sheet, add your favorite sauce, cheese, and toppings, brush the crust with more olive oil, and bake for 10 to 12 minutes.

Crusty Bean Pie

4 to 6 servings

Easily made ❤ by omitting the cheese

For this recipe, use your favorite piecrust. Our go-to can be found in How to Cook Everything Vegetarian *by Mark Bittman. But if you don't want to make your own, don't let that stop you from making this or any savory pie: Buy piecrusts from the store and keep them in your freezer so you have them handy when the inspiration hits you.*

Oil for sautéing
1 onion, chopped
1 carrot, chopped
3 stalks celery, chopped
3 cups cooked kidney
   beans, or two 15-ounce
   cans, rinsed and drained
Pinch of cayenne pepper

1 teaspoon ground cumin
1 tablespoon tamari
One 9-inch prepared
   piecrust, store-bought
   or homemade, at room
   temperature
⅓ cup (or more) grated
   cheddar cheese

Preheat the oven to 350°F. Heat the oil in a skillet and briefly sauté the onion, carrot, and celery. Gently stir in the beans, cayenne, cumin, and tamari. Adjust seasoning to taste and turn the mixture into the piecrust. Bake about 25 minutes, remove from the oven, sprinkle with the cheese, and bake 5 minutes more.

Walnut Cheddar Loaf

1 loaf; about 6 servings

This vegetarian version of meat loaf is especially nice served with whole walnuts sprinkled on top.

2 tablespoons oil
1 large onion, chopped
1 cup coarsely chopped
   walnuts
1 cup grated cheddar
   cheese
Juice of ½ lemon

2 eggs, beaten
½ teaspoon salt
2 tablespoons nutritional
   yeast
1 teaspoon caraway seeds
1¼ cups cooked brown
   rice (½ cup uncooked)

Preheat the oven to 350°F. Heat the oil in a pan and sauté the onion until translucent. Mix the onion with the remaining ingredients in a bowl and put the mixture in an oiled 9 × 5-inch loaf pan, smoothing the top. Bake for 30 minutes, or until edges are browned. Allow to cool and cut into slices.

Snacks and Sweets

In the original *Diet*, I included desserts because I wanted people to see I'm no purist. Yes, we should all try to limit our sugar intake, but indulging in the occasional homemade treat is not a problem! One of the best ways to reduce sugar in our diets is to cut out sugary drinks, including sodas, sports drinks, energy drinks, imitation fruit drinks, and sweetened iced teas or coffees. (Consider that just one large fancy coffee drink can catapult you beyond the World Health Organization's upper daily sugar limit for an adult—about 6 teaspoons.)

Cinnamon Roasted Nuts

6 to 8 servings

Serve as a party snack or offer as a treat after a big meal. Or you can enjoy these with yogurt or oatmeal for breakfast.

1 teaspoon ground
   cinnamon
½ teaspoon ground
   nutmeg
Pinch of salt
2 tablespoons coconut oil,
   melted

3 tablespoons maple syrup
   (use more or less to
   adjust for sweetness)
2 cups mixed nuts
   (walnuts, cashews,
   pecans, almonds, etc.)

Preheat the oven to 300°F. Mix the spices and salt in a large bowl with the coconut oil and maple syrup. Add the nuts and massage the spice mix into the nuts. Pour the nuts onto a parchment-lined baking sheet and bake for 25 minutes, stirring once halfway through. Allow to cool and enjoy.

Peanut Butter–Date Spread

4 to 6 servings

This simple-to-make spread is rich and creamy. It's delicious scooped on ice cream, oatmeal, yogurt, or toast. Prepare and enjoy it throughout the week.

1½ cups dates, soaked in
    water for 2 to 3 hours
    and drained
¼ cup smooth peanut
    butter

¼ cup chopped peanuts,
    walnuts, or pecans
Pinch of salt

Pulse the dates and peanut butter in a food processor until creamy. Fold in the nuts and a pinch of salt. Enjoy!

Coconut Tahini Balls with Sesame Seeds

12 to 18 pieces

Enjoy these when you're craving something sweet and rich. The tahini and peanut butter will keep you satisfied in between meals, and the shredded coconut adds an additional layer of flavor.

1 cup pitted dates, finely chopped in a food processor
¼ cup tahini
¼ cup smooth peanut butter
2 tablespoons maple syrup
¼ cup sesame seeds
¼ cup chopped pecans or walnuts
¼ teaspoon ground cinnamon
Shredded unsweetened coconut

In a bowl, mix together the dates, tahini, peanut butter, maple syrup, sesame seeds, chopped nuts, and cinnamon. Combine the ingredients thoroughly with your hands. You can also use a food processor to blend them together for a smoother texture. In the palm of your hand, divide and shape the mixture into 12 to 18 small balls, then roll them in a bowl of shredded coconut to coat. Chill for a few hours until firm—and enjoy!

Sesame and Oat Dream Bars

12 squares

A heavenly taste combination. Enjoy when you're in the mood for a snack that has subtle sweetness and crunch.

Base Layer

1 cup pecans or walnuts
1 cup rolled oats
Pinch of salt
2 tablespoons maple
    syrup
2 tablespoons oil

Top Layer

1 egg
¼ cup maple syrup
½ teaspoon vanilla
2 tablespoons flour
½ cup shredded
    unsweetened coconut
¼ cup sesame seeds

For the base layer, preheat the oven to 350°F. In a food processor, pulse the nuts, oats, and salt until finely chopped. Add the maple syrup and oil and continue pulsing until a wet, crumbly mixture forms. Using a spatula and your hands, shape the mixture into a 6 × 8-inch rectangle. Bake on a parchment-lined baking sheet for 5 minutes.

In a small bowl, whisk all the top layer ingredients together. Spread it evenly over the cookie base and bake for 20 minutes. Let cool for 30 minutes before cutting into squares. Store in an airtight container in the refrigerator and enjoy throughout the week.

Frozen Peach Treat with Lemon Zest

4 to 5 servings

This refreshing and easy-to-make treat was contributed by Claire Greens-felder, who also contributed several other recipes to the first edition. This is a fabulous way to put those almost-too-far-gone peaches to work. Depending on the sweetness of your fruit, you may need no honey at all. The recipe is easy to scale up or down, depending on your peach supply.

4 ripe peaches, peeled, pitted, and roughly chopped

½ cup plain yogurt (this works especially well with European yogurt)

Zest of 1 lemon, or more to taste

Juice of ½ lemon, or more to taste

Honey to taste (optional)

In a large bowl, crush the peaches with a potato masher or back of a fork. Add the yogurt, lemon zest, and lemon juice. Stir well. Add more lemon and yogurt to taste and, depending on the sweetness of the peaches, add honey (if using). Ladle the mixture into 4 or 5 small individual ramekins or bowls. Set in the freezer for at least 2½ hours. Serve straight from the freezer.

Alicia's Salted Chocolate-Almond Cookies

15 to 30 cookies, depending on size

Despite this being a cookie, its texture is decidedly more brownie-like. This was a fan favorite back in the day when I was selling baked goods at farmers' markets, and it goes especially great with nondairy vanilla bean ice cream. —Alicia Kennedy

1 cup chocolate chunks
1 cup coarsely chopped almonds
2³⁄₈ cups all-purpose flour
1 scant cup cocoa powder
¾ teaspoon baking soda
1 teaspoon kosher salt
3 tablespoons arrowroot
1 cup loosely packed dark brown sugar
⁷⁄₈ cup cane sugar

½ cup unsweetened almond milk
16 tablespoons vegan butter, preferably Miyoko's Creamery, cut into chunks, at room temperature
Coarse sea salt for sprinkling

Set aside the roughly chopped chocolate and almonds in one bowl. Measure the flour, cocoa, baking soda, salt, and arrowroot into one bowl and whisk to combine well. Measure both sugars into another bowl, then pour the nondairy milk into a measuring cup. Set aside.

In the bowl of a stand mixer fitted with the paddle attachment (or a mixing bowl and using a hand mixer), beat the butter on medium speed until creamy. Add the sugars and continue to beat on medium until the butter has a sandy texture and all the sugar has been incorporated. Turn the mixer to low and add the dry ingredients in three parts, letting each addition incorporate fully into the dough before adding more. After the dry ingredients have been added, stream in the nondairy milk, continuing to beat the dough on low. It should form into a ball around the paddle. Add the chopped chocolate and almonds, using the mixer or a wooden spoon to incorporate them. Place the dough in a sealable container or wrap it tightly in plastic wrap and chill for at least 1 hour.

When you're ready to bake, preheat the oven to 350°F and line a large baking sheet with parchment paper. Using your hands or an ice cream scoop, measure out between 1 tablespoon and ⅓ cup of dough per cookie—depending upon the desired size. Place each ball of dough on the parchment-lined sheet about 2 inches apart (they won't spread much). Sprinkle them with coarse sea salt before baking. (If making more than one sheet at a time, keep the ready-to-bake cookies in the fridge or freezer rather than at room temperature.) Bake each sheet for 12 to 16 minutes, depending on the size of the cookies. As they cook to perfect doneness, they'll lose their shine and become matte in appearance.

Let cool to room temperature before eating.

—Contributed by Alicia Kennedy

Cypress Point Carrot Cake with Cream Cheese Frosting

8 ample slices

Cypress Point refers to my former home in Point Richmond, California, where I wrote the first edition of Diet for a Small Planet, *nestled between San Francisco Bay and a Chevron oil refinery. For this version, we cut the soy flour and sesame seeds and swapped the honey and buttermilk sauce for a richer cream cheese frosting, which works well with this cake.*

½ cup oil, plus more for the pan
2 cups all-purpose flour
2 teaspoons ground cinnamon
½ cup light brown sugar
2 teaspoons baking soda
2 cups grated carrots, about 4 medium carrots
1 cup canned crushed pineapple, drained
3 eggs
¾ cup buttermilk
½ cup chopped walnuts (optional)

Cream Cheese Frosting

8 ounces cream cheese, at room temperature
¼ cup (½ stick) unsalted butter, at room temperature
1 teaspoon vanilla extract
¼ teaspoon salt
1 cup powdered sugar, plus more if needed
Grated lemon zest (optional)

To make the cake, preheat the oven to 350°F. Prep a 9-inch cake pan: Trace the shape of the bottom of the pan on a large piece of parchment, cut out the circle, and place it in the bottom of the pan; grease the sides with oil. In a bowl, combine the flour, cinnamon, sugar, and baking soda. In another bowl, mix the carrots, pineapple, eggs, oil, and buttermilk. Add the wet mixture to the dry and, with a rubber spatula, mix well. Fold in the walnuts, if using. Pour into the prepared pan. Bake for about 1 hour; a knife or toothpick should come out clean. Cool completely on a rack.

For the frosting, in the bowl of a stand mixer, blend the cream cheese and butter. Add the vanilla and salt, and gradually mix in the powdered sugar. You can add more powdered sugar if you would like it sweeter or thicker. If you want the frosting to have a pop of tartness, mix in some lemon zest to taste. Make sure the cake is completely cool before you cover with the frosting.

Poppy Seed Cake
with Lemony Crème Fraîche Frosting

8 ample slices

This recipe can be whipped together in just a few minutes. The final result is a moist, not-too-sweet cake. You can make it with a more traditional frosting, like a lemon buttercream, or serve it with the tart and tangy crème fraîche recipe included here. This dessert, originally contributed by a close friend, was a favorite of my children.

1½ tablespoons poppy
   seeds
1 cup milk
¾ cup oil, plus more for
   the pan
2 eggs
¾ cup honey or maple syrup
½ teaspoon vanilla extract
2 cups all-purpose flour
Dash of ground cinnamon
2½ teaspoons baking
   powder

*Lemony Crème Fraîche
Frosting*

¾ cup crème fraîche (one
   7.5-ounce container)
3 tablespoons powdered
   sugar, or more to taste
Juice of ½ lemon, or
   more to taste
Zest from 1 lemon, plus
   more for serving

Make the cake: Soak the poppy seeds in the milk in a large bowl while prepping the other ingredients. Preheat the oven to 350°F and place a rack in the middle. Prep a 9-inch cake pan: Trace the shape of the bottom of the pan on a large piece of parchment, cut out the circle, and place it in the bottom of the pan; grease the sides with oil. Add the eggs, oil, honey, and vanilla to the poppy seeds and mix together. In another bowl, mix together the flour, cinnamon, and baking powder. Add the wet ingredients to the dry and mix. Pour the batter into the prepared pan and bake for 45 minutes. A knife or tooth-pick should come out clean. Allow to cool for a few minutes in the pan, then carefully flip it out onto a wire rack to cool completely.

While the cake is cooling, prepare the frosting. Mix the crème fraîche, powdered sugar, lemon juice, and zest together in a stand mixer or large bowl. Adjust for taste, then whip to your desired consistency. Flip the cake from the cooling rack to a large serving platter. Using a spatula, spread the frosting evenly across the cake. Sprinkle lemon zest across the top. Save any extra frosting to enjoy with pancakes or waffles for a special breakfast.

Book Two Contributors

Chef José Andrés is one of the world's most renowned chefs and restaurateurs, often credited with introducing tapas to American eaters. His ThinkFoodGroup currently comprises 28 acclaimed restaurants around the world. In 2010, José began his efforts to use food as a powerful agent of positive change and founded World Central Kitchen, which has since earned him the title of "Humanitarian of the Year" from the James Beard Foundation. He has twice been named to *Time*'s "100 Most Influential People" list.

Mark Bittman is the author of more than 20 acclaimed books, including the How to Cook Everything series. He wrote for *The New York Times* for more than two decades and became the country's first food-focused Op-Ed columnist for a major news publication. His most recent book is *Animal, Vegetable, Junk*.

Luz Calvo and Catriona Rueda Esquibel are ethnic studies professors and the authors of *Decolonize Your Diet: Plant-Based Mexican-American Recipes for Health and Healing*. They live in Oakland, California, where they tend a backyard food garden.

Brooks Headley is the owner/operator of Superiority Burger in Manhattan's East Village. It's a vegetarian restaurant that skews vegan at times. Brooks is also the author of two cookbooks, *Fancy Desserts* and *Superiority Burger Cookbook*.

Mollie Katzen is best known as the author of the vegetarian classics *Moosewood Cookbook* and *The Enchanted Broccoli Forest*. She was influenced and inspired by Frances Moore Lappé's original publication of *Diet for a Small Planet* (which preceded the first publication of *Moosewood* by several years) and is delighted to be part of this 50th anniversary edition.

Alicia Kennedy is a writer based in San Juan, Puerto Rico. She has a weekly newsletter on food culture, justice, and media and is writing a book about veganism for Beacon Press.

Yasmin Khan is an author and broadcaster who is passionate about sharing people's stories through food. Her critically acclaimed cookery books, *The Saffron Tales* and *Zaitoun*, chronicle her culinary adventures through Iran and Palestine, sharing recipes and stories that celebrate the beauty and power of the human spirit in regions more commonly associated with conflict. Her third book, *Ripe Figs*, explores the food of the eastern Mediterranean. Before working in food, Yasmin was a human rights campaigner for a decade, with a special focus on the Middle East.

Padma Lakshmi is an internationally renowned food expert, model, actress, and bestselling author. She serves as host and executive producer of Bravo's Emmy-winning series *Top Chef* and Hulu's *Taste the Nation*. Her memoir, *Love, Loss, and What We Ate*, was published in 2016, and her cookbooks include *Easy Exotic* and *Tangy Tart Hot & Sweet*. Lakshmi is also an avid activist for immigrants' rights and women's reproductive rights, serving as an artist ambassador for the ACLU and as a Goodwill Ambassador for the UN Development Programme.

Anna Lappé is a national bestselling author and advocate for sustainability and justice along the food chain. A James Beard Leadership honoree, Anna has contributed to 13 books and co-authored or authored three, most recently *Diet for a Hot Planet: The Climate Crisis at the End of Your Fork and What You Can Do*

About It. Anna is the founder or co-founder of three national organizations, including Real Food Media. For 20 years she has managed the Small Planet Fund, and she currently leads a food-focused grantmaking program at the Panta Rhea Foundation.

Wendy Lopez is a registered dietitian/nutritionist, recipe developer, and co-founder of Food Heaven, an online platform that provides resources on cooking, intuitive eating, and body respect. She is the co-author of the *28-Day Plant-Powered Health Reboot* cookbook and is the co-host of the *Food Heaven Podcast.* She also has a food and nutrition column in *Self* magazine, where she explores the intersection of food, class, race, and culture.

Anthony Myint is a chef and climate activist who is the co-founder of Mission Chinese Food and a trailblazer of the pop-up genre. His nonprofit, Zero Foodprint (ZFP), leads a public-private collaboration with California State agencies to scale agricultural climate solutions rooted in healthy soil. ZFP was awarded the 2020 James Beard award for Humanitarian of the Year.

Louisa Shafia is the author of the cookbook *The New Persian Kitchen.* She is an authority on Iranian food and partners with restaurants around the country to host Persian dinners. Her food writing for a variety of publications focuses on immigrant cooking traditions.

Oglala Lakota chef **Sean Sherman**, founder of The Sioux Chef, is decolonizing our food system. From growing up on Pine Ridge Reservation in South Dakota to an epiphany on a beach in Mexico, chef Sean Sherman shares his journey of discovering, reviving, and reimagining Native cuisine.

Aileen Suzara, MPH, is a cook, educator, and food justice advocate who uplifts the role of culturally rooted foods as medicine. She launched the food project Sariwa ("fresh" in Filipino) to reclaim her community's healing wisdom. As part of this journey, she is honored to grow with Sama Sama Cooperative and Asian Farmers Alliance and as a Castanea Fellow.

Bryant Terry is a James Beard award–winning chef, educator, and author renowned for his activism to create a healthy, just, and sustainable food system. Since 2015 he has been the chef-in-residence at the Museum of the African Diaspora (MoAD) in San Francisco, where he creates public programming that celebrates the intersection of food, farming, health, activism, art, culture, and the African diaspora. Bryant's sixth book, *Black Food*, will be published in the fall of 2021.

Alice Waters is a chef, food activist, and owner of Chez Panisse restaurant in Berkeley, California, which first opened its doors the same year *Diet for a Small Planet* was published—1971. Alice has been a champion of local sustainable agriculture ever since. In 1995 she founded the Edible Schoolyard Project, which advocates for a free regenerative school lunch for all children and a sustainable food curriculum in every public school. She is the author of 16 books, including her critically acclaimed memoir, *Coming to My Senses: The Making of a Counterculture Cook*.

Acknowledgments

Acknowledgments for the 50th Anniversary Edition

My daughter Anna Lappé's contribution to this new edition has been enormous, as she has overseen the recipe development and more. What fun it's been to work with her again.

We are both deeply grateful for the stellar assistance of our team at the Small Planet Institute: Heather Packard, for your steadfast, good-spirited oversight; Annalise Sheppard, for your essential, expert research and its coordination; Olivia Smith, for your consistent passion for getting all the facts right. And to the rest of our great team we offer our heartfelt thanks: Rachel Madison, Avisha Goyal, Grace Killian, Hannah Nesson, David Snower, and Mia Thacker.

In addition, we profoundly appreciate the insightful feedback of colleagues—Raj Patel, Ricardo Salvador, Molly Anderson, and Timothy A. Wise, as well as invaluable input from Jules Pretty, James Galloway, Gray Tappan, Chris Reij, Roland Bunch, Tony Rinaudo, Dennis Garrity, Suzanne Simard, Satheesh Periyapatna, Leah Penniman, Keefe Keeley, Jacob Grace, Eric Adams, Rachel Atcheson, and Christopher Gardner. We are grateful to Richard Rowe for his consistent support and insightful feedback.

We couldn't have redone the recipes in this edition without the hard work of Wendy Lopez. Not only is Wendy a gifted recipe developer, she is a complete joy to work with. Her creativity infuses the pages of Book Two. Thanks go as well to Aimée Mazara, whom we had the pleasure of working with on the all-new illustrations. We are also forever grateful to the wonderful recipe contributors. Their work in the world is an inspiration, and they are among the many culinary leaders showing the diversity and deliciousness of plant-rich diets. Thank you to José Andrés, Mark Bittman, Luz Calvo and Catriona Rueda Esquibel, Brooks Headley, Mollie Katzen, Alicia Kennedy, Yasmin Khan, Padma Lakshmi, Anthony Myint, Sean Sherman, Louisa Shafia, Aileen Suzara, Bryant Terry, and Alice Waters. For the recipe development, we received support from several donors without whom this work would not have been possible. Thank you in particular to the William and Elizabeth Patterson Family Fund. We also thank the Small Planet Institute interns, friends, and family who tested recipes and gave great feedback, including Aliana Ruxin, Carter Smith, Georgia Ezell, David Snower, Mia Thacker, Alison Eddy, Clarice Lappé, Claire Greensfelder, and Susan Kanaan. We are also appreciative of the dozens of *Diet for a Small Planet* fans who contributed smoothie recipe ideas. They all looked delicious! Further appreciation goes to Bryant Terry, Kendra Klein, and Tanya Kerssen who provided stellar feedback. As always, any mistakes are our responsibility alone.

Finally, we are indebted to our editor, Emily Hartley, for her insight and dedication to this book.

Acknowledgments for 20th Anniversary Edition

In the first edition of this book I included a special acknowledgment to my parents. As I appreciate them even more today than I did ten years ago, I would like to repeat those words: "I wish to thank my parents, John and Ina Moore, who, by having always set the finest example of critical openness to new ideas, made this inquiry possible."

I am indebted to Nick Allen, of the Institute's staff, for his support for this project from its inception and for his inspired and very significant editorial contribution.

Mary Sinclair, Cindy Crowner, and Perri Sloane each contributed cooking talent and other skills to improve the recipes in this book and test the many contributions sent in from around the country. For testing and improving recipes I also appreciate the help of Elizabeth Rivers, Julia Rosenbaum, Claire Greensfelder, Myra Levy, Charles Varon, Katie Allen, Vince Bielski, Elinor Blake, Maria Torres McKay, and the Davis, California, Food for All group—especially Laurie Rubin.

Special thanks go to Jennifer Lovejoy and JoNina Abron, who handled many of my Institute responsibilities so that I could be free to work on this book.

Debbie Fox was the loyal and talented typist of most of this manuscript. Her good humor and her willingness to put up with umpteen drafts will never be forgotten.

Research for this book depended on the help of dozens of people. My special thanks go to Sandy Fritz, Jenny Robinson, and John Moore. I also appreciated the help of Mort Hantman, Tracey Helser, Jim Wessel, Erik Schapiro, David Kinley, Vince Bielski, and Fred Brauneck.

This book benefited greatly from the valuable suggestions of friends and colleagues around the country. I am indebted to Michael Jacobson of the Center for Science in the Public Interest, Marty Strange of the Center for Rural Affairs, William Shurtleff of the Soyfoods Center, to Judy Stone, Robert Greenstein, and Steve Daschle of the Project on Food Assistance and Poverty, to Rick Weissbourd, Cheryl Rogers, and Tom Joe of the Center for the Study of Welfare Policy of the University of Chicago, and to Bard Shollenberger of the Community Nutrition Institute. I also appreciate the time and thought given to this book by Joan Gussow, Nevin Scrimshaw, Isabel Contento, Keith Akers, Robin Hur, Alex Hershaft, Georg Borgstrom, Douglas McDonald, Donald R. Davis, Stan Winter, Jim Spearow, and V. James Rhodes.

I would also like to thank those to whom I am indebted for recipe sections in the first two editions of this book. Many of the recipes they contributed or helped to develop remain in this edition. First, Ellen Ewald who back in 1970 helped acquaint me with the unknown world of whole foods. Second, Susan Kanor whose special kitchen touch and hard work made developing the recipes for the second edition a great adventure.

For other recipes that I have retained in this new book, I am grateful to Barbara Peter, Carol Ackerman Albiani, Sandye Carroll, Diane Coleman, Nancy Posselt, Jackie Potts, Paul Prensky, Joy Gardner, Nancy Meister, Robin McFarlane, and Jamie Seymour.

For their ideas and editorial suggestions I also want to thank Joseph Collins, Charles Varon, Regina Fitzgerald, Jess Randall, and my parents, John and Ina Moore.

And I appreciate all those at the Institute who put up with me during the period of stress to meet this deadline: Gretta Goldenman, JoNina Abron, Joseph Collins, David Kinley, Jim Wessel, Nick Allen, Jess Randall, Annie Newman, and Diana Dillaway.

Finally, I am grateful to my agent, Joan Raines, for her strong support for my work.

Appendixes

Here, I've kept several of the original appendixes from *Diet for a Small Planet*. I want to share them—despite some outdated numbers—because they were such a key part of the original. I removed the detailed Protein Tables and Tips for Complementing Proteins to help eliminate concern about complementing proteins, which was key in my first edition but eliminated by subsequent science.

Three are updated for the 50th anniversary edition: Appendix A lists great resources in Tools for Learning and Action; Appendix C highlights plant-protein foods meeting protein needs without exceeding calorie allowances; and Appendix D offers up-to-date plant, dairy, and meat protein-price comparisons.

Appendix A.

Tools for Learning and Action: Recommended Books, Organizations, and Websites

It can be hard to sustain hope and energy for change when we are bombarded each day by the news: threats to democracy, pandemics, climate disasters, hunger, and poverty . . . we may easily feel overwhelmed. To develop an understanding of how one's own efforts can make a difference, to learn about work for deep system change, we need to expand the news and analysis coming into our lives. We can select news about citizen initiatives that would rarely appear in the daily paper or on the evening news.

Since the 20th anniversary edition of *Diet for a Small Planet*, I have been so pleased to see many great books and amazing plant-forward cookbooks published. Consider the recommendations below simply a launching point, by no means the only great resources out there on sustainable food, farming, and living democracy.

More Related Lappé Books

Lappé, Anna. *Diet for a Hot Planet: The Climate Crisis at the End of Your Fork and What You Can Do About It*. New York: Bloomsbury, 2010.

Lappé, Frances Moore. *EcoMind: Changing the Way We Think, to Create the World We Want*. New York: Nation Books, 2011.

Lappé, Frances Moore, and Joseph Collins. *World Hunger: Ten Myths*. New York: Grove Press, 2015.

Lappé, Frances Moore, and Adam Eichen. *Daring Democracy: Igniting Power, Meaning, and Connection for the America We Want*. Boston: Beacon Press, 2017.

Lappé, Frances Moore, and Anna Lappé. *Hope's Edge: The Next Diet for a Small Planet*. New York: Jeremy P. Tarcher, 2002.

Other Books at the Top of Our Bookshelf

Bowens, Natasha. *The Color of Food: Stories of Race, Resilience and Farming*. Gabriola Island, BC: New Society Publishers, 2015.

Carson, Rachel. *Silent Spring & Other Writings on the Environment*. Edited by Sandra Steingraber. New York: Library of America, 2018.

Chappell, M. Jahi. *Beginning to End Hunger: Food and the Environment in Belo Horizonte, Brazil, and Beyond*. Oakland: University of California Press, 2018.

Genoways, Ted. *The Chain: Farm, Factory, and the Fate of Our Food*. New York: HarperCollins, 2014.

Hauter, Wenonah. *Foodopoly: The Battle over the Future of Food and Farming in America*. New York: The New Press, 2014.

Kimmerer, Robin Wall. *Braiding Sweetgrass: Indigenous Wisdom, Scientific Knowledge, and the Teachings of Plants*. Minneapolis: Milkweed Editions, 2013.

Nestle, Marion. *Food Politics: How the Food Industry Influences Nutrition and Health*. Berkeley: University of California Press, 2007.

Patel, Raj. *Stuffed and Starved: The Hidden Battle for the World Food System*. Brooklyn, NY: Melville House, 2012.

Penniman, Leah. *Farming While Black: Soul Fire Farm's Practical Guide to Liberation on the Land*. White River Junction, VT: Chelsea Green Publishing, 2018.

Philpott, Tom. *Perilous Bounty: The Looming Collapse of American Farming and How We Can Prevent It*. New York: Bloomsbury, 2020.

Thompson, Gabriel. *Chasing the Harvest: Migrant Workers in California Agriculture*. New York: Verso, 2017.

Wise, Timothy A. *Eating Tomorrow: Agribusiness, Family Farmers, and the Battle for the Future of Food*. New York: The New Press, 2019.

Learning More and Making Connections in the Food and Democracy Movements

To join in the Food and Democracy Movements, find connection and inspiration in these organizations. Enjoy!

Black Farmer Fund www.blackfarmerfund.org

Brennan Center for Justice www.brennancenter.org

Civil Eats www.civileats.com

Common Cause www.commoncause.org

Corporate Accountability www.corporateaccountability.org

Declaration for American Democracy www.dfadcoalition.org

Democracy Initiative www.democracyinitiative.org

Democracy Movement www.democracymovement.us

Demos www.demos.org

Environmental Working Group www.ewg.org

Fair Vote www.fairvote.org

Food Chain Workers Alliance www.foodchainworkers.org

Food First www.foodfirst.org

Food Tank www.foodtank.org

Food and Water Watch www.foodandwaterwatch.org

Friends of the Earth www.foe.org

Hawai'i Alliance for Progressive Action www.hapahi.org

HEAL Food Alliance www.healfoodalliance.org

Institute for Agriculture and Trade Policy www.iatp.org

International Panel of Experts on Sustainable Food Systems (IPES-Food) www.ipes-food.org

National Black Food & Justice Alliance www.blackfoodjustice.org

National Sustainable Agriculture Coalition
www.sustainableagriculture.net

Pesticide Action Network of North America www.panna.org

Practical Farmers of Iowa www.practicalfarmers.org

Public Citizen www.citizen.org

Real Food Generation www.realfoodgen.org

Real Food Media www.realfoodmedia.org

Savanna Institute www.savannainstitute.org

Seed Savers Exchange www.seedsavers.org

Slow Food International www.slowfood.com

Soul Fire Farm www.soulfirefarm.org

Southeastern African American Farmers' Organic Network
(SAAFON) www.saafon.org

The Counter www.thecounter.org

The Center for Popular Democracy www.populardemocracy.org

Union of Concerned Scientists www.ucsusa.org

United Food Workers www.ufw.org

Enjoy these great cookbooks for plant- and planet-centered meals featuring *Diet for a Small Planet* contributors:

Note: For authors who've written more than one cookbook, we recommend them all! We're highlighting just one below.

Andrés, José. *Made in Spain: Spanish Dishes for the American Kitchen*. New York: Clarkson Potter, 2008.

Bittman, Mark. *Animal, Vegetable, Junk: A History of Food, From Sustainable to Suicidal*. New York: Houghton Mifflin Harcourt, 2021.

Bittman, Mark. *How to Cook Everything Vegetarian: Completely Revised Tenth Anniversary Edition*. New York: Houghton Mifflin Harcourt, 2017.

Calvo, Luz, and Catriona Rueda Esquibel. *Decolonize Your Diet: Plant-Based Mexican-American Recipes for Health and Healing*. Vancouver, BC: Arsenal Pulp Press, 2016.

Headley, Brooks. *Superiority Burger Cookbook: The Vegetarian Hamburger Is Now Delicious*. New York: W. W. Norton, 2018.

Jones, Jessica, and Wendy Lopez. *28-Day Plant-Powered Health Reboot: Reset Your Body, Lose Weight, Gain Energy & Feel Great*. Salem, MA: Page Street Publishing, 2017.

Katzen, Mollie. *The Moosewood Cookbook*. 40th anniversary ed. Berkeley, CA: Ten Speed Press, 2014.

Khan, Yasmin. *Zaitoun: Recipes from the Palestinian Kitchen*. New York: W. W. Norton, 2018.

Lakshmi, Padma. *Tangy Tart Hot & Sweet: A World of Recipes for Every Day*. New York: Hachette Books, 2007.

Lappé, Anna, and Bryant Terry. *Grub: Ideas for an Urban Organic Kitchen*. New York: Penguin, 2006.

Shafia, Louisa. *The New Persian Kitchen*. Berkeley, CA: Ten Speed Press, 2013.

Sherman, Sean, with Beth Dooley. *The Sioux Chef's Indigenous Kitchen*. Minneapolis: University of Minnesota Press, 2017.

Terry, Bryant. *Vegetable Kingdom: The Abundant World of Vegan Recipes*. Berkeley, CA: Ten Speed Press, 2020.

Waters, Alice. *The Art of Simple Food: Notes, Lessons & Recipes from a Delicious Revolution*. New York: Clarkson Potter, 2007.

And for children:

Katzen, Mollie. *Pretend Soup and Other Real Recipes*. New York: Random House Children's Books, 1994.

Katzen, Mollie. *Honest Pretzels and 64 Other Amazing Recipes for Kids Who Love to Cook*. New York: Random House Children's Books, 1999.

Katzen, Mollie. *Salad People and More Real Recipes*. New York: Random House Children's Books, 2005.

Appendix B.

Basic Cooking Instructions for Beans, Grains, Nuts, and Seeds

Definitions

Soy grits (or soy granules) = partially cooked cracked soybeans

Soy powder = soybean flour

Bulgur wheat = partially cooked (parboiled) wheat, usually cracked

Ground sesame seed = sesame meal (can be made easily at home; see cooking instructions below)

Seasoned stock = any leftover liquid from cooking beans, vegetables, etc., *or* water with a small amount of powdered or cubed vegetable seasoning (available without additives in health food stores; can be substituted for stock in any recipe)

Here are instructions for preparing the basic ingredients often called for.

Cooking Beans

1. Regular cooking: Wash beans in cold water, and soak overnight in three times the volume of water; *or* bring the beans and water to a boil, cover tightly, and let sit for 2 hours. Simmer the beans, partially covered, adding water if necessary, for about 2 hours, depending on the type of bean and the consistency you want. If you want to mash or purée the beans, you will want to cook them until they are quite soft.

2. Pressure cooking: A pressure cooker is a real advantage in cooking beans as well as grains. Since the foods cook so much more quickly, a meal doesn't require as much forethought. Pressure cooking also gives you a more tender bean. Soaking or precooking saves a little time, but with pressure cooking it really is not necessary. Bring the washed beans and three to four times their volume in water to a boil in the cooker. Cover and bring to 15 pounds pressure. Cook beans for 25 to 45 minutes. Cool immediately. Don't attempt to cook split peas, or any bean that tends to foam, in a pressure cooker or you may find yourself with a clogged cooker and a big mess.

3. Roasting: Cook beans by one of the above methods for a firm bean. Spread the beans on a lightly oiled baking sheet. Sprinkle with salt, if desired, and bake at 200°F for about 1 hour, until they are well browned. When they are hot, they will be crunchy outside and tender inside. When they are cool, they will be hard and crunchy throughout. You can also roast the beans in a lightly oiled frypan over medium heat on top of the stove. Stir constantly. Soybeans, when roasted, or when chopped or ground in a blender, can be eaten alone. They make a garnish to be sprinkled on a variety of dishes; or use them when nuts or nutmeal are called for.

4. Making tofu (soybean curd): Tofu is now widely available throughout the United States at most natural food stores and at many supermarkets. Tofu has the best flavor and is least expensive when made at home. For an easy to follow recipe that gives consistently good results, see *The Book of Tofu* (Ballantine paperback), which also contains over 250 recipes for using the eight basic types of tofu, plus detailed nutritional information and a list of U.S. tofu shops.

Cooking Grains

1. Regular cooking: Wash the grains in cold water. Bring stock or water, equal to twice the volume of the grains, to a boil (for millet or buckwheat, use three times the volume). Put in the grains, bring to a boil again, lower heat, and simmer (covered) for 30 to 45 minutes, until all of the liquid is absorbed.

2. Pressure cooking: In the pressure cooker follow the same method, but instead of simmering the grains, bring to 15 pounds pressure and cook for about 20 minutes. Cool under cold water when cooking time is up. You may wish to vary the amount of water in order to create the texture of grain you prefer. If you have trouble with sticking, here's the trick I use: Put about 1 inch of water in the bottom of the pressure cooker. Put the grain into a stainless-steel bowl that will fit easily into the pressure cooker (with plenty of room between the top of the bowl and the lid of the pressure cooker). Add water to the level of about ¾ inch above the level of the grain. Put the bowl inside the pressure cooker, cover, and begin cooking. This method is also handy when I need to cook both grains and beans at the same time, but separately. I merely put the small stainless-steel bowl inside the pressure cooker. I then put the beans with adequate water around the outside of the bowl, and the grains inside the bowl.

3. Sautéing: This method is most frequently used in cooking bulgur wheat and buckwheat groats but can be used with any grain to achieve a "nuttier" flavor. Wash the grains and put in a dry saucepan or pressure cooker over low heat. Stir until dry. Add just enough oil to coat each kernel. Sauté the grains, stirring constantly, until all of the grains are golden. Stir in boiling water or stock (amounts as for regular cooking, above) and bring the mixture to a boil. Cover and simmer 30 to 45 minutes; or, if using a pressure cooker, bring to 15 pounds pressure and cook 20 minutes. Cool cooker immediately.

Cooking Nuts and Seeds

1. To roast whole seeds or nuts: Place in a dry pan and roast over medium flame until they have desired brownness; or spread them on a baking sheet and toast them in a 200°F oven. Use the roasted seeds whole, or grind them in a blender, a few at a time, or with a mortar and pestle. Add salt if desired.

2. To roast or toast ground seeds or nuts: Buy the meal or, to make it yourself, grind the seeds or nuts in a blender. Then roast the meal in a dry pan, stirring constantly, adding salt if desired. Or spread the meal on a baking sheet and bake at 200°F, stirring often. (You can also grind small quantities of whole grains in your blender.)

3. Nut and seed butters: It is easy to make your own fresh nut and seed butters if you have a blender. From whole roasted or raw seeds or nuts: Grind as for meal, adding a little oil to "start" the butter; continue adding as many nuts or seeds as your blender can handle. From roasted or raw ground nuts or seeds: Stir a little oil, and honey if desired, into the meal, and you will have creamy nut or seed butter.

Appendix C.

A Look at Protein in Plant Foods

A good way to demonstrate the protein richness of plant foods is to ask: Do plant foods provide adequate protein without exceeding calorie needs? By this measure, many plant foods qualify, and some excel, as you'll see.

To make that judgment, first, from a day's diet, let's subtract those foods that provide no protein—oil, butter, sugar, honey, alcohol, and most fruits. In the diet of people conscious of the need for moderation in fat and sugar, these foods provide roughly a quarter of the calories. (In the day's menu in Figure 10, such foods provide about this share of the calories.)

Then, to assess what plant foods meet our protein needs without exceeding our calorie allowances, let's start with the midpoint caloric allowance for average adult males and females of 2,300 calories per day, recommended by the Department of Health and Human Services (Health.gov). Assuming the quarter of calories just mentioned contain no protein, the remaining 75 percent of one's calories—or 1,725—must come from food containing protein. The analogous protein midpoint allowance would be 51 grams per day. Since each gram of protein has 4 calories, we need an average of 204 calories from protein out of our total 1,725 calories from foods with protein, or

12 percent. Now we have a basis for judging what foods will meet the average person's protein needs on a plant-food diet.

Using this guideline, if a food has 12 percent or more of its calories from protein, it qualifies as a protein source that can fill our protein needs without exceeding our calorie limit.

Percent of Calories from Protein in a Wide Range of Plant Foods

NOTE: FOOD WITH 12% OR HIGHER PROTEIN CAN MEET PROTEIN NEEDS WITHOUT EXCEEDING CALORIE ALLOWANCES			
		Pintos	19%
		Chickpeas	17%
		Lima Beans	17%
		Peanuts	17%
		Radish	17%
Watercress	51%	Wheat (hard spring)	17%
Mushroom	46%	Cucumber	16%
Corn	40%	Iceberg Lettuce	16%
Soybeans	31%	Oatmeal	15%
Spinach	30%	Okra	14%
Lentils	24%	Black Walnuts	13%
Collards	23%	Bulgar	13%
Peas	23%	Cabbage	13%
Green Onion	21%	Millet	13%
Broccoli	20%	Sesame Seeds	13%
Kale	20%	Sunflower Seeds	13%
Cauliflower	19%	Turnips	13%

Appendix D.

Comparing the Cost of Protein: Plants, Dairy, and Meat

In the original *Diet for a Small Planet*, I included an appendix to highlight the affordability of plant sources of protein. We updated the numbers with today's prices, and, once again, they show that choosing plant protein is either less costly or on par with meat protein options.

Product Cost Per Gram of Protein

PLANT FOODS

Peanut Butter	$0.03
Black Beans (dry)	$0.03
Chickpeas/Garbanzo Beans	$0.04
Lentils	$0.05
Tofu	$0.05
Almonds	$0.09
Pumpkin Seeds	$0.10
Quinoa	$0.15
Mushrooms (white)	$0.16

DAIRY

Eggs	$0.03
Milk	$0.04
Greek Yogurt	$0.07
Parmesan Cheese	$0.08

MEAT

Chicken Breast (boneless and skinless)	$0.05
Steak	$0.06
Ground Beef	$0.08
Ham (sliced)	$0.10

Prices are based on the average found across three grocery stores—Stop & Shop, Star Market, and Whole Foods—in Boston, Massachusetts, August 2020. Price per gram of protein was calculated based on grams of protein listed in ingredient labels or, for bulk foods, on protein per gram data.

Appendix E.

Whole Wheat Flour Compared to White Flour

	Composition of Whole Wheat Flour (per 100 g, or 3½ oz)	Composition of All-Purpose White Flour Compared to Whole Wheat Flour			
		White Flour		Enriched White Flour	
1. Protein	13.3 g	10.5 g	79%	10.5 g	79%
2. Minerals					
Calcium	41 mg	16 mg	39%	16 mg	39%
Phosphorous	372 mg	87 mg	23%	87 mg	23%
Iron	3.3 mg	0.8 mg	24%	2.9 mg	88%
Potassium	370 mg	95 mg	26%	95 mg	26%
Sodium	3 mg	2 mg	67%	2 mg	67%
3. Vitamins					
Thiamin	0.55 mg	0.06 mg	11%	0.44 mg	80%
Riboflavin	0.12 mg	0.05 mg	42%	0.26 mg	216%
Niacin	4.3 mg	0.9 mg	21%	3.5 mg	81%

Appendix F.

Brown Rice Compared to Other Types of Rice

	Composition of Brown Rice (per 100 g, or 3½ oz)	Composition of Other Types of Rice					
		White Rice		Enriched White Rice		Converted Rice (Enriched)	
1. Protein	7.5 g	6.7 g	90%	6.7 g	90%	7.4 g	99%
2. Minerals							
Calcium	32 mg	24 mg	75%	24 mg	75%	60 mg	190%
Phosphorous	221 mg	94 mg	43%	94 mg	43%	200 mg	90%
Iron	1.6 mg	0.8 mg	50%	2.9 mg	180%	2.9 mg	180%
Potassium	214 mg	92 mg	43%	92 mg	43%	150 mg	70%
Sodium	9 mg	5 mg	56%	5 mg	56%	9 mg	100%
3. Vitamins							
Thiamin	0.34 mg	0.07 mg	21%	0.44 mg	130%	0.44 mg	130%
Riboflavin	0.05 mg	0.03 mg	60%	0.03 mg	60%	0.03 mg	60%
Niacin	4.7 mg	1.6 mg	34%	3.5 mg	74%	3.5 mg	74%

Appendix G.

Sugars, Honey, and Molasses Compared

	White Sugar (Granulated)	Brown Sugar (Beet or Cane)	Molasses (Third Extraction or Blackstrap)	Honey (Strained or Extracted)	Maple Sugar
1. Minerals	mg	mg	mg	mg	mg
Calcium	0	85	684	5	143
Phosphorus	0	19	84	6	11
Iron	0.1	3.4	16.1	0.5	1.4
Potassium	3.0	344	2927	51	242
Sodium	1.0	30	96	5	14
2. Vitamins					
Thiamin	0	0.01	0.11	trace	—
Riboflavin	0	0.03	0.19	0.04	—
Niacin	0	0.2	2.0	0.3	—

Composition (per 100 g, or 3½ oz)

Source: "Composition of Foods," Agriculture Handbook, No. 8, USDA. Values given vary in other sources.

Notes

Our Choice, Our Power:
Introduction to the 50th Anniversary Edition

1. Larry Buchanan, Quoctrung Bui, and Jugal K. Patel, "Black Lives Matter May Be the Largest Movement in U.S. History," *New York Times,* July 3, 2020, https://www.nytimes.com/interactive/2020/07/03/us/george-floyd-protests-crowd-size.html.

2. "The State of Food Security and Nutrition in the World 2020" (Rome: FAO, IFAD, UNICEF, WFP, and WHO, 2020), 3, http://www.fao.org/documents/card/en/c/ca9692en; Max Roser and Hannah Ritchie, "Food Supply," *Our World in Data,* March 5, 2013, https://ourworldindata.org/food-supply; "World," Food and Agriculture Organization of the United Nations, accessed October 2020, http://faostat.fao.org/static/syb/syb_5000.pdf.

3. Julia A. Wolfson and Cindy W. Leung, "Food Insecurity and COVID-19: Disparities in Early Effects for US Adults," *Nutrients* 12, no. 6 (June 2, 2020): 1, https://doi.org/10.3390/nu12061648.

4. Brad Plumer, "Humans Are Speeding Extinction and Altering the Natural World at an 'Unprecedented' Pace," *New York Times,* May 6, 2019, https://www.nytimes.com/2019/05/06/climate/biodiversity-extinction-united-nations.html; S. Díaz et al., *The Global Assessment Report on Biodiversity and Ecosystem Services: Summary for Policymakers* (Bonn, Germany: Intergovernmental

Science-Policy Platform on Biodiversity and Ecosystem Services, November 25, 2019), https://doi.org/10.5281/zenodo .3553579.

5. *David Attenborough: A Life on Our Planet,* directed by Alastair Fothergill, aired 2020 on Netflix, https://www.netflix.com/ title/80216393; for more information, see website for Attenborough's documentary *A Life on Our Planet,* www.ourplanet.com.

6. Thomas Filk, "It Is the Theory Which Decides What We Can Observe (Einstein)," chap. 5 in *Contextuality from Quantum Physics to Psychology,* ed. E. Dzhafarov et al., vol. 6, *Advanced Series on Mathematical Psychology,* eds. H. Colonius and E. Dzhaharov (Singapore: World Scientific, 2016), 77–92, https://www .worldscientific.com/doi/abs/10.1142/9789814730617_0005.

7. Brian Rosenwald, *Talk Radio's America: How an Industry Took Over a Political Party That Took Over the United States* (Cambridge, MA: Harvard University Press, 2019). "Who We Support," Koch Foundation, updated January 2020, https://www.charleskoch foundation.org/who-we-support.

8. "Reagan Talk to World Bank and I.M.F.," *New York Times,* September 30, 1981, https://www.nytimes.com/1981/09/30/ business/reagan-talk-to-world-bank-and-imf.html.

9. Dan Roberts, "Wall Street Deregulation Pushed by Clinton Advisers, Documents Reveal," *Guardian,* April 19, 2014, https://www.theguardian.com/world/2014/apr/19/wall -street-deregulation-clinton-advisers-obama; Yun Li, "The Five Biggest Stocks Are Dwarfing the Rest of the Stock Market at an 'Unprecedented' Level," CNBC, January 13, 2020, https:// www.cnbc.com/2020/01/13/five-biggest-stocks-dwarfing-the -market-at-unprecedented-level.html.

10. Noah Kirsch, "The 3 Richest Americans Hold More Wealth Than Bottom 50% of the Country, Study Finds," *Forbes,* November 9, 2017, https://www.forbes.com/sites/noahkirsch/ 2017/11/09/the-3-richest-americans-hold-more-wealth-than -bottom-50-of-country-study-finds/#32333dc3cf86.

11. U.S. Department of Agriculture, *2017 Census of Agriculture Highlights: Farm Economics,* ACH17-1 (April 2019), https://www .nass.usda.gov/Publications/Highlights/2019/2017Census _Farm_Economics.pdf; Adrian Torchiana, "What Percentage of Cropland Acres Are Absentee Owned?" Granular, February 15, 2018, https://granular.ag/blog/absentee-owned

-cropland-2/; "Farming and Farm Income," U.S. Department of Agriculture Economic Research Service, accessed September 29, 2020, https://www.ers.usda.gov/data-products/ag-and-food-statistics-charting-the-essentials/farming-and-farm-income/.

12. "In Views of U.S. Democracy, Widening Partisan Divides Over Freedom to Peacefully Protest," Pew Research Center, September 2, 2020, https://www.pewresearch.org/politics/2020/09/02/in-views-of-u-s-democracy-widening-partisan-divides-over-freedom-to-peacefully-protest/.

13. "Gini Index (World Bank Estimate)," The World Bank, accessed September 14, 2020, https://data.worldbank.org/indicator/SI.POV.GINI?most_recent_value_desc=false&view=map&year=1981.

14. Robert B. Reich, *The System, Who Rigged It, and How We Can Fix It* (New York: Alfred A. Knopf, 2020), 15.

15. "Seed Industry Structure Is Characterized by Growth and Consolidation," in *The Seed Industry in U.S. Agriculture*, Agriculture Information Bulletin No. AIB-786 (Washington, DC: USDA Economic Research Service, February 2004), 26, accessed October 13, 2020, https://www.ers.usda.gov/webdocs/publications/42517/13605_aib786g_1_.pdf?v=0.

16. Food & Water Watch, *The Economic Cost of Food Monopolies* (November 2012), 2, accessed October 13, 2020, http://www.cagj.org/wp-content/uploads/CostofFoodMonopolies.pdf.

17. Hayley Peterson, "The Grocery Wars Are Intensifying with Walmart and Kroger in the Lead and Amazon Poised to 'Cause Disruption,'" *Business Insider,* January 30, 2020, https://www.businessinsider.com/walmart-kroger-dominate-us-grocery-amazon-gains-share-2020-1.

18. "Farmer's Share of the Food Dollar Falls to All-Time Low," National Farmers Union, April 25, 2019, https://nfu.org/2019/04/25/farmers-share-of-the-food-dollar-falls-to-all-time-low/.

19. Jacob Bunge and Jesse Newman, "To Stay on the Land, American Farmers Add Extra Jobs," *Wall Street Journal,* February 25, 2018, https://www.wsj.com/articles/to-stay-on-the-land-american-farmers-add-extra-jobs-1519582071.

20. U.S. Department of Agriculture Economic Research Service, "Recent Trends in GE Adoption," accessed October 16, 2020, https://www.ers.usda.gov/data-products/adoption-of

-genetically-engineered-crops-in-the-us/recent-trends-in-ge
-adoption.aspx.

21. Emily S. Cassidy et al., "Redefining Agricultural Yields: From Tonnes to People Nourished per Hectare," *Environmental Research Letters* 8, no. 3 (August 2013): table 2, https://doi.org/10.1088/1748-9326/8/3/034015.

22. Ibid., 5.

23. J. Poore and T. Nemecek, "Reducing Food's Environmental Impacts through Producers and Consumers," *Science* 360, no. 6392 (June 1, 2018): 4, https://doi.org/10.1126/science.aaq0216.

24. Dana Gunders, "Wasted: How America Is Losing Up to 40 Percent of Its Food from Farm to Fork to Landfill," NRDC, August 16, 2017, https://www.nrdc.org/resources/wasted-how -america-losing-40-percent-its-food-farm-fork-landfill.

25. Chris Vogliano and Katie Brown, *The State of America's Food & Opportunities to Make a Difference* (Academy of Nutrition and Dietetics, 2016), 5, https://eatrightfoundation.org/wp-content/uploads/2016/09/The-State-of-Americas-Food-Waste-Report .pdf.

26. Dana Gunders, op. cit.

27. World Resources Report, *Creating a Sustainable Food Future* (World Resources Institute, 2018), 14, https://research.wri.org/sites/default/files/2019-07/creating-sustainable-food-future_2_5 .pdf.

28. A. W. Geiger, "How Americans See Their Country and Democracy," Pew Research Center, July 4, 2018, https://www .pewresearch.org/fact-tank/2018/07/04/how-americans-see -their-country-and-their-democracy/.

29. Pippa Norris and Max Grömping, *Electoral Integrity Worldwide*, The Electoral Integrity Project, 2019, fig. 1, https://www .electoralintegrityproject.com/the-year-in-elections-2019.

30. Robert B. Reich, op. cit.

31. "Lobbying Data Summary," Open Secrets/Center for Responsive Politics, accessed September 21, 2020, https://www .opensecrets.org/federal-lobbying?inflate=Y; "Ranked Sectors," Open Secrets/Center for Responsive Politics, accessed September 17, 2020, https://www.opensecrets.org/federal-lobbying/ranked-sectors?cycle=2019.

32. Lee Drutman, *The Business of America Is Lobbying* (New York: Oxford University Press, 2015), 9, 71; "Lobbying," Open Secrets/

Center for Responsive Politics, accessed January 14, 2021, https://www.opensecrets.org/lobbying.

33. Martin Gilens and Benjamin I. Page, "Testing Theories of American Politics: Elites, Interest Groups, and Average Citizens," *Perspectives on Politics* 12, no. 3 (September 2014): 575, https://doi.org/10.1017/S1537592714001595.

34. Bradley Jones, "Most Americans Want to Limit Campaign Spending," Pew Research Center, May 8, 2018, https://www.pewresearch.org/fact-tank/2018/05/08/most-americans-want-to-limit-campaign-spending-say-big-donors-have-greater-political-influence/.

35. Roberto Foa and Yascha Mounk, "Are Americans Losing Faith in Democracy?" *Vox*, December 18, 2015, https://www.vox.com/polyarchy/2015/12/18/9360663/is-democracy-in-trouble.

36. "All Are Responsible," Evolve, August 8, 2018, http://evolve.reconstructingjudaism.org/all-are-responsible.

37. Srinivasan S. Pillay, *Life Unlocked* (New York: Rodale, 2011), 183.

38. *The State of Food Security and Nutrition in the World 2020* (Rome: FAO, IFAD, UNICEF, WFP, and WHO, 2020), 36, http://www.fao.org/documents/card/en/c/ca9692en; "Hunger and Food Insecurity," Food and Agriculture Organization of the United Nations, accessed September 23, 2020, http://www.fao.org/hunger/en/; UNICEF, World Health Organization, World Bank Group, *Levels and Trends in Child Malnutrition*, March 31, 2020, https://www.who.int/publications/i/item/jme-2020-edition.

39. Pete Smith et al., "Interlinkages Between Desertification, Land Degradation, Food Security and Greenhouse Gas Fluxes: Synergies, Trade-offs and Integrated Response Options," chap. 6 in *Climate Change and Land: An IPCC Special Report on Climate Change, Desertification, Land Degradation, Sustainable Land Management, Food Security, and Greenhouse Gas Fluxes in Terrestrial Ecosystem* (International Panel on Climate Change, 2019), 551–672.

40. Michael A. Clark et al., "Global Food System Emissions Could Preclude Achieving the 1.5° and 2°C Climate Change Targets," *Science* 370, no. 6517 (November 6, 2020): 705–8, https://science.sciencemag.org/content/370/6517/705.

41. Adam Satariano, "The Business of Burps: Scientists Smell Profit in Cow Emissions," *New York Times*, May 1, 2020,

https://www.nytimes.com/2020/05/01/business/cow
-methane-climate-change.html.

42. Food and Agriculture Organization of the United States, *Food
Wastage Footprint: Impacts on Natural Resources; Summary Report*
(Rome: FAO, 2013), 6, http://www.fao.org/3/i3347e/i3347e
.pdf.

43. Jennifer M. Poti, Bianca Braga, and Bo Qin, "Ultra-Processed
Food Intake and Obesity: What Really Matters for Health—
Processing or Nutrient Content?" *Current Obesity Reports* 6, no. 4
(December 2017): 423, https://doi.org/10.1007/s13679-017
-0285-4; Melanie Warner, *Pandora's Lunchbox: How Processed Food
Took Over the American Meal* (New York: Scribner, 2013), 98.

44. Susan M. Krebs-Smith et al., "Americans Do Not Meet Federal
Dietary Recommendations," *Journal of Nutrition* 140, no. 10 (October 2010): 1832–38, https://doi.org/10.3945/jn.110.124826.

45. Ashkan Afshin et al., "Health Effects of Dietary Risks in 195
Countries, 1990–2017: A Systematic Analysis for the Global
Burden of Disease Study 2017," *Lancet* 393, no. 10184 (May
2019): 1961, https://doi.org/10.1016/S0140-6736(19)30041-8.

46. "Long-Term Trends in Diabetes," CDC's Division of Diabetes Translation, April 2017, https://www.cdc.gov/diabetes/
statistics/slides/long_term_trends.pdf; "Statistics About Diabetes," American Diabetes Association, accessed August 31, 2020,
https://www.diabetes.org/resources/statistics/statistics-about
-diabetes.

47. Thomas R. Frieden and Peter A. Briss, "We Can Reduce Dietary Sodium, Save Money, and Save Lives," *Annals of Internal
Medicine* 152, no. 8 (April 20, 2010): 526–27, https://doi.org/
10.7326/0003-4819-152-8-201004200-00214.

48. "Chicken Noodle Soup," Campbell Soup Company, accessed
January 15, 2021, https://www.campbells.com/products/
condensed/chicken-noodle-soup/.

49. "Why Public Health Is Necessary to Improve Healthcare," National Association of Chronic Disease Directors, 2012, https://
chronicdisease.org/resource/resmgr/white_papers/cd_white
_paper_hoffman.pdf.

50. USDA Economic Research Service, "Recent Trends in GE
Adoption," last updated July 17, 2020, https://www.ers.usda
.gov/data-products/adoption-of-genetically-engineered-crops

-in-the-us/recent-trends-in-ge-adoption.aspx; Reuters, "W.H.O. Report Links Ingredient in Roundup to Cancer," *New York Times,* March 20, 2015, https://www.nytimes.com/2015/03/21/business/who-report-links-ingredient-in-roundup-to-cancer.html; International Agency for Research on Cancer/World Health Organization, *Some Organophosphate Insecticides and Herbicides,* vol. 112, *IARC Monographs on the Evaluation of Carcinogenic Risks to Humans* (Lyon, France: International Agency for Research on Cancer, 2017), 398.

51. "Where Is Glyphosate Banned?" Baum Hedlund Aristei & Goldman, July 2020, https://www.baumhedlundlaw.com/toxic-tort-law/monsanto-roundup-lawsuit/where-is-glyphosate-banned/.

52. Carey Gilliam, Monsanto Papers (Washington, DC: Island Press, 2021).

53. Athanasios Valavanidis, "Glyphosate, the Most Widely Used Herbicide: Health and Safety Issues; Why Scientists Differ in Their Evaluation of Its Adverse Health Effects," ResearchGate, March 2018, https://www.researchgate.net/publication/323727351_Glyphosate_the_Most_Widely_Used_Herbicide_Health_and_safety_issues_Why_scientists_differ_in_their_evaluation_of_its_adverse_health_effects.

54. Nathan Donley, "The USA Lags Behind Other Agricultural Nations in Banning Harmful Pesticides," *Environmental Health* 18, no. 1 (June 7, 2019): 44.

55. Wolfgang Boedeker et al., "The Global Distribution of Acute Unintentional Pesticide Poisoning: Estimations Based on a Systematic Review," *BMC Public Health* 20, no. 1 (December 7, 2020): 1875, https://doi.org/10.1186/s12889-020-09939-0; "NIOSH Pesticide Poisoning Monitoring Program Protects Farmworkers," CDC/National Institute for Occupational Safety and Health, December 2011, https://doi.org/10.26616/NIOSHPUB2012108; "Farmworkers," Pesticide Action Network, accessed September 9, 2020, https://www.panna.org/frontline-communities/farmworkers.

56. Jef Feeley, Tim Loh, and Bloomberg, "Bayer to Pay $12 Billion to Settle Roundup Lawsuits and Payments," *Fortune,* June 25, 2020, https://fortune.com/2020/06/25/bayer-monsanto-billion-payment-settlement/.

57. Carey Gillam, "Dicamba Fact Sheet," U.S. Right to Know, June 12, 2020, https://usrtk.org/pesticides/dicamba/; Carey Gillam, "Updated: Court Overturns EPA Approval of Bayer Dicamba Herbicide; Says Regulator 'Understated the Risks,'" U.S. Right to Know, June 3, 2020, https://usrtk.org/pesticides/court-orders-epa-approvals-of-bayer-dicamba-herbicide-vacated-says-regulator-understated-the-risks/.

58. "About Genetically Engineered Foods," Center for Food Safety, accessed August 31, 2020, https://www.centerforfoodsafety.org/issues/311/ge-foods/about-ge-foods.

59. Marc Lappé and Britt Bailey, *Against the Grain: Biotechnology and the Corporate Takeover of Your Food* (Monroe, ME: Common Courage Press, 1998).

60. Jonathan R. Latham, "Growing Doubt: A Scientist's Experience of GMOs," Independent Science News for Food and Agriculture, August 31, 2015, https://www.independent sciencenews.org/health/growing-doubt-a-scientists-experience-of-gmos/.

61. "Humans Have Destroyed 83% of Wild Mammals, Biomass Census Shows," Global Agriculture, May 23, 2018, https://www.globalagriculture.org/whats-new/news/en/33211.html; "Do Not Waste Nature's 'Capital': David Attenborough," Phys.org, April 11, 2019, https://phys.org/news/2019-04-nature-capital-david-attenborough.html. Livestock Systems, Food and Agriculture Organization, UN, 2021. http://www.fao.org/livestock-systems/global-distributions/cattle/en/.

62. Yinon M. Bar-On, Rob Phillips, and Ron Milo, "The Biomass Distribution on Earth," *Proceedings of the National Academy of Sciences* 115, no. 25 (June 19, 2018): 6506–11, https://doi.org/10.1073/pnas.1711842115.

63. "Factory Farm Nation: 2015 Edition," Food & Water Watch, May 27, 2015, https://www.foodandwaterwatch.org/insight/factory-farm-nation-2015-edition; "Animal Factories and Public Health," Center for Food Safety, accessed September 16, 2020, https://www.centerforfoodsafety.org/issues/307/animal-factories/animal-factories-and-public-health; "Evaluation of Nitrate Concentrations and Potential Sources of Nitrate in Private Water Supply Wells in North Carolina," National Environmental Health Association, May 2018, https://www.neha.org/node/59958; "CAFOs and Environmental Justice: The Case

of North Carolina," *Environmental Health Perspectives* 121, no. 6 (June 1, 2013): 183, https://doi.org/10.1289/ehp.121-a182.

64. David Pimentel, "Soil Erosion: A Food and Environmental Threat," *Environment, Development and Sustainability* 8, no. 1 (February 2006): 119, https://doi.org/10.1007/s10668-005 -1262-8.

65. Chris Arsenault, "Only 60 Years of Farming Left if Soil Degradation Continues," *Scientific American*, December 5, 2014, https://www.scientificamerican.com/article/only-60-years-of -farming-left-if-soil-degradation-continues/.

66. "Product Gallery," Water Footprint Network, accessed October 13, 2020, https://waterfootprint.org/en/resources/ interactive-tools/product-gallery/; Mesfin M. Mekonnen and Arjen Y. Hoekstra, "A Global Assessment of the Water Footprint of Farm Animal Products," *Ecosystems* 15, no. 3 (April 1, 2012): 401–15, table 3, https://doi.org/10.1007/s10021-011 -9517-8.

67. Bridget R. Scanlon et al., "Groundwater Depletion and Sustainability of Irrigation in the US High Plains and Central Valley," *Proceedings of the National Academy of Sciences* 109, no. 24 (June 12, 2012): 9324, https://doi.org/10.1073/pnas .1200311109; "KGS—Aquifer's Replenishment Rate Is Low, Says New Survey Report," Kansas Geological Survey, accessed September 21, 2020, http://www.kgs.ku.edu/General/News/ 2004/recharge.html.

68. Bridget R. Scanlon et al., "Groundwater Depletion and Sustainability of Irrigation in the US High Plains and Central Valley," *Proceedings of the National Academy of Sciences* 109, no. 24 (June 12, 2012): 9320, https://doi.org/10.1073/pnas .1200311109; "Aquifer's Replenishment Rate Is Low, Says New Survey Report," Kansas Geological Survey News Release, February 9, 2004, http://www.kgs.ku.edu/General/News/2004/ recharge.html.

69. James N. Galloway et al., "Nitrogen Footprints: Past, Present and Future," *Environmental Research Letters* 9, no. 11 (November 3, 2014): 2, https://doi.org/10.1088/1748-9326/9/11/115003.

70. Jan Willem Erisman et al., "An Integrated Approach to a Nitrogen Use Efficiency (NUE) Indicator for the Food Production– Consumption Chain," *Sustainability* 10, no. 4 (April 2018): 925, https://doi.org/10.3390/su10040925; Robert W. Howarth et

al., "Nitrogen Use in the United States from 1961–2000 and Potential Future Trends," *Ambio* 31, no. 2 (March 2002): 92, http://www.jstor.org/stable/4315220.

71. "NOAA Forecasts Very Large 'Dead Zone' for Gulf of Mexico," National Oceanic and Atmospheric Administration, June 12, 2019, https://www.noaa.gov/media-release/noaa-forecasts-very-large-dead-zone-for-gulf-of-mexico.

72. "Dead Zone," National Geographic, January 21, 2011, http://www.nationalgeographic.org/encyclopedia/dead-zone/; Jenny Howard, "Dead Zones, Explained," National Geographic, updated July 2019, https://www.nationalgeographic.com/environment/oceans/dead-zones/.

73. Robert W. Howarth et al., "Nitrogen Use in the United States from 1961-2000 and Potential Future Trends," *Ambio* 31, no. 2 (2002): 92, http://www.jstor.org/stable/4315220.

74. Elizabeth Kolbert, *The Sixth Extinction: An Unnatural History* (New York: Henry Holt, 2014); "Earth's Sixth Mass Extinction Event under Way, Scientists Warn," *Guardian,* accessed October 13, 2020, https://www.theguardian.com/environment/2017/jul/10/earths-sixth-mass-extinction-event-already-underway-scientists-warn.

75. Michael DiBartolomeis et al., "An Assessment of Acute Insecticide Toxicity Loading (AITL) of Chemical Pesticides Used on Agricultural Land in the United States," *PLOS One* 14, no. 8 (August 6, 2019): 1, https://doi.org/10.1371/journal.pone.0220029; Francisco Sánchez-Bayo and Kris A. G. Wyckhuys, "Worldwide Decline of the Entomofauna: A Review of Its Drivers," *Biological Conservation* 232 (April 1, 2019): 8, https://doi.org/10.1016/j.biocon.2019.01.020.

76. Michael DiBartolomeis, op. cit.; Francisco Sánchez-Bayo and Kris A. G. Wyckhuys, op. cit.

77. Gilbert Waldbauer, "The Importance of Insects in the Web of Life," Mother Earth News, May 3, 2012, https://www.motherearthnews.com/nature-and-environment/wildlife/importance-of-insects-ze0z1205zsie.

78. "US Pollinator Information," U.S. Department of Agriculture/Research, Education, and Economics, accessed October 18, 2020, https://www.ree.usda.gov/pollinators.

79. R.E.A. Almond, M. Grooten, and T. Petersen, eds., *Living Planet Report 2020: Bending the Curve of Biodiversity Loss* (Gland, Switzer-

land: World Wildlife Fund, 2020), fig. 1, https://edepot.wur.nl/531235; "What's Driving Deforestation?" Union of Concerned Scientists, February 8, 2016, https://www.ucsusa.org/resources/whats-driving-deforestation; "Big Meat Is Growing in the South," GRAIN, October 13, 2010, https://www.grain.org/en/article/entries/4044-big-meat-is-growing-in-the-south.

80. UN Environment Programme, "Agroecology—a Contribution to Food Security?" UN Environment Programme, October 15, 2020, http://www.unep.org/news-and-stories/story/agroecology-contribution-food-security.

81. "UN Report: Nature's Dangerous Decline 'Unprecedented'; Species Extinction Rates 'Accelerating,'" United Nations Sustainable Development, accessed October 20, 2020, https://www.un.org/sustainabledevelopment/blog/2019/05/nature-decline-unprecedented-report.

82. Anna Lappé, *Diet for a Hot Planet: The Climate Crisis at the End of Your Fork and What You Can Do about It* (New York: Bloomsbury USA, 2011).

83. Marco Springmann et al., "Analysis and Valuation of the Health and Climate Change Cobenefits of Dietary Change," *Proceedings of the National Academy of Sciences* 113, no. 15 (April 12, 2016): 4146–51, https://doi.org/10.1073/pnas.1523119113.

84. University of Minnesota, "Live Longer? Save the Planet? Better Diet Could Nail Both," ScienceDaily, November 12, 2014, accessed October 13, 2020, https://www.sciencedaily.com/releases/2014/11/141112132057.htm; David Tilman and Michael Clark, "Global Diets Link Environmental Sustainability and Human Health," *Nature* 515, no. 7528 (November 2014): 518–22, https://doi.org/10.1038/nature13959.

85. Sean Sherman, "This Healthy Diet Has Stood the Test of Time," *Bon Appétit,* October 18, 2017, https://www.bonappetit.com/story/healthy-native-american-diet.

86. David Tilman and Michael Clark, op. cit.

87. Kate E. Jones et al., "Global Trends in Emerging Infectious Diseases," *Nature* 451, no. 7181 (February 2008): 991, https://doi.org/10.1038/nature06536; "Agroecology—a Contribution to Food Security?" UN Environment Programme, October 15, 2020, http://www.unep.org/news-and-stories/story/agroecology-contribution-food-security.

88. Matthew N. Hayek and Rachael D. Garrett, "Nationwide

Shift to Grass-fed Beef Requires Larger Cattle Population,"
Environmental Research Letters 13, no. 8 (July 25, 2108), https://
iopscience.iop.org/article/10.1088/1748-9326/aad401.

89. William J. Ripple et al., "Ruminants, Climate Change and
Climate Policy," *Nature Climate Change* 4, no. 1 (January 2014):
2–5, https://www.nature.com/articles/nclimate2081.epdf?no
_publisher_access=1&r3_referer=nature. Valerie Brown, "Can
Responsible Grazing Make Beef Climate-Neutral?" Civil
Eats, April 10, 2018, https://civileats.com/2018/04/10/can
-responsible-grazing-make-beef-climate-neutral/.

90. "Eating Better—for Us and the Planet," UN Environment Programme, October 15, 2020, http://www.unep.org/news-and
-stories/story/eating-better-us-and-planet.

91. Elḥam A. Ghabbour et al., "National Comparison of the Total
and Sequestered Organic Matter Contents of Conventional
and Organic Farm Soils," chap. 1 in *Advances in Agronomy,*
vol. 146 (Cambridge, MA: Academic Press, 2017), 10–28.

92. William J. Ripple et al., "Ruminants, Climate Change and Climate Policy," *Nature Climate Change* 4, no. 1 (January 2014): 2–5,
https://doi.org/10.1038/nclimate2081.

93. Robert W. Howarth et al., "Nitrogen Use in the United States
from 1961–2000 and Potential Future Trends," *Ambio* 31, no.
2 (March 2002): 92, http://www.jstor.org/stable/4315220; Jan
Willem Erisman et al., "An Integrated Approach to a Nitrogen
Use Efficiency (NUE) Indicator for the Food Production–
Consumption Chain," *Sustainability* 10, no. 4 (April 2018): 925,
https://doi.org/10.3390/su10040925.

94. François Mariotti and Christopher D. Gardner, "Dietary Protein and Amino Acids in Vegetarian Diets—A Review," *Nutrients*
11, no. 11 (November 4, 2019): 2661, https://doi.org/10.3390/
nu11112661.

95. Henk Westhoek et al., "Food Choices, Health and Environment: Effects of Cutting Europe's Meat and Dairy Intake,"
Global Environmental Change 26 (May 2014): 196–205, https://doi
.org/10.1016/j.gloenvcha.2014.02.004.

96. Julia Baudry et al., "Association of Frequency of Organic Food
Consumption With Cancer Risk: Findings From the NutriNet-
Santé Prospective Cohort Study," *JAMA Internal Medicine* 178,
no. 12 (December 1, 2018): 1597–1606, https://doi.org/10

.1001/jamainternmed.2018.4357; "More Organics, Less Cancer," Living on Earth, September 4, 2020, https://www .loe.org/shows/segments.html?programID=20-P13-00036& segmentID=1.

97. "Noncommunicable Diseases," World Health Organization, June 1, 2018, https://www.who.int/news-room/fact-sheets/ detail/noncommunicable-diseases; Yan Zheng et al., "Association of Changes in Red Meat Consumption with Total and Cause Specific Mortality among US Women and Men: Two Prospective Cohort Studies," *BMJ* 365 (June 12, 2019): I2110, https://doi.org/10.1136/bmj.l2110.

98. "Red Meat: Avoid the Processed Stuff," Harvard Health Publishing/Harvard Medical School, August 2010, https:// www.health.harvard.edu/newsletter_article/red-meat-avoid -the-processed-stuff; "Red Meat and Processed Meat Consumption," National Cancer Institute/Cancer Trends Progress Report, accessed September 14, 2020, https://progressreport .cancer.gov/prevention/red_meat#field_related_cancers; Carrie R. Daniel et al., "Trends in Meat Consumption in the USA," *Public Health Nutrition* 14, no. 4 (April 2011), https:// www.ncbi.nlm.nih.gov/pmc/articles/PMC3045642/.

99. Tilman, David, and Michael Clark. "Global Diets Link Environmental Sustainability and Human Health." *Nature* 515, no. 7528 (November 12, 2014): 518–22. https://doi.org/ 10.1038/nature13959.

100. Abdus Samad Ansari et al., "Glycemic Control Is an Important Modifiable Risk Factor for Uveitis in Patients with Diabetes: A Retrospective Cohort Study Establishing Clinical Risk and Ophthalmic Disease Burden," *Journal of Diabetes and Its Complications* 32, no. 6 (June 2018): 602–8, https://doi.org/10.1016/ j.jdiacomp.2018.03.008; "Type 2 Diabetes Is a Reversible Condition," ScienceDaily, September 13, 2017, https://www .sciencedaily.com/releases/2017/09/170913084432.htm; Michelle McMacken and Sapana Shah, "A Plant-Based Diet for the Prevention and Treatment of Type 2 Diabetes," *Journal of Geriatric Cardiology* 14, no. 5 (May 2017): 342, https://www.ncbi .nlm.nih.gov/pmc/articles/PMC5466941/.

101. "Nutrition and Food," Gallup.com, accessed January 14, 2021, https://news.gallup.com/poll/6424/Nutrition-Food.aspx.

102. Anna Lappé, "Food Without Fields?" *Earth Island Journal*, Autumn 2019, https://www.earthisland.org/journal/index.php/magazine/entry/food-without-fields.

103. Rachel Rabkin Peachman, "Meat Gets a Makeover," *Consumer Reports*, August 29, 2019, https://www.consumerreports.org/nutrition-healthy-eating/meat-gets-a-makeover/.

104. Steve Curwood, "Lappe's Cookbook for the Revolution," *Boston Globe*, June 26, 1975.

105. "U.S. Certified Organic Cropland Has Increased Most Years Since 2002," Economic Research Service/U.S. Department of Agriculture, July 18, 2017, https://www.ers.usda.gov/data-products/chart-gallery/gallery/chart-detail/?chartId=84362.

106. Sara Clarke, "5 States with the Most Organic Farms," *US News & World Report*, March 15, 2019, https://www.usnews.com/news/best-states/slideshows/5-states-with-the-most-organic-farms.

107. Ibid.

108. Mark Strauss, "Americans Are Divided over Whether Eating Organic Foods Makes for Better Health," Pew Research Center, November 26, 2018, https://www.pewresearch.org/fact-tank/2018/11/26/americans-are-divided-over-whether-eating-organic-foods-makes-for-better-health/.

109. "Organic Industry Survey," Organic Trade Association, accessed October 12, 2020, https://ota.com/organic-market-overview/organic-industry-survey.

110. Daniel Imhoff with Christina Badaracco, "Local Food," chap. 23 in *The Farm Bill: A Citizen's Guide* (Washington, DC: Island Press, 2019), 189.

111. "Menus of Change" ("Introduction & Overview" brochure, 8th Annual Leadership Summit, July 22–August 26, 2020), 3, https://www.menusofchange.org/images/uploads/pdf/2020MOC_OVERVIEW.pdf.

112. Real Food Generation, https://www.realfoodgen.org/.

113. Center for Good Food Purchasing, https://goodfoodpurchasing.org/, accessed January 29, 2021.

114. "About Farmers Markets," Farmers Market Coalition, accessed January 14, 2021, https://farmersmarketcoalition.org/education/qanda/; Agricultural Marketing Service/U.S. Department of Education, accessed October 18, 2020, https://

www.ams.usda.gov/services/local-regional/farmers-markets
-and-direct-consumer-marketing.

115. "Community Supported Agriculture," National Agricultural
Library/U.S. Department of Agriculture, accessed September 16, 2020, https://www.nal.usda.gov/afsic/community
-supported-agriculture.

116. Raychel Santo and JH Bloomberg School of Public Health,
"FPC Map," accessed January 15, 2021, http://www
.foodpolicynetworks.org/fpc-map/.

117. "Here's the Dirt on Park Trends: Community Gardens Are
Growing," Trust for Public Land, August 22, 2018, https://
www.tpl.org/blog/here%E2%80%99s-dirt-park-trends
-community-gardens-are-growing; U.S. Department of Agriculture, *2017 Census of Agriculture Highlights: Black Producers* ACH17-
9 (October 2019), 1, https://www.nass.usda.gov/Publications/
Highlights/2019/2017Census_Black_Producers.pdf.

118. Sasha Feldstein and James Barham, "Running a Food Hub,
Learning From Food Hub Closures" (USDA Rural-Business
Cooperative Service, August 2017), 11, https://www.rd.usda
.gov/files/publications/SR77_FoodHubs_Vol4_0.pdf; Regional Food Hub Resource Guide, http://www.ams.usda
.gov/sites/default/files/media/Regional%20Food%20Hub
%20Resource%20Guide.pdf.

119. John Francis Ficara and Juan Williams, "'Black Farmers in
America,'" NPR, February 22, 2005, https://www.npr.org/
2005/02/22/5228987/black-farmers-in-america.

120. Anna Brones, "Karen Washington: It's Not a Food Desert,
It's Food Apartheid," *Guernica,* May 7, 2018, https://www
.guernicamag.com/karen-washington-its-not-a-food-desert-its
-food-apartheid/; Soul Fire Farm, accessed October 19, 2020,
https://www.soulfirefarm.org/.

121. "Farming Practices," Soul Fire Farm, accessed January 14,
2021, https://www.soulfirefarm.org/theland/farming
practices/; Personal communication with Soul Fire Farm staff,
emails, and virtual training, October 2020.

122. Steve Curwood interview with Leah Penniman, "Farming
While Black: Soul Fire Farm's Practical Guide to Liberation on
the Land," Living on Earth, November 23, 2018, https://loe
.org/shows/shows.html?programID=18-P13-00047; "BIPOC
Immersions & Programs," Soul Fire Farm, accessed Janu-

ary 14, 2021, https://www.soulfirefarm.org/food-sovereignty
-education/immersion/; personal communication with Leah
Penniman.

123. "About Us—SAAFON," Southeastern African American
Farmers' Organic Network (SAAFON), accessed October 18,
2020, https://saafon.org/about-us/.

124. Gosia Wozniacka, "Less than 1 Percent of US Farmworkers
Belong to a Union. Here's Why," Civil Eats, May 7, 2019,
https://civileats.com/2019/05/07/less-than-1-percent-of-us
-farmworkers-belong-to-a-union-heres-why/.

125. "About FLOC," Farm Labor Organizing Committee, AFL-
CIO, accessed September 16, 2020, http://www.floc.com/
wordpress/about-floc/.

126. "Baldemar Velasquez, President, Farm Labor Organizing
Committee (FLOC, AFL-CIO)" Labor and Community for an
Independent Party, October 4, 2019, https://lcipcampaign.org/
2019/10/04/floc-endorses-campaign-for-a-new-labor-based
-party/; Dan La Botz, "Farm Labor Organizer Is Murdered
in Mexico," Labor Notes, April 29, 2007, https://labornotes
.org/2007/04/farm-labor-organizer-murdered-mexico
?language=en.

127. "Campaign for Fair Food," Coalition of Immokalee Workers,
accessed December 3, 2020, https://ciw-online.org/campaign
-for-fair-food/; "About CIW," Coalition of Immokalee Workers, accessed January 12, 2021, https://ciw-online.org/about/.

128. Garrett Graddy-Lovelace, "Farmer and Non-Farmer Responsibility to Each Other: Negotiating the Social Contracts and
Public Good of Agriculture," *Journal of Rural Studies* (in press):
1–3, https://doi.org/10.1016/j.jrurstud.2020.08.044.

129. Cass R. Sunstein, *The Second Bill of Rights: FDR's Unfinished Revolution and Why We Need It More than Ever* (New York: Basic Books,
2004).

130. Nicholas Lemann, "The Unfinished War," Atlantic Online,
December 1988.

131. Robert B. Reich, *Supercapitalism: The Transformation of Business,
Democracy, and Everyday Life* (New York: Alfred A. Knopf, 2007),
36–39.

132. Dylan Matthews, "Poverty in the 50 Years Since 'The Other
America,' in Five Charts," *Washington Post,* July 11, 2012,
https://www.washingtonpost.com/news/wonk/wp/2012/

07/11/poverty-in-the-50-years-since-the-other-america-in-five
-charts/.

133. Nicholas Lehman, "The Unfinished War," Atlantic Online,
December 1988.

134. "Federal Farm Subsidies: What the Data Says," USAFacts,
June 4, 2019, https://usafacts.org/articles/federal-farm
-subsidies-what-data-says/.

135. "The United States Farm Subsidy Information," Environmental Working Group Farm Subsidy Database, accessed January
12, 2021, https://farm.ewg.org/region.php?fips=00000&
statename=UnitedStates; "Agricultural Policy," *A Place at the
Table* (blog), accessed December 14, 2020, https://tinyurl.com/
y6uke9tc.

136. Roger Johnson, "We Must Reject the 'Go Big or Go Home'
Mentality of Modern Agriculture," The Hill, October 8, 2019,
https://thehill.com/opinion/finance/464856-we-must-reject
-the-go-big-or-go-home-mentality-of-modern-agriculture.

137. Nick Hanauer and David M. Rolf, "The Top 1% of Americans
Have Taken $50 Trillion From the Bottom 90%—and That's
Made the US Less Secure," *Time*, September 14, 2020, https://
time.com/5888024/50-trillion-income-inequality-america/
?amp=true.

138. Leah Penniman, *Farming While Black: Soul Fire Farm's Practical
Guide to Liberation on the Land* (White River Junction, VT: Chelsea
Green Publishing, 2018); Monica M. White, *Freedom Farmers:
Agricultural Resistance and the Black Freedom Movement* (Chapel Hill:
University of North Carolina Press, 2018).

139. "Mini Gulf Tour: Federation & Mississippi," America
the Bountiful Tours, October, 29, 2109, https://www
.americathebountiful.org/post/mini-gulf-tour-federation
-mississippi.

140. Ryan Nebeker, "Hundreds of Community Organizations Press
for Nationwide Moratorium on CAFOs," FoodPrint, September 16, 2020, https://foodprint.org/blog/cafo-moratorium/;
"300 Diverse Advocacy Groups Endorse the Farm System Reform Act and Urge Quick Passage in Congress," Food & Water
Watch, September 9, 2020, https://www.foodandwaterwatch
.org/news/300-diverse-advocacy-groups-endorse-farm-system
-reform-act-and-urge-quick-passage-congress.

141. Ibid.

142. "Fact Sheet: Corporate Tax Rates" (2014), Americans for Tax Fairness, accessed January 12, 2021, https://americansfortax-fairness.org/tax-fairness-briefing-booklet/fact-sheet-corporate-tax-rates/.

143. Kevin Shalvey, "Tax Abuse and Offshore Havens Are Costing Governments $427 Billion a Year," *Business Insider*, November 20, 2020, https://www.businessinsider.com/tax-abuse-tax-havens-cost-tax-justice-network-study-2020-11.

144. Jesse Pound, "These 91 Companies Paid No Federal Taxes in 2018," CNBC, December 16, 2019, https://www.cnbc.com/2019/12/16/these-91-fortune-500-companies-didnt-pay-federal-taxes-in-2018.html.

145. Karisha Kuypers and OAA Staff, "Mexico Announces New Agricultural Support Programs," USDA Foreign Agricultural Service, *GAIN Report* no. MX9016 (April 5, 2019), 5, https://apps.fas.usda.gov/newgainapi/api/report/downloadreportby filename?filename=Mexico%20Announces%20New %20Agricultural%20Support%20Programs_Mexico_Mexico _4-5-2019.pdf.

146. "Pesticide Action Network Contributions to the CFS Policy Convergence Process," Pesticide Action Network International (November 27, 2019), 10, http://www.fao.org/fileadmin/templates/cfs/Docs1920/Agroecology_an_other_innovative/PAN_Int_Input_Agroecology_and_Other_Innovative _Approaches.pdf.

147. Frank Viviano, "This Tiny Country Feeds the World," *National Geographic*, September 2017, https://www.nationalgeographic .com/magazine/2017/09/holland-agriculture-sustainable -farming/; "Top 10 Agricultural Exporters," Humboldt, July 5, 2018, https://humboldt.global/top-agricultural-exporters/.

148. Ibid.

149. "Helping Farmers Go Organic in Thailand," Asian Development Bank, June 16, 2017, https://www.adb.org/results/helping-farmers-go-organic-thailand; Mary Wales, "Four Countries Supporting Organic Agriculture the Most," February 28, 2019, https://www.naturespath.com/en-us/blog/four -countries-supporting-organic-agriculture/; "The Danish Model," Danish Agriculture & Food Council, accessed January 12, 2020, https://agricultureandfood.dk/danish-agriculture -and-food/organic-farming.

150. Angelique Chrisafis, "French Law Forbids Food Waste by Supermarkets," *Guardian*, February 4, 2016, https://www .theguardian.com/world/2016/feb/04/french-law-forbids -food-waste-by-supermarkets.

151. Jules Pretty et al., "Assessment of the Growth in Social Groups for Sustainable Agriculture and Land Management," Global Sustainability, vol. 3 (August 2020), 2, http://dx.doi.org/10 .1017/sus.2020.19.

152. Ibid., 5.

153. Jeffrey Ashe and Kyla Jagger Neilan, *In Their Own Hands: How Savings Groups Are Revolutionizing Development* (San Francisco: Berrett Koehler Publishers, 2014).

154. Jules Pretty et al., "Global Assessment of Agricultural System Redesign for Sustainable Intensification," *Nature Sustainability* 1, no. 8 (August 2018): 441–46, https://doi.org/10.1038/s41893 -018-0114-0.

155. Max Roser and Hannah Ritchie, "Hunger and Undernourishment," Our World in Data, 2019, https://ourworldindata.org/ hunger-and-undernourishment.

156. Roland Bunch, "Case Studies of Regenerative Agriculture" (California State University, Chico, revised April 2020), https://www.csuchico.edu/regenerativeagriculture/_assets/ documents/case-studies-roland-bunch.pdf; Roland Bunch, *Restoring the Soil*, 2nd ed. (ECHO Inc., 2019).

157. C. Reij, G. Tappan, and M. Smale, "Re-Greening the Sahel: Farmer-Led Innovation in Burkina Faso and Niger" in *Millions Fed: Proven Successes in Agricultural Development*, chap. 7 (Washington, DC: International Food Policy Research Institute, 2009); UN Environment Programme, World Bank, and World Resources, *Roots of Resilience: Growing Wealth of the Poor* (Washington, DC: World Resources Institute, 2008), 149; personal communication with Gray Tappan and Chris Reij, emails, September 2020.

158. C. Reij, G. Tappan, and M. Smale, op. cit., 56.

159. Personal communication, Gray Tappan, U.S. Geological Survey, October 2020.

160. "The Forest Maker," World Vision Australia, accessed October 18, 2020, https://www.worldvision.com.au/global-issues/work -we-do/poverty/forest-maker; personal communication with Tony Rinaudo, emails, September 2020.

161. Jacob Grace, "Savanna Institute Receives Grant to Support Midwest Farmers Planting Tree Crops," Association for Temperate Agroforestry, accessed January 12, 2020, https://www .aftaweb.org/146-2020-vol-26/volume-26-no-2-june-2020/268 -savanna-institute-receives-grant-to-support-midwest-farmers -planting-tree-crops.html; Kevin J. Wolz and Evan H. DeLucia, "Black Walnut Alley Cropping Is Economically Competitive with Row Crops in the Midwest USA," *Ecological Applications* 29, no. 1 (2019): e01829, https://doi.org/10.1002/.

162. IPCC, "Food Security," chap. 5 in *Special Report on Climate Change and Land* (2019), section 5.5.1.3, https://www.ipcc .ch/srccl/chapter/chapter-5/; "Global CO2 Emissions in 2019—Analysis," International Energy Agency, February 11, 2020, https://www.iea.org/articles/global-co2-emissions-in -2019. (Global annual emissions (33.3) divided by the maximum technical potential (5.7) equals a 5.8-fold difference.)

163. Rattan Lal et al., "The Carbon Sequestration Potential of Terrestrial Ecosystems," *Journal of Soil and Water Conservation* 73, no. 6 (November 1, 2018): 145A–152A, https://doi.org/10.2489/ jswc.73.6.145A.

164. J. M. Sillick and W. R. Jacobi, "Healthy Roots and Healthy Trees," fact sheet 2.926, Colorado State University Extension, December 2013, https://extension.colostate.edu/topic-areas/ yard-garden/healthy-roots-and-healthy-trees-2-926/.

165. Diane Toomey, "Exploring How and Why Trees 'Talk' to Each Other," Yale Environment 360, September 1, 2016, https:// e360.yale.edu/features/exploring_how_and_why_trees_talk_to _each_other.

An Extraordinary Time to Be Alive: Introduction to the 20th Anniversary Edition

1. National Academy of Sciences, "Alternative Agriculture," Washington, DC, September 1989.

2. Marty Strange, *Family Farming: A New Economic Vision* (Lincoln and San Francisco: University of Nebraska Press and the Institute for Food and Development Policy, 1988).

3. Helvetius, *de l'esprit*, Paris, 1758, cited in Jane Mansbridge,

Beyond Self-Interest (Chicago: University of Chicago Press, 1990), 6.

4. John Adams, quoted by Clinton Rossiter, *Conservatism in America*, 2d ed., rev. (New York: Vintage, 1962), 111.

5. See, for example, Frances Moore Lappé, *Rediscovering America's Values* (New York: Ballantine Books, 1989), Part II, "What's Fair?" and Kevin Phillips, *The Politics of Rich and Poor* (New York: Random House, 1990).

6. Adam Smith, *The Theory of Moral Sentiments,* ed. D. D. Raphael and A. L. Macfie (Indianapolis: Liberty Classics, 1982), pt. 1, sec. 1, ch. 5, 25.

7. Charles R. Darwin, *The Descent of Man, and Selection in Relation to Sex* (New York: D. Appleton, 1909), pt. 1, 121.

8. Martin L. Hoffman, "The Development of Empathy," in J. Philippe Rushton and Richard M. Sorrentino, eds., *Altruism and Helping Behavior* (Hillsdale, NJ: Lawrence Erlbaum Associates, 1981).

9. Alfie Kohn, *The Brighter Side of Human Nature* (New York: Basic Books, 1990).

10. See, for example: *In Defense of the Land Ethic: Essays in Environmental Philosophy* (Albany: State University of New York Press, 1989), and *Companion to A Sand County Almanac: Interpretive and Critical Essays* (Madison: University of Wisconsin Press, 1987).

11. "Marx Meets Muir, Toward a Synthesis of the Progressive Political and Ecological Visions," *Tikkun,* vol. 2, no. 4, Sept./Oct. 1987.

12. Jim Mason and Peter Singer, *Animal Factories* (New York: Crown, 1980).

13. John Robbins, *Diet for a New America* (Walpole, NH: Stillpoint Publishing, 1987).

14. Wes Jackson, "Making Sustainable Agriculture Work," *The Journal of Gastronomy,* vol. 5, no. 2, Summer/Autumn 1989, 133.

15. "Democracy's Next Generation," People for the American Way, Washington, DC, 1989.

16. Harry C. Boyte, *CommonWealth: A Return to Citizen Politics* (New York: Free Press, 1989).

17. Harry C. Boyte, *Community Is Possible: Repairing America's Roots* (New York: Harper and Row, 1984).

18. Bernard Crick, *In Defence of Politics* (Baltimore: Penguin, 1964), 25.

19. Kentuckians for the Commonwealth, P.O. Box 1450, London, KY 40743.

20. Bill Elasky, "Becoming" in *Democracy & Education*, 1990 Conference Issue (Athens, OH: Institute for Democracy in Education, 1990).

21. Barry Commoner, *Making Peace with the Planet* (New York: Pantheon, 1990).

22. Frances Moore Lappé and Family, *What To Do After You Turn Off the TV* (New York: Ballantine Books, 1985).

23. Listening Project, Rural Southern Voice for Peace, 1898 Hannah Ranch Road, Burnsville, NC 28714.

Book One: Diet for a Small Planet
PART I. RECIPE FOR A PERSONAL REVOLUTION

Chapter 2. My Journey

1. *Impact of Market Concentration on Rising Food Prices*, Hearing Before the Subcommittee on Antitrust, Monopoly and Business Rights of the Committee on the Judiciary, United States Senate, 96th Congress, 1st Session on Rising Food Prices in the United States, April 6, 1979, U.S. Government Printing Office, 1979. Testimonies of Drs. Russell Parker, John Conner, and Willard Mueller. (Based on their testimony of $10 to $15 billion in 1975, I estimate monopoly overcharges to have reached close to $20 billion by 1981.)

2. U.S. Agency for International Development, Congressional Presentation, Fiscal Year 1982, main volume, p. 239.

3. Ibid., p. 250.

4. William Lin, George Coffman, and J. B. Penn, *U.S. Farm Numbers, Size and Related Structural Dimensions: Projections to the Year 2000*, Technical Bulletin No. 1625, Economics and Statistics Service, U.S. Department of Agriculture, 1980, p. iii.

5. U.S. Department of Agriculture, *Landownership in the United States*, 1978, p. 1.

6. Donald Paarlberg, *Farm and Food Policy: Issues of the 1980s*, University of Nebraska Press, 1980, p. 68.

7. *Impact of Market Concentration*, op. cit.

8. Industry profits from *Handbook of Agriculture Charts*, 1980, U.S. Department of Agriculture, p. 39. Overcharges estimate from

Impact of Market Concentration, op. cit., adjusted upward to account for increased profits and inflation since 1975.

9. *Washington Resource Report,* Environmental Policy Center, Washington, D.C., July 1981.

10. "The Pesticide Industry: What Price Concentration?" *Farmline,* U.S. Department of Agriculture, March 1981, p. 10.

11. Council on Wage and Price Stability, Executive Office of the President, *Report on Prices for Agricultural Machinery and Equipment,* Washington, D.C., 1976.

12. U.S. Department of Agriculture, *Status of the Family Farm,* Second Annual Report to Congress, Economics and Statistics Service, Agricultural Economic Report No. 441, 1979, p. 40.

13. James Rowen, "Oxy Takes a Very Big Bite," *The Nation,* October 31, 1981, p. 435.

14. V. James Rhodes, "The Red Meat Food Chain: Horizontal Size and Vertical Linkages," presented at Midwestern Conference on Food, Agriculture and Public Policy, S. Sioux City, Nebraska, November 18, 1980.

15. *Western Livestock Journal,* August 1979.

16. *An Analysis of the Futures Trading Activity in Live and Feeder Cattle Contracts of Large (Reporting) Traders on the Chicago Mercantile Exchange,* staff report to the Small Business Committee of the House of Representatives, September 1980, pp. 13, 21, 23.

17. Our estimate comes from the following sources: Profits in the late 1960s averaged $14 million/yr. according to *Feedstuffs,* January 11, 1969. Profits for 1979 estimated at $150 million by *Business Week,* April 16, 1979. In constant 1967 dollars this is a 441 percent increase; in current dollars, over 1,000 percent increase.

18. "Cargill: Preparing for the Next Boom in Worldwide Grain Trading," *Business Week,* April 16, 1979, pp. 3ff.

19. *Multinational Corporations and United States Foreign Policy,* Hearing Before the Subcommittee on Multinational Corporations, Senate Foreign Relations Committee, June 18, 23, 24, 1976, Part II, p. 241.

20. *Wall Street Journal,* March 6, 1979.

21. Dan Morgan, *Merchants of Grain* (Viking, 1979), pp. 234–235.

22. *Feedstuffs,* November 1, 1979, p. 1.

23. Ibid.

24. *Small Business Problems in the Marketing of Meat and Other Commodi-*

ties (Part 3—Beef in America: An Industry in Crisis), by the staff of the Committee on Small Business, House of Representatives, 96th Congress, 2nd Session, October 1980, U.S. Government Printing Office, 1980, pp. 28–29.

25. *Relationship Between Structure and Performance in the Steer and Heifer Slaughtering Industry,* Committee on Small Business, House of Representatives, 96th Congress, 2nd Session, September 1980, U.S. Government Printing Office, 1980, p. 44. (This study indicates that 30 percent of the rise in beef prices in recent years can be attributed to concentration in the industry. But the study is widely disputed.)

26. *Impact of Market Concentration on Rising Food Prices,* op. cit.

PART II. DIGGING TO THE ROOTS ON OUR SMALL PLANET

Chapter 1. One Less Hamburger?

1. *Food and Agriculture Organization, Production Yearbook,* Rome, 1979.

2. *World Hunger, Health, and Refugee Problems, Summary of a Special Study Mission to Asia and the Middle East* (Washington, D.C.: U.S. Government Printing Office, 1976), p. 99.

3. Letter from Dr. Marcel Ganzin, Director, Food Policy and Nutrition Division, FAO, Rome, April 1976.

4. Calculations based on Food and Agriculture Organization, *Yearbook of International Trade Statistics,* 1974; *Production Yearbook,* 1974 and 1975; and *Trade Yearbook,* 1975. For a complete discussion see Chapter 11, *Food First: Beyond the Myth of Scarcity* (Ballantine Books, 1979).

5. Food and Agriculture Organization, *Report on the 1960 World Census of Agriculture,* Rome, 1971. (And since then, landholdings in most countries have become even more concentrated.)

6. Food and Agriculture Organization, *State of Food and Agriculture,* 1978, Rome, pp. 66–71.

7. Ho Kwon Ping, "Profit and Poverty in the Plantations," *Far Eastern Economic Review,* July 11, 1980, pp. 53ff.

8. James Parsons, "Forest to Pasture: Development or Destruction?" *Revista de Biologia Tropical,* vol. 24, Supplement 1, 1976, p. 124.

9. The first part of *Food First: Beyond the Myth of Scarcity* by Frances Moore Lappé and Joseph Collins (Ballantine, 1979), discusses

the reasons behind the high birthrates in the Global South and includes references to many excellent sources.

10. U.S. Agency for International Development, *Congressional Presentation,* Fiscal Year 1980, p. 128.

Chapter 2. Like Driving a Cadillac

1. *Raw Materials in the United States Economy 1900–1977;* Technical Paper 47, prepared under contract by Vivian Eberle Spencer, U.S. Department of Commerce, U.S. Department of Interior Bureau of Mines, p. 3.

2. Ibid., Table 2, p. 86.

3. U.S. Department of Agriculture, *Livestock Production Units, 1910–1961,* Statistical Bulletin No. 325, p. 18, and *Agricultural Statistics, 1980,* p. 56. Current world imports from *FAO At Work,* newsletter of the liaison office for North America of the Food and Agriculture Organization of the United Nations, May 1981.

4. David Pimentel et al., "The Potential for Grass-Fed Livestock: Resource Constraints," *Science,* February 22, 1980, volume 207, pp. 843ff.

5. David Pimentel, "Energy and Land Constraints in Food Protein Production," *Science,* November 21, 1975, pp. 754ff.

6. Robert R. Oltjen, "Tomorrow's Diets for Beef Cattle," *The Science Teacher,* vol. 38, no. 3, March 1970.

7. The amount varies depending on the price of grain, but 2,200 to 2,500 pounds is typical. See note 13 for more detailed explanation of grain feeding.

8. U.S. Department of Agriculture, Economic Research Service, *Cattle Feeding in the United States,* Agricultural Economics, Report No. 186, 1970, p. 5.

9. Ibid., p. iv.

10. U.S. Department of Agriculture, *Agricultural Statistics, 1979 and 1980,* Tables 76 & 77.

11. Norman Borlaug in conversation with Frances Moore Lappé, April 1974.

12. U.S. Department of Agriculture, *Agricultural Statistics, 1980,* Table 76.

13. How many pounds of grain and soy are consumed by the American steer to get 1 pound of edible meat?

    (a) The total forage (hay, silage, grass) consumed: 12,000 pounds (10,000 pre-feedlot and 2,000 in feedlot). The

total grain- and soy-type concentrate consumed: about
2,850 pounds (300 pounds grain and 50 pounds soy
before feedlot, plus 2,200 pounds grain and 300 pounds
soy in feedlot). Therefore, the actual percent of total feed
units from grain and soy is about 25 percent.

(b) But experts estimate that the grain and soy contribute
more to weight gain (and, therefore, to ultimate meat
produced) than their actual proportion in the diet. They
estimate that grain and soy contribute (instead of 25
percent) about 40 percent of weight put on over the life of
the steer.

(c) To estimate what percent of edible meat is due to the
grain and soy consumed, multiply that 40 percent (weight
gain due to grain and soy) times the edible meat produced
at slaughter, or 432 pounds: $.4 \times 432 = 172.8$ pounds of
edible portion contributed by grain and soy. (Those who
state a 7:1 ratio use the entire 432 pounds edible meat in
their computation.)

(d) To determine how many pounds of grain and soy it took
to get this 172.8 pounds of edible meat, divide total grain
and soy consumed, 2850 pounds, by 172.8 pounds of edible meat: $2850 \div 172.8 = 16-17$ pounds. (I have taken the
lower figure, since the amount of grain being fed may be
going down a small amount.) These estimates are based on
several consultations with the USDA Economic Research
Service and the USDA Agricultural Research Service,
Northeastern Division, plus current newspaper reports of
actual grain and soy currently being fed.

14. U.S. Department of Agriculture, Economic Research Service
and Agricultural Research Service, Northeastern Division,
consultations with staff economists.

15. In 1975 I calculated this average ratio and the return to us
in meat from *Livestock-Feed Relationships,* National and State
Statistical Bulletin #530, June 1974, pp. 175–77. In 1980 I
approached it differently and came out with the same answer.
I took the total grain and soy fed to livestock (excluding dairy)
from *Agricultural Statistics, 1980.* The total was about 145 million
tons in 1979. I then took the meat and poultry and eggs consumed that year from *Food Consumption, Prices, and Expenditures,*
USDA-ESS, Statistical Bulletin 656. (I included only the por-

tion of total beef consumed that was put on by grain feeding, about 40 percent, and reduced the total poultry consumed to its edible portion, i.e., minus bones.) The total consumption was about 183.5 pounds per person, or 20 million tons for the whole country. I then divided the 145 million tons of grain and soy fed by the 20 million tons of meat, poultry, and eggs produced by this feeding and came up with the ratio of 7 to 1. (Imports of meat are not large enough to affect this calculation appreciably.)

16. Calculated as follows: 124 million tons of grain "lost" annually in the United States × 2,000 pounds of grain in a ton = 248 billion pounds "lost" divided by 4.4 billion people = 56 pounds per capita divided by 365 days equals .153 pounds per capita per day × 16 ounces in a pound − 2.5 ounces per capita per day—⅓ cup of dry grain, or 1 cup cooked volume.

17. R. F. Brokken, James K. Whittaker, and Ludwig M. Eisgruber, "Past, Present and Future Resource Allocation to Livestock Production," in *Animals, Feed, Food and People, An Analysis of the Role of Animals in Food Production*, R. L. Baldwin, ed., An American Association for the Advancement of Science Selected Symposium (Boulder, CO: Westview Press, 1980), pp. 99–100.

18. J. Rod Martin, "Beef," in *Another Revolution in U.S. Farming?*, by Lyle Schertz and others, U.S. Department of Agriculture, Washington, D.C., 1979, p. 93.

19. D. E. Brady, "Consumer Preference," *Journal of Animal Science*, vol. 16, p. 233, cited in H. A. Turner and R. J. Raleigh, "Production of Slaughter Steers from Forages in the Arid West," *Journal of Animal Science*, vol. 44, no. 5, 1977, pp. 901ff.

20. *Des Moines Register*, December 8, 1974.

21. *Cattle Feeding in the United States*, op. cit., pp. 78–79.

22. "Past, Present and Future Resource Allocation to Livestock Production," op. cit., p. 97.

23. Ibid., p. 91.

24. U.S. Department of Agriculture, Economics and Statistics Service, *Status of the Family Farm*, Second Annual Report to the Congress, Agricultural Economic Report No. 434, p. 48.

25. Quantities of each fuel used from *Energy and U.S. Agriculture: 1974 and 1978*, U.S. Department of Agriculture, Economic and Statistics Service, April 1980. Conversions to BTUs used in Cervinka, "Fuel and Energy Efficiency," in David Pimentel,

ed., *Handbook of Energy Utilization in Agriculture* (Boca Raton, Fla.: CRC Press, 1980). Fossil fuel imports from *Monthly Energy Review,* March 1981, U.S. Department of Energy, Energy Information Administration, p. 8.

26. Georg Borgstrom, Michigan State University, presentation to the Annual Meeting of the American Association for the Advancement of Science (AAAS), 1981.

27. Ibid.

28. "The Browning of America," *Newsweek,* February 22, 1981, pp. 26ff.

29. To arrive at an estimate of 50 percent, I used *Soil Degradation: Effects on Agricultural Productivity,* Interim Report Number Four of the National Agricultural Lands Study, 1980, which estimates that 81 percent of all water consumed in the United States is for irrigation. And I used the *Fact Book of U.S. Agriculture,* U.S. Department of Agriculture, Misc. Publication No. 1065, November 1979, Table 3, which shows that about 64 percent of irrigated land is used for feed crops, hay, and pasture. Sixty-four percent of 81 percent is 52 percent.

30. Philip M. Raup, "Competition for Land and the Future of American Agriculture," in *The Future of American Agriculture as a Strategic Resource,* edited by Sandra S. Batie and Robert G. Healy, A Conservation Foundation Conference, July 14, 1980, Washington, D.C., pp. 36–43. Also see William Franklin Lagrone, "The Great Plains," in *Another Revolution in U.S. Farming?,* Lyle Schertz and others, U.S. Department of Agriculture, ESCS, Agricultural Economic Report No. 441, December 1979, pp. 335–61. The estimate of grain-fed beef's dependence on the Ogallala is from a telephone interview with resource economist Joe Harris of the consulting firm Camp, Dresser, McKee (Austin, Texas), part of four-year government-sponsored study: "The Six State High Plains Ogallala Aquifer Agricultural Regional Resource Study," May 1980.

31. William Franklin Lagrone, "The Great Plains," op. cit., pp. 356ff.

32. "Report: Nebraska's Water Wealth Is Deceptive," *Omaha World-Herald,* May 28, 1981.

33. Giannini Foundation of Agricultural Economics, *Trends in California Livestock and Poultry Production, Consumption, and Feed Use: 1961–1978,* Information Series 80-5, Division of Agricultural

Sciences, University of California Bulletin 1899, November 1980, pp. 30–33.

34. General Accounting Office, *Ground Water Overdrafting Must Be Controlled,* Report to the Congress of the United States by the Comptroller General, CED 80–96, September 12, 1980, p. 3.

35. Donald Worster, *Dust Bowl: The Southern Plains in the 1930s* (New York: Oxford University Press, 1979), p. 236.

36. William Brune, State Conservationist, Soil Conservation Service, Des Moines, Iowa, testimony before Senate Committee on Agriculture and Forestry, July 6, 1976. See also Seth King, "Iowa Rain and Wind Deplete Farmlands," *New York Times,* December 5, 1976, p. 61.

37. Curtis Harnack, "In Plymouth County, Iowa, the Rich Topsoil's Going Fast. Alas," *New York Times,* July 11, 1980.

38. David Pimentel et al., "Land Degradation: Effects on Food and Energy Resources," in *Science,* vol. 194, October 1976, p. 150.

39. National Association of Conservation Districts, Washington, D.C., *Soil Degradation: Effects on Agricultural Productivity,* Interim Report Number Four, National Agricultural Lands Study, 1980, p. 20, citing the 1977 National Resources Inventory.

40. Calculated from estimates by Medard Gabel for the Cornucopia Project, c/o Rodale Institute, 11 Siegfriedale Rd., Kutztown, PA 19530.

41. Seth King, "Farms Go Down the River," *New York Times,* December 10, 1978, citing the Soil Conservation Service.

42. Ned D. Bayley, Acting Assistant Secretary for Natural Resources and Environment, "Soil and Water Resource Conservation Outlook for the 1980's," 1981 Agricultural Outlook Conference, Washington, D.C.

43. *Soil Degradation: Effects on Agricultural Productivity,* op. cit., p. 21.

44. W. E. Larson, "Protecting the Soil Resource Base," *Journal of Soil and Water Conservation,* vol. 36, number 1, January-February 1981, pp. 13ff.

45. Soil and Water Resources Conservation Act—Summary of Appraisal, USDA Review Draft, 1980, p. 18.

46. David Pimentel, "Land Degradation: Effects on Food and Energy Resources," op. cit., p. 150, estimates $500 million costs of sediment damage. E. Phillip LeVeen, in "Some Considerations for Soil Conservation Policy," unpublished manuscript, Public Interest Economics, 1981, p. 29, estimates $1 billion.

47. *Soil Degradation: Effects on Agricultural Productivity,* op. cit., p. 28.

48. U.S. Department of Agriculture, Economics and Statistics Service, *Natural Resource Capital in U.S. Agriculture: Irrigation, Drainage and Conservation Investments Since 1900,* ESCS Staff Paper, March 1979.

49. *Ag World,* April 1978, citing work of Clifton Halsey, University of Minnesota conservationist.

50. U.S. Department of Agriculture, *Handbook of Agricultural Charts,* 1979, p. 19.

51. U.S. Department of Agriculture, *Fertilizer Situation,* 1980, p. 14.

52. Medard Gabel, Cornucopia Project, Preliminary Report, Rodale Institute, 11 Siegfriedale Rd., Kutztown, PA 19530, p. 33.

53. C. A. Wolfbauer, "Mineral Resources for Agricultural Use," in *Agriculture and Energy,* ed. William Lockeretz (New York: Academic Press, 1977), pp. 301–14. See also *Facts and Problems,* U.S. Bureau of Mines, 1975, pp. 758–868.

54. General Accounting Office, *Phosphates: A Case Study of a Valuable, Depleting Mineral in America,* Report to the Congress by the Comptroller General of the United States, EMD-80-21, November 30, 1979, p. 1.

55. *Environmental Science and Technology,* vol. 4, no. 12, 1970, p. 1098.

56. Barry Commoner, *The Closing Circle* (Knopf, 1971), p. 148.

57. Georg Borgstrom, *The Food and People Dilemma* (Duxbury Press, 1973), p. 103.

58. U.S. Department of Agriculture, Economics and Statistics Service, *Natural Resource Capital in U.S. Agriculture: Irrigation, Drainage and Conservation Investments Since 1900,* ESCS Staff Paper, March 1979.

59. General Accounting Office, *Federal Charges for Irrigation Projects Reviewed Do Not Cover Costs,* Report to the Congress of the United States from the Comptroller General, PAD-81-07, March 3, 1981, p. 43.

60. Ibid., p. 26.

61. Julia Vitullo-Martin, "Ending the Southwest's Water Binge," *Fortune,* February 23, 1981, pp. 93ff.

62. Ibid.

63. *Federal Charges,* op. cit., pp. 3–4.

64. "Ending the Southwest's Water Binge," op. cit.

65. U.S. Department of Agriculture, *Farmline,* September 1980.

66. Milton Moskowitz, Michael Katz, and Robert Levering, eds., *Everybody's Business: An Almanac* (Harper and Row, 1980), p. 643.

67. U.S. Department of Agriculture, Economics and Statistics Service, *Status of the Family-Farm*, Second Annual Report to the Congress, Agricultural Economic Report No. 434, p. 47.

68. Ibid., p. 45.

69. Joseph C. Meisner and V. James Rhodes, *The Changing Structure of U.S. Cattle Feeding*, Special Report 167, Agricultural Economics, University of Missouri-Columbia, November 1974, p. 13.

70. "Past, Present and Future Resource Allocation to Livestock Production," in *Animals, Feed, Food and People, An Analysis of the Role of Animals in Food Production*, op. cit.

71. U.S. Department of Agriculture, *Agricultural Statistics, 1979*, pp. 435–38.

Chapter 3. The Meat Mystique

1. Winrock International Livestock Research and Training Center, *The World Livestock Product, Feedstuff, and Food Grain System: An Analysis and Evaluation of System Interactions Throughout the World, with Projections to 1985*, Winrock, Arkansas, 1981.

2. U.S. Department of Agriculture, *Utilization of Grain for Livestock Feed*, Washington, D.C., May 1, 1980, pp. 4–6.

3. Kenneth Bachman and Leonardo Paulino, *Rapid Food Production Growth in Selected Developing Countries: A Comparative Analysis of Underlying Trends, 1961–76*, Research Report 11, International Food Policy Research Institute, October 1979, p. 29.

4. "Replacing Energy as the Inflation Villain: Agriculture," *Business Week*, June 1, 1981, p. 71.

5. Maurice Brannan, "Trade Patterns," *Feedstuffs*, September 1, 1980.

6. Interview with J. Dawson Ahalt, Chairman, World Food and Agricultural Outlook and Situation Board, U.S. Department of Agriculture, July 1980.

7. For a complete discussion of promotion of agricultural exports by the U.S. government, see *Food First: Beyond the Myth of Scarcity*, by Frances Moore Lappé and Joseph Collins with Cary Fowler (Ballantine Books, 1979), Parts VII and IX.

8. C. W. McMillan, "Meat Export Federation to Be Newest Co-operator," *Foreign Agriculture* 13 (May 26, 1975), p. 14.

9. Ibid.

10. U.S. Department of Agriculture, *Handbook of Agricultural Charts 1980*, pp. 63, 69.

Chapter 4. Democracy at Stake

1.   General Accounting Office, Report by the Comptroller General of the United States, *An Assessment of Parity as a Tool for Formulating and Evaluating Agricultural Policy*, CED 81-11, October 10, 1980, p. 18.

2.   U.S. Department of Agriculture, *Status of the Family Farm*, Second Annual Report to Congress, 1979, p. 3.

3.   Marvin Duncan, "Farm Real Estate: Who Buys and How," *Monthly Review of the Federal Reserve Bank of Kansas City* (June 1977), p. 5.

4.   William Lin, George Coffman, and J. B. Penn, *U.S. Farm Numbers, Size and Related Structural Dimensions: Projections to the Year 2000*, Technical Bulletin No. 1625, Economics and Statistics Service, U.S. Department of Agriculture, 1980, p. iii.

5.   Lyle Schertz and others, *Another Revolution in U.S. Farming?*, Agricultural Economic Report No. 441, Economics and Statistics Service, U.S. Department of Agriculture, 1979, pp. 300ff.

6.   Diocesan Coalition to Preserve Family Farms, *Fourteen-County Land Ownership Study 1980*, Diocese of Sioux City, Iowa, 1980.

7.   U.S. Department of Agriculture, *A Time to Choose: Summary Report on the Structure of Agriculture*, Washington, D.C., January 1981. Table 24, p. 58, indicates that 100 percent of the economies of scale are, on average, reached when sales average $133,000. From Table 5, p. 43, one can calculate that roughly 50 percent of sales are from farms above this size.

8.   Leo V. Mayer, *Farm Income and Farm Structure in the United States*, Congressional Research Service, Library of Congress, Report No. 79-188 S, September 1979, Table 11, p. 31. The lowest per-unit costs of production—expenses per dollar of gross farm income—are found on farms with gross sales between $20,000 and $99,999 a year; the highest on farms with sales over $200,000.

9.   *A Time to Choose*, op. cit., p. 56.

10. *Another Revolution in U.S. Farming?*, op. cit., p. 31.

11. *A Time to Choose*, op. cit., pp. 46–47, 144–45.

12. Ibid.

13. E. Phillip LeVeen, "Towards a New Food Policy: A Dissenting

Perspective," *Public Interest Economics-West*, April 1981, Berkeley, California, Table 1.

14. Alfred J. Kahn and Sheila B. Kamerman, "Social Assistance: An Eight-Country Overview," *Journal of the Institute for Socioeconomic Studies* 8, no. 4 (Winter 1983–4), 93–112.

15. Warren Weaver, "House Unit Finds Aged Getting Poorer," *New York Times*, May 2, 1981.

16. National Advisory Council on Economic Opportunity, *Critical Choices for the 1980s*, 12th Report, August 1980, p. 15.

17. Ibid., pp. 16–17.

18. Census Bureau figures, as quoted in the *San Francisco Chronicle* of August 21, 1981.

19. Mike Feinsilber, *Philadelphia Inquirer*, December 24, 1980, quoted by Loretta Schwartz-Nobel, *Starving in the Shadow of Plenty* (G. P. Putnam's Sons, 1981).

20. Tom Joe, Cheryl Rogers, and Rick Weissbourd, *The Poor: Profiles of Families in Poverty*, Center for the Study of Welfare Policy, University of Chicago, Washington office, March 20, 1981, p. iii.

21. Ibid.

22. Robert Greenstein, Director on Food Assistance and Poverty (former administrator of the Food and Nutrition Service, U.S. Department of Agriculture), statement before the Senate Committee on Agriculture, Nutrition and Forestry, April 2, 1981.

23. Interview with Robert Greenstein, May 30, 1981.

24. Nick Kotz, *Hunger in America: The Federal Response*, (Field Foundation, 1979), p. 13.

25. Interview with Dr. Livingston by research assistant Sandy Fritz, May 1981.

26. President's Commission for a National Agenda for the Eighties, *Government and the Advancement of Social Justice, Health, Welfare, Education and Civil Rights in the Eighties*, Washington, D.C., 1980, p. 33.

27. M. E. Wegman, *Pediatrics*, December 1980, p. 832.

28. Ibid.

29. *Statistical Abstract*, 1978.

30. "Infant Mortality Highest in Capital," *New York Times*, December 13, 1981.

31. *Starving in the Shadow of Plenty*, op. cit.

32. *Hunger in America*, op. cit.

33. Robert Greenstein, testimony (see note 22).

34. *Access to Food: A Special Problem for Low-Income Americans,* Community Nutrition Institute, Washington, D.C., April 1, 1979, p. 17.
35. Interview with Nancy Amidei of the Food Research and Action Center, December 1981.
36. Greenstein, testimony, and Gar Alperovitz and Jeff Faux, "Controls and the Basic Necessities," *Challenge,* May–June 1980.
37. "Poverty Rate on Rise Even Before Recession," *The New York Times,* February 20, 1982.
38. *Dietary Goals for the United States,* Second Edition, prepared by the staff of the Select Committee on Nutrition and Human Needs, U.S. Senate, December 1977, reproduced by the Library of Congress, Congressional Research Service, March 31, 1978, p. xxxi.

Chapter 5. Asking the Right Questions

1. U.S. Department of Agriculture, *Food Consumption, Prices and Expenditures,* Economics and Statistics Service, Statistical Bulletin No. 656, February 1981, pp. 4–5.
2. *Wall Street Journal,* May 8, 1981.

PART III. OUR DANGEROUS DIET—WE CAN DO BETTER!

Chapter 1. America's Experimental Diet

1. Patricia Hausman, *Jack Sprat's Legacy: The Science and Politics of Fat and Cholesterol,* Center for Science in the Public Interest (Richard Marek Publishers, 1981), p. 97.
2. *Dietary Goals for the United States,* Second Edition, prepared by the staff of the Select Committee on Nutrition and Human Needs, United States Senate, December 1977, reproduced by the Library of Congress, Congressional Research Service, March 31, 1978, p. xxviii. See also W. Haenszel and M. Kurihara, "Studies of Japanese Migrants," *Journal of the National Cancer Institute,* vol. 40, 1968, p. 43.
3. M. Hindhede, "The Effect of Food Restriction During War on Mortality in Copenhagen," *Journal of the American Medical Association,* vol. 74, no. 6 (February 7, 1920), p. 381, cited by Keith Akers, *A Vegetarian Sourcebook.* See also H. C. McGill, Jr., "Appraisal of Dietary Fat as a Causative Factor in Atherogenesis," *American Journal of Clinical Nutrition,* vol. 32, 1979, pp. 2637–43.

4. Erik Eckholm and Frank Record, "The Affluent Diet: A World-wide Health Hazard," in *Sourcebook on Food and Nutrition*, First Edition, Dr. Ioannis S. Scarpa and Dr. Helen Chilton Kiefer, eds. (Chicago: Marquis Academic Media, 1978), p. 20.

5. *Journal of the American Dietetic Association*, vol. 77, July 1980, p. 66.

6. Letitia Brewster and Michael Jacobson, *The Changing American Diet*, Center for Science in the Public Interest, pp. 64–65.

7. Ibid., pp. 35, 43.

8. *Dietary Goals*, op. cit., p. xl.

9. Lindsay H. Allen et al., "Protein-induced Hypercalciuria: A Longer Term Study," *The American Journal of Clinical Nutrition*, vol. 32, April 1979, pp. 741–49; and *Journal of Dental Research*, vol. 60, 1971, p. 485.

10. *Jack Sprat's Legacy*, op. cit., pp. 58–59.

11. *Dietary Goals*, op. cit., p. xxx.

12. *Jack Sprat's Legacy*, op. cit., pp. 105–106.

13. Ibid., p. 59, and *Clinical and Developmental Hypertension*, vol. 3, no. 1, 1981, pp. 27–28.

14. *The Changing American Diet*, op. cit., p. 22.

15. Charles Frederick Church and Helen Nichols Church, *Food Values of Portions Commonly Used*, Tenth Edition, J. B. Lippincott Co., 1975.

16. *Dietary Goals*, op. cit., p. 46.

17. Jane Brody, *Jane Brody's Nutrition Book* (W. W. Norton, 1981), p. 397.

18. *Dietary Goals*, op. cit., p. 46.

19. *The Changing American Diet*, op. cit., p. 46, and U.S. Department of Agriculture, Economics and Statistics Service, *Food Consumption, Prices and Expenditures*, Statistical Bulletin No. 656, February 1981, p. 2.

20. *Dietary Goals*, op. cit., p. 32.

21. *The Changing American Diet*, op. cit., p. 17.

22. *Dietary Goals*, op. cit., p. 31.

23. Ibid., p. 31.

24. Milton Moskowitz, Michael Katz, and Robert Levering, *Everybody's Business: An Almanac* (Harper and Row, 1980), p. 66.

25. *The Changing American Diet*, op. cit., 44–45.

26. *Everybody's Business*, op. cit., p. 34.

27. *Dietary Goals*, op. cit., pp. 40–49.

28. Ibid., p. 49.

29. *Jane Brody's Nutrition Book,* op. cit., p. 397.

30. U.S. Department of Agriculture, *The Sodium Content of Your Food,* Home and Garden Bulletin No. 233, pp. 11–12.

31. Ibid., pp. 17, 19.

32. Ibid., p. 28.

33. Gene A. Spiller with Ronald J. Amen, *Topics in Dietary Fiber Research* (Plenum Press, 1978), p. 78.

34. U.S. Department of Agriculture, *Handbook of Agricultural Charts, 1978,* p. 56.

35. Dr. Sharon Fleming, personal correspondence, February 26, 1981.

36. M. G. Hardinge, A. C. Chambers, H. Crooks, and F. J. Stare, "Nutritional Studies of Vegetarians III. Dietary Levels of Fiber," *American Journal of Clinical Nutrition,* 1958, 6:523.

37. *The Changing American Diet,* op. cit., p. 25.

38. Ibid., p. 30.

39. Ibid., p. 13.

40. *Everybody's Business,* op. cit., p. 785.

41. Wayne Anderson, "More Meat—or Less—on the Dinner Table," *Feedstuffs,* May 12, 1975, p. 116.

42. *The Changing American Diet,* op. cit., p. 58.

43. *Everybody's Business,* op. cit., p. 784.

44. *The Changing American Diet,* op. cit., pp. 27–28.

45. "Antibiotic Feed Additives: The Prospect of Doing Without," *Farmline,* U.S. Department of Agriculture, December 1980.

46. U.S. Department of Health, Education and Welfare, Public Health Service, Food and Drug Administration, Bureau of Foods, *Compliance Program Report of Findings,* FY77 Total Diet Studies—Adult (7320.73), pp. 8, 9.

47. Talbot Page, Joel Babien, and Stephanie Harris, "The Effect of Diet on Organochlorine Concentration in Breast Milk," unpublished study. Contact through the Environmental Defense Fund, Washington, D.C. For report of women eating no animal food, see Jeffrey Hergenrather, Gary Hlady, Barbara Wallace, and Eldon Savage, Ethos Research Group, letter to the *New England Journal of Medicine,* March 26, 1981, p. 792. See also *Birthright Denied: The Risks and Benefits of Breast-Feeding,* by Stephanie G. Harris and Joseph H. Highland, Second Edition, revised, The Environmental Defense Fund, Washington, D.C., 1977.

48. *Compliance Program Report,* op. cit., p. 10.
49. Randall Ment, "Pestiscam," *Greenpeace Examiner,* Spring 1981, p. 25.
50. *The Changing American Diet,* op. cit., p. 50.
51. Graham T. Molitor, "The Food System in the 1980s," *Journal of Nutrition Education,* volume 12, no. 2, Supplement 1, 1980, pp. 103ff.
52. *The Changing American Diet,* op. cit., p. 58.
53. *New England Journal of Medicine,* vol. 304, no. 16 (April 6, 1981), pp. 930–33.
54. *Journal of the American Dietetic Association,* vol. 77, July 1980, p. 67.

Chapter 2. Who Asked for Froot Loops?

1. Daniel Zwerdling, "The Food Monsters: How They Gobble Up Each Other—and Us," *The Progressive,* March 16, 1980, p. 20.
2. "Judge Admonishes ITT Bakery Division on Price Tactics," *San Francisco Chronicle,* May 13, 1981.
3. Frances Moore Lappé and Joseph Collins with Cary Fowler, *Food First: Beyond the Myth of Scarcity* (Ballantine, 1979), p. 324ff. discusses agri-business expansion abroad.
4. Milton Moskowitz, Michael Katz, and Robert Levering, *Everybody's Business: An Almanac* (Harper and Row, 1980), p. 1.
5. *Impact of Market Concentration on Rising Food Prices,* Hearing Before the Subcommittee on Antitrust, Monopoly and Business Rights of the Committee on the Judiciary, United States Senate, 96th Congress, 1st Session on Rising Food Prices in the United States, April 6, 1979. U.S. Government Printing Office, 1979, Testimonies of Drs. Russell Parker, John Connor, and Willard Mueller, p. 46.
6. Ibid. (These authorities estimated consumer overcharges to be as much as $15 billion a year by 1975. From this, I estimate them to have reached about $20 billion a year by 1982.)
7. "FTC Asserts Big 3 Cereal Makers Reap Over $1 Billion," *Wall Street Journal,* October 2, 1980.
8. Frederick F. Clairmonte, "U.S. Food Complexes and Multinational Corporations, Reflections on Economic Predation," *Economic and Political Weekly,* vol. XV, nos. 41, 42, 43, special no. 1980, p. 1815.
9. *Everybody's Business,* op. cit., p. 29.
10. "FTC Asserts" (see note 7).

11. *Impact of Market Concentration,* op. cit., p. 13.

12. Ibid., p. 47.

13. "The Food Monsters," op. cit., p. 22.

14. *Impact of Market Concentration,* op. cit., p. 47.

15. "The Food Monsters," op. cit., p. 22.

16. A. Kent MacDougall, "Market-Shelf Proliferation—Public Pays," *Los Angeles Times,* May 27, 1979, pp. 1ff.

17. Anthony E. Gallo and John M. Connor, "Packaging in Food Marketing," *National Food Review,* U.S. Department of Agriculture, Spring 1981.

18. "Market-Shelf Proliferation—Public Pays," op. cit.

19. Ibid.

20. *Everybody's Business,* op. cit., p. 45.

21. U.S. Department of Agriculture, *Handbook of Agricultural Charts,* 1978, p. 31.

22. David Pimentel et al., "Land Degradation: Effects on Food and Energy Resources," *Science,* vol. 194, no. 4261, October 8, 1976, pp. 151–55.

23. Georg Borgstrom, *The Food and People Dilemma* (Duxbury Press, 1973), pp. 102–103.

24. *San Francisco Examiner,* May 3, 1981.

25. Graham T. Molitor, "The Food System in the 1980s," *Journal of Nutrition Education,* vol. 12, no. 2, Supplement, 1980, p. 109.

26. Judith J. Wurtman, "The American Eater: Some Nutritional Problems and Some Solutions," *Vital Issues,* Center for Information on America, vol. XXIX, no. 2, Washington, Conn. 06793.

27. *Everybody's Business,* op. cit., p. 19.

28. "Market-Shelf Proliferation—Public Pays," op. cit.

29. *Everybody's Business,* op. cit., p. 66.

30. Ibid., p. 127.

31. Ibid., p. 64.

32. "Branded Foods," *Forbes,* January 5, 1981.

33. *Everybody's Business,* op. cit., p. 49.

34. Ibid., pp. 28–29.

35. Robert Choate, Chairman, Council on Children, Media and Merchandising, in *Edible TV: Your Child and Food Commercials,* prepared by the Council on Children, Media and Merchandising for the Select Committee on Nutrition and Human Needs, United States Senate, September 1977, U.S. Government Printing Office, p. 9.

36. Ibid., p. 21.
37. Ibid., p. 63.
38. Ibid., p. 66.
39. Ibid., p. 69.
40. "Branded Foods," *Forbes,* January 5, 1981.
41. Kathryn E. Walker, "Homemaking Still Takes Time," *Journal of Home Economics,* vol. 61, no. 8, October 1969, pp. 621ff.
42. Michelle Marder Kamhi, "Making Diets Healthy at P.S. 166," *Nutrition Action,* January 1980.

Chapter 3. Protein Myths: A New Look

1. "Dietary Guidelines for Americans, 2020-2025," Department of Health and Human Services 2020, A 1-2 p.133, Appendix 1, https://www.dietaryguidelines.gov/sites/default/files/2020-12/Dietary_Guidelines_for_Americans_2020-2025.pdf.
2. "Are You Getting Too Much Protein?" Mayo Clinic News Network, accessed January 26, 2021, https://newsnetwork.mayoclinic.org/discussion/are-you-getting-too-much-protein/.
3. Jessica Wade et al., "Evidence for a Physiological Regulation of Food Selection and Nutrient Intake in Twins," *The American Journal of Clinical Nutrition,* vol. 34, February 1981, pp. 143–47.
4. "Pregnancy Diet: Focus on These Essential Nutrients," Mayo Clinic, accessed January 26, 2021, https://www.mayoclinic.org/healthy-lifestyle/pregnancy-week-by-week/in-depth/pregnancy-nutrition/art-20045082.; "Pregnancy Nutrition," American Pregnancy Association, April 27, 2012, https://americanpregnancy.org/healthy-pregnancy/pregnancy-health-wellness/pregnancy-nutrition-1008/.; "Eating Right Before and During Pregnancy," University of California San Francisco Health, accessed January 26, 2021, https://www.ucsfhealth.org/Education/Eating_Right_Before_and_During_Pregnancy.
5. "Are You Getting Too Much Protein?" Mayo Clinic News Network, accessed January 26, 2021, https://newsnetwork.mayoclinic.org/discussion/are-you-getting-too-much-protein/; "When It Comes to Protein, How Much Is Too Much?" Harvard Health, accessed January 26, 2021, https://www.health.harvard.edu/nutrition/when-it-comes-to-protein-how-much-is-too-much.
6. "When It Comes to Protein, How Much Is Too Much?" Harvard Health, accessed January 26, 2021, https://www.health

.harvard.edu/nutrition/when-it-comes-to-protein-how-much-is
-too-much.

7.   "Dietary Guidelines for Americans, 2020-2025," Department
     of Health and Human Services 2020, A 1-2 p.133, Appendix
     1, https://www.dietaryguidelines.gov/sites/default/files/2020
     -12/Dietary_Guidelines_for_Americans_2020-2025.pdf.

Book Two: Plant- and Planet-Centered Cooking
for Everyone, 50th Anniversary

1.   François Mariotti and Christopher D. Gardner, "Dietary
     Protein and Amino Acids in Vegetarian Diets—A Review," *Nu-
     trients* 11, no. 11 (November 4, 2019), https://doi.org/10.3390/
     nu11112661.

Part I: Kitchen Tips for Eating Well on a Small Planet

1.   Dana Gunders, "Wasted: How America Is Losing Up to 40
     Percent of Its Food from Farm to Fork to Landfill," NRDC,
     August 16, 2017, https://www.nrdc.org/resources/wasted-how
     -america-losing-40-percent-its-food-farm-fork-landfill.

2.   Federal Insecticide, Fungicide, and Rodenticide Act (FIFRA),
     "pesticide" is defined broadly as including "any substance or
     mixture of substances intended for preventing, destroying,
     repelling, or mitigating any pest." 7 U.S.C. § 136(u).

3.   Anket Sharma et al., "Worldwide Pesticide Usage and Its
     Impacts on Ecosystem," *SN Applied Sciences* 1, no. 11 (October
     2019), https://doi.org/10.1007/s42452-019-1485-1.

4.   Polyxeni Nicolopoulou-Stamati et al., "Chemical Pesticides and
     Human Health: The Urgent Need for a New Concept in Ag-
     riculture," *Frontiers in Public Health* 4 (July 2016): 148, https://
     doi.org/10.3389/fpubh.2016.00148. We also recommend the
     book *Living Downstream: An Ecologist's Personal Investigation of Cancer
     and the Environment* by Sandra Steingraber (Cambridge, MA: Da
     Capo Press, 2010).

5.   See, for example, research from Dr. Virginia Rauh and
     colleagues on chlorpyrifos: Virginia A. Rauh et al., "Brain
     Anomalies in Children Exposed Prenatally to a Common Or-

ganophosphate Pesticide," *Proceedings of the National Academy of Sciences* 109, no. 20 (May 15, 2012): 7871–76, https://doi.org/10.1073/pnas.1203396109.

6. See, for example, the many publications that have come from the Agricultural Health Study, which has involved more than 89,000 farmers and their spouses in Iowa and North Carolina since 1993: https://aghealth.nih.gov/news/publications.html. For farmworker impacts, see, for example, the many publications from the Center for the Health Assessment of Mothers and Children of Salinas (CHAMACOS) Study. Started in 1999, CHAMACOS is "the longest running longitudinal birth cohort study of pesticides and other environmental exposures among children in a farmworker community." Publications from the research can be found at https://cerch.berkeley.edu/research-programs/chamacos-study.

7. See, for example, Julia Baudry et al., "Association of Frequency of Organic Food Consumption With Cancer Risk: Findings From the NutriNet-Santé Prospective Cohort Study," *JAMA Internal Medicine* 178, no. 12 (December 1, 2018): 1597–1606, https://doi.org/10.1001/jamainternmed.2018.4357. See also Vanessa Vigar et al., "A Systematic Review of Organic Versus Conventional Food Consumption: Is There a Measurable Benefit on Human Health?" *Nutrients* 12, no. 1 (December 18, 2019): 7, https://doi.org/10.3390/nu12010007.

8. "Arsenic in Your Food," *Consumer Reports*, November 2012, https://www.consumerreports.org/cro/magazine/2012/11/arsenic-in-your-food/index.htm; "How Much Arsenic Is in Your Rice?" *Consumer Reports*, November 18, 2014, https://www.consumerreports.org/cro/magazine/2015/01/how-much-arsenic-is-in-your-rice/.

9. Bob Klein, "Op-ed: Will the Real 'Whole Grain' Please Stand Up?" Civil Eats, August 28, 2020, https://civileats.com/2020/08/28/op-ed-will-the-real-whole-grain-please-stand-up/.

10. Charles M. Benbrook, "Trends in Glyphosate Herbicide Use in the United States and Globally," *Environmental Sciences Europe* 28, no. 1 (2016): 3, https://www.ncbi.nlm.nih.gov/pmc/articles/PMC5044953/.

11. "Current Eating Patterns in the United States," in *2015–2020 Dietary Guidelines for Americans*, 8th ed., (Washington, DC: U.S.

Department of Health and Human Services and U.S. Department of Agriculture, 2015), 38–43, https://health.gov/our-work/food-nutrition/2015-2020-dietary-guidelines/guidelines/chapter-2/current-eating-patterns-in-the-united-states/#figure-2-1.

Permissions Acknowledgments

Alicia Kennedy: "Alicia's Salted Chocolate-Almond Cookies" by Alicia Kennedy. Used by permission of Alicia Kennedy.

Wendy Lopez: "Wendy's Maple Amaranth Porridge" by Wendy Lopez. Used by permission of Wendy Lopez.

Anthony Myint: "Anthony's Leek, Shitake, and Miso Butter 'Casserole'" and "Soy-Pickled Peppers" reprinted by permission of Anthony Myint.

W. W. Norton & Company, Inc.: "Eggplant and Feta Kefte" from *Zaitoun: Recipes from the Palestinian Kitchen* by Yasmin Khan, copyright © 2018 by Yasmin Khan; "Superiority Burger" from *Superiority Burger Cookbook: The Vegetarian Hamburger Is Now Delicious* by Brooks Headley, copyright © 2018 by Brooks Headley. Reprinted by permission of W. W. Norton & Company, Inc.

Aileen Suzara: "Aileen's Gintaang Gulay-Coconut Simmered Vegetables" by Aileen Suzara. Used by permission of Aileen Suzara.

Ten Speed Press, an imprint of Random House, a division of Penguin Random House LLC: "Louisa's Garlicky Eggplant and Tomato Spread (Mirza Ghasemi)" from *The New Persian Kitchen: A Cookbook* by Louisa Shafia, text copyright © 2013 by Louisa Shafia. Reprinted by permission of Ten Speed Press, an imprint of Random House, a division of Penguin Random House LLC.

Bryant Terry and Ten Speed Press, an imprint of Random House, a division of Penguin Random House LLC: "Bryant's Slow-Braised Mustard Greens" adapted from *Afro-Vegan: Farm-Fresh African, Caribbean & Southern Flavors Remixed* by Bryant Terry (Emeryville, CA: Ten Speed Press, 2014). Used by permission of Bryant Terry and Ten Speed Press, an imprint of Random House, a division of Penguin Random House LLC.

University of Minnesota Press: "Roasted Corn with Wild Greens Pesto" from *The Sioux Chef's Indigenous Kitchen* by Sean

Sherman with Beth Dooley (Minneapolis, MN: University of Minnesota, 2017), 13, 24, copyright © 2017 by Ghost Dancer, LLC. Reprinted by permission of University of Minnesota Press.

Alice Waters: "Alice's Creamy Meyer Lemon Dressing" adapted from *The Art of Simple Food II: Recipes, Flavor, and Inspiration from the New Kitchen Garden* by Alice Waters (New York: Clarkson Potter, 2013). Reprinted by permission of Alice Waters.

Index

About the Author

FRANCES MOORE LAPPÉ is an American original. *New York* magazine dubbed her "the Movement Mother," while the Smithsonian described her first book, *Diet for a Small Planet,* as "one of the most influential political tracts of the times." *Gourmet* magazine named Lappé one of 25 people—from Thomas Jefferson to Julia Child—whose work has changed the way America eats. She has been featured in *Harper's, The New York Times Magazine,* and *O: The Oprah Magazine,* among others. Her media appearances range from the *Today* show to *Hardball with Chris Matthews,* from *Fox and Friends* to the BBC and PBS's *Retro Report.*

The recipient of 20 honorary degrees, Lappé has authored 20 books, most recently *Daring Democracy,* co-authored with Adam Eichen, and *It's Not Too Late.* A sought-after public speaker, Lappé has been a visiting scholar at MIT and U.C. Berkeley. In 1987, Lappé received the Right Livelihood Award, often called "the alternative Nobel Prize." She is a founding member of the World Future Council and serves on the National Advisory Board of the Union of Concerned Scientists.

Lappé is co-founder of three national organizations: the Oakland-based Food First, the Center for Living Democracy (1991–2000), and her current home, the Cambridge-based Small Planet Institute, co-founded with her daughter, Anna Lappé.

smallplanet.org
Twitter: @fmlappe

About the Illustrator

AIMÉE MAZARA is an illustrator from the Dominican Republic, focusing on independent graphic journalism. Her work is inspired by childhood nostalgia, traditional culture, and biodiversity and showcases the communities and experiences she surrounds herself with, using a range of mediums and styles to represent their vibrancy.

About the Type

This book was set in Baskerville, a typeface designed by John Baskerville (1706–75), an amateur printer and typefounder, and cut for him by John Handy in 1750. The type became popular again when the Lanston Monotype Corporation of London revived the classic roman face in 1923. The Mergenthaler Linotype Company in England and the United States cut a version of Baskerville in 1931, making it one of the most widely used typefaces today.